Climbing Roses of the World

Climbing Roses
of the World

Charles Quest-Ritson

TIMBER PRESS
Portland • Cambridge

Published in 2003 by
Timber Press, Inc.
The Haseltine Building
133 S.W. Second Avenue, Suite 450
Portland, Oregon 97204, U.S.A.

Timber Press
2 Station Road
Swavesey
Cambridge CB4 5QJ, U.K.

Printed in Hong Kong

Library of Congress Cataloging-in-Publication Data

Quest-Ritson, Charles.
    Climbing roses of the world / Charles Quest-Ritson.
        p.   cm.
    Includes bibliographical references (p.   ).
    ISBN 0-88192-563-2
    1. Climbing roses. I. Title.

SB411.65.C55 Q47 2003
635.9'33734–dc21

                                2002072790

This book is dedicated to two people:
my wife, Brigid, who knows more about roses than I do,
and Gianfranco Fineschi, who has done more for the rose in one lifetime
than the Empress Josephine herself.

Contents

Acknowledgements

I would like to thank the following people who have helped me in the course of researching this book: Tid Alston, Walter Branchi, Helle Brumme, John Clements, Nan Cocker, Maurice and Rosemary Foster, Barry Futter, Bill Grant (a constant source of encouragement), Hedi Grimm, Pierre Guillot, Peter Harkness, François Joyaux, Gregg Lowery, Neal Maillet, Michael Marriott, Clare Martin, Odile Masquelier, John Mattock, Bill McNamara, Jon Nieuwesteeg, Trevor and Margaret Nottle, Roger Phillips, Elena Pizzi, Ruth Randle, Martyn and Alison Rix, Henry and Susie Robinson, David Ruston, David Stone, Barbara Tcherchoff, Sharon Van Enoo, Rudy Velle, and Dwayne Wilson. I also acknowledge a great debt to Brent Dickerson for his compilations of useful source materials, which have given me a lot of useful leads. I have always consulted his sources before quoting them, and I have sometimes adopted a different editorial interpretation.

Introduction

It was at L'Haÿ-les-Roses on 4 June 1992, as I sat musing on the glories of French rose breeding, while the memories of Cavriglia were but two days behind me, that the idea of writing the story of climbing and rambling roses first started to my mind. I did not realise how large a subject it would prove to be. Nearly sixteen hundred climbing and rambling roses are still in cultivation, and some four hundred are available from nurseries throughout the world.

A full-length study of climbing roses is long overdue. Only two comprehensive books on this subject have ever been published: G. A. Stevens's *Climbing Roses* (1933) and Graham Stuart Thomas's *Climbing Roses Old and New* (1965), which was revamped in 1994 as part of a three-in-one edition with his two other rose books. Stevens's book never had the success it deserved; even now, his judgements on roses stand out for their accuracy and the wry humour with which he wrote. Graham Stuart Thomas is a remarkably acute observer of plants who analyses their qualities with erudition and lucidity, but his viewpoint is rather Anglo-centric.

You may wonder whether a monograph which sets out to describe so many cultivars can serve any useful purpose. The answer is yes, because no previous writer on climbing roses has had the means to undertake such a comprehensive overview. Travel, communications, and the electronic revolution make it possible to collect and analyse horticultural information as never before. In so doing, problems of nomenclature are resolved and value judgements are possible as we have our eyes opened to the beauties of other traditions. My hope was that I could achieve something worthwhile by extensive research in half a dozen languages, such as no writer on roses had attempted before, and by taking a truly international perspective. In the event, I found even more valuable the opportunity to study roses closely, one by one, so that my descriptions of them are based wherever possible on what I have seen for myself and not upon the judgments of earlier writers.

It is easy to set out with the intention of being comprehensive. It is more difficult to present sixteen hundred roses in a logical and accessible format—the botanical classes are often too large. Sometimes the answer is to break them down into the work of individual breeders and describe the roses in the context of their raisers' circumstances, including the market and social conditions in which they lived. But it is important to treat every breeder and every rose fairly. Graham Stuart Thomas wrote in *Climbing Roses Old and New* (1965) that he had omitted 'Chaplin's Pink Climber' and 'American Pillar' from his book because they were "blatant, almost scentless, and would not be included in my own garden, however large." I believe that such judgements owe more to fashion than to an impartial appreciation of beauty.

I have tried to include every climbing rose now grown in some part of the world, although I realise that a few recent introductions may have escaped me, especially if they are not yet widely available and grown. Unfortunately, I have been able to unearth little about the many excellent cultivars of climbing roses grown in the old gardens of China. Nor is it appropriate to include roses which have been reintroduced under modern names. I have therefore excluded 'Miss Jekyll' and 'Janet B. Wood', while making an exception for such long-established names as 'Rambling Rector' and 'Fiamma Nera'.

It is not always easy to decide whether a particular rose should qualify as a climbing rose. In cases of uncertainty, I considered how a cultivar was categorised by its original breeder or introducer and how it grows in the conditions where that person lived. Take David Austin's English roses, for example. If you live in southern California, you may be surprised to find that I have included 'Constance Spry' but omitted 'Graham Thomas' and 'The Pilgrim'. This is because 'Constance Spry' grows to 3 m in central England, where the other two bushes reach 1.5–2.0 m. I have seen 'Chinatown' 4 m high at the Huntington Botanical Gardens in San Marino, California, and 'Buff Beauty' at least 5 m high at Quarryhill in the Sonoma Valley, California. But neither is anything more than a shrub back home in northern Europe.

Most of the leading writers on roses have been English, American, or French. In the course of researching this book, I discovered how woefully previous writers have overlooked or underestimated the German contribution to the history of roses and rose growing. It is an imbalance which I have tried to redress. Another consequence of the English domination of rose literature is that people in such places as Australia and California try to grow roses which are not the best cultivars for their very different climates. I wish garden writers in Australia and California would realise that most roses grow better in their climates than in mine and boast about it. The truth is that roses in English gardens survive at the margins of cultivation—roses fare better in a warm, dry climate than in a cool, wet one. The first flush of roses in Texas or Italy is usually superior to the rain-sodden, wind-bashed, first blooming in Oregon or Ireland. In contrast, the autumn reflowering is more successful after a temperate summer than a hot, dry one.

The Classification of Roses

The classification of any intensely hybridised genus is a nightmare. The problem of taxonomy is well illustrated by the white-flowered rambler 'Rudolphus', which was described in 1891 as a Prairie rose by Scipion Cochet, the editor of *Journal des Roses*; a Sempervirens Hybrid in the published list of roses grown at L'Haÿ-les-Roses in 1902; and an Arvensis Hybrid by Rivoire and Ebel in *Roses et Rosiers* (1933). The descriptions of this charming cultivar do not enable us to classify it easily; however, because 'Rudolphus' has not been recorded in cultivation for at least sixty years and is almost certainly extinct, the problem of categorising this particular rose need detain us no further.

There are two possible approaches to classification. One is to follow the historic precedent—if the raiser called his rose a Wichurana, then it must be treated as a Wichurana. The trouble with this method is that some raisers have been known to change the classification of their own roses from year to year. It is worth remembering that Joseph Pemberton introduced 'Moonlight' as a Hybrid Tea. Because of its name, 'Tea Rambler' has often been lumped with the Tea roses, rather than with the Multiflora Ramblers. 'Ards Rambler', a popular Hybrid Tea introduced at about the same time, suffered the reverse fate. The English rosarian Norman Young (1971) pointed out that roses were usually allocated to their maternal section, even though the resemblance might be small after a couple of generations. If you cross *Rosa wichurana* with a Tea rose like 'Perle des Jardins', you may get a Wichurana Hybrid like 'Jersey Beauty'. If you then cross 'Jersey Beauty' with the China × Tea hybrid 'Comtesse du Cayla', you may obtain a plant like 'Emily Gray', and this too will be called a Wichurana Hybrid despite the fact that it is three-quarters Tea rose and only one-quarter *R. wichurana*.

The other approach is to classify roses according to their botanical characteristics. So far as climbing roses are concerned, where you are trying to classify a large and heterogeneous group, you have to decide which specific characteristics predominate in a particular cultivar—not always an easy task. I have allowed myself a little latitude in assigning cultivars to the various categories in this book. If, for example, the offspring of a cross between a Wichurana Rambler and a Climbing Floribunda more closely resembles a Multiflora Rambler than either of its parents, I have allocated it to the chapter on Multifloras. This may sound high-handed, but it is important to remember that many of our garden roses are complex hybrids whose genes will, on occasion, recombine with surprising results. In other words, it may not be obvious how a particular cultivar could have been bred from its putative parents. Of course, it is possible that the quoted parentage is wrong and may even have been deliberately misrepresented by the originator. (It has been estimated that at least 10 per cent of published rose parentages are incorrect.) Every horticultural taxonomist hopes that DNA analysis will eventually answer the questions which conventional learning does not.

In this book I distinguish and examine such clearly defined strains as the 'Gloire de

Dijon' line and the 'Blue Multiflora' group and describe the work of leading breeders, if possible, in homogeneous groups. In practice, this may mean placing some roses in chapters or sections where strictly they do not belong, for example, by including Peter Lambert's few Wichurana Ramblers in the section on his Multiflora Ramblers. In these cases, I have pointed out that such anomalies do not belong where I have placed them. This practice also means that, on some occasions, a breeder's work has to be spread between two or three chapters according to taxonomic considerations. Most chapters have a final section of miscellaneous cultivars, in which I describe the leftovers that cannot be incorporated thematically into the rest of the chapter.

I have used the older terms *Polyantha* and *Floribunda*, in preference to the orthodox modern *cluster-flowered rose*, to avoid confusion with such roses as Noisettes, Wichuranas, and Multiflora Hybrids, which are often described as cluster flowered. Similarly I have used the more familiar term *Hybrid Tea* in preference to *large flowered*. Most of the climbing sports mentioned in this book derive from bush cultivars which were known as Hybrid Teas or Floribundas. I have not adopted the American usage of the term *Grandiflora*, which serves only to thicken an already dense taxonomic jungle. Climbing sports of Grandifloras are therefore distributed between the Climbing Hybrid Teas and the Climbing Floribundas, as most appropriate to each cultivar.

With regard to hybrid terminology, I use, for instance, "a *Rosa gigantea* hybrid" to indicate a hybrid with *R. gigantea* as one of its parents and "a Gigantea Hybrid" to indicate a hybrid with *R. gigantea* somewhere in its ancestry. The latter would, for example, include a rose whose ancestry was (*R. gigantea* × Hybrid Tea) × (*R. gigantea* × Noisette).

The Names of Roses

When researching a rose, I have often been surprised by the extent to which it differs from its descriptions in such old sources as the introducer's catalogue. Most are correctly named, and any distinctions between the published description and the living rose are usually minor. However, when there is a substantial variance—for example, when the original rose is described as "yellow" but the rose I see is actually pink—I have to decide whether the early description is wrong (which does happen) or whether the name of the rose has mistakenly been attached to another cultivar.

In this book, I have sought to establish and use the correct names for roses, but I am only too aware that I have failed to spot similarities (a cultivar is known by more than one name, of which only one is correct) and disparities (a rose grown under a wrong name). However, I hope that in years to come others will take up the torch and shed more light on areas of nomenclatural darkness. I trust, in particular, that readers will write to me with their observations on problems of nomenclature, correcting me wherever possible, so that together we can put an end to the mistakes and anomalies which have been handed down to us from previous generations. I hope also that readers will tell me that roses which I have omitted because I believe them to be extinct are in fact alive and well in gardens known to them. For instance, just as this book was going to print, I discovered the Multiflora Ramblers 'Grevinde Sylvia Knuth', 'Jutlandia', and 'Selandia' flourishing in the collection of Poulsen hybrids at Gerlev in Denmark.

Names are lost: we still cannot put the correct name to 'Bleu Magenta'. Wrong names are attached: the rose that Australians and New Zealanders call 'Wedding Day' is in fact 'Polyantha Grandiflora', and I have seen no fewer than four different roses all claiming to be the true 'Geschwind's Nordlandrose'. We call our roses by the names under which we receive them. Mistakes of nomenclature are perpetuated and handed down by the unwitting deceiver to the unwittingly deceived. There are too many roses called 'Astra Desmond' or 'Awakening' in nurseries' catalogues and in the gardens of their customers. (There are very few exceptions which qualify, in my opinion, for an exemption from the rules for cultivar names laid down by the Tokyo Convention—perhaps only 'Mme A. Meilland'. The cultivar is known as 'Gloria Dei' in Germany, 'Gioia' in Italy, and 'Peace' in the English-speaking world.) The trouble is that foreign names are often a barrier to popularity and commercial success. Many of the best German roses are ignored abroad because of their names. 'Großherzogin Eléonore von Hessen' and 'Herzogin Viktoria-Adelheid von Coburg-Gotha' may be difficult to remember and impossible for non-Germans to pronounce, but there can be no excuse for ignoring such exceptional roses as 'Regierungsrat Rottenberger', 'Frau Eva Schubert', or 'Rosarium Uetersen'.

The Americans are the worst offenders when it comes to renaming non-American roses for the home market. How many Americans realise that 'Blaze Superior' should properly be called 'Demokracie'? The definitive American stud-book *Modern Roses* is wrong to claim that 'Danse du Feu' is the name whereby 'Spectacular' is known in Europe. It would be truer to say that 'Spectacular' is the name by which 'Danse du Feu' is known in the United States. As for introduction dates, the year in which a rose was first offered for sale in the United States is often cited as the year in which a rose was first introduced worldwide, when in fact it was introduced in Europe several years earlier. Indeed, we Europeans have something to complain about.

Climbers Versus Ramblers

At the Royal Horticultural Society's Great Autumn Show in London in 1980, I attended a lecture on climbing roses by Graham Stuart Thomas, the man who knew more about roses than anyone then living. Thomas was the champion of old-fashioned and forgotten cultivars. He had rescued them from obscurity and returned them to pride of place in every fashionable garden in England. His first words came as rather a shock: "I feel I am here on rather false pretences," he declared. "There is no such thing as a climbing rose." Then he went on to explain that "all roses are shrubs . . . and they range from tiny dwarfs to gigantic plants achieving 50 ft [16 m] in height. These very strong growers are not self-reliant but hoist themselves up through shrubs and trees by means of their hooked prickles." Thomas's definition of a climbing rose is still good enough for me, although the same point has been made rather more stylishly by the English garden writer Hugh Johnson (1979, 92): "No rose climbs in the sense that a vine does by deliberately taking a grip on the next hand-hold in the direction of the light. The rose method is to put up canes, sometimes of amazing length, in the hope that support will be forthcoming." Their thorns (technically prickles) help to anchor them as they climb.

What then is the difference between a climber and a rambler? Hugh Johnson (1979) has the answer again: "*Climbers* are those which tend to produce stiff stems in relatively small numbers (not 'breaking' very often from the base); *ramblers* usually have more pliable and whippy shoots in larger numbers, tending not to grow so long because new ones are regularly coming from ground level to take over." To this I add that the long, thin, pliable canes of ramblers often trail along the ground, taking root where they touch it and eventually building up into a low thicket.

All ramblers are climbers, but not all climbers are ramblers. Ramblers have a greater admixture of wild roses in their more immediate ancestry, usually a species from the Synstylae section such as *Rosa wichurana* or *R. arvensis*, whereas climbing roses are more closely related to such complex hybrids as the Hybrid Teas and Floribundas. Some ramblers are in fact sports of bushy varieties. Floriferousness is not a distinguishing factor—all roses, both climbers and ramblers, bloom most profusely at their first flowering in spring or summer. Many ramblers flower only once, whereas many climbers produce flowers intermittently throughout the summer and autumn. Being closer to their wild ancestors, ramblers have an old-fashioned look more often than climbers do. The quartered flower of the rambler 'Albéric Barbier' is very different from the modern climbers 'Schoolgirl' or 'Dreaming Spires'. These are all generalisations, however, and there are exceptions to every rule. For most purposes, it does not matter whether a rose is a climber or a rambler.

Less vigorous ramblers are sometimes known as *semi-climbers*. Likewise, less vigorous climbers may be called *pillar roses*. If pruned to protect them from wind damage, both make good shrubs. Most pillar roses in the early days were vigorous Hybrid Perpetuals and Bourbons such as 'Général Jacqueminot' and 'Reine des Violettes'. Today these cultivars are again grown as shrubs. Pillar roses are not vigorous enough to be called climbers, and their wood is too stiff and short to ramble, but the terms have always been used fairly loosely. The Franco-American rosarian Jean H. Nicolas (1930) observed that 'Paul's Scarlet Climber' is a pillar rose, 'Turner's Crimson Rambler' does not ramble, and 'American Pillar' is one of the most vigorous climbers. The problem also exists in other languages: the Frenchman Jean Sisley rejected the word *grimpant* (climbing), because it suggested tendrils, crampons, and suckers. Nevertheless it continues to be used to describe climbing sports, whereas the delightful *sarmenteux* is applied to ramblers (*Journal des Roses* 1893).

When is a climber not a climber? When it is a shrub. Climate and growing conditions have a considerable effect upon roses. Dean Hole (1901) of Rochester, England, wrote that "Roses generally may be induced to climb, if planted in rich soil against a wall, facing south or east. In half a dozen summers many of the Hybrid Bourbon, Hybrid China, and Gallican Roses will reach the eaves of an ordinary dwelling, as I have proved with 'Charles Lawson' and 'Coupe d'Hébé'." The Tea roses are particularly variable in habit; their vigour depends upon heat, and thus upon their planting position, more than any other type. 'Isabella Sprunt', a pale yellow sport of 'Safrano', was described by an American nurseryman as recently as 1985 as 60–90 cm, but a correspondent of the National Rose Society of Great Britain in 1917 reported that "on a west aspect [it] quickly covers a wall 15 ft [450 cm] high" (Dickerson 1992).

The Descriptions of Roses

Roses differ enormously from place to place and from year to year. Height, colour, size, and resistance to disease are all directly affected by growing conditions. Flowering times and hardiness too vary according to the climate. Climbing Hybrid Teas generally flower earlier in the season the hotter the climate. A rose such as 'Albertine', which my fellow-countrymen regard as hardy in any situation, will not survive the winter in Prague or Chicago (plate 2). 'Climbing Peace' grows vigorously and flowers repeatedly in Cape Town, but is a bad grower and a worse bloomer in Ireland or Denmark. Each nation is concerned to breed roses which are suited to its climate. The American Rose Society in its early days had an evangelising spirit: "to nationalize the love for roses in America, with a rose for every home and a bush for every garden is our declared purpose" wrote its President Robert Pyle in 1921. This meant championing the development of new hardy roses which would be "as sturdy as our pioneer forefathers who tamed the Wild West."

There is surprisingly little information on the hardiness of climbing roses, although it is safe to say that no one in New York or Budapest could grow the Tea roses in chapter 6 except in a glasshouse. Any rose selected for the climate of central Europe by such breeders as Peter Lambert and Rudolph Geschwind, however, will be hardy in New England, just as the Pennsylvanian Walter Van Fleet's Wichurana Ramblers will flourish in Berlin or Vienna.

Gardeners in Africa or Australia have the opposite problem—trying to work out what will do well for them in a climate which is much hotter, and often much drier, than European and American garden writers can comprehend. For the Australian rosarian Susan Irvine (1997) the problem is even more complicated: "It would be impossible to write accurately about growing roses 'in Australian conditions' because these conditions vary so radically." She found that in some of the harsher climatic zones of Australia, for instance Western Australia and far western Queensland, roses described as "delicate" in English books turned out to be robust. Irvine also discovered that in many parts of Australia the Tea roses are the most reliable.

Chapter 1

Scent is difficult to quantify and describe, and everyone's perception of scent differs. Many people used to smoke tobacco, which affected their sense of smell; until recently, therefore, some roses have been described as scentless when in fact they are not. One of the earliest descriptions of 'Sombreuil', for example, said that it had "odeur nul," although this was soon corrected by other writers (*Le Journal des Roses et des Végétales* 1856). Some writers regard only the sweet damask fragrance of roses as a true scent, treating the musky scent as if it did not exist, let alone give pleasure. I am wary of generalising about scents, but it does seem to me that most rose scents are sweet, foetid, musky, tealike, myrrhy, fruity, or combinations of these six types. I am also sceptical of those whose sense of smell seems to be influenced by colour. Graham Stuart Thomas, for example, tells us that 'Lady Hillingdon' smells of apricots. It may be an apricot-coloured rose, but it certainly does not smell of apricots to me.

Many rose descriptions in the standard works are regurgitations of the breeder's original, overlaudatory descriptions. Errors are perpetuated from one generation to the next, not through any desire to mislead, but simply as a result of ignorance and a failure to look again at the rose in question. Any nineteenth-century description of a deep, lasting, rich yellow rose usually turns out to be pale lemon rose which fades to cream. There is a tendency for such authorities as August Jäger, the author of the invaluable *Rosenlexikon* (1960), to describe the colour of the flowers when they first open and never to mention that they usually fade, sometimes losing their colour altogether. Nor is Jäger alone in this: many of the overenthusiastic descriptions of roses in such publications as *Journal des Roses* were picked up and perpetuated by *Modern Roses*. The colours always seem better, richer, and more complex on the printed page than they do to us in the garden. Anyone who buys 'Albéric Barbier' expecting a rose with flowers which are "rich apricot" or "yolk-yellow" will be disappointed when the overall impression of this cultivar turns out to be milky white. And colours are variable—they differ according to the weather and from day to day, season to season, and year to year. At the International Heritage Rose Conference at Lyon in 1999, Professor Maurice Jay pointed out that the magenta colours in roses are affected by the pH of the soil in which they grow: a low pH produces darker magenta tones, whereas a high pH makes them pale and pinker.

Roses frequently have different colours on the two sides of their petals. This characteristic seldom elicits comment, unless the contrast is extreme. But the interaction between the two colours is crucial to the overall effect of the flower and the way light is reflected at the centre, giving rise to distinctive shadows, tones, and hues which are one of the charms of roses. It also helps to distinguish and identify individual cultivars.

When noting how many flowers there are in a cluster, the original introducers have tended to exaggerate the number of flowers. Wherever possible, I give the size of a typical cluster on a healthy, mature plant at its first flowering of the year, which is always the most productive. All roses tend to make smaller clusters on old wood and larger ones on new. This explains why the autumn clusters are often very much larger than the original spring-flowering ones.

Taking a World View: Choosing the Best

I was brought up in the world of English horticulture, which many non-English people consider a fount of true knowledge. Writing this book has been a humbling experience. I have learned to admire and appreciate the rose traditions of many other people, especially the French, Germans, and Americans, and to realise how different they are from my own and in some ways better. We are too often persuaded that home-grown roses are the only ones which will succeed for us. Nationalism, introspection, isolationism, tariff controls, ignorance, and complacency have much to answer for. The truth is that there are many excellent roses which grow in other countries but are unknown in our own. Many of the Kordesii climbers which made such an impact upon European gardens in the late twentieth century failed to become popular in those parts of North America where they would have greatly enhanced people's gardens. Alister Clark's hybrids of *Rosa gigantea*, still the backbone of climbing roses in his native Australia, have had some measure of success in California but none in the western Mediterranean region, where they would be well adapted to climatic and growing conditions. It is important to look around the world for your roses and to pick the best. Some of the least-known were bred in countries with small home markets, for instance, Belgium, Denmark, and Hungary.

It is difficult to make a proper assessment of a cultivar's value from a cursory encounter in a single garden, but I believe there are many first-rate old roses which have never had a chance to establish a claim to our attention. Breeders who introduce a large number of similar cultivars within a few years of each other are happy for the open market to assess their relative merits. For example, between 1902 and 1909 Barbier introduced eight hybrids of *Rosa wichurana* bred by crossing the species with 'Souvenir de Catherine Guillot'. It is little wonder that only one ('Léontine Gervais') is still widely grown, while 'Adélaïde Moullé' and 'Pinson' have disappeared entirely from cultivation. 'Léontine Gervais' may indeed be the best of these Barbier hybrids, but there are seasons when such cultivars as 'Alexandre Tremouillet' or 'Jean Guichard' seem to excel. Nor does the best invariably establish itself as the popular favourite.

The earlier work of a breeder is seldom as good as his later achievements. Such is the excitement and novelty of rose breeding that first introductions are often of inferior quality; the breeder, however, is certain that all ugly ducklings are swans. Jack Harkness began rose breeding in 1962; later, he was ashamed to say that from that year's crosses he subsequently introduced twenty-four new roses, some of them ill advisedly. But with the passing of the years, a breeder learns discrimination and will introduce a rose only if it represents a marked advance upon what is already available. The public perception is different, however. It is the breeder's early work which catches the eye of the market, precisely because it is different from what has gone before. The first of a series is often the most popular—it continues to outsell its successors even though the breeder knows that subsequent introductions are distinctly better. 'New Dawn' was the first rose to be registered under the U.S. plant patent laws. It achieved enormous popularity for its vigour, beauty, scent, health, and, above all, for its remontancy. 'New Dawn' was widely used by breeders in every continent, and its genes have been responsible for many excellent climbing roses over the last seventy years. Yet, none of its offspring or remoter issue has ever enjoyed such esteem as 'New Dawn' itself.

It is true, nevertheless, that for nearly two hundred years the rose trade has been driven by novelty. The popularity of a particular cultivar is always followed by a reaction, a period in which its qualities are found to be faults. Disparagement follows renown as night follows day. Time and again when writing this book, it became apparent that many of the best roses are rare, threatened, or even extinct, while mediocrities remain widely available. The qualities which distinguish the great from the merely competent are vigour, health, grace of carriage, abundance and duration of flowering, and adaptability to many different soils and climates. The most immediately attractive qualities of the rose—colour and scent—are incidentals. A truly great rose must have a distinctive personality which sets it apart from the other great roses.

The Conservation of Our Rose Heritage

All rosarians owe an inestimable debt to such collections as L'Haÿ-les-Roses in France, Cavriglia in Italy, Gerlev in Denmark, Coloma in Belgium, and the Ruston garden in South Australia. But it is important to remember, above all, what a stunning collection of old roses has been preserved for nearly a century in the European Rosarium at Sangerhausen (plate 3). Hundreds of roses of every class survive here, and only here, and would have been extinct but for the tenacity of its staff and supporters over the years.

In this book I have recorded nearly sixteen hundred climbing roses still in existence. Another thirteen hundred have been allowed to disappear altogether during the last hundred years. Many forgotten or unnamed roses are grown in nurseries, public collections, and private gardens. Their conservation represents an important part of our social and cultural history and helps to fill the gaps in our understanding of the history of the rose itself. I hope that no rose which I have seen, described, and photographed will ever be allowed to fade from cultivation and slip into extinction.

The Chinese Synstylae and Other Species

All our rambling roses and most of our modern garden roses are descended from Synstylae species. The Synstylae are a group within the genus *Rosa*, which includes such important species as *R. multiflora* and *R. wichurana*, each of which has been extensively used to breed garden hybrids. There is one characteristic which distinguishes the Synstylae roses from all others: they have a projecting column of fused styles at the centre of the flower. The untrained eye will not see it but, once it was pointed out to me as a boy, I remember how obvious the exserted style of *R. arvensis* seemed.

Synstylae roses tend to have lots of small white flowers in large clusters. They also tend (but there are exceptions here, too) to have a strong musky scent. This differs from species to species in both quality and degree. Some such as *Rosa setigera* are commonly scentless, but muskiness is unique to the Synstylae and very distinctive. Another characteristic of the section is of horticultural significance—they flower late. When this characteristic is transmitted to their garden progeny, we can enjoy climbing roses until late into the season, as with the 'Turner's Crimson Rambler' tribe of small-flowered rambling roses.

One of the most important events in the history of the rose was the development of dwarf, bushy, repeat-flowering growth among the garden roses of China. This is usually thought to have occurred as a mutation in *Rosa chinensis*, but the phenomenon also occurs within the Synstylae section. I have seen flowers on young plants of *R. helenae*, *R. wichurana*, and *R. multiflora*, only two or three months old. If genetic analysis showed that the old China roses contained a trace of Synstylae genes, it would also explain why those cultivated roses carry their flowers in small clusters, whereas their non-Synstylae ancestors *R. chinensis* and *R. gigantea* bear their flowers singly.

The Synstylae roses are native of every continent in the Northern Hemisphere, from North America across Europe and all of Asia, with a concentration of species in a rapid state of evolution in the Himalayas and western China. Few taxonomists in recent years have had the courage or the field experience to work on them. Some species are distinct and immediately recognisable (e.g., *Rosa soulieana*), but others dissolve in a confusion of subspecies, varieties, and forms. The pan-Asian groups of *R. brunonii* and *R. longicuspis* are among the most difficult to unravel because they merge with other species at the edges of their natural distributions. The roses which end this chapter (*R. banksiae*, *R. laevigata*, and *R. bracteata*) are not members of the Synstylae, but all are native to the same warm lowlands of China.

Rosa brunonii and Its Hybrids

Rosa brunonii displays so much natural variability that it is best regarded as a group of species or as a single species in a state of rapid evolution. It grows naturally throughout the Himalayas, from Kashmir and Afghanistan to the mountains of western Sichuan, and has given rise to many horticultural hybrids and selections, including the rose known as *R. moschata*.

Rosa brunonii Lindley. Himalayan musk rose. This deciduous shrub has arching stems 5–12 m high, which can grow taller up a tree, thanks to its short, stout, hooked prickles. The leaves are large (15–25 cm long) with prickly, glandular rachis. The leaflets are 7 cm long, drooping, narrowly ovate to elliptic, acute or acuminate, greyish green or glaucous above, and occasionally hairy or downy beneath; the margins have simple, regular teeth. The stipules are narrow and hairy or glandular, as are the pedicels and receptacles. The flowers are creamy white in bud but open pure white, single, 3–4 cm across, and carried in large corymbose clusters fairly late in the season. These clusters are often combined into one huge compound inflorescence measuring as much as 35 cm across. The flowers have a strong musky scent. The long sepals reflex during flowering, then drop off. The hips are round or obovoid, red, shiny, and 1–2 cm across.

Rosa moschata Miller is a cultivated plant and variable in its characteristics. Its many forms need to be sorted out by a botanist with a sense of historical discipline. *Rosa moschata* is said to be less vigorous than *R. brunonii*, with greener leaves, broader leaflets, larger flowers, acuminate petals, and larger corymbs. Semi-double and double forms have been known since the seventeenth century. The semi-double *R. brunonii* 'Autumnalis' is sometimes attributed to *R. moschata*. *Rosa phoenicia* Boissier is close to *R. moschata* but not in cultivation outside its native Turkey. Phillips and Rix (1993) distinguish it by its "stems 5 m, leaflets usually five, 2–4.5 cm long, densely short-hairy beneath, with distinct very broad, coarse teeth."

Lindley named *Rosa brunonii* for Robert Brown, a botanist who worked for the Horticultural Society of London. There are many collections in cultivation, including the pink cultivar known as 'Betty Sheriff'. The form known as 'La Mortola', which Graham Stuart Thomas introduced in the mid-1950s, comes from the Hanbury Garden between Ventimiglia and Menton in Italy. It has particularly large flowers and large leaves which are greyish green, limp, and breathtakingly beautiful.

Several clones of *Rosa brunonii* 'Autumnalis' are grown; they vary in many characteristics, including their exact season of flower. Two additional remontant cultivars are almost certainly hybrids with *R. chinensis* and possibly *R. gigantea*: 'Princesse de Nassau' and 'Nastarana'. The rose now in cultivation as 'Princesse de Nassau' was reintroduced by Graham Stuart Thomas in the 1970s. The original rose was bred by Laffay in about 1830. It is fully double, opens cream but fades to white, is medium sized (5–7 cm), flat, and strongly musk scented. 'Nastarana' (syn. 'Pissardii') [W. Paul, 1879] is a short climber with fairly small (5 cm), pale pink flowers which are fully double; almost all the stamens make little petaloids, giving it a distinct form. The leaves are attractively glaucous. The Belgian amateur botanist Yvan Louette believes that 'Nastarana' is probably descended as much from *R. freytagii* as *R. brunonii*. He noted that *R. freytagii* has a circular stigma like 'Nastarana' (it is columnar in *R. brunonii*). These Moschata Hybrids merge with such early Noisettes as 'Blanc Pur' (see chapter 6).

Western Hybrids of *Rosa brunonii*

Rosa brunonii is one of the finest of climbers for temperate climates. Its hybrids are often hardier than the species. They are among the most rewarding of all small-flowered ramblers.

'Banksiaeflora'. Probably a hybrid between *Rosa arvensis* or *R. sempervirens*, crossed with a form of *R. moschata*. It has small, very double, pure white flowers with a cream centre and reflexing petals.

'Francis E. Lester' [Lester, 1946]. 'Kathleen' seedling. This is a very handsome and vigorous rose. Its flowers open apple-blossom pink, with a creamy centre, then fade to white but do not brown off, so the colour always looks pure. The flowers are set off, at first, by bright yellow stamens. They have a strong fruity scent and are profusely carried in medium-sized clusters (twenty to thirty) which, because the individual flowers are comparatively large for a single-flowered rambler (5.0–5.5 cm), seem enormous. It grows thickly and vigorously to 5–6 m and reblooms occasionally after the first spectacular burst. The leaves are a bright, rich green. The handsome, widely spaced clusters of hips are very attractive in autumn.

'Mme d'Arblay' syn. 'Wells's White' [Wells, 1835]. Allegedly *Rosa multiflora* × *moschata*, the reverse cross to 'The Garland', but very different. 'Mme d'Arblay' has small (2.5–3.0 cm), very double white flowers in dense, distinctly conical clusters. They are musk scented, with rather short petals. The plant grows vigorously, if not as luxuriantly as 'The Garland', to about 5 m and is excellent for rambling through a tree. It is very hardy and was once recommended as a rootstock.

'Paul's Himalayan Musk' [W. Paul, 1916]. *Rosa brunonii* seedling. This rose is one of the most widely grown once-flowering ramblers in the world—universally popular for its vigour and ease of cultivation (plate 4). Its flowers are 3 cm, fully double, and soft lilac pink fading to white. They are strongly musk scented, offset by lush green leaves, and borne in large clusters of thirty to fifty. Planted in the most unpromising of situations at the foot of a fairly tall tree, it will make its way up in a few years and cascade out of the branches in eye-catching profusion.

'Polyantha Grandiflora' syn. *Rosa × gentiliana* [Bernaix, 1886]. Parentage unknown, probably *R. multiflora* hybrid × *R. moschata* hybrid. This has fairly small (4–5 cm), single, pure white flowers, each with a very handsome boss of orange stamens which turn quickly to brown. The flowers come in fairly large clusters and are strongly scented. They also have conspicuous reddish brown glands on the pedicels, which run down to become little prickles on the stems. The leaves are large, pale to medium green, and glossy, with red midribs when young. The plant grows vigorously to about 5 m and is reasonably hardy. The flowers are not recurrent, but are followed by many orange red hips which last well into late autumn. More than one cultivar is grown under this name.

'The Garland' syn. 'Wood's Garland', 'Wells's Garland', 'Splendid Garland' [Wells, 1835]. Perhaps *Rosa moschata × multiflora*. The slender buds open to elegant, semi-double flowers (4 cm) on long stems in very large, conical clusters of up to forty, sometimes more (plate 5). Pale peachy pink at first, the flowers fade to white as they open out; they are held upright and have a strong musky scent. The petals are distinctively reflexed along their sides and the stamens at the centre form a crown around the stigma; these two characteristics distinguish 'The Garland' from every other climbing rose. The plant is exceptionally vigorous, rather late to flower, very free-flowering, but not recurrent. The stems are very prickly and the prickles are large.

Rosa filipes and Its Hybrids

Of all the tall Asiatic species of climbing roses, *Rosa filipes* is probably the most widely grown, usually in its exceptionally vigorous form 'Kiftsgate'. Because its size makes it unsuitable for small gardens, it has become a status symbol among those who garden on a large scale. *Rosa filipes* has also begotten a growing range of equally vigorous hybrids of somewhat uneven quality.

Rosa filipes Rehder & Wilson is a large shrub, growing to about 10 m high, with arching and climbing stems armed with a few small prickles about 1 cm long (plate 6). The leaves have five or seven thin leaflets, which are coppery red when young, with glabrous rachis and petioles, sparsely prickly, and sometimes glandular. The slender leaflets are narrowly elliptic, 3.5–8.0 cm long, 2.5–5.0 cm wide, acuminate, glabrous above but usually downy on the veins beneath, and with shallowly toothed margins. The stipules are slender and fringed with glands. The flowers are musk scented and open white from cream-coloured buds. Flowers measure about 2.5 cm wide and are borne in huge corymbose panicles of as many as one hundred flowers, often 40 cm or even 50 cm wide. The pedicels are slender, glandular, not downy, and 3–4 cm long. The sepals have slender tips and are glandular and slightly downy or hairless on the back; they reflex and eventually fall after flowering. The petals are distinctly obovate and seldom overlap, which gives the flowers an airy look. The stamens are large and very numerous, with golden yellow anthers. The fruits are usually round, 1 cm across, orange or scarlet, and very impressive on their long pedicels in huge clusters.

Rosa filipes is a native of western China. Reginald Farrer (1916) described it as "a huge rampageous bush, diffusing an intense sweetness so keen and entrancing that all the air quivers with the intoxicating deliciousness of it for half a mile around." The flowers owe their impact to their glorious stamens; long, widely spaced pedicels; and long, slender sepals. *Rosa filipes* is among the last species to flower and is said to be less tolerant of shade than other Asiatic species, although that is not my experience. *Rosa filipes* is now represented almost exclusively by the fine clone 'Kiftsgate', which Graham Stuart Thomas admired at Diany Binny's Kiftsgate Court in Gloucestershire and introduced in 1954. His admiration was for the size and vigour of the plant, which has reached some 25 m up a copper beech tree at Kiftsgate Court; the plant is widely considered the largest of all roses in cultivation in northern Europe. 'Kiftsgate' is said to be slow to get growing, but Diany Binny gave me a mass of hardwood cuttings some years ago which rooted and grew so quickly that some were as much as 5 m high a year later. Mrs Binny was concerned that seedlings of 'Kiftsgate' were being sold as the original clone and that many of the plants which people grew as 'Kiftsgate' were incorrectly named.

Rosa filipes hybridises freely in the garden and sows itself around, so that any garden owner with a flowering specimen of 'Kiftsgate' begins to chance upon seedlings which are often hybrids. Not all are garden-worthy, but among the best are 'Brenda Colvin', 'Suzon', and 'Treasure Trove'. Louis Lens used *R. filipes* and 'Kiftsgate' fairly extensively in his species breeding programme. His best seedling is the vigorous 2-m shrub rose 'Dentelle de Bruxelles' [Lens, 1986].

'Brenda Colvin' [Colvin, introduced by Sunningdale, 1970]. This is the best of the simpler Filipes Hybrids. It grew in Oxfordshire at Filkins, the garden belonging to the influential designer Brenda Colvin. Its flowers are small (3 cm) and lightly semi-double. The overall impression is of apple-blossom pink: I have several specimens in my own garden which smother old apple trees with flower so that the trees seem to blossom for a second time. The flowers have a good, strong, sweet-musky scent and are most abundantly carried in nicely spaced, open corymbs. The plant is enormously vigorous, and well-furnished with handsome, rich green leaves.

'Diany Binny' [Binny, c. 1975]. This seedling occurred at Kiftsgate but is not one of the best. The flowers are slightly larger than 'Kiftsgate' (5 cm) and musk scented, but carried on short stems in rather congested, medium-sized clusters (typically ten to twenty). They are single, pure white, with conspicuous yellow stamens. The distinctive grey leaves contrast with coppery red new growths. The plant is very hardy and extremely vigorous.

'Rosemary Foster' [Foster, 1997]. This promising new seedling received an Award of Merit from the Royal Horticultural Society in London in 1997. The single, musk-scented flowers are 3 cm and medium pink before fading to white, but remain slightly darker at the edges and on the undersides of the petals. The orange stamens survive for about a day and the flowers shatter well when spent. The plant grows extremely vigorously to 15 m and produces enormous pyramidal corymbs.

'Suzon' [Eve, 1994]. 'Suzon' and 'Suzy' are sister-seedlings from a cross between 'Kiftsgate' and 'Joseph's Coat'. 'Suzon' is a striking orange climber with 8-cm, semi-single flowers which fade to coral. They come in large, open corymbs on long pedicels, with a sweet musky scent. The plant grows to at least 8 m. It is, to my thinking, the best of Eve's Filipes Hybrids.

'Suzy' [Eve, 1994]. The French rosarian Odile Masquelier considers 'Suzy' the best of André Eve's 'Kiftsgate' crosses. The flowers are fully double, medium to large (10 cm), and rather cupped in shape, largely because they are very closely held together in their clusters. The flowers are pale peach at first and said to smell of peaches. 'Suzy' is very vigorous, growing to at least 10 m. With its many petals, it may prefer a dry, warm climate. Mme Masquelier says that it flowers early and freely over a long period. It is much beloved of bees.

'Toby Tristram' [c. 1970]. The flowers are 3 cm, single, and musk scented. They are cream at first, opening from small pink buds, but fade quickly to white. They are carried in large, spacious clusters earlier in the season than most Filipes Hybrids and are followed by beautiful, pendant hips. This hybrid is said to flower repeatedly, but I have not noticed this. There is a fine archway wreathed in 'Toby Tristram' at L'Haÿ-les-Roses.

'Treasure Trove' [Treasure, 1977]. This is a vigorous climbing rose of supreme loveliness, with 6-cm butterscotch flowers which fade to buff, pale pink, and cream. The beautiful colouring, combined with the loosely double form of the flowers and the limp red new growths, makes 'Treasure Trove' the best of all the Filipes Hybrids. The flowers come in spacious clusters of about fifteen. The plant is free-flowering, sweetly scented, once-flowering, and hardy, and grows to 8 m.

Rosa helenae and Its Hybrids

Rosa helenae is widespread in west and central China, through eastern Sichuan and western Hubei, and south into Vietnam, Laos, and Cambodia. It was introduced to the West by Ernest Wilson for the Arnold Arboretum in 1900 and named after his wife, Helen. It is said to be closely allied to *R. brunonii*, although hardier and less vigorous, and could be regarded as its eastern counterpart: intermediates between the two are found in Sichuan. *Rosa helenae* is among the hardiest of the Asiatic musk roses and has been used to breed subzero roses in Ottawa.

Rosa helenae Rehder & Wilson is a large shrub which grows to about 7 m high, with arching and climbing stems armed with short, backward-hooked prickles which are about 1 cm long. The leaves are 7–18 cm long and have seven to nine leaflets which are 2–6 cm long, usually ovate, acute, bright green and hairless above, grey beneath and glabrous, with downy veins and simple-toothed margins. The flowers are white (although the base of the petals turns pink with age and the unusually pale stamens intensify the whiteness), single, musk scented, and 4 cm across. The petals reflex after flowering and later fall away. The sepals are about 1 cm long, with lateral lobes. The pedicels are 2–3 cm long and the flowers come in flat, spacious corymbs of thirty to fifty. The hips are small (about 1 cm), ovoid, and orange red; they hang down gracefully and distinctively.

'Hélène Maréchal' [Lens, 1995]. As the name suggests, this is a cross between *R. helenae* and 'Maréchal Niel'. Lens maintained that from *R. helenae* it inherited supple long stems and its creamy white colour passing to white. From 'Maréchal Niel' came small (5-cm), double flowers in the style of a Tea rose and a delicate scent.

'Longford' [Preston, pre-1938]. *Rosa helenae × gallica*. The plant at Sangerhausen under this name owes more to the latter parent. It has small flowers (3.5 cm) in clusters of five to ten which are a very rich crimson but scentless. It flowers late and grows to 3–4 m.

'Lykkefund' [Olsen, 1930]. This putative seedling of a *Rosa helenae* seedling is a very beautiful, once-flowering, thornless rambler with strongly scented, small (4 cm), loosely semi-double flowers profusely borne in medium-sized clusters of ten to twenty (plate 7). Small pink buds open to pale mother-of-pearl flowers which fade quickly to white. Dark golden stamens attract the eye of the beholder. The leaves are fairly small, bright green, and copious, while the whole plant exudes a distinctive airy elegance. A specimen at Sangerhausen has grown 10 m up a tree. As with so many thornless roses, the undersides of the leaves still have small barbs or prickles along their midribs—there is no such thing as a rose without a thorn.

'Patricia Macoun' [Preston, 1945]. This *Rosa helenae* seedling has small (4.5 cm), white, loosely double, scented flowers. They open out flat to show their stamens and are carried in fairly large clusters of fifteen to twenty-five. The foliage is dark and glossy. The plant is vigorous and very free-flowering but does not repeat. It is a useful climbing rose for extremely cold climates, although the flowers are sensitive to rain.

Rosa longicuspis and Its Hybrids

Rosa longicuspis is a native of the lower ranges of northeastern India, western China, and Burma. It is fairly closely related to *R. brunonii*, although the leaves of *R. longicuspis* are tougher and more glabrous and the clusters contain fewer flowers. Intermediates grow in the eastern Himalayas and western China. Some of the plants in cultivation as *R. longicuspis* are actually forms of *R. rubus* or *R. mulliganii*.

Rosa longicuspis Bertoloni syn. *R. lucens* Rolfe syn. *R. sinowilsonii* Hemsley is a large evergreen or semi-evergreen shrub which scrambles and climbs to 8 m, thanks to its very vigorous reddish mahogany shoots and copious covering of short, stout, flat, straight prickles which are also dark red when young. The leaves are up to 20 cm long, eventually dark shiny green, with five to seven leaflets, each 5–10 cm long, ovate to elliptic, leathery, and glabrous. The margins have small, simple teeth. The flowers open from narrow buds; they are white, 4–5 cm across, single, and have a fruity scent. They are borne in loose clusters of five to fifteen. The silky backs to the petals are distinctive. The pedicels are quite long, about 3 cm. The sepals are about 2–3 cm long, reflex after flowering, and eventually fall. The hips are round, 1.5–2.0 cm, and red or orange. Some forms have a tendency to be mildly stoloniferous. Some authorities consider 'Lime Kiln' [Brooke, 1970] close to *R. longicuspis*. It has small flowers (about 3 cm) which are fairly double, lightly scented, and borne in small clusters (typically five or six flowers). The medium-sized leaves are medium to dark green with seven leaflets; the rachis and pedicels are likewise green. 'Lime Kiln' flowers in midseason, but is not very distinguished. It was a chance seedling in the garden at Lime Kiln in Suffolk, which belonged to Humphrey Brooke, one of the few Westerners to visit Sangerhausen in the 1960s and 1970s.

Rosa lucens Rolfe is best regarded as a variety of *R. longicuspis*. The only botanical differences are that *R. longicuspis* var. *lucens* has glabrous petal-backs, not silky, and slightly shorter leaflets. *Rosa sinowilsonii* Hemsley & Wilson also belongs with *R. longicuspis*, as *R. longicuspis* var. *sinowilsonii*. This rose is rather more distinct: it has more rounded buds and much larger flower clusters than pure *R. longicuspis*. Its foliage is also larger, up to 35 cm long, and the young leaves are grey, with crimson rachis. The rampant climber 'Wedding Day' [Stern, 1950] is an open-pollinated seedling of a hybrid between *R. longicuspis* var. *sinowilsonii* and *R. moyesii*. It has large clusters of small (3 cm), single flowers with a strong fruity scent. The pale apricot buds open to cream-coloured flowers which fade quickly to dirty white with crimson blotches in rainy weather. The plant will easily reach 8 m. It was named 'Wedding Day' because it flowered for the first time on 26 June, which was Sir Frederick and Lady Stern's wedding anniversary (Stern 1960). The rose grown as 'Wedding Day' in Australia is 'Polyantha Grandiflora'.

Rosa glomerata Rehder & Wilson is also fairly close to *R. longicuspis* and, according to Wilson, easily distinguished by its large leaflets with strong reticulate venation and villous pubescence on the underside, short-peduncled dense corymbs, and the villous tomentum on the pedicels. However, in these features it also resembles some forms of *R. rubus*.

Other Chinese Synstylae Species

Rosa rubus Léveillé & Vaniot. This vigorous shrub has purplish stems which clamber up to 6 m, thanks to its scattering of short, hooked prickles. The leaves are 10–20 cm long, with three to five (typically five) leaflets which are 3–9 cm long, elliptic-ovate to oblong-obovate, acute, hairless above, and greyish and usually downy beneath. The margins have simple, large, coarse teeth. The receptacle is glandular-bristly. The flowers are white, about 4 cm across, single, scented, with broad overlapping petals on pedicels 1–2 cm long and borne in dense clusters. The sepals are downy and glandular on the back, usually entire, reflexing after flowering and falling. The hips are 1.0–1.5 cm in diameter, round, dark red, and glandular-bristly. *Rosa rubus* comes from western and central China. Reginald Farrer praised its "blossom of such a fragrance that all the air is drunk with its sweetness" and commented that the scent is only noticeable after midday. It flowers early with attractive young foliage very like that of a *Rubus* but has never been common in gardens, nor used for hybridisation. *Rosa cerasocarpa* Rolfe is very near to *R. rubus* and probably no more than a glabrous form of it. *Rosa mulliganii* Boulenger is a horticultural selection raised in the Royal Horticultural Society Garden at Wisley from seeds collected by Forrest during his 1917 expedition to Yunnan. *Rosa henryi* Boulenger, *R. gentiliana* sens. Rehder & Wilson, in part, not Léveillé & Vaniot, is also very close to *R. rubus*.

Rosa soulieana Crépin. This upright shrub has strong, thick stems that reach 5 m or more and forms a broad thicket as much as 10 m across. The stems have many pale, stout, decurved, compressed, broad-based prickles. The leaves are 6–10 cm long, deciduous, with seven to nine greyish green leaflets 1–3 cm long, oval to elliptic, acute to obtuse, glabrous on both sides except sometimes along the midrib beneath. The margins have fine, simple teeth. The flowers are pale yellow in bud and open cream, 3–4 cm across, single, scented, and produced rather late in the season in large clusters (of fifteen to thirty). The sepals are usually entire or with a few lateral lobes; they reflex and fall after flowering. The dainty hips are small (no more than 1 cm), ovoid, and orange. The grey foliage and large prickles give *R. soulieana* great ornamental value when it is not in flower or fruit, but it has never been systematically used to breed new climbers or shrub roses. Its best-known seedling is the beautiful 'Wickwar' [Steadman, c. 1960], a probable hybrid with *R. brunonii* which grew in Keith Steadman's garden at Wickwar, in Gloucestershire. It has greyish glaucous foliage and substantial, musk-scented, creamy white, single, 5-cm flowers in great abundance, followed by small red hips in autumn. Keith Steadman was a wealthy plantsman with relaxed ideas about garden maintenance and a passion for unusual trees and shrubs. 'Sir Cedric Morris' [Beales, 1979] is a garden hybrid between *R. soulieana* and *R. longicuspis*. It is a late-flowering climber with large prickles, large leaves, and slender leaflets. The small (4 cm), creamy white, musk-scented, single flowers come in large, airy clusters (twenty to thirty). It grows very vigorously to at least 8 m. The clusters of round hips are very attractive and last well into late autumn. Sir Cedric Morris was a wealthy amateur whose garden at Benton End, Hadleigh, Suffolk was a treasure-house of rare plants. 'Kew Rambler' [Kew, 1912] is a putative cross between *Rosa soulieana* and 'Hiawatha' (plate 8). It has large clusters of small (4 cm), scented, single, blush pink flowers that fade to ivory white rather late in the season. They are best when just starting to flower. Its glossy leaves show its Wichurana ancestry, but 'Kew Rambler' grows vigorously to 8 m.

The Banksian Roses

The Philadelphia nurseryman Robert Buist declared in 1844 that the Banksians were "the most graceful, luxuriant, and beautiful of roses." They are also the first to flower (a month before other roses) and among the most vigorous. The largest rose-tree in the world is a plant of the double white *Rosa banksiae* var. *banksiae* on the corner of Fourth Street and Toughnut in Tombstone, Arizona, which was planted in 1886. By 1969 its trunk had a circumference of nearly 2.5 m and the plant was spread over a trellis of more than 550 m^2. Now it is said to cover 800 m^2.

Banksian roses have long been popular in China, where there are records of cultivated forms as far back as the sixteenth century. *Rosa banksiae* var. *banksiae* was the first to be introduced to the West; the following description is widely drawn to embrace both the wild species and the three cultivars (double white, double yellow, and single yellow) which were known in Western gardens and described earlier.

Rosa banksiae Robert Brown in Ait. This shrub has strong, slender, glabrous stems which grow to 15 m high (plate 9). The stems are usually unarmed but occasionally bear very sparse, hooked prickles. The leaves are evergreen, with three to five (occasionally seven) leaflets, 2–6 cm long, 1–2 cm wide, oblong-lanceolate, glossy and glabrous on both surfaces, with wavy margins and simple teeth. The flowers are single or double, white or yellow, and small (2.5–3.0 cm across), carried in large umbels of up to fifty. The styles are free and not exserted; the flowers come on long stalks; and the fruits are 0.5–1.0 cm, round, and usually red, but sometimes orange or yellow. The plant forms a substantial trunk, with shaggy, russet brown bark.

The wild rose is known as *Rosa banksiae* var. *normalis* Regel. It has single, white, violet-scented flowers with distinctive petals and long wispy stamens. The plant has hooked prickles, and is widely distributed in China, from Gansu to Yunnan, often on steep, rocky hillsides or as a boundary hedge in agricultural areas. It was first described from the wild by Augustine Henry nearly a hundred years after the original introduction of the double-flowered form (Henry 1902).

Rosa banksiae var. *banksiae* was first described in 1811: Robert Brown is said to have named it after Sir Joseph Banks's wife. John Lindley considered it the most elegant of the genus. *Rosa banksiae* var. *banksiae* has small (1.5–2.0 cm), very double flowers which are intensely scented of violets. So strong and carrying is this scent that the English plantsman Canon Ellacombe (1982) recounted "I once heard an old gardener declare that when in full flower he could smell it although more than a hundred yards [90 m] away." The flowers are small (little more than 1 cm across) and very double, like miniature cherry blossoms. The leaves are glossy and bronze when young, which sets off the flowers very attractively. The plant is completely thornless. The characteristics which distinguish it from the wild single-flowered form suggest that it is a hybrid, rather than a naturally occurring form. Martyn Rix maintains that the double white form which is most commonly seen as a hedging plant in the Lijiang Valley has prickles and more closely resembles a simple double-flowered form of *R. banksiae* var. *normalis*.

A single form with yellow flowers was introduced from China in the mid-nineteenth century as *Rosa banksiae* f. *lutescens*. It is sweetly scented (but not of violets), and its slightly larger flowers (2.0–2.5 cm) indicate that it is a hybrid with a form of *R. chinensis*. It sets vast quantities of yellow hips and was extensively used by Quinto Mansuino to raise his Banksian Hybrids. Its yellow colouring, as well as that of *R. banksiae* var. *lutea*, probably came from a cultivated form of *R. chinensis*. (Martyn Rix has also advanced a theory that it might be a hybrid with *R. xanthina*, whose distribution overlaps considerably with *R. banksiae*.)

Lindley named the double yellow Banksian rose *Rosa banksiae* var. *lutea*. It was collected in Nankin by John Parks on behalf of the Horticultural Society of London in 1824 and has large clusters of small (1.0–1.5 cm), fully double, straw yellow flowers with a green eye. They are scentless but borne in immense profusion. The plant usually has five leaflets and few prickles. It is the hardiest of the Banksians: the English rosarian Rose

Kingsley wrote of a fine specimen at Chillon Castle in Switzerland. Banksian roses flourish in hot, dry climates: Western Australia, Cape Province, Morocco, and California can all boast specimens which have grown as much as 20 m high. The finest plants of *R. banksiae* var. *lutea* that I have seen are exuberantly intertwined with purple *Wisteria sinensis* in the gardens of the Generalife at Granada in southern Spain.

There is a hybrid between *Rosa banksiae* and *R. gigantea* which grows in several Riviera gardens and can be traced back to 'La Mortola'. It has single, white, medium-sized flowers (7 cm) in small umbels and was presumably imported by Sir Thomas Hanbury in the latter half of the nineteenth century. It is not listed in the *Hortus Mortolensis* of 1937, but Phillips and Rix have a fine photograph of it in *Conservatory and Indoor Plants* (1997). The cultivar known as 'Anemonaeflora', introduced from China by Fortune in 1846, is probably a hybrid between *R. banksiae* and a form of *R. multiflora*. It has large clusters of very small (1 cm) and very double flowers which are pale pink, fading to white. The petals are very narrow, like those of daisies, with the inner ones shorter than the outer. The plant is evergreen or semi-evergreen, not very hardy, with wiry growth, little prickles and small, hard glossy leaves (for a full description, see *Rosen-Zeitung* 1899). It is said to have the sweet, violet scent of the Banksians, but I have not noticed this. One additional hybrid of *R. banksiae* came as a garden cultivar from China, the incomparable 'Fortuneana'.

> 'Fortuneana' syn. 'Fortuniana' [= *Rosa ×fortuniana*]. Crépin considered 'Fortuneana' a hybrid between *R. laevigata* and *R. banksiae*, but this parentage is questionable because no one has ever succeeded in crossing *R. laevigata* with *R. banksiae*. Its flowers are larger than other Banksian roses, about 6 cm across, although 'Fortuneana' flowers at the same time as they do, very early in the season. It was named in honour of Robert Fortune (1812–1880) by John Lindley in 1850. 'Fortuneana' is an important rootstock in Western Australia, where heat, drought, and poor soil are a challenge to cultivation.

There has been little breeding with *Rosa banksiae* in the West. Buist mentioned a fellow nurseryman who offered twenty-one cultivars in 1844, and Nietner had a list of thirteen in 1880. But it was two Italians, Attilio Ragionieri and Quinto Mansuino, who exploited the possibilities inherent in this vigorous and drought-resistant species. Dottore Ragionieri was a gentleman amateur from Castello near Florence. He found *R. banksiae* difficult to use in breeding: 'Ibrido di Castello' was the only seedling he was able to flower (there is a full account of this beautiful cultivar in *Gardener's Chronicle*, 1924, part II, p. 73). Commendatore Mansuino lived at Poggio di San Remo and worked with many unusual species. He admired *R. banksiae* for its elegant foliage, ruddy wood, early flowering, lack of prickles, and petal shape. He hoped that hybridising it would give repeat flowering, greater colour, more petals, and fewer flowers in the cluster. Mansuino began by crossing *R. banksiae* f. *lutescens* with a red-flowered form of *R. chinensis* but, of all the seventeen hundred seedlings he raised, he considered only one worthy of additional work. He crossed it with the old Noisette 'Lamarque' and, after five more generations of inbreeding and backcrossing, he obtained his first 'Mansuino' rose, a race of elegant and distinctive bushes that are far too little known outside Italy. Mansuino's only climber was 'Purezza', a first-generation cross with a Tea rose, which is the only perpetual-flowering or remontant Banksian climber.

'Ibrido di Castello' [Ragionieri, c. 1920]. *Rosa banksiae* 'Lutescens' × 'Lamarque'. Perhaps the prettiest of all the Banksian roses, the flowers of 'Ibrido di Castello' are about 4 cm in diameter, cream at first and fading to white, fully double, sometimes with a button eye, but always with many small petals inside and usually borne in small clusters. Their scent is delicious, a mixture of Tea and violets. The plant has typical *R. banksiae* foliage and a slight tendency to blackspot. The new growths are a bronze colour, which would indicate chlorosis in other roses but is common in the young leaves of *R. banksiae* hybrids. 'Ibrido di Castello' is less vigorous than 'Lutescens' but hardier. An established plant also has the fat, excorticating trunk typical of all the Banksians.

'Purezza' [Mansuino, 1961]. This hybrid is more widely grown than 'Ibrido di Castello' and is in flower for many months in the year. It was an early by-product of Mansuino's work with *Rosa banksiae*. The flowers are pure white, 3.5–4.0 cm across, loosely petalled, and less double than 'Ibrido di Castello'. They come in rather crowded clusters unlike, for example, the more widely spaced clusters of 'Fortuneana'.

Fairly closely allied to *Rosa banksiae* is *R. cymosa* Trattinick (syn. *R. microcarpa* Lindley), which is the most widespread of all Chinese roses and found in all the warmer areas. Although rather variable across its range, all forms have very small (1 cm) white flowers with conspicuous stamens in fairly large, open cymes, set off by crimson sepals and beautiful deep crimson young leaves which tend to hang limply when they first open. Its styles are not united into a column, but they are exserted. *Rosa cymosa* is clearly related to the Synstylae. It has a sweet scent, which some describe as resembling violets, and more prickles than *R. banksiae*. The flowers are sometimes said to resemble those of an elder (*Sambucus*) or whitebeam (*Sorbus*). *Rosa cymosa* flowers about four weeks later than *R. banksiae*.

Rosa bracteata and Its Hybrids

Rosa bracteata is a very handsome and distinct species, whose flowers are subtended by a ruff of green bracts. Although native to the coastal lowlands of southeastern China and possibly to Taiwan, it has also spread widely through the southern states of the United States. Indeed, so long has it been grown in Florida and Louisiana that it is sometimes said, without any proof, to have been introduced into pre-European America by Chinese who came to trade with Colorado Indians. *Rosa bracteata* was certainly used as a hedging plant from North Carolina to Texas during the nineteenth century and in some places is now an invasive menace.

Rosa bracteata Wendland. The 'Macartney' Rose is an evergreen shrub with thick, sturdy stems, covered with brownish down and armed with pairs of stout, broad-based, hooked prickles. The leaves have five to eleven leaflets which are 2–5 cm long and 1.0–2.5 cm wide, dark green, glossy, hairless above, usually downy beneath (if only on the midrib), and finely toothed. The flowers are pure white, 5–8 cm across, usually solitary, and single; they smell distinctly of peardrops, are borne singly on very short stalks, and are framed by several large, laciniated, downy bracts. The sepals are entire and brown and woolly on their backs; they fall after flowering. The styles are free, not exserted. The fruits are round, orange red, 2.5–4.0 cm across, and covered in the same woolly brown fluff.

Horticulturists have long admired *R. bracteata* for its very handsome, dense, bright green foliage and its comparatively large flowers set among rich golden stamens. The curious bracts have always excited interest, too. *Rosa bracteata* is late flowering, a characteristic which it has passed on to its offspring, and produces an occasional flower throughout the summer. Although classed among the climbers and capable of clambering up to a considerable height, it is usually seen as a free-standing shrub, about 2.5 m high and 5 m across.

It is surprising that such a handsome and distinct shrub as *Rosa bracteata* has not been more widely employed to breed new types of roses. The Catalan breeder Pedro Dot did some work with *R. bracteata* (half his crosses in 1937–38 were on this species), but he introduced no offspring. More recently, Louis Lens used *R. bracteata* fairly extensively in his species breeding programme, culminating in the exquisite shrub rose 'Pink Surprise' and the very hardy 'Jelena de Belder'. Among the climbers, only the double-flowered 'Maria Léonida' and the pale yellow 'Mermaid' have ever achieved popularity.

'Maria Léonida' syn. 'Alba Odorata' [Lemoyne, 1832]. *Rosa bracteata* cross, probably with a Tea rose. The flowers are white, with a cream-coloured centre, fully double, medium sized (6–8 cm), fully quartered, and lightly scented. 'Maria Léonida' lacks the subtending bracts of the species but has splendid glossy green foliage. It flowers very late and is no more hardy than the species, but is tolerant of heat and drought. Indeed, the flowers ball up in wet weather and open best to reveal their exquisite beauty when it is hot and dry.

'Mermaid' [W. Paul, 1918]. *Rosa bracteata* × a Tea rose. 'Mermaid' has fairly large (10–11 cm) single flowers which are soft, fresh yellow and fading to cream, around a beautiful brush of golden stamens which remains for several days after the petals fall (plate 10). The lightly scented flowers are enhanced by fine, glossy, bright, dark green leaves. They start late in the season but continue through until late autumn, although the flowers are short lived, so the plant is never spectacularly covered in flowers. 'Mermaid' is slow to get going and resents root disturbance, so it is usually supplied pot-grown and, increasingly, on its own roots. Once settled, it is extremely vigorous, throwing up prickly growths as long as 10–12 m. The plant requires little pruning and is best trained when young because the wood becomes very brittle later. 'Mermaid' is a little hardier than the species and will flower in shade. This popular cultivar is widely regarded as one of the finest of all climbers.

Rosa laevigata and Its Hybrids

Rosa laevigata is known as the Cherokee rose, because it has spread over much of the American South. Indeed, it was first described in 1803 from specimens collected in Georgia, where it is now the state flower. The Australian rosarian Susan Irvine (1997) wrote that "like the Banksias, it has become part of *our* landscape. It might eventually achieve wild rose status here too." *Rosa laevigata* is not hardy in New England or central Europe.

Rosa laevigata Michaux is a vigorous shrub which naturally clambers up trees to a height of 10 m, aided by scattered, strong, reddish brown, hooked prickles. The evergreen leaves have three to five (usually three) leaflets and are brilliant, shiny, dark green, and quite hairless on both sides. The leaflets are variable in size and shape, but usually 4–9 cm long and 2–5 cm wide, hard, leathery, and short stalked. The midribs are sometimes crimson and may also have prickles underneath. The flowers are white, invariably solitary, single, scented (of gardenia), and 6–9 cm across. They are borne on bristly stalks, with bristly receptacles and bristly sepals which persist for a long time. The styles are free, not exserted. The handsome golden stamens are very striking. The fruits are 3.5–4.0 cm across, egg shaped, orange or red, and very bristly.

Rosa laevigata is native to lowland areas of southern China and Indo-China. In warm climates, it is one of the most beautiful of all single roses, especially when covered with its brilliant white flowers, which are large for a species and wonderfully set off by their great boss of yellow stamens and the dark, glossy leaves. It has been little used for hybridising, although a double-flowered form was reported from California in 1900.

'Anemonenrose' syn. 'Anemone', 'Anemonoides', 'Pink Cherokee' [Schmidt, 1896]. *Rosa laevigata* × a Tea rose. 'Anemonenrose' was actually bred by Rudolph Geschwind and merely distributed by Schmidt. It has lightly scented, attractive, single, medium pink flowers which fade to silvery pink and are 5–6 cm across (plate 11). It is less vigorous than *R. laevigata*, but hardier. A much darker pink sport of 'Anemonenrose' was introduced as 'Ramona' by Dietrich and Turner in 1913. It remains a popular rose in warm climates, where the colour is a deep glowing carmine, although always paler on the backs of the petals.

'Cooper's Burmese' [Cooper, 1927]. Although sometimes (wrongly) described as a hybrid with *Rosa gigantea*, 'Cooper's Burmese' is best thought of as a cultivar of *R. laevigata*. It was collected as seed by Roland Cooper, who worked in the 1920s as superintendent of the Maymyo Botanic Garden in the Shan Hills of Burma. It is the commonest cultivar in European gardens.

Rosa gigantea and *Rosa chinensis*

These two Chinese species, together with the European *Rosa gallica*, are the most important ancestors of our garden roses. There is scarcely a climbing or rambling rose in this book that does not carry their genes in some degree. Both were well known in the West, through their cultivated forms and hybrids, long before the original species were found in the wild. And most of the cultivated roses of Southeast Asia were grown for hundreds of years before European botanists subjected the Asian garden flora to the disciplines of Western empiricism. It is here that we need to look for the origins of modern garden roses, in the unresearched, ignored, and sometimes disparaged history of cultivated Chinese plants. No doubt much will be revealed in the years to come by genetic studies, but the greatest gap today in our understanding of modern roses is our simple ignorance of Chinese and Japanese horticultural history.

Rosa gigantea is the largest flowered of all wild roses and one of the most rampant growers—there are records of plants which have grown as much as 25 m high. (The museum at Kew has a walking stick made from a single stem of *R. gigantea*.) The species was first described by the Belgian botanist François Crépin (1830–1903), who immediately recognised its horticultural possibilities: "If one were able to introduce it to Europe and grow it, *Rosa gigantea* would enrich rose collections by its enormous flower size and handsome leaves. It would, moreover, by crossing it with other types, become the source of hybrids which were probably superior to those of *Rosa* [*chinensis*]." Realising that it would fare better in a warmer climate, he sent plants to gardens and institutes in southern Europe. *Rosa gigantea* flowered for the first time in Europe at the Lisbon Botanic Garden in 1896. The following year, it flowered in another Portuguese garden, belonging to the Barão Soutelinho, who had received his plant from Kew. In 1898 it also flowered for the English Lord Brougham at his famous Château Eléonore. In due course, garden owners discovered that *R. gigantea* grows even better in such climates as California, Australia, and New Zealand and that it looks especially fine growing up a deciduous tree, because the pale evergreen leaves give colour all through the year.

At the northern limit of its natural range, *Rosa gigantea* is commonly found either as a bushy form, which grows to no more than 2 m high, or hybridised with *R. chinensis*. The description which best captures the excitement of finding this legendary species in the wild is Frank Kingdon-Ward's (1952, 45–46) account of his plant-hunting expedition to Manipur in 1948: "The chubby leaves, still soft and limp, were a deep red; the slim, pointed flower buds a pale daffodil yellow; but when the enormous flowers opened they were ivory white, borne singly all along the arching sprays, each petal faintly engraved with a network of veins like a watermark." Kingdon-Ward was there in March, when the previous year's fruit still hung on the branches "like crab apples . . . yellow, with rosy cheeks when ripe, thick and iron hard."

> *Rosa gigantea* Collett ex Crépin syn. *R. odorata* var. *gigantea* (Crépin) Rehder & Wilson. This is a vigorous climbing shrub attaining 25 m in height, whose young shoots may grow 6–7 m in one season and are armed with stout, scattered, uniform, hooked prickles (absent from the flowering branches). The leaves are evergreen or semi-evergreen, dark glossy green, up to 25 cm long, and usually with seven leaflets (sometimes five); the rachis and petiole are glabrous and slightly prickly. The leaflets are 4–10 cm long, 1–3 cm wide, elliptic to ovate, rounded or tapered at the base, acuminate at the apex, hairless on both sides, with fine, simple and often glandular teeth. The narrow stipules have slender, spreading tips, not glandular at the edge. The flowers are solitary (rarely in sets of two or three), single, 10–15 cm, and scented; the petals are white or cream and open from slender, yellow buds, with broad silky petals overlapping for most of their length, and with a broad boss of white stamens and golden anthers in the centre. The pedicels are 1–3 cm long, smooth, and glabrous. The sepals are entire, narrowly triangular, not constricted at the base, 2.5–4.0 cm long, smooth on the back, and reflexed; they fall after flowering or, at any rate, before the fruits are fully ripe. The styles are free, the stigmas very downy. The fruits are quite large (2–4 cm), spherical or pear shaped, smooth, red or yellow flushed with red, with a thick wall and a small cavity.

The First Western Hybrids of *Rosa gigantea*

One of the botanists to receive a plant of *Rosa gigantea* from François Crépin was Henri Cayeux, a young Frenchman in charge of the Botanic Garden in Lisbon. When it flowered, in 1896, this specimen turned out to be a form with fairly large flowers, some 13 cm in diameter. Cayeux remembered Crépin's prediction that hybrids of *R. gigantea* would make superior garden plants, and in 1897 he set about crossing it with pollen from several Tea roses and Hybrid Perpetuals. Cayeux's ambition was to breed Gigantea Hybrids that would be hardy in Paris. He introduced five hybrids: 'Belle Portugaise' and 'Étoile de Portugal' in 1903; 'Amateur Lopes', 'Lusitania', and 'Palmira Feijas' in 1905. 'Étoile de Portugal', bred from a cross between *R. gigantea* and 'Reine Marie Henriette' was certainly the first to bloom. 'Lusitania' was a seedling of 'Souvenir de Mme Léonie Viennot', whereas 'Amateur Lopes' (bred from 'Mme Bérard') was named after Alberto Lopes, a Portuguese acquaintance of Cayeux's who had himself raised hybrids of *R. gigantea* using 'Rêve d'Or' and 'Général Jacqueminot' as the seed parents. 'Belle Portugaise' is the only one still in existence and is very widely grown.

> 'Belle Portugaise' syn. 'Belle of Portugal', 'Bela Portuguesa' [Cayeux, 1903]. *Rosa gigantea* × 'Reine Marie Henriette'. The flowers of 'Belle Portugaise' are as much as 15 cm across and barely semi-double. They are pure pink, slightly darker on the outside of the petals and paler towards the tips. The buds are tall, slender, elegant, and about 10 cm long, with narrow stems which drop down under the weight of the flowers. This makes them easy to enjoy if they open out fully, revealing a boss of yellow stamens, though most remain half-closed. The light scent is a mixture of sweet damask and tea. This rose flowers only once, but it is very profuse and lasts a long time. The foliage is pure *R. gigantea*: long, narrow, pale green, and drooping when young. 'Belle Portugaise' is extremely vigorous, reaching 5–10 m, with a thick, excorticating trunk. There is a white-flowered sport in commerce known as 'Belle Blanca' (plate 12).

Lord Brougham's head gardener at Château Eléonore in Cannes, Mr. Busby, is remembered still for one splendid and very vigorous climber he bred.

> 'La Follette' syn. 'Sénateur la Follette' [Busby, 1910]. The flowers are large (13 cm), double, and open from a long pointed bud; they are a good rose pink with some cream and coppery salmon on the outside, and sometimes a little carmine. The flower has a distinct scent. Like all Gigantea Hybrids, it flowers early, long, and profusely, with an occasional later flower. The foliage is almost evergreen and the plant grows very vigorously, with a thick excorticating trunk, to 5–10 m. 'La Follette' has always been popular in large Riviera gardens, where it is often seen cascading through an olive tree or cypress in opulent profusion.

Breeding with *Rosa gigantea* was then taken up by a Catholic priest in California called George Schoener (1864–1941). Only one of his hybrids is thought to be in existence: 'Glory of California' was given a special award at the Bagatelle annual competitions in 1935 and is said to grow still at Sangerhausen, but the plant there is pale pink, whereas Schoener's original 'Glory of California' was yellow. Another Santa Barbara amateur, the Italian-born Barone Franchetti, crossed *R. gigantea* with *R. moschata* in the 1920s and obtained 'Madeleine Lemoine', 'Montecito', and 'Montearioso'. The original plant of 'Montecito' has recently been rediscovered in the very overgrown grounds of his house above Santa Barbara and has now found its way once again into commerce (plate 13).

In the 1920s Paul Nabonnand introduced seven hybrids of *Rosa gigantea* from his French Riviera Nursery. All were once flowering and first-generation crosses with Teas, Noisettes, or Hybrid Teas. They flowered so early that Nabonnand's richer clients were able to enjoy them before the Riviera season came to an end at Easter. Paul Nabonnand was never so able a nurseryman as his father and grandfather, and five of his hybrids are extinct: 'Comtesse de Chaponnay' [1924], which was pale creamy pink; 'Comtesse Prozor' [1922], pale yellow with a hint of salmon; 'Fiammetta' [1922], pale yellow with salmon red in the bud; 'Lady Johnstone' [1922], pale pink with a cream-coloured base; and 'Noella Virebent' [1922], peachy pink fading to creamy pink. Still cultivated are:

'Emmanuela de Mouchy' [P. Nabonnand, 1922]. *Rosa gigantea* × 'Lady Waterlow'. Of all the Gigantea Hybrids, none has fuller flowers than 'Emmanuela de Mouchy', a great, round, ruffled mass of long, delicate petals (plate 14). The bud is pale pink, long, and elegant, and the flowers open apricot pink but fade slowly to pearly pink, so that the centre is always darker than the edges and the flowers take on a translucent quality. The flowers are borne on long stems, singly or in small clusters, and have a distinct, light scent. There is only one flowering, but it comes early and lasts long. The plant is leafy and vigorous, easily reaching 8 m. It is also fairly hardy, flourishing in the open at L'Haÿ-les-Roses, south of Paris.

'Sénateur Amic' [P. Nabonnand, 1924]. *Rosa gigantea* × 'General MacArthur'. This is another very vigorous Gigantea Hybrid, reaching 8–10 m up a tree. The pale crimson buds, with scarlet patches and long sepals, open into a pink flower—a particularly intense, glowing, dark pink, occasionally flecked with white. They are about 11–12 cm in diameter, well scented, and lightly double. 'Sénateur Amic' is still occasionally seen on the Riviera.

Alister Clark: The Great Australian Rose Breeder

Alister Clark was born in Victoria in 1864, the younger son of a first-generation immigrant from Scotland who had made a fortune during the gold rush and built himself a fine country house called Glenara, rather like a Scottish shooting lodge, some 30 km north of Melbourne. Orphaned at the age of eight, Alister was educated in Scotland. He married a rich New Zealander in 1888, which enabled him to buy Glenara and its 413 ha from his father's estate. Clark's main interests, apart from gardening, were racing and fox hunting. His biographer complained that he "never seriously applied himself to any business activity," while adding that he was also very handsome and charming (Garnett 1990).

Clark said that it was the sight of *Rosa gigantea* growing up an *Acacia salicina* tree that first inspired him to raise a new race of Gigantea Hybrids suitable to the Victorian climate. He ordered the species from William Paul in England and noted, twenty-seven years later, that its great quality was vigour. Clark's aim was to raise a race of perpetual-flowering bush roses which had *R. gigantea* for at least one of their grandparents, with foliage that was immune to disease and with the ability to survive without water in the hot, dry Australian summer. His ideal rose "will make a pleasing bush, hold itself well and, while blooming through the autumn, will be able to last in water and keep its colour when picked."

Clark would only release a new rose if he felt certain that it was quite distinct from the best that North America and Europe could offer. One result is that almost all his roses, not just the Gigantea hybrids, look quite different from roses raised by anyone else. Clark wanted that flower produced in the open air without coddling—hence his early Gigantea Hybrids 'Jessie Clark', 'Flying Colours', 'Harbinger', and 'Golden Vision'—and he also valued scent.

Clark was too indolent to keep a detailed pedigree of all his seedlings. The colour and habit of 'Lorraine Lee' [1924] he considered unsurpassed by any of his later hybrids. The Melbourne newspaper, *The Argus*, used to run an annual popularity poll among its readers: 'Lorraine Lee' constantly topped the list of bush roses. It was even suggested that these Gigantea Hybrids should be known as "Clarkianas" to honour their originator, just as 'Pernetiana' and 'Lambertiana' bestowed a similar distinction on Joseph Pernet-Ducher and Peter Lambert. Clark never made any money out of his rose breeding, however. His usual practice was to present a new cultivar to one of the state rose societies to promote for the benefit of the society's own funds. Many were never introduced through nurseries, but just given away to friends. Thus, some of the names are still a little tentative.

Clark released more than 130 named roses. Some suffered a decline in their popularity in the years immediately following his death, but there has been a great resurgence of interest in his work in recent years. Susan Irvine put together a national collection of them at her Gisborne garden and another has recently been made at Werribee Park in Victoria. But the main credit for identifying Alister Clark's roses, propagating them, and putting them into circulation again must lie with a handful of nurserymen with an enthusiasm for Australia's horticultural heritage, most especially the remarkable Jon Nieuwesteeg of Tarrawarra, whose collection of old Australian roses is one of the best-kept secrets in Victoria. Almost all Clark's roses are still in cultivation. They include the single greatest corpus of Gigantea Hybrids ever bred, each with a distinctive wave to their petals and infinitely variable in shape and form.

'Cicely Lascelles' [Clark, introduced by National Rose Society of Victoria, 1937]. Allegedly 'Frau Oberhofgärtner Singer' × 'Scorcher', the rose now in cultivation under this name is very much a Gigantea Hybrid. The long-stemmed flowers are large (12 cm), scented, semi-double, and pink. The broad petaloids at the centre tend to fold themselves over the stamens and, because the petals have a darker underside, the flower appears pale pink on the outside and quite a dark pink in the middle. It makes a vigorous plant, growing to 5 m, with large leaves. 'Cicely Lascelles' flowers early and recurs right through to autumn.

'Courier' [Clark, introduced by Brundrett, 1930]. *Rosa gigantea* × 'Archiduc Joseph'. This delicately coloured climber has shapely pale pink buds which open out into double flowers of the palest creamy pink, slightly darker towards the centre. The flowers are medium sized (8–9 cm), borne in small clusters, and appear early in the season. The foliage is large, lush, and healthy and carried on a plant which is very vigorous, quickly reaching 8 m, but dislikes hard pruning. In a frost-free climate, 'Courier' is one of the loveliest harbingers of spring.

'Doris Downes' [Clark, introduced by National Rose Society of Victoria, 1932].

Parentage unknown. 'Doris Downes' is never more than a pillar rose, 2.5 m at most, but very vigorous and nearly thornless. The sweetly scented flowers are large (11–15 cm), semi-double, and open pink but then darken to pale crimson. They are borne on long stems in great numbers in spring, with only a few flowers later in the season. The foliage is very clean and healthy.

'Editor Stewart' [Clark, 1939]. Parentage unknown. This rose has large (11–15 cm), lightly scented, semi-double flowers of a good crimson (with an occasional white fleck), fading to a very striking dark pinkish purple. The colour is set off by a large ring of prominent yellow stamens and the flowers are very attractive to bees. They are held on long, elegant stems, facing out horizontally so that you can look straight at them. The petals have a distinctive ripple which transforms the flowers into objects of great beauty. The young foliage is also a rich wine red. 'Editor Stewart' is very free-flowering and continuously in bloom from early spring to late autumn.

'Flying Colours' [Clark, introduced by Hazelwood, 1922]. This was one of Clark's first-generation *Rosa gigantea* hybrids. The lightly scented flowers are nearly single, fairly large (12 cm), and deep cherry pink, with white at the base of the petals and paler undersides. They are very profusely borne during their single, early flowering season, on a plant that will quickly reach to 7–8 m.

'Glenara' [Clark, 1951]. This seedling from the Glenara estate was introduced post-humously. The flowers are little more than single, dark pink (fading to medium pink, with pale yellow stamens), and only medium sized (9–10 cm). However, it repeats well (it is always in bloom) and its flowers do have some scent. 'Glenara' is of moderate vigour, about 2.5–3.0 m high, which makes it a good pillar rose.

'Golden Vision' [Clark, introduced by National Rose Society of Victoria, 1922]. Supposedly 'Maréchal Niel' × *Rosa gigantea*. 'Golden Vision' is smaller than 'Maréchal Niel', but the medium-sized (7 cm), semi-double flowers are just the same overall shade of pale creamy yellow, and it flowers extremely early in the season. The buds are char-treuse green and often split, but the flowers are very attractive when they first come out. The colouring is variable: parts are yellow and parts cream or white, giving a charming lopsided look. Some flowers are darker than others. 'Golden Vision' dies badly—the flowers turn greenish and look tired. The petals are very strongly recurved, unlike any other Gigantea Hybrid and it has a light scent of French fern. The plant is floriferous, leafy, and vigorous, growing to 7–8 m or even more.

'Harbinger' [Clark, introduced by Hackett, 1923]. There is doubt whether this is still in cultivation, although an attractive namesake is available again in Australia. It has large (12 cm), single, lightly scented, pink flowers which open medium pink and fade to pale silvery pink. It makes a fairly vigorous plant to about 6–7 m and has the lush drooping leaves of *Rosa gigantea*.

'Jessie Clark' [Clark, introduced by Law, Somner & Co., 1915]. *Rosa gigantea* × 'Mme Martignier'. This was the first of Clark's hybrids. The flowers are large (12 cm), single, clear rose pink and fading to silvery pink, but borne in great abundance on a vigorous leafy plant. It is one of the earliest to flower in spring, and lasts for several weeks, but does not repeat. The flowers have a light tea scent from their pollen parent. The plant quickly reaches 7–8 m high.

'Kitty Kininmonth' [Clark, 1922]. Unnamed seedling × *Rosa gigantea*. This is one of Clark's most popular Gigantea Hybrids, not least because it blooms very early and in incredible profusion (plate 15). The sweetly scented flowers are large (12 cm), semi-double, and bright pale crimson, a glowing colour which they hold well; the petals do not fade until just before they drop. The undersides of the petals are notably paler (no more than medium pink) and the petals themselves reflex slightly at the ends, with a distinctive roll to their middles. The plant is very vigorous, quickly reaching 7–8 m high, with lush foliage and few prickles.

'Lorraine Lee (Climbing)' [McKay, 1932]. The bush form was bred by Clark from 'Jessie Clark' × 'Captain Millet' and introduced in 1924. The climbing sport, one of Australia's favourite roses, is correspondingly more vigorous and one of the tallest roses in existence, easily reaching 12–15 m. It blooms spectacularly well in early spring, and intermittently thereafter. 'Climbing Lorraine Lee' has elegant, pointed buds which open out to reveal yellow stamens and semi-double flowers. The colour is pink with a hint of coral and slightly darker on the outside than the inside. The flowers are strongly scented. Other sports of 'Lorraine Lee' include 'Lady Mann', 'Baxter Beauty' (which is apricot coloured), and 'Yellow Baxter Beauty'.

'Mrs Richard Turnbull' [Clark, 1945]. *Rosa gigantea* hybrid. The elegant, yellow buds open out into huge (14 cm) single flowers which are cream coloured and fade to white at the edges. They have a large ring of yellow stamens and a strong scent. 'Mrs Richard Turnbull' is a vigorous grower, reputed to reach 7 m high. The magnificent specimen at Oaklands north of Melbourne which is about fifty years old has scaled the top of a 15-m oak tree, from which it cascades down.

'Nancy Hayward' [Clark, 1937]. 'Jessie Clark' seedling. The single, scented flowers are a deep glowing pink, a wonderfully attractive and vivid colour, and exactly the same on both sides of the petals. It also looks exceptionally good under artificial light and lasts much longer as a cut flower than many double-flowered roses. In Australia 'Nancy Hayward' remains a very popular rose, seldom out of flower, growing vigorously to 6 m or more. Its only misfortune is that the lady after whom it was named disliked it intensely.

'Pennant' [Clark, 1941]. I have not seen this once-flowering, recently reintroduced Gigantea Hybrid. It is apparently medium pink, semi-double, scented, and very profuse in its flowering.

'Tonner's Fancy' [Clark, introduced by Gill & Searle, 1928]. *Rosa gigantea* hybrid. The flowers of this attractive, once-flowering climber open pale apricot and fade to cream, but the colour is always darker at the base of the petals. They are semi-double at most, but the flowers are enhanced by red filaments and a light sweet scent. The original plant still grows at Glenara as a free-standing bush with branches about 5 m long.

'Traverser' [Clark, 1928]. *Rosa gigantea* hybrid. 'Traverser' has recently reappeared in commerce in Australia and seems identical to an old plant of this name at Glenara. It has fairly large (11 cm), semi-double to double flowers, which open primrose yellow but fade to cream, although the centre of the flower stays yellow throughout. The blooms are lightly scented, borne singly or in small clusters, and carried on a vigorous plant which grows to about 5 m.

Rosa chinensis

It was long thought that *Rosa chinensis* was no more than a race of garden roses. *Rosa chinensis* is a crimson cultivar properly known as *R. chinensis* var. *chinensis*, but is usually called *R. chinensis* var. *semperflorens*. Like all the forms that were introduced to Europe from 1750 onwards, it was the result of more than 1000 years of mutation, intercrossing, and selection in the gardens of China.

> *Rosa chinensis* var. *spontanea* is an evergreen branched shrub of scandent habit, scrambling into trees for more than 3 m. There are usually five leaflets which are oval to lanceolate, wedge shaped at the base, acuminate, serrated, 2.5–6.0 cm long, 2–3 cm wide (the terminal leaflet is sometimes larger, up to 8 cm long, and twice the length of the side leaflets), glabrous on both sides, firm, light or dark green above, and sometimes purple when young (plate 16). There is a scattering of small hooked prickles on the leaf-stalks and on the midribs; the stipules are narrow, persistent, and glandular-bristly. The flowers are produced singly on short glabrous pedicels. The five calyces are lanceolate, 1.5–3.0 cm long, entire, and reflexing after the flowers open. The flowers are 5–8 cm across, with five ovate petals, quite variable in colour but usually white, pink, or crimson, and lightly scented (of peardrops). Fruit is yellow or orange and 2 cm in diameter.

The distinctive feature about *Rosa chinensis* is the sheer variability of its flowers' colour. Moreover, some plants produce flowers which change from very pale pink to crimson. This important characteristic has been passed down to many of its horticultural descendants. Every garden rose which darkens with age owes this phenomenon to *R. chinensis*. Recent collectors working with Mikinori Ogisu have emphasised that the flowers may be white, buff, yellow, pink, or red. Some have related this to changes in altitude, but the plants growing at Quarryhill in the Sonoma Valley, California, from the Erskine, Flieder, Howick, and McNamara collection throw doubt on this. They were grown from seed collected at about 740 m near Nanba in Sichuan in 1988 from a single scrambling shrub about 3 m high. Of the twenty plants at Quarryhill, one has red flowers, three are pink, and the remaining sixteen are white. There is some variability in their growth, but no evidence of hybridity or introversion. The only safe conclusion is that *R. chinensis* is a species in an active state of evolution.

During the early twentieth century botanists realised that *Rosa chinensis* had hybridised in the wild with *R. gigantea* and that some of the early Western collections were from hybrid populations. The cultivated forms tend to be dwarf growing and repeat flowering (indeed, their Chinese name means "monthly roses"), whereas the wild *R. chinensis* is a once-flowering climber. The unsung heroes of rose breeding are the old gardeners, nurserymen, and plant lovers of China, who selected and refined their native species for hundreds of years. Their efforts meant that when the four stud roses celebrated by Dr Hurst were crossed in the nineteenth century with "European" roses, Western breeders could take the credit for advances that would otherwise have required several centuries to achieve. It is curious that Chinese and Japanese gardeners never developed such strains as the Wichurana Ramblers and Teas because their gardens had long contained all the necessary genes. The cultivated forms of China roses and their hybrids almost invariably carry their flowers in clusters, whereas the flowers of *R. chinensis* and *R. gigantea* are solitary, borne on short laterals from the previous season's wood. It may be that the gene for repeat-flowering, which is Asia's greatest gift to modern roses, came not from *R. chinensis* or *R. gigantea* but from a mutation of one of the Synstylae roses such as *R. multiflora* or *R. moschata*.

The China roses were once especially popular in cold-winter areas among people of modest means who could not afford heated glasshouses and conservatories in which to grow the more fashionable Teas and Noisettes. Recent travellers to China from Western countries have collected and established in cultivation many garden cultivars which fall within the *Rosa chinensis* group (and ought properly to be called China Hybrids). As they become better known, they will become a rich addition to Western gardens.

'Beauty of Rosemawr' [Van Fleet, introduced by Conard & Jones, 1904]. China × Tea hybrid. The lightly scented flowers are fairly large, medium pink at first, but darkening to pale crimson as they open, which creates a contrast between the dark outer petals and the pale inner ones. They often have flecks of white at the base. The flower is loosely petalled but fully double and the leafy plant grows to about 2 m, or more against a wall. 'Beauty of Rosemawr' is hardy and flowers perpetually.

'Belmont' [Vibert, 1846]. This is a charming rose, with palest pink flowers, no more than mother-of-pearl or blush white, with a delicious tea scent. It is fairly hardy and grows to about 3 m.

'Empress of China' [Jackson, introduced by Elizabeth Nurseries, 1896]. This is a very hardy scrambler. The flowers are semi-double to double, open out attractively, measure about 6 cm, and have a light fruity scent. Unlike most China roses, 'Empress of China' pales as it ages, starting very dark pink and passing to medium pink, especially at the edges of the petals. It has a slight tendency to mildew on its pedicels, but this does not stop it from flowering almost perpetually. It has small leaves, a slender habit, and dense leafy growth to 3–4 m.

'Fellemberg' syn. 'La Belle Marseillaise' [Fellemberg, 1835]. China × Noisette hybrid. Its crimson buds open out to dark carmine pink flowers which fade to mauve pink but always retain a distinct satiny brightness. They are sweetly scented, fully double, about 6 cm across, and carried in small clusters. The plant has slightly bluish foliage which is small and neat, but densely borne because the internodes are short. 'Fellemberg' grows to about 2.5–3.0 m.

'Hume's Blush Tea-Scented Rose' syn. 'Odorata'. This was one of the more important garden cultivars to be introduced from China at the start of the nineteenth century and undoubtedly had a large portion of *Rosa gigantea* as well as *R. chinensis* in its genetic makeup. The flowers were pale pearly pink, fading to creamy white at the edges, large, fully double, and tea scented. A rose known locally as 'Spice' has recently been introduced from Bermuda as 'Hume's Blush Tea-Scented Rose'. DNA analysis will shortly enable us to determine whether the attribution is correct. It is a handsome lax bush about 2.5 m tall, but higher when allowed to climb.

'Indica Major'. Although sometimes attributed to Vibert, this is probably a genuine Chinese cultivar brought to Europe early in the nineteenth century. It was very widely used in hot climates both as a hedging rose and as a rootstock. 'Indica Major' was propagated by late summer cuttings and had the great advantage of reacting quickly to irrigation, so that one could regulate the growth of the plants at will; no other stock possessed this characteristic. It is an attractive and distinctive early-flowering cultivar with small to medium-sized (6–7 cm), fully double flowers in clusters which open pink and fade to white. It is rather a prickly plant and grows to 3.0–3.5 m as a hedge, but to 5 m or more as a climber.

'Malton' syn. 'Joséphine Malton', 'Fulgens' [Guérin, 1830]. This underestimated climber is an important ancestor of the Hybrid Perpetual roses. The flowers are crimson, with much paler undersides (almost white) and white flecks at the base, and hold their colour well until the petals fall. The petals are rounded, short, incurved, and numerous. The flower-stalks are long and slender, so that the flowers hang down elegantly in small clusters. The flowers are medium sized (7–8 cm), strongly tea scented, and appear inter-mittently throughout the season after the first abundant flush. The leaves are dark and small, and the plant makes long new wands of about 3 m, or 5 m up a wall.

'Mutabilis' syn. 'Tipo Ideale'. Origin unknown. In cool climates, the flowers open bright orange, and fade first to buff before turning to pink and finally pale crimson; in hot weather they pass quickly to crimson and the colour is darker. It is the graceful tenure of the petals which distinguishes this cultivar: the flowers are single and the petals do not overlap but reflex in innumerable different but elegant ways. The flowers are about 7 cm and carried in small clusters on long slender crimson stems. The young leaves are crimson, later bronze, as are the large prickles. The plant will grow to 6 m up a wall. It also makes a spectacular mass planting. At La Landriana, south of Rome, Lavinia Taverna planted an entire hillside with this one cultivar.

CHAPTER 4

The Ayrshire and Evergreen Roses

The old Ayrshire and Evergreen roses are a fine, healthy, vigorous, hardy group of climbing roses which have recovered much of their lost popularity in recent years. Their ability to thrive in difficult situations, including dry shade and poor soils, has long been unmatched by other climbers. Their habit of growth, characterised by very slender trailing stems, means that they are excellent for covering trees, arches, sheds, and roofs. When grown in the open, they will mound up into dense thickets. Late in the season, long after they have flowered, they suffer from mildew, but this seems never to affect their remarkable vigour or subsequent growth. If Ayrshire and Evergreen roses have a weakness, it is that their single season of flower is rather short, but this is more than compensated for by their floriferousness. Their soft petals spoil easily in heavy rain, but they flourish surprisingly well in hot climates, for instance, in southern California. Several breeders experimented with breeding Ayrshires, especially in the years 1810–30, and these roses still offer the breeder much of value—namely their vigour, hardiness, scent, relaxed habit, and ability to grow in unpromising sites.

The group is burdened by misnaming and multiple synonyms. We keenly need an international trial of cultivars from gardens and nurserymen across the world, backed by chromosome analysis and a re-evaluation of all the historical sources. The Ayrshire roses are hybrids of *Rosa arvensis* and the Evergreen roses are hybrids of *R. sempervirens*, the only two Synstylae species widely distributed in Europe. *Rosa arvensis* is most common in the western and central parts of the continent, and *R. sempervirens* in the southwestern and Mediterranean regions. Most of the hybrids are obscure in origin, especially the Ayrshire roses. Their attribution to Ayrshire in southwestern Scotland, where *R. arvensis* is dubiously native, is also suspect. Many Ayrshires were bred from an extinct rose known as 'Ayrshirea', variously described as an improved form of *R. arvensis* or a hybrid between *R. arvensis* and *R. sempervirens*. Professor Maurice Jay's discovery that such roses as 'Reine des Belges' and 'Flore' appear to carry both species in their genes gives this theory credence.

Rosa arvensis Hudson. A trailing shrub which grows up to 1.5 m tall, but is capable of clambering up to 5 m over other shrubs and trees. The long stems are very slender, glabrous, much branched, purple where exposed to light, and sparsely armed with short, stout, hooked prickles. The leaves have five to seven oval leaflets which are 1.5–4.0 cm long, sometimes slightly rounded, dark green above, slightly paler and clearer beneath, glabrous on both sides, their margins with simple, eglandular teeth. The petioles have short prickles on their backs and an enlarged bract at the base. The stipules are narrow. The flowers are white, with a strong musky scent, either solitary or up to eight in a cyme or corymb, 2.5–5.0 cm in diameter, and borne on slender pedicels, 2–5 cm long. The petals are strongly notched and sometimes turn pink with age. The purplish green sepals are long, pointed, smooth, and reflexed, with lateral lobes. The styles are exserted, columnar, and usually quite glabrous. The fruits are 1–2 cm, usually rounded, occasionally ovoid, but always red, and they shed their sepals as they ripen. *Rosa arvensis* is native of western, central, and some parts of southern Europe; in the British Isles *R. arvensis* is commonest in southern England and very rare in Scotland.

The wild form of *Rosa arvensis* is useful for its ability to thrive in the shade of trees. It is a particular favourite of mine and grew in our hedgerows when we lived at Corsley in west Wiltshire. Its strong musky scent is for me one of its greatest attractions: indeed, it was Shakespeare's own musk rose. Gertrude Jekyll (1902) mentions two good forms: "one with large single flowers and strong rambling habit, an old favourite of mine, and another, half double, equally good and still more free of bloom." Neither equates to the cultivar now known as 'Miss Jekyll'. Louis Lens introduced a double form called 'Plena', found wild in the Province of Namur in 1982 but probably of hybrid origin. It is pinkish white, with three rows of petals. Lens used it to produce such hybrids as the beautiful shrub rose 'Porcelaine de Chine' [1996].

'Alice Grey' syn. 'Alice Gray', 'Scandens' [unknown origin, pre-1840]. The rose grown under this name is a vigorous, once-flowering climber with semi-double flowers which reach about 5 cm across in clusters of up to fifteen. They open pearly pink and fade to cream, but are darker on the undersides and edges of the petals. They have a strong musky scent and characteristic red stems. 'Alice Grey' is definitely a hybrid, and the record cards at L'Haÿ-les-Roses suggest *arvensis × gallica*. Some writers identify it with a form of *Rosa sempervirens* known as 'Scandens', but that rose had corymbs of small, single, white flowers.

'Ayrshire Queen' syn. 'Reine des Ayrshire' [Rivers, 1835]. 'Blush Ayrshire' × 'Tuscany'. This semi-double, purplish crimson hybrid has the flower shape of an Arvensis, but the rich colour of its Gallica parent. It is less vigorous than most Ayrshires—a pillar rose or short climber. Some of the roses grown or sold under this name are such other cultivars as 'Splendens'.

'Bennet's Seedling' syn. 'Thoresbyana' [Bennet, 1840]. Although launched as a double form of *Rosa arvensis*, 'Bennet's Seedling' is a hybrid, perhaps with a Noisette. The semi-double flowers open very pale pink (from pink buds) but fade quickly to white (plate 17). They are small to medium sized (5 cm), have prominent stamens and strongly notched petals, giving the flowers their distinctive carriage, and a strong musky scent. This rose is free-flowering and the flowers are borne in large clusters fairly late in the season. The plate in *Journal des Roses* (1907, 188) is of another rose, probably a Multiflora Hybrid. The editor claimed that 'Thoresbyana' was distinct from 'Bennet's Seedling', but I can find no evidence for this.

'Duc de Constantine' [Soupert & Notting, 1857]. This is an Ayrshire rose of the second or third generation, much more like a Bourbon or Hybrid Perpetual. It is an extremely attractive cultivar, with pure rose pink flowers which measure 7–8 cm across. Its sweet, damask scent has no trace of musk. The fully double, cupped flowers come early in the season and fade to silvery pink. 'Duc de Constantine' is one of the prettiest of all once-flowering ramblers. The plate in *Journal des Roses* (1898, 136) is a good resemblance.

'Dundee Rambler' [Martin, c. 1830]. *Rosa arvensis* × a Noisette. This is the most double and one of the earliest to flower of the Ayrshires; some regard it as the best of all. The small to medium-sized flowers (5 cm) open pale rose pink and fade to pure white; they come in medium-sized clusters. The elongated hips indicate its Noisette heritage, but 'Dundee Rambler' is nevertheless very hardy. It is also exceptionally vigorous, growing to at least 5 m, and floriferous. Its scent is light, but both sweet and musky. It succeeds even in hot climates, and I have seen it flourishing at Carrick Hill near Adelaide.

'Reine des Belges' syn. 'Queen of the Belgians' [Jacques, 1832]. This vigorous, hardy, once-flowering rambler has the typically long, slender, reddish stems of *Rosa arvensis* and will grow 4–5 m in a year. The clusters of small (4–5 cm) flowers are fully double and open out to show their stamens. They are pure white, sometimes with a pinkish tinge as they age, and have a light musky scent. I have long suspected that the rose at L'Haÿ-les-Roses, illustrated in *Journal des Roses* (1897, 136), owed more to *R. arvensis* than to *R. sempervirens*; recent chromosome analysis by Maurice Jay has revealed both species in its ancestry, in addition to the China rose 'Parson's Pink'. 'Reine des Belges' is one of the prettiest of early-flowering roses.

'Ruga' [c. 1820]. I have seen several roses purporting to be the true 'Ruga', a presumed hybrid between *Rosa arvensis* and *R. chinensis* which was sent from Italy to John Lindley at the Horticultural Society in London. Descriptions vary: pink, white, opening pale pink and fading to white, or opening cream and fading to pink. Most authorities call it double, some very double, and others only semi-double. All agree that it is very hardy and has a Tea rose scent. The form I believe closest to the original cultivar has semi-double, small to medium-sized flowers (5–6 cm). They open creamy pink, fade to cream, and come in clusters of four to ten. 'Ruga' flowers once, blooms early to midseason, has long prickly stems, and produces elegant, slender, vigorous growths of up to 4 m a year.

'Splendens' syn. 'Ayrshire Splendens' [c. 1835]. One of the best-known Arvensis Hybrids, this looks spectacular when its heavy, crimson buds open up to reveal the pale creamy pink flowers inside. The flowers fade to white, with just a tinge of pink at the edges. They are semi-double, medium sized (6–7 cm), strongly and pungently scented of myrrh, and borne in great quantity on a very hardy, densely leafy, vigorous plant. The hips are an autumn bonus.

'Sublaevis' [= ×*sublaevis*]. Presumed *Rosa arvensis* × *gallica* hybrid. This rose grows at Cavriglia and has attractive salmon pink, single flowers in small clusters which fade to rose pink.

'Venusta Pendula' [Origin unknown, reintroduced by Kordes, 1928]. 'Venusta Pendula' has semi-double flowers which are 6–8 cm in diameter and white (with pink outside petals; plate 18). They open out gracefully to show their dark stamens, and their strong scent carries freely in the air. The crimson new wood is typical of *R. arvensis* and its hybrids, but is fairly prickly. 'Venusta Pendula' grows very vigorously to at least 5 m, and its tendency to mildew does nothing to reduce this vigour.

'Virginian Rambler' possibly a synonym for 'Virginalis Superbissima' [c. 1800]. The flower is pale pink, small to medium sized (6 cm), and fairly double. The plant is early blooming and very vigorous with few prickles, not unlike a blush pink version of 'Dundee Rambler'.

Several Ayrshire cultivars are foundlings. 'Janet B. Wood' [reintroduced by Peter Beales, 1990] is a midseason bloomer with small to medium-sized (6 cm), creamy white, nearly double flowers, reddish pedicels, and a strong musky scent. It is quite close to 'Dundee Rambler', and there is no evidence to link it to 'Orangefield Rambler'. Likewise, 'Miss Jekyll' is small (4–5 cm), double flowered, white with a splash of pink on the bud and outer petals, and a strong musky scent. I can find no evidence to link it to Gertrude Jekyll, although at the National Rose Society of Great Britain conference at Salisbury in 1900, George Paul did mention that Jekyll had selected a superior form of *Rosa arvensis* in the wild known as 'Miss Jekyll's Arvensis'.

Rosa sempervirens was one of several rose species which the Paris rose breeders worked with in the early nineteenth century. Descemet and Vibert both raised seedlings, but Antoine Jacques bred the best and the most lasting. For many years, Jacques worked for the Duc d'Orléans, later King Louis-Philippe. He was a botanist, horticulturist, writer, and administrator but, when he died at age eighty-four in 1867, his obituarist wrote that "Jacques lived and died a poor man." All the Jacques hybrids are beautiful and distinctive. Their only weakness is a tendency not to shatter when they have finished flowering but to retain their brown petals indefinitely.

Some observers say that the Sempervirens roses lack fragrance. I enjoy their musky scent which, in such cultivars as 'Flore', has that distinctive bitterness described as "myrrh." All are easy to grow, and they flourish in most soils and situations. Sempervirens roses have small, neat, dark shiny green leaves. The foliage is entirely evergreen in warm climates, where plants retain their leaves until the spring. This makes them particularly valuable as screening roses and offers great possibilities for further hybridisation. It seems incredible that there has been no development of the Sempervirens Hybrids since they first appeared in the 1820s and early 1830s. Several French rosarians and horticultural historians are actively researching the development of horticultural cultivars in the first half of the nineteenth century. One surprise has been the discovery by Professor Maurice Jay of Lyon University that *Rosa arvensis* played a part in the development of some cultivars previously assumed to be pure Sempervirens Hybrids.

All the Sempervirens Hybrids are enormously vigorous, especially if grown on their own roots; they take easily and have occasionally been used as stocks. Sempervirens

Hybrids grow rapidly, and their long, flexible growths make them particularly well adapted for training and trailing over arches, pillars, and trelliswork. All must be sparingly pruned. Old wood will always bear good quantities of flowers on the spurs that grow from the old axils, but hard winter-pruning encourages the growth of vigorous new growths which will not produce flowering wood until the following year. The most the Sempervirens Hybrids require is the removal of the older branches (three or four years old) which have begun to go back and produce fewer flowers.

> *Rosa sempervirens* L. A trailing or climbing shrub, 2 m high as a free-standing specimen, but as much as 6 m when clambering over other shrubs and trees (plate 19). The stems may be unarmed or carry a few small hooked prickles. The leaves are evergreen (they persist through the winter and do not drop until spring) with typically five or seven leaflets, which are rather thick, tough, dark green, glossy and glabrous on both sides, and 3–7 cm long. The leaflets are ovate, acuminate with simply toothed margins; the terminal leaflet is noticeably larger than the laterals. The stipules are narrow, glandular at the edge, and not toothed. The flowers are white, simple, 2.5–5.0 cm across, and open from small ovoid buds. They have a fairly strong musky scent and are borne in pyramidal panicles of up to ten flowers, typically five. The pedicels are 4–9 cm long. The sepals are elliptic, glandular on the back, and reflexed; they fall after flowering. The styles are united in an exserted column. The fruits are usually smooth, round or ovoid, vermilion red, and 1–2 cm across. The species is native to the Mediterranean region and overlaps with *R. arvensis*; hybrids and intermediates are found where this occurs, which has led to considerable confusion in the past. Lindley, for example, attributed many of the forms and hybrids of *R. arvensis* to *R. sempervirens*. Horticulturally, there should be no difficulty in distinguishing the two groups of hybrids: the red stems and limp leaves of the Ayrshires are as distinctive as the brilliant green leaves of the Evergreen roses. And, unlike the Ayrshires, the flowers of the Evergreen hybrids are borne in clusters of ten to thirty.

Many natural variations of *Rosa sempervirens* are recorded from about 1750 onwards. The most important horticulturally were the early double-flowered forms, including a cultivar known as 'Sempervirens Major' which may have been the parent of the Jacques hybrids. There is also an early hybrid still in cultivation in Europe known as 'Sempervirens Pleno' or 'Blanc à Fleurs Pleines', which was raised by Laffay in the 1820s and was probably the result of crossing the species with a Noisette.

> 'Adélaïde d'Orléans' syn. 'Léopoldine d'Orléans' [Jacques, c. 1826]. *Rosa sempervirens* × 'Parson's Pink'. A loosely cupped flower, reminiscent of a flowering crab or cherry, distinguishes 'Adélaïde d'Orléans' from all other Sempervirens (plate 20). The buds are small and dark pink, although the flower opens creamy pink and soon fades to cream and white. The flowers are 6–7 cm across, at best semi-double, their centres filled with scores of little petaloids. The flower-stalks are long and slender, so that the flowers hang down gracefully. The plant is extremely vigorous, with long, slender growths and a lax, sprawling habit which makes it ideal for training. There is a famous archway of 'Adélaïde

d'Orléans' in the collection of old roses at Mottisfont Abbey in England. This hybrid flowers only once, but the last few flowers are produced over a long period.

'Anatole de Montesquieu' [van Houtte, c. 1850]. This late-flowering Sempervirens × Noisette hybrid still grows at Sangerhausen among the Noisettes. The pink buds open to pure white flowers and are borne in large, open clusters of ten to thirty. They have a musky scent. The growth is vigorous and the stems prickly, while the elongated capsules indicate its hybrid origins.

'Donna Maria' syn. 'Doña Maria' [Vibert, c. 1830]. Vibert originally described this as a semi-double form of *Rosa sempervirens*, white with a hint of pink. Then Laffay introduced an Arvensis Hybrid with the same name around 1835—pure white, small, and double. No plates or drawings accompany the few references to these roses in the nineteenth century, so it is difficult to know whether either equates to the cultivar now sold in Australia as 'Donna Maria'. The small clusters of medium-small flowers (5–6 cm) with a sweet musky scent could belong to almost any section, but the foliage of the Australian rose resembles a Multiflora of *R. wichurana* origin. There was, moreover, much confusion from the beginning between 'Donna Maria' and 'Princesse Marie'.

'Félicité-Perpétue' syn. 'Félicité et Perpétue' [Jacques, c. 1827]. *Rosa sempervirens* × 'Parson's Pink'. This rose has several synonyms, variations on "Félicité" and "Perpétue," but the spelling Jacques used in his catalogue of roses in 1830 must be considered correct. 'Félicité-Perpétue' is the most widely grown of the Sempervirens. The flowers are about 3.5–4.0 cm across, globular at first, then opening flat to little rosettes with a mass of neat petals around a button eye. They are blush pink but fade quickly to cream and then white, with a strong musky scent. The flowers come late in the season, in large clusters and in great quantities. The only defect of 'Félicité-Perpétue' is that it does not drop its petals, which remain on the plant, turning an unsightly brown. Henderson introduced a dwarf, repeat-flowering mutant called 'White Pet' in 1879 which remains a popular small bedding rose; the reversion introduced by Corboeuf in 1894 as 'Climbing White Pet' is indistinguishable from 'Félicité-Perpétue'.

'Flore' syn. 'Flora' [Jacques, 1829]. (*Rosa sempervirens* × *arvensis*) × 'Parson's Pink'. This is one of the hardiest and best of the Sempervirens Hybrids (plate 21). The buds are crimson, but open to ruffled flowers which have pink petals towards the outside and are creamy white towards the centre. They are nicely set off by the crimson stains which remain on the outside of the outer petals. Sometimes the flowers have a button eye. They are 6–7 cm across, attractively carried in small loose clusters, and have a delicious musky scent.

'Laure Davoust' syn. 'L'Abbandonata' [Laffay, 1834]. This hybrid between *Rosa sempervirens* and a Noisette is an exceptionally attractive rose when it first opens. The flowers are cupped, sometimes imbricated but more usually quartered, and open out to reveal a mass of beautifully incurved petals. These are dark pink at the outside and paler towards the centre, with a neat button eye, recalling the popular dwarf cherry *Prunus glandulosa* 'Sinensis'. Unless grown in shade, the colour fades almost completely, so that by midseason each cluster is a mass of sugar-almond pink and white. The plant, which is so enchanting when it opens, later becomes one of the least attractive of roses because the clusters are too congested and the individual flowers die badly, turning brown without dropping their petals. The neat, dark, luxuriant foliage is typically Sempervirens. Growth and vigour depend entirely upon the presence or absence of heat; in hot climates 'Laure Davoust' will grow to 8 m.

'Princesse Louise' [Jacques, c. 1828]. *Rosa sempervirens* × 'Parson's Pink'. This beautiful and vigorous climber has larger flowers (5–7 cm) than 'Félicité-Perpétue', with many layers of rather loosely held petals. The crimson buds open to pale pink flowers which turn quickly to white, but the crimson buds remain an attractive contrast to the white ruffles of the flowers themselves. The clusters usually have five to twelve flowers, occasionally more, and are set off by the neat, dark leaves.

'Spectabilis' syn. 'Spectabile' [pre-1839]. Probably *Rosa sempervirens* × a Noisette. 'Spectabilis' has fully double flowers which open from dark crimson buds. The neat incurved petals are rich pink with a hint of lilac at first, but fade almost to white. The flowers are borne in small, loose clusters and possess a strong musky scent. 'Spectabilis' is particularly late flowering and sometimes produces an occasional flower or two in autumn. I have always grown this as a lax shrub, which allows it to ramble and scramble after the manner of 'Raubritter' or 'Scintillation'. In hot climates it will reach 4 m, but the colour is less vivid.

There is a handsome Sempervirens of the Jacques type at L'Haÿ-les-Roses called 'Gallande' about which nothing is known. It has larger flowers than 'Félicité-Perpétue' and is slightly darker pink. The bigger mystery, however, surrounds the rose known as 'Princesse Marie' introduced by Jacques in about 1828. There are many early descriptions of the rose. From these it seems clear that 'Princesse Marie' was similar to the other Jacques hybrids—very double, quartered, opening a fairly rich pink but fading to pale pink, cupped at first, but opening out flat later. These characteristics all accord with the plate in *Journal des Roses* (1886, 8). There are three cultivars in commerce under this name at the moment. Two are available from French nurseries: one is 'Reine des Belges', the other I cannot identify. In England the confusion is greater, because several nurseries offer as 'Princesse Marie' either a seedling of 'Dorothy Perkins' called 'Ethel' [Turner, 1912] or a mysterious pink Multiflora Rambler apparently from Ireland known as 'Belvedere'. Only a proper examination of all the evidence can help us to identify the true 'Princesse Marie'.

∝ CHAPTER 5 ∝

Rosa setigera (the Prairie Rose) and the Boursault Roses

Early American Hybrids

The great advantage of *Rosa setigera* to rose breeders has always been its remarkable hardiness. Rose growers in warm climates would do well to ponder a remark made by the American rosarian Steve Stevens (1933, 22): "Hardiness is a difficult term to explain because those who live in moderate climates cannot conceive the extent of the damage which severe cold causes."

> *Rosa setigera* Michaux (= *R. rubifolia* Robert Brown). *Rosa setigera* is North America's only native Synstylae rose, growing from Ontario to Florida, extending west to Kansas and Texas. The old name *R. rubifolia* referred to the distinctive bramble-like leaves. The flowers come in loose clusters of five to fifteen which measure 12–20 cm across; the flowers are single, occasionally fragrant, and 5.0–7.5 cm. They vary from crimson to the palest pink (typically a striking bright pink) and fade to pale pink or nearly white. The styles are exserted, the stigmas hairless. The sepals are ovate, pointed, about 3 cm long, have lateral lobes, and are very downy and glandular-bristly on the back. *Rosa setigera* flowers in June and July in the wild, later in cooler climates. The glandular stalks and receptacles develop into graceful clusters of fruits which are 1 cm across, spherical, vermilion, bristly, and set off by rich autumn leaf colour. Leaves are deciduous, with typically three large leaflets, up to 8 cm long, deep green and glabrous above, pale and downy on the veins beneath, the margins with coarse simple teeth. *Rosa setigera* makes a loose spreading shrub, with slender flexible stems that trail or stretch up to 5 m into trees. Its prickles, although few, are stout, broad based, and straight (slightly curved at the tip), although *R. setigera* var. *serena* is thornless. Striped and semi-double cultivars are available commercially.

Early American nurserymen used *Rosa setigera* to breed a race of hardy garden-worthy climbers. Samuel and John Feast of Baltimore were among the first. In 1836 they sowed seeds of the common species and crossed the resultant seedlings with pollen from cultivated varieties, mainly Gallica roses. Right from the start, the best known and most popular were 'Baltimore Belle' and 'Queen of the Prairies', and they have remained the most

52

widely grown ever since. Other breeders included the Prince Nursery (founded in Flushing, Long Island, by Robert Prince in 1737) and an amateur from Washington, D.C., named Joshua Pierce, who raised about ten cultivars.

The Setigera Hybrids, or Prairie roses as they were known in the United States and Canada, have many good qualities. Foremost is their hardiness. Robert Buist wrote in 1844 of the species itself: "Its constitution is such that it will bear without injury the icy breezes of the St. Lawrence, or the melting vapours of the Mississippi." They are also easy to propagate by layering in July. Buist explained: "Give the shoot of the present year's growth a twist, and then bury the twisted part six inches [15 cm] under ground; in November it will be well rooted, and can then be cut off and transplanted in any desired situation." Prairie roses grow rapidly. Their luxuriant foliage is rough, large, and handsome; their wood is strong, thin, and pliable. Their late blooming fills a space between the first and second blooming of the remontant roses. They tend to be poorly scented and once flowering.

One of the great promoters of the Setigera Hybrids was the young nurseryman Henry B. Ellwanger of Rochester, New York. He thought the prairie rose to be the most valuable of all the nonremontant climbers, and he had no doubt that they should be crossed with other types of roses to obtain hardy climbing varieties with larger flowers, truly remontant and in a wide choice of colours. In practice he found this difficult, because the varieties he chose, 'Gem of the Prairies' and 'Baltimore Belle', were nearly sterile as female parents. Ellwanger died young in 1883, at age thirty-two. Had he lived longer, there can be no doubt that Ellwanger would have transformed the whole history of rose breeding by developing from *R. setigera* the range of hybrids that Barbier and Lambert were to breed from *R. wichurana* and *R. multiflora*, respectively.

Only five of the many Prairie roses recorded in the nineteenth century survive. I have a list of an additional twenty which were once fairly common but must now be presumed extinct.

'Baltimore Belle' syn. 'Belle de Baltimore' [Feast, 1843]. *Rosa setigera* × a Noisette. The flowers (3–4 cm) are very double and pale pink fading to white with an occasional dark petal; they have a button centre and sometimes a green eye (plate 22). The large clusters droop down, whereas the individual pedicels turn their flowers towards the sun. The thin petals turn mushy in wet weather. The fresh medium green leaves are comparatively resistant to disease. 'Baltimore Belle' has pliable stems and grows quickly to at least 4 m.

'Bijou des Prairies' syn. 'Gem of the Prairies' [Burgess, 1865]. 'Queen of the Prairies' × 'Mme Laffay'. This is one of the few nineteenth-century second-generation Setigera Hybrids to have survived. The flowers are medium sized (6–7 cm), full, with a very dark centre, fading almost to white at the edges. They are sweetly scented and borne in medium-sized clusters on a vigorous plant which reaches 3–4 m.

'Eva Corinne' [Pearce, introduced by Feast, 1843]. This rose is said to be in cultivation still, although I have not seen it. The flowers have reddish buds and open bright but fade to medium pink. The flowers (3–4 cm) are cupped and very double. 'Eva Corinne' is very floriferous, but flowers only once, and grows to 4–5 m.

'Mill's Beauty' [Origin unknown]. Generally classified as a Setigera Hybrid, this rose may also have a trace of *Rosa arvensis*. The rather cupped, semi-double flowers (3–4 cm) open from pale pink buds and darken with age, ending deep carmine to almost crimson. This sequence suggests a China rose parentage. The flowers come in upright clusters of fifteen to twenty. The leaves are medium green, with broad, ribbed leaflets. The plant is very hardy and vigorous, growing to about 5 m.

'Queen of the Prairies' syn. 'Prairie Queen', 'Beauté des Prairies', 'Beauty of the Prairies' [Feast, 1843]. *Rosa setigera* × a Gallica. The flowers (7 cm) open bright crimson (although with paler petal-backs) but then fade through every shade of pink and lilac pink almost to white. They then hang on and turn brown. Although reasonably double and cupped, the flowers are somewhat inelegant. I find 'Queen of the Prairies' to be strongly scented, although others disagree. The flowers come in clusters of ten to fifteen on a very hardy plant which grows to about 3 m. The large leaves are dark green and corrugated, with toothed leaflets.

The Work of Rudolph Geschwind

The next breeder to explore the possibilities of *Rosa setigera* was a Hungarian, Rudolph Geschwind. He was born in 1829 at Teplice (Bohemia) and died in 1910 at Krupina (now Slovakia). Geschwind wrote the first book in German on raising new roses from seed. His exhaustive *Die Hybridation und Sämlingszucht der Rosen* (1863) became the foundation of German rose breeding; it covers the same ground and anticipates much of the work of Geschwind's contemporary Gregor Mendel. Geschwind was an educated man, and he wrote clearly and well. Throughout his working life, he was employed as an official of the royal and imperial forestry service. Geschwind was offered the chair of botany at the German University in Prague, but declined it to concentrate upon his rose breeding. He was not just a theorist, but a practical hands-on breeder himself.

Geschwind's abiding preoccupations were winter hardiness, health, and freedom of flowering, which led him to explore the inherent possibilities of more wild rose species than any breeder before or since—and all at a time when his rose breeding contemporaries in the German-speaking world were concentrating upon breeding tender Tea roses. Geschwind wrote a small book on Tea roses and raised a few new ones himself, but it was to such species as *Rosa setigera* and *R. californica* and such tough old hybrids as the Alba roses, 'De La Grifferaie', and 'Louise Odier' that he looked for real advances in rose breeding. He wrote a definitive study of hardiness and roses, *Die Rose in Winter* (1884), which deals exhaustively with every aspect of the breeding, choosing, cultivation, and protection of roses in cold climates.

In 1886 Ketten frères of Luxembourg introduced thirteen rose hybrids that Geschwind had asked them to distribute in western Europe as "Hardy Hungarian Climbing Roses." Ketten announced that Geschwind's preference was for climbing roses, "of which he currently has more than 2000 seedlings, among them some remarkable varieties. The one characteristic which these thirteen varieties share is complete hardiness, complete insensibility to freezing." Not everyone appreciated the qualities of these Hungarian Climbers; many were so far in advance of their time that their rugose leaves or purplish pink flowers were regarded with uncomprehending suspicion.

Part of Geschwind's problem was that he remained an amateur. He could experiment with unusual crosses but he had problems getting his roses known. Because he lived on the eastern fringes of central Europe, he never enjoyed easy contact with the great rose breeders of France and England, and he worked outside the mainstream of rose breeding. Geschwind's younger German colleagues, notably Peter Lambert and Ernst Metz, wrote extensively about his mould-breaking breeding work in *Rosen-Zeitung*, although (then as now) this publication of record was little read outside the German-speaking world. Lambert distributed some of Geschwind's novelties, but did not always acknowledge him as the breeder. When Ketten, Schmidt, or Lambert exported his roses to North America, Britain, and France, they translated the original names: 'Zigeuner-knabe' is still more commonly known in the United States as 'Gypsy Boy' and 'Erlkönig' flourishes in France as 'Roi des Aunes'. And so it came about that the importance of Geschwind's work was never fully appreciated. Geschwind himself knew its value, however; in a letter to *Rosen-Zeitung* dated 18 January 1910, he stated, "such roses as 'Freya', 'Griseldis', 'Siwa' and 'Wachhilde' are not 'Eliterosen' but nevertheless well-filled, vigorous and fully remontant right through until winter, and good seed-bearers too, so that they are quite good enough for the raising of new varieties."

Geschwind used *Rosa setigera* extensively. Many of his roses are said to be hybrids of the Prairie rose but, because some are remontant, it is clear that they derive from second- or even third-generation crosses. Although his stud book is rumoured still to exist somewhere in Slovakia, we shall probably never know the origins of Geschwind's hybrids until all have been tested genetically. And, because his work was for so long neglected, it is difficult to be sure that all the names we give to Geschwind's roses are correct. More than any other breeder, it is open to question whether the right names are attached to the right roses. Many were named after fairy-tale characters ('Prinz Hirzeprinzchen'), popular songs ('Aennchen von Tharau'), and ancient or Nordic deities ('Freya' and 'Wodan').

'Alpenfee' [Geschwind, pre-1890]. Probably a cross between *Rosa setigera* and a Hybrid Perpetual. This cultivar has light pink, fully double, but scentless flowers (6 cm across), carried in clusters on a plant which grows to 2–3 m.

'Aurelia Liffa' [Geschwind, 1886]. *Rosa setigera* × 'Marie Baumann'. Rather a late-flowering climber, 'Aurelia Liffa' has purplish red flowers (4–6 cm) which are very double and borne singly or in clusters of up to five. The plant is fairly vigorous and very hardy, growing to about 3 m, with long, prickly stems and rich green leaves.

'Erinnerung an Brod' [Geschwind, 1886]. *Rosa setigera* hybrid × 'Génie de Château-briand'. The very full flat flowers (8 cm) have neatly imbricated petals and a strong, sweet scent (plate 23). The violet purple pales towards the centre, and the undersides of the petals are paler, too. The plant is fairly vigorous, with flexible branches and lush green leaves that show their hybrid origin. It grows to about 2.5 m and is strongly remontant; in warm climates it flowers all through the winter. It is the parent of 'Veilchenblau' [Kiese, 1908] and thus the grandparent of all the blue roses.

'Eurydice' [Geschwind, 1887]. *Rosa setigera* × 'Louise Odier'. The rose in commerce is an attractive, pale pink rose with a very strong scent, but there is some uncertainty if it is the true 'Eurydice', because it looks more like an Alba Hybrid of the 'Aennchen von Tharau' type. Some French authorities say that it is indistinguishable from 'Michigan Miledgeville', a natural variant of *R. setigera*, now extinct.

'Geschwind's Nordlandrose II' [Geschwind, introduced by Chotek, 1929]. More Multiflora than Setigera in appearance, this rose has a strong musky scent; large, bright green, Multiflora-type leaves; few prickles; and double, cup-shaped flowers with wavy edges. They are deep pink at first, but later rose pink, and always paler on the underside. The plant is vigorous and grows to about 5 m.

'Himmelsauge' syn. 'Francesco Dona' [Geschwind, introduced and renamed by Schmidt, 1894]. *Rosa setigera* hybrid × *R. rugosa* 'Rubra Plena'. The flowers open dark crimson and fade to medium pink, with an occasional white stripe in the inner petals (plate 24). The petals are numerous, some quill shaped. The flowers (4–6 cm) are strongly scented and carried in small to medium-sized clusters which are not always neat, but very striking en masse. Later in the year it has clusters of handsome hips. 'Himmelsauge' is floriferous and grows to about 3 m.

'Ovid' [Geschwind, 1890]. The older descriptions call this a Setigera Hybrid. The flowers are lively pink with creamy pink petal-edges. The large, double flowers open flat in once-flowering clusters of three to five; the strong branches grow vigorously to about 2 m. Three different cultivars are now grown as 'Ovid' in major collections. At L'Haÿ-les-Roses there is a deep purplish pink, scented rose, more like a Bourbon or Hybrid Perpetual; at Sangerhausen a semi-double purple rose, fading to dark pink, with a conspicuous white centre and a suggestion of China rose ancestors; at Baden bei Wien a floriferous pink Wichurana Rambler. None matches the early descriptions.

'Virago' [Geschwind, 1887]. Setigera Hybrid. The flowers (6 cm) are semi-double, rose pink, scentless, full, cup-shaped at first (later opening out flat), and carried in small clusters. 'Virago' flowers only once, but in great abundance, and makes a bushy, very hardy plant, about 2.5 m tall. This rose was definitely a climber at Dolná Krupá, but grown as a large, free-standing shrub at Sangerhausen in the 1920s. I think it has Bourbon ancestors.

Geschwind's Hybrids of 'De La Grifferaie'

Geschwind called his hardy hybrids "Nordlandrosen." They had their origins in the collection of rose species he had made from all over the world and crossed with garden roses. He eventually bred two excellent mother-plants, one pink and one white, which were frost-hardy to −30° Réamur (−37.5°C), flowered continuously from May until the autumn, and were vigorous and healthy, forming round bushes; both were semi-double and both set fertile seed. Geschwind's policy was to cross and backcross these two good mothers with the hardiest garden roses in his collection to obtain better colours, more petals, and a better habit. These seedlings he called his Nordlandrosen, and he divided them according to their hardiness: good at −20°C, −25°C, −30°C, and so on. Geschwind bred roses throughout his life. Although he grumbled that no one was interested in his breeding of Nordlandrosen, he was certain that his life's work had been a worthy endeavour because everyone wanted roses that were really hardy in a central European winter (*Praktischer Ratgeber* 1901, 403–404). Geschwind called them "Die Rosen der Zukunft," the roses of the future.

Geschwind's collection of roses was inherited by his patron, Gräfin Chotek. Some two thousand bushes were replanted at her country house of Dolná Krupá in Hungary (later Slovakia). She tested them, picked out some of the better ones, and introduced them towards the end of the 1920s. 'Geschwind's Schönste' and 'Geschwind's Unermüdliche' did not come out until 1930. Chotek lauded Geschwind as one of the most intelligent of the old breeders, whom the world of roses had all-too-soon forgotten. But his reputation began to recover in the 1990s, thanks to the patient work of a young Austrian scholar, Erich Unmuth. Now there is a near-complete collection of Geschwind's surviving hybrids in a place of honour at the Austrian National Rose Garden in Baden bei Wien.

Geschwind also used the old Multiflora × Gallica cross 'De La Grifferaie' in the breeding of his hardy Nordlandrosen. Because they are very different from most Multiflora Hybrids, I include them in this chapter. Unless otherwise indicated, all are crosses between 'De La Grifferaie' and an unknown Bourbon or Hybrid Perpetual.

'Asta von Parpart' [Geschwind, introduced by Lambert, 1909]. This is one of the prettiest of all roses (plate 25). The flowers (4–5 cm) come in small clusters and open flat from fat buds to reveal a mass of crinkly petals around a quilled and quartered centre. They are dark pink or pale crimson with a hint of purple, paler at the edges and on the undersides. The foliage is neat, glaucous, almost blue with reddish margins, and accompanied by large prickles. The scent is a mixture of musk and sweetness. The plant is moderately vigorous, hardy, and grows to 3 m.

'Caroline Bank' [Geschwind, pre-1890]. This has rich crimson semi-double flowers, flecked with white, which fade to pink and take on a mauve hue. They open out flat to show some of their stamens. I detect a light scent. The plant grows to about 3 m and is very hardy.

'Corporal Johann Nagy' [Geschwind, 1890]. The scentless pale crimson flowers (6–7 cm) are neat and round, a very Geschwind shape, and open from fat buds. The rounded Gallica-type leaves have a purple tinge when young. The plant grows to about 3 m and is very hardy, one of the few climbing roses to survive the 1939–40 winter at Sangerhausen.

'Erlkönig' syn. 'Roi des Aunes' [Geschwind, 1885]. This has probably been available in commerce ever since it was first introduced. The full, rounded flowers (5–6 cm) open carmine crimson and fade to medium pink, although the petal undersides are at most silvery pink. They have a muddled centre, and come in medium or large clusters. The leaves are a distinctive bright green. It does not repeat, but the prickly bush grows vigorously to about 3 m.

'Ernst G. Dörell' [Geschwind, 1887]. The cup-shaped flowers (3–4 cm) are deepest pink, the shade called cherry pink, and very full, with incurved petals. The pedicels are slender, so the flowers hang their heads, a distinct asset in a tall rose. It grows to about 3 m and is extremely floriferous.

'Futtaker Schlingrose' [Geschwind, c. 1900; introduced by Chotek, 1923]. The flowers (4–5 cm) are lightly double, dark pink, and streaked with crimson with slightly paler edges (plate 26). They have a strong, sweet scent and are profusely carried in elegant long sprays, followed by good hips in autumn. The plant has smooth medium green leaves and long flexible stems; it grows to about 3 m.

'Geisha' [Geschwind, 1913]. Geschwind's 'Geisha' (there have been others of this name) has brilliant rich crimson, double flowers (8 cm) with conspicuous white streaks and paler, less brilliant petal-backs. They remind some people of a camellia in flower. The leaves are slightly puckered, with short pedicels, which gives them a superficially congested look. The plant is nearly thornless, vigorous, and grows to about 3 m.

'Geschwind's Nordlandrose' [Geschwind, 1884; introduced by Chotek, 1926]. Gräfin Chotek explained when she introduced this rose in October 1926 that she had wanted to do so for a long time, but World War I had intervened. The flowers were medium sized, fully double, three to five in a cluster, and a beautiful unfading 'Hermosa' pink. The buds were attractively shaped and shaded slightly darker on the underside. It was very floriferous and repeated a little in autumn. The plant now in cultivation under this name is lightly double, with loose flowers about 6 cm across which fade from pink almost to white and often have a slightly dark streak down the middle of the petal. Despite the differences, I am inclined to think it is correctly named.

'Geschwind's Orden' syn. 'Décoration de Geschwind' [Geschwind, 1885]. The flowers open from plump buds and are a very attractive shape, cupped, and quartered. The outer petals are broad, flat, and palest pink, whereas the many inner ones are crimson or purple, curved, and narrow. All are rather thin, but the overall effect is exquisite. The flowers are lightly but sweetly scented and carried in small clusters. The leaves are wrinkled but healthy, and the plant grows to about 3 m. It is very hardy but not remontant. 'Geschwind's Orden' is one of the prettiest of his roses.

'Geschwind's Schönste' [Geschwind, c. 1900; introduced by Chotek, c. 1930]. The flowers are a stunning, very bright crimson, with that brilliant sheen associated with China roses (plate 27). Although introduced as a Multiflora Hybrid, the way the petals turn white at the base suggests a 'Turner's Crimson Rambler' × 'Gruß an Teplitz' cross. The flowers (6 cm) are cupped with incurved petals and keep their colour well. The clusters are small, with six to ten flowers, but solid. 'Geschwind's Schönste' is immensely floriferous throughout its one long flowering period and grows to 2.5–3.0 m.

'Gilda' [Geschwind, 1887]. The flowers (5–6 cm) are pleasantly scented, double, neatly imbricated, and open from small round buds. They are pale pink towards the outside of the flower, white at the edge, and very dark pink (almost purple) in the centre, fading to lilac. The leaves are pale bright green with rather rounded leaflets. The plant grows vigorously to about 2.5 m.

'Josephine Ritter' [Geschwind, pre-1900]. The tight clusters of rich pink flowers (6–7 cm) have a very full, cabbage shape of soft petals that can ball in damp weather. They open out quartered and quilled and fade to silvery pink. The scent is a mixture of musk and damask. The plant is fairly dark green and has large matt leaves and very prickly, slender growth. It is once-flowering, hardy, and grows vigorously to 2.5–3.0 m.

'Leopold Ritter' [Geschwind, 1900]. This cultivar can also be grown as a lax bush, reaching about 2 m. The flowers (5–7 cm) are brilliant velvety red, fading to purplish crimson, very strongly scented, lightly double, and borne in small clusters (up to eight flowers). The plant has rather large leaves and prickly stems. It is vigorous and hardy and repeats occasionally in autumn.

'Mercedes' [Geschwind, 1886]. I have not seen this hybrid, which still grows at Zvolen in Slovakia. Its flowers are said to be pale lilac pink, medium sized, and shell-shaped; the plant is vigorous, floriferous, prickly, and 3 m high.

'Nymphe Tepla' [Geschwind, 1886]. The sweetly scented full flowers (6–7 cm) are cupped at first, but the inner petals open loosely later. The light crimson flowers fade to pink, with faint lilac stripes in some of the petals, and white bases. They are borne in short-stemmed, medium-sized clusters on a vigorous but very prickly plant which climbs to 3–4 m.

'Prinz Hirzeprinzchen' [Geschwind, introduced by Lambert, 1912]. Erich Unmuth gave me a plant of the true 'Prinz Hirzeprinzchen'. Its flowers (5–6 cm) are rich crimson red, with slightly paler undersides, semi-double, and scented and have the flashes of white that often appear on red roses of China descent. They are carried in rather tight clusters of up to twenty flowers on a very hardy plant that grows to about 3 m. I find it a vigorous, energetic grower, but susceptible to blackspot.

'Trompeter von Säckingen' [Geschwind, pre-1890]. The lightly scented dark crimson flowers (5–6 cm) are borne in small clusters, rarely more than six. As they age, they turn to cerise and then medium pink, paler still at the edges, although they always have a few darker flecks and stripes, too. The much paler undersides give character to the flat quartered flowers because the petals are rather short and wavy. The plant makes a lax shrub or a moderate climber to 2.5 m. It is named for Joseph Victor von Scheffel's nineteenth-century verse epic *Der Trompeter von Säckingen*.

'Wodan' [Geschwind, 1890]. The semi-double flowers (4–6 cm) are deep cerise or crimson, with white bases to the petals, paler undersides, and conspicuous yellow stamens. They are lightly scented, cupped, and borne in clusters of five to ten. The leaves have rather round leaflets, and the plant is very prickly, but grows fairly vigorously to about 2.5 m.

GESCHWIND'S HYBRIDS OF HARDY EUROPEAN ROSES

No other breeder ever employed so many rose species to such good effect, more than thirty-five of them, including such hardy Americans as *Rosa acicularis, R. arkansana, R. blanda, R. californica,* and *R. carolina.* Time and again, Geschwind shows us what an inventive breeder he was, the most experimental ever known. He wrote in 1894 that he had been breeding with *R. canina* for thirty years; the attraction of a hardy native plant was overwhelming, and some of his best hybrids came from crossing it with Tea roses and Bourbons.

Geschwind's hybrids fit into no known categories. To this day, such roses as 'Gruß an Teplitz' remain outside mainstream rose history, despite the considerable debt which subsequent breeders owe to them. It is now clear that Geschwind presented us with a gene pool of enormous value to draw on for the future development of the rose. But even his friends and supporters in Germany did not build upon the remarkable new lines which he created, and his roses remain largely untapped some hundred years later. One can but wonder how the rose would have evolved in the twentieth century had Geschwind found a disciple to carry on the work he began. The following section represents some of his more offbeat work on the breeding of hardy climbing roses.

'Aennchen von Tharau' [Geschwind, 1886]. Alba (pink) × Arvensis Hybrid. The flowers (7 cm) are very double, with incurved petals, and creamy mother-of-pearl, with a pink radiation at the centre (plate 28). They are richly and sweetly scented and come in small clusters (up to seven flowers) on slender stems. The plant is tall and lanky (it grows to about 3 m) with glaucous leaves. It is vigorous, hardy, late flowering, and rather prickly, but a ravishing combination of graceful habit, rich sweet scent, and delicate colouring. It is named after the popular song by Friedrich Silcher.

'Crême' [Geschwind, 1895]. (*Rosa canina* × unknown Tea) × (*R. canina* × unknown Bourbon). 'Crême' has masses of pale creamy pink flowers (4–5 cm) with creamy white edges and conspicuous yellow stamens which are borne in clusters of ten to fifteen. They are strongly musk scented and late flowering, but repeat well in autumn. The plant is prickly and very hardy; it mounds up to at least 3 m and will climb to twice that height.

'Fatinitza' [Geschwind, 1886]. This complex hybrid of Multiflora and Ayrshire descent has striking semi-single flowers (7 cm across) borne in medium-sized clusters. They are crimson at the edges but white elsewhere, as if a white rose were dipped in crimson and the colours allowed to run. But the colour fades quickly, the stamens turn brown, and the flower dies a dirty white. The bush is vigorous and grows to about 3 m.

'Forstmeister's Heim' [Geschwind, 1886]. Bourbon × Boursault. The exceedingly attractive flower has a Bourbon shape—very full, with many concentric circles of short, rounded petals. It is dark pink, with a slightly purple hue, and silvery pink in the centre. The undersides of the petals are slightly paler. The flowers are borne on sturdy, upright pedicels in medium-sized clusters but are, alas, scentless. The plant is vigorous and almost thornless and grows to about 3 m.

'Freya' [Geschwind, 1910]. This semi-double, early-flowering, and remontant *Rosa canina* hybrid (more petals than 'Macrantha' but fewer than 'Daisy Hill') bears pale pink, sweetly scented flowers (4–5 cm) in small clusters. The leaves have conspicuous reddish rachis, and the plant grows vigorously to 3–4 m.

'Griseldis' [Geschwind, 1895]. (*Rosa canina* × a Hybrid Tea) × (*R. canina* × a Bourbon rose). The flowers (8–9 cm) are semi-double, dark pink (almost crimson at the centre, with paler edges), fading to pale pink, very sweetly scented, and with all the charm of a wild rose (plate 29). They are carried in small clusters on a vigorous climber which grows to 2.5–3.0 m and has rather rounded leaflets. It flowers again in autumn.

'Nymphe Egeria' [Geschwind, 1893]. Allegedly a Multiflora Hybrid, this looks more like a *Rosa canina* × Bourbon cross. The flowers (4–5 cm) are globular and attractive, deep pink fading to pure pink, and very abundant, usually in small clusters. They are fully double and borne on a vigorous climber which will reach 4 m or more.

'Theano' [Geschwind, 1894]. Two roses, both attributed to Geschwind, grow under this name. One is the tall, stoloniferous shrub rose also known as 'Californica Plena'; the other has clusters of semi-double, cupped flowers which are deep pink (fading to pale pink, sometimes with white flecks) with white centres and rather cleft petal-tips. It has a fused style and drops its petals cleanly. The clusters are tight, typically six or seven well-scented flowers. It makes tall, arching growths of prickly dark brown wood which are about 3.5 m high. Erich Unmuth considers it the true 'Theano', although some of the early descriptions refer to "peach-yellow" flowers (e.g., *Rosen-Zeitung* 1900, 93) and others call it a hybrid between *Rosa californica* and 'Turner's Crimson Rambler' (which Geschwind did not see until a year after 'Theano' was introduced).

'Walküre' [Geschwind, 1909]. This *Rosa canina* cross has a delicate beauty. The flowers (6 cm) hang their heads. They are medium pink (paler at the edges) and fade as they age. The fully double flowers have incurved petals but open flat and quartered in clusters of up to seven. The scent suggests raspberries. The plant is once flowering, hardy, and vigorous; it grows to about 3 m.

Michael Horvath

Michael Horvath is the only other breeder to have worked extensively with *Rosa setigera*. Little is known of his early life, except that he was born in Hungary, graduated in forestry, and came to the United States as a young man in about 1890. At first, he worked in New Jersey, where he bred Wichurana Ramblers for Manda & Pitcher of South Orange. Later he was employed as a dendrologist in Cleveland, Ohio, and lived at Mentor, not far from Lake Erie. Horvath discovered that almost the only large-flowered climbers which would survive a Midwestern winter were the old *R. setigera* hybrids 'Baltimore Belle' and 'Queen of the Prairies'. He disliked the fashionable small-flowered ramblers and decided that he would have to raise his own hardy, large-flowered roses. So competent did he become, it is said, that he ended up breeding roses to specification for rich clients who could not find what they wanted in nursery catalogues. Horvath later became a trustee of the American Rose Society.

Horvath's first batch of large-flowered climbers, issued in 1934, had names associated with *Treasure Island*: 'Captain Kidd', 'Doubloons', 'Jean Lafitte', and 'Long John Silver' are all of real merit still. His later climbers were perhaps overshadowed by the work of his contemporaries Jean Nicolas and Walter and Josephine Brownell. Horvath was less interested in Hybrid Tea roses, although he did name a fine pale yellow seedling after his wife. He did, however, introduce some bushy cluster-flowered roses by backcrossing his vigorous first-generation Setigera Hybrid climbers to Hybrid Tea roses: 'Mabelle Stearns', for instance, is a strongly scented ground-cover rose of Setigera descent.

All Horvath's Setigera Hybrids are awesomely vigorous, capable of growing as much as 10 m up a tree. The gawky and uncomely plants lack the pliability of the Wichurana Ramblers, but the flowers are carried on long, strong stems, which are good for cutting, and all are extremely hardy. They bloom rather late in the season, when most garden roses have finished.

'Captain Kidd' [Horvath, 1934]. *Rosa setigera* seedling × 'Hoosier Beauty'. The least known of Horvath's four Treasure Island seedlings has open, cupped, double, crimson flowers (10 cm) which are moderately scented and borne on long, strong stems. The plant is once flowering, with dark leathery foliage and long prickles. No longer in commerce, it is still grown in old gardens.

'Doubloons' [Horvath, 1934]. Setigera Hybrid × a yellow Hybrid Tea. Although initially hailed as a hardy yellow climber, 'Doubloons' was later criticised because the flowers (5–7 cm) fade from deep yellow to lemon yellow. They are lightly double, cupped when open, and well scented. The flowers are profusely borne in large clusters at the height of the rose season and intermittently through to autumn. 'Doubloons' is still available from a few nurseries, and an established plant in full bloom is an impressive sight.

'Iceland Queen' [Horvath, 1935]. This vigorous climber has double, creamy white flowers (7–9 cm), but its popularity has suffered from its introduction immediately after the four Treasure Island climbers. It is only occasionally seen in nursery catalogues now.

'Jean Lafitte' [Horvath, 1934]. *Rosa setigera* seedling × 'Willowmere'. The soft clear pink flowers (deeper at the centre) are very full, cupped, 7–8 cm, and carried in rather tightly bunched clusters. The buds are prettiest half open, when they show the contrast between the nearly white outer and deep pink inner petals. I have not been able to detect a scent. The plant is very vigorous, and the conspicuously prickly stems grow to about 3 m, clambering eventually to twice that height.

'Long John Silver' [Horvath, 1934]. *Rosa setigera* seedling × 'Sunburst'. This is the best-known of Horvath's Setigera Hybrids (plate 30). The silvery white flowers (11 cm) have a fair scent and are very double. They are carried in large clusters, which can get congested because the individual flowers are long-lasting. 'Long John Silver' is occasionally remontant. The leaves are large and convex, a very distinctive feature. The plant is stiff and gawky, but grows quickly to 5–6 m high with impressive vigour.

'Mrs F. F. Prentiss' [Horvath, 1925]. (*Rosa setigera* × *wichurana*) × 'Lady Alice Stanley'. Although widely exhibited and still grown at Sangerhausen, the first of Horvath's Setigera Hybrids was never really launched commercially. Horvath used it extensively for breeding additional hybrids. It is an immensely vigorous, once-flowering climber with rather short stems and attractive pale pink flowers (7–9 cm) which are borne in clusters of five to ten. They have a musky scent and an imbricated shape when they open out flat to reveal their stamens.

'Thor' [Horvath, 1940]. The sumptuous crimson red flowers (10–12 cm) are very double and fairly strongly scented. When they open out, the numerous ruffled petals and the dark shades in the centre of the flower are reminiscent of a paeony. The attractive deep green foliage is very healthy, and the prickly plant grows very vigorously to at least 5 m. 'Thor' is spectacular when in full flower and best when several plants are wound round the same pole together.

Many of Horvath's better roses have faded from the catalogues. Some may even be extinct, despite being bred comparatively recently and introduced by substantial nurseries. Some have survived only in such collections as Sangerhausen in Germany. I know of eleven additional Setigera Hybrids which Horvath introduced between 1925 and 1955 which are currently lost to cultivation. I hope that the rose rustlers of New England and the Midwest will shortly direct their energies to hunting down Horvath's missing roses and restore them to cultivation.

Latest Developments

It is a pity that, apart from Horvath, so few twentieth-century breeders understood the potential of *Rosa setigera* for breeding vigorous, healthy, hardy roses. The principal breeders to have seen the opportunities were Isabella Preston and Jan Böhm. Preston bred ornamental garden plants to survive a Canadian winter at the Central Experimental Farm at Ottawa in the 1930s and 1940s and is best known for her lilacs. Only one of her crosses with *R. setigera* has survived: a cross between the species and 'Ännchen Müller' called 'Langford'. Jan Böhm also took up breeding with Geschwind's hybrids, to continue the quest for hardy Nordlandrosen, but his work was brought to an untimely end by political changes in his native Bohemia.

'Langford' [Preston, c. 1940]. *Rosa setigera* × 'Ännchen Müller'. Preston considered this the best of her Setigera Hybrids. It has densely double, dark pink flowers, almost red when they first open, in medium-sized clusters and with large, dark, crinkly leaves. 'Langford' flowers once, late in the season.

'Stratosféra' [Böhm, 1934]. 'Geschwind's Nordlandrose' × *Rosa centifolia*. This rose survives only at Sangerhausen, where it has semi-single, pale pink flowers (4–6 cm) in small clusters and grows to about 2 m, perhaps more if allowed to ramble freely.

'Tolstoï' [Böhm, 1938]. A very vigorous *Rosa setigera* hybrid, 'Tolstoï' has flowers (8–10 cm) which are globular, pale pink, and slightly darker on the undersides of the petals. It has a very sweet, rich scent, and broad leaves.

'Zeus' [Kern, 1959]. 'Doubloons' seedling. This is an improved 'Doubloons': the colour lasts longer. But the flower is smaller (4–6 cm), semi-double, and rather an unexciting yellow. Nevertheless, the plant is hardy in Ontario and grows vigorously to about 5 m.

The Boursault Roses

The Boursaults are the original thornless roses. No climbing roses are naturally thornless, because wild roses need prickles to clamber towards the sun. The Boursaults are a small group of hybrids bred from *Rosa pendulina*, a European shrub from the Alps and the Pyrenees. Most date from the nineteenth century and are rather disappointing as garden roses. Their great assets were thornlessness, hardiness, and early flowering, but this does not compensate for misshapen flowers, lack of scent, and thin-petalled sensitivity to rain. Yet, on the rare occasions when a bush of 'Mme Sancy de Parabère' is covered in large, well-formed flowers, weeks before other ramblers, the Boursaults earn their place in the garden.

Rosa pendulina is a thornless bush, an alpine rose which makes a shrub about 1.5 m high. It flowers very early and has small (4.0–4.5 cm), crimson blooms with creamy white anthers. It makes stout, stiff growth with crimson stems, especially on their sunny sides, and has a natural tendency to be stoloniferous. The hips are flagon shaped or urn shaped, like many of the Cinnamomeae section of the genus *Rosa*, of which this is the only representative in Europe.

The Boursault roses were named after a Parisian amateur rose breeder of that name in the 1820s. It is claimed that they are hybrids between *Rosa pendulina* and one or more China roses, although this is unlikely because *R. pendulina* is tetraploid and the China roses are all diploid. Some Boursaults are shrubs, including the purple-flowered 'L'héri-tierana' which reaches no more than 1.5 m. Others are gawky climbers. The Boursaults are usually profuse, grow well in light shade, and are characterised by reddish maroon stems. They were once used as rootstocks, although their tendency to sucker made them unpopular. And, although known as thornless roses, they sometimes have a prickle or two at the base of their stems. Most cultivars have many synonyms and are habitually mis-named. All are very hardy and flower early.

'Amadis' syn. 'Crimson Boursault' [Laffay, 1829]. This cultivar has medium-sized (6–7 cm), loosely double, rather cup-shaped flowers which open purplish red and fade to a more lilac tone. Most have a conspicuous white stripe. The petals do not drop when they have finished flowering. The blooms come in small clusters. The plant is very hardy and fairly vigorous. 'Amadis' is floriferous, reaches 3–4 m, and makes a vigorous free-standing shrub. The flowers look best when the plant is trained up a little. The leaves are thin and pale, whereas the thornless stems are green at first and maroon later, especially on their sunny sides.

'Blush Boursault' syn. 'Calypso' [Noisette, 1826]. The flowers are medium sized (6–7 cm), fairly full, globular, and deep creamy pink, although paler (almost white) towards the edges of the petals. They hang down attractively in small clusters. The plant is vigorous (as tall as 6 m), with long, thornless, purple growths. 'Blush Boursault' is attractive when grown well, but Gertrude Jekyll's (1902) reservations are worth recording: "Would be worthy of a place in every garden if it were not that the flowers are seldom perfect. Every now and then there is a good one, and then it is the loveliest thing in the garden."

'Inermis Morletii' syn. 'Morletii' [Morlet, 1883]. When first introduced, this cultivar was described as rose pink, but the plant we now grow as 'Inermis Morletii' or 'Morletii' is dark pink, with a hint of purple when the flowers first open. It has masses of small (4–5 cm), semi-double flowers which open out flat. They come in small clusters on a vigorous plant with beautiful, smooth, red stems which grow to about 4 m.

'L'Orléanaise' [Vigneron, 1899]. 'Mme Sancy de Parabère' × 'Blush Boursault'. At Sangerhausen, this is the best of the pink Boursault roses. The flowers are medium sized (7–8 cm) and very full. They come singly or in small clusters on long stems. The outer petals are pale pink, whereas the inner petals are dark pink and form a dense, muddled, and sometimes quartered centre. All the colours start much darker and pale significantly as they age. The plant is thornless and grows to about 2.5 m, but can also be grown as a shrub.

'Mme Sancy de Parabère' syn. 'Mme de Sancy de Parabère', 'Mme Sancy' [Bonnet, 1874]. This is the best of the pink Boursaults, although some writers consider it an old cultivar renamed (for example, Geier 1936). The flowers are medium to large (10–11 cm), paeony shaped, with a circle of flat guard petals around the outside and a mass of smaller petals at the centre (plate 31). They are a bright rose pink and lightly scented of cloves. The blooms are generously borne in small clusters (three to five), but their soft petals are susceptible to wind and rain. 'Mme Sancy de Parabère' is slightly less hardy than other Boursaults, but has the same thornless stems and grows to about 4 m. 'Weiß-rote Mme Sancy de Parabère' is a form spotted by Wernt Grimm in the Wilhelmshöhe rose garden at Kassel in about 1980. The outer petals are pink but the centre is white; otherwise it resembles the type.

'Ornement des Bosquets' [Jamain, 1860]. The flowers are small (5 cm), dark pink, fading to lilac pink, with white bases to the petals, fully double, and carried in clusters of up to fifteen. This cultivar is fairly hardy and has attractive, small, rather glaucous leaves.

'Zigeunerblut' [Geschwind, 1889]. This Boursault hybrid is said to have large, cup-shaped flowers of deep crimson, ringed with purple.

The Noisettes and Tea Roses

Early Noisettes and Noisette Hybrids

The Noisettes are all-American roses. They flourish in the southern states and California better than almost anywhere else in the world, and they owe their origins to a small-time rice farmer in Charleston, South Carolina, named John Champneys (1743–1820). Champneys raised a vigorous and once-flowering hybrid between the bushy China rose 'Parson's Pink' and a form of *Rosa moschata*. This happened in about 1802, and the rose became known as 'Champneys' Pink Cluster'.

We cannot say whether 'Champneys' Pink Cluster' was the result of deliberate pollination but we do know that it was common at that time throughout the American South to grow fruit trees from open-pollinated seeds, so it is fair to suppose that roses too would be treated this way, especially by farmers who used them as hedging. Champneys was described many years later as a "rose lover" but, so far as we know, he never introduced another rose. Thus, it is probably fair to surmise that 'Champneys' Pink Cluster' was a chance seedling.

'Champneys' Pink Cluster' is a good seed-setter. A resident of Charleston named Philippe Noisette, a florist or nurseryman by trade, sowed some of the seeds and raised a repeat-flowering rose which became known as 'Blush Noisette'. Once again, we do not know whether the seedling was the result of deliberate pollination, although one account says that Philippe Noisette pollinated 'Champneys' Pink Cluster' with a paintbrush.

In about 1814, Philippe Noisette sent propagating material of 'Blush Noisette', probably several plants, to his brother Louis, a famous Parisian horticulturist. Paris was at that time the centre of the rose world, where more hybrids were raised in one year than throughout the eighteenth century. The Musk × China hybrids became known as Noisette roses and reached standards of extraordinary beauty later in the nineteenth century at the hands of French nurserymen, first in Paris and later at Lyon. As noted by Francis E. Lester in 1942, "The French rose-growers created; the English and Americans bought."

Many Noisette roses were introduced in the 1820s and 1830s. Some were bred in the United States, some even in Charleston, but it was above all the nurserymen of France who developed the Noisettes. Laffay, Cochet, Desprez, Mauget, and Vibert all introduced one or more Noisettes in the 1820s. One report suggested that ten years after the introduction into France of 'Blush Noisette', more than one hundred cultivars were in existence. Vibert listed twenty-five in 1824. Some of the thirty-five roses Philippe Noisette introduced in 1827 were certainly Noisettes, and Mrs Gore listed ninety-three by name in 1838. The colour range began to include some deeper pinks, deep enough even to be called crimson, and one or two were sweetly scented.

'Blush Noisette' is actually rather a shy seed-setter. It has been suggested that 'Champneys' Pink Cluster' was a more important parent and that many introductions were open-pollinated or selfed seedlings of it. What we do know is that the class developed very quickly, mainly as a result of crosses with Tea roses, so that the later Noisettes actually owed more to the Teas than to the original 'Champneys' Pink Cluster'.

The early Noisettes are a fairly homogeneous group. They have large clusters of small flowers, as many as forty in a single upright corymb. They flower repeatedly and are usually hardy as far north as Richmond, Virginia. Their greyish leaves, vigorous growth, and long receptacles are other characteristics shared by all. But when they began to be crossed, naturally or artificially, with Tea roses and other complex hybrids, they became quite variable and difficult to classify. Indeed, in 1898 the French botanist Sirodot looked back over their development and divided the Noisettes into no fewer than ten groups.

In this chapter, therefore, we will look first at the old Noisettes, before examining some of the Tea roses with which they were later crossed. The largest section will explain the importance of 'Gloire de Dijon' and its descendants, at which point it is useful to examine the work of such individual breeders as Levet, Guillot, Bernaix, Drögemüller, and Nabonnand. Other strains emerged under the influence of such important cultivars as 'Rêve d'Or'. Finally we shall discuss the Noisettes' decline and fall from grace in the first decade of the twentieth century. However, it must be remembered that, despite their demise in response to the rise of the Wichuranas, Multifloras, and Climbing Hybrid Teas, the Noisettes remain by far the most beautiful and satisfactory climbing roses for hot climates.

'Aimée Vibert' syn. 'Unique' [Vibert, 1828]. Allegedly 'Champneys' Pink Cluster' × *Rosa sempervirens* hybrid. When this rose first flowered as a seedling, in 1826, Vibert wrote to his agents in England "Je viens d'obtenir une nouvelle et magnifique Rose, devant laquelle tous les Anglais doivent se mettre à genoux" (I have just raised a magnificent new rose, before which all the English should genuflect; Lee 1881). He was, as ever, wrong about the English, but right about his rose, which has small (5 cm), double, creamy white flowers in medium-sized clusters. The pinkish buds open into white rosettes with their stamens visible at the centre and a strong musky scent. 'Aimée Vibert' grows vigorously to 5 m but, because it produces many new stems from the base, also makes a large loose shrub or hedging plant (and roots easily from cuttings). The stems are nearly thornless and the semi-evergreen leaves darkly handsome. It is still the hardiest Noisette climber and one of the most remontant.

'Belle Vichysoise' [Lévêque, 1895]. This is an old Noisette which Lévêque found at the spa town of Vichy and reintroduced under a temporary name (plate 32). Its true identity remains a mystery. Lévêque described the flowers of 'Belle Vichysoise' as small or medium sized, pinkish white or creamy pink together on the same panicle, and borne in corymbs of twenty to thirty. This matches the Noisette still grown as 'Belle Vichysoise' at Sangerhausen; it has a delicious scent and grows to about 4 m.

'Blanc Pur' [Mauget, 1827]. This early Noisette has small to medium-sized flowers in large upright clusters. They are strongly scented, double, and, of course, pure white. The plant grows lushly to 4–5 m and has fairly large prickles.

'Blush Noisette' syn. 'Noisette Carnée' [Noisette, 1815]. 'Champneys' Pink Cluster' seedling. This rose may be thought of as the first of the true Noisettes—a vigorous, upright, tall shrub or short climber. It has been much confused with 'Champneys' Pink Cluster', which is taller, once flowering, and without the hint of mauve. 'Blush Noisette' has crimson buds in large upright clusters; its floriferousness is one of its determining characteristics, especially noticeable in autumn or after hard pruning. The flowers are small (4 cm), pale lilac pink (but fading to white at the edges), cupped, fully double, but with yellow stamens at the centre. They have an unusual leafy scent, neither sweet nor musky. The buds tend to ball in damp weather, although it is extremely hardy and flourishes unprotected at Baden bei Wien in Austria. 'Blush Noisette' grows to 3.0–3.5 m. The dark leaves often have crimson midribs, and the reddish stems are almost thornless.

'Bougainville' [Vibert, 1822]. This excellent cultivar is best described as a darker version of 'Blush Noisette' (plate 34). The flowers are small (about 4 cm across) and bright pink, fading to pale pink. The backs of the petals are always paler. They open from round, crimson purple buds in large clusters of up to fifty flowers with a light scent. 'Bougainville' is more prickly than 'Blush Noisette' and slightly less vigorous, growing to about 2.5 m as a dense, leafy shrub, but more against a wall. It is constantly in flower.

'Bouquet de la Mariée' syn. 'Bouquet de Marie' [Demaizin, 1858]. I have seen this rose only at Sangerhausen, where it makes a tall, prickly climber with sweetly scented, fully double, pure white, 6-cm flowers with rather papery petals. It has lots of pale green foliage.

'Bouquet Tout Fait' [Laffay, pre-1836]. More than one rose is grown under this name—the correct one has flowers which more closely resemble *Rosa moschata* than any other. The small (3–4 cm), semi-double flowers open out to a muddled shape with a glimpse of yellow stamens at the centre. They are pure white (apart from an occasional hint of mother-of-pearl in the slender, elegant buds) and distinct in their long, foliolate sepals and long slender hips. The flowers come in large clusters: up to forty in the first flowering and even more in the autumn. The leaves have a pale bluish grey tint. The plant grows to 4 m as a climber or makes a 2-m free-standing shrub or hedge. 'Bouquet Tout Fait' is seldom without flowers.

'Caroline Marniesse' syn. 'Duchesse de Grammont' [Roeser, 1848]. This attractive Noisette opens pure white from a pink bud. Its neat, compact flowers are small (5 cm in diameter), fully double, and carried in small clusters, typically of three to nine flowers with a light musky scent. It is a shrubby climber of bushy growth, 2.0–2.5 m high, fairly hardy, and continuously in flower.

'Champneys' Pink Cluster' [Champneys, c. 1805]. It has long been assumed that the most important rose ever bred in the American South was a hybrid between a form of *Rosa moschata* and 'Parson's Pink'; this assumption may soon be tested by DNA analysis. 'Champneys' Pink Cluster' makes a very vigorous, once-flowering climber which grows up to 4 m tall and carries its pale pink, double flowers in large, dense clusters. They have long receptacles, like a damask rose, and a light musky scent. 'Champneys' Pink Cluster' is still fairly widely grown and appreciated for its hardiness in cold areas.

'Manettii' [Rivers, c. 1840]. Probably a cross between 'Blush Noisette' and 'Slater's Crimson'. Giuseppe Manetti sent seed to Rivers in 1834, followed by a grafted specimen in 1836 or 1837. This hybrid was distributed as a useful understock and is still offered commercially. Sometimes seen as a relic of a long-dead rose, 'Manettii' itself is fairly unexciting; it produces small (3–4 cm), deep pink, scentless, single flowers in small clusters.

'Mme Plantier' [Plantier, 1835]. Many regard this remarkable rose of unknown origin an early Noisette hybrid; I consider it a Noisette × Boursault hybrid. It is most remarkable for its hardiness and its adaptability to different climates: *Rosen-Zeitung* (1925, 79) described 'Mme Plantier' as a proper Nordlandrose that was hardy in St Petersburg, whereas in steamy Florida it was even used as a rootstock during the nineteenth century. The flowers are medium sized (6–7 cm across), reflexing, pure white (sometimes with a hint of pink in the bud), fully double (and sometimes with a button eye), and a light leafy scent. They are borne in clusters of ten to twenty flowers on a vigorous, bushy, thornless shrub with small pale green leaves. 'Mme Plantier' flowers only once, in midseason, and reaches 3–4 m.

'Narrow Water' [Daisy Hill Nurseries, 1883]. This is a mystery rose. It was introduced by the Irish nursery of Daisy Hill as an old cultivar whose name had been lost and, although it has since travelled all over the world, 'Narrow Water' remains its temporary name. The rose was found at Narrow Water Castle, an 1830s country house at Warrenpoint in County Down. It is a typical, early Noisette, with small to medium-sized (5–6 cm), pale pink flowers which are nicely held on sturdy, upright pedicels in large airy clusters of up to forty flowers. It has some scent and is reliably remontant, throwing out flushes of flowers all through the year in hot climates.

The Original Tea Roses

There was once an English geneticist by the name of Dr Charles Hurst, whose passion for roses led him to forsake his academic career for the chance to manage a rose nursery. He had some original ideas about the evolution of the genus *Rosa*, now sadly discredited, and a particular interest in historical pedigrees. Hurst was the first man to identify the four stud Chinas which contributed so richly to the development of garden roses between 1800 and 1850. All four were themselves horticultural cultivars of long cultivation in the gardens of China, somewhat distantly descended from *R. gigantea* and *R. chinensis*. Two of these stud roses, 'Parson's Pink' and 'Slater's Crimson', leaned more towards the hardier *R. chinensis*, whereas 'Hume's Blush' and 'Parks' Yellow' were more tender and became the ancestors of the Tea roses.

'Hume's Blush' may be trained as a climber, but it also makes a lanky, once-flowering bush with arching branches and strongly scented flowers. 'Parks' Yellow' was a dwarf, repeat-flowering bush with flowers that were at best semi-double and only very lightly scented. It was introduced by John Parks for the Horticultural Society of London in 1824. Thomas Rivers described seeing it some years later, sold in pots in the Paris markets, flowering in summer and autumn. All the early descriptions emphasise the brightness of its yellow colouring. The rose now in commerce under the name 'Parks' Yellow' is a tall, once-flowering, pale buff Noisette hybrid in search of a correct name.

Tea roses take their name not from the Bostonian beverage, as often believed, but from the scent of fresh tea leaves. Eminent rosarians disagree on the precise brand, but the fragrance of Tea roses is one of their glories; most commentators describe it as "rich" or "delicious." The breeding of Tea roses was very much the preserve of French horticulturists; demand was fuelled by the sudden growth of the market in cut flowers in the 1850s. Tea roses produced an uninterrupted succession of blooms throughout the year, and Teas became fashionable. They were symbols of wealth and plenty. In New York, cut roses were worth up to one dollar a bud in 1871, especially 'Bon Silène', 'Safrano', 'Maréchal Niel', and 'Lamarque'.

Teas are still the best of roses for hot climates, including California, Argentina, and Australia. The rich Philadelphia amateur Captain George Thomas, who moved to California so that he could grow better roses, noted in 1924 that the Teas there "grow to prodigious size, and the best do splendidly on their own roots." But the best testimonial comes from an Englishman who emigrated to California's Santa Cruz Mountains and never looked back: Francis E. Lester (1942) maintained that "under average conditions they require no spraying. They rather resent pruning and, indeed, are at their best when left unpruned. The Tea roses and their near relatives the Noisettes, formerly called the Tea-Noisettes, were the backbone of the rose gardens of the Pacific coast and the South a few generations ago. So easy to grow, so readily started from slips, they were passed on from one garden lover to another. And when you note these old rose treasures, so indifferent to neglect, you find yourself asking whether any modern Hybrid Tea rose possesses the same keen will to live."

> 'Adam' syn. 'President' [Adam, 1838]. This popular rose is typical of the Teas in its buff colouring, beetroot new leaves, and powerful scent of tea. The flowers are medium sized (7–9 cm) and semi-double to double, and the petals, on examination, are pink outside and more yellow inside, which creates an attractive contrast. 'Adam' suffers somewhat from mildew, but this does not affect its vigour or its floriferousness. It grows as a bush in cool conditions, but will willingly climb much higher in a warm climate. Roger Phillips has it growing 4 m high in Eccleston Square, London.

'Fortune's Double Yellow' syn. 'Beauty of Glazenwood' [introduced from China by Robert Fortune, 1845]. This Tea hybrid is a most striking, early-flowering rose when well grown. Its loose, untidy, medium-sized (7–8 cm), and semi-double flowers are carried in extraordinary abundance and are rather variable in colour. The overall effect is of coppery pink, but the individual flowers tend to open pink and change to buff yellow before fading to ivory. They are lightly tea scented. The plant has neat foliage and a mass of iniquitous hooked prickles. It flowers superbly in California, Australia, and the Mediterranean region.

'Hume's Blush'. This is the rose from which most of the Tea roses bred in Europe and the United States are descended. It is an old Chinese cultivar, imported into England in about 1808 from Canton and named after Lady Amelia Hume. The rose has elegant buds which open to large (9–10 cm), pale pink flowers which are cream at the base. They are fairly full, strongly tea scented, and have large petals. The plant is vigorous, but very prickly.

'Mme de Tartas' [Bernède, 1859]. This is a good example of those Tea roses which grow as bushes in a cool climate and as climbers in the heat. The flowers are fairly large, full, strongly scented, and a mixture of pink, cream, and pale yellow. 'Mme de Tartas' was also an important parent of early Hybrid Teas.

'Roi de Siam' [Laffay, 1825]. All the original descriptions of this early tea-scented rose describe its flowers as pale pink and cream, large, and semi-double. The cultivar now grown under this name is deep cherry pink, strongly scented, with perhaps a bit of Bourbon or Hybrid Perpetual in it.

'Rosabelle' [Bruant, 1899]. 'Fortune's Yellow' × 'Mme de Tartas'. This is a fine example of one of the last Tea climbers to be bred with little or no Noisette influence. It has very handsome, large, bright pink flowers, with just a hint of salmon on the undersides. They open out wide and flat, and have a fair scent of tea. The plant is prickly, remontant, and grows fairly vigorously to at least 3.5 m.

The Early Tea-Noisettes

"Nearly 300 varieties of Tea Roses have been described and listed" wrote a French observer in 1845, when they were already hopelessly hybridised with the Noisettes. The effect of crossing them with the Tea roses was to turn the Noisettes, originally a fairly homogeneous group of hardy, small-flowered climbers, into large-flowered, elegant, scented beauties which could only comfortably be grown outside in warm climates. Most Tea roses had previously been bush roses; the Noisettes gave great vigour to what became a race of beautiful, large-flowered climbers sometimes known as the Tea-Noisettes.

Both the Teas and the Noisettes tended to have pale flowers—commonly white, buff, or pale pink—but occasionally darker, especially towards the end of the nineteenth century. By then, the word "Tea" was again generally used to describe only bush roses, whereas "Noisette" was attached to climbers. The verdict of the New York nurseryman Henry Brooks Ellwanger is as good now as it was in 1880: "In the southern states they [the Tea-Noisette roses] are by far the finest Climbers that can be grown" (Ellwanger 1893).

'Céline Forestier' syn. 'Lusiadas' [Trouillard, 1860]. 'Champneys' Pink Cluster' × a Tea rose, probably 'Parks' Yellow'. The flowers are pale yellow, buff, or pink, always more deeply coloured towards the centre and fading as they age. They are 6–8 cm across, fully double, often quartered, with a good tea scent. They are borne in small clusters, sometimes singly, almost without cease. 'Céline Forestier' makes a large loose shrub, 2 m high, or twice that when grown as a climber.

'Chromatella' syn. 'Cloth of Gold' [Coquereau, 1843]. 'Lamarque' seedling. The pendulous, scented flowers open golden yellow but quickly fade to cream, while remaining slightly darker at the centre and paler on the petal-backs. They are quite variable in the depth of their colour—sometimes there is just one yellow patch on an otherwise nearly white flower. The petallage also varies, although the flowers are usually fully double and quartered. 'Chromatella' dislikes cool conditions, but there are records of plants in warm, dry climates producing more than ten thousand flowers in a season.

'Coquette des Blanches' [Lacharme, 1871]. 'Mlle Blanche Laffitte' × 'Sappho'. This vigorous, leafy climber has fairly large flowers (10 cm across) which open from fat buds. The flowers are pure white, very full, with lots of little quill-like petals in the centre. The plant has short internodes, which gives the impression of rather dense growth, and slightly glaucous leaves. It is seldom grown in Europe, but is deservedly popular in North America. Lacharme bred three additional Noisette hybrids from the same parents. 'Louise d'Arzens' [1861] and 'Lady Emily Peel' [1862] are fairly similar to 'Coquette des Blanches'. The third, 'Coquette des Alpes' [1867], was white with a pale pink middle, medium sized, double, and very remontant (plate in *O Jornal de Horticultura Practica* 1887, XVIII: 128). It is said to be in cultivation still in France and the United States.

'Deschamps' syn. 'Longworth Rambler' [Deschamps, 1877]. This is a very attractive and floriferous climber. The flowers are medium sized (6–7 cm across) and rich pale crimson or dark pink and open out attractively. They are carried in small clusters on a very prickly plant which grows to about 3 m and repeats well all through the season.

'Desprez à Fleurs Jaunes' syn. 'Desprez', 'Jaune Desprez' [Desprez, 1830]. 'Blush Noisette' × 'Parks' Yellow'. This is a vigorous climber, with little clusters of flowers at the end of each long shoot. Their colour is variable, not really yellow—rather more creamy pink or mother-of-pearl, with an occasional buff patch. The flowers are medium sized (about 6 cm across), with a damask scent. They open rather unevenly and are often split. 'Desprez à Fleurs Jaunes' fares best in hot, dry climates. The large leaves are lush and pale. Because the colour of the flowers is so variable, the belief has arisen that there are two distinct roses, one properly called 'Desprez' and the other 'Desprez à Fleurs Jaunes', but there is no evidence for this.

'Duarte de Oliveira' [Brassac, 1879]. 'Ophirie' × 'Rêve d'Or'. This beautiful rose has medium-sized (7–8 cm) Tea flowers which grow singly or in small clusters. The colour is pale coral or salmon pink, slightly darker towards the centre and cream at the edges. The flowers are very full and tea scented; they droop down under their own weight. Because the petals are thin, this cultivar does better in hot, dry climates. The plant is vigorous and repeats well, starting into flower rather late. A sport with variegated foliage was introduced as 'Souvenir de Mme Ladvocat' [Veysset, 1899] and is still in cultivation in the United States. The yellow sport 'Gruß an Friedberg' was discovered by Ernst Metz of Friedberg in Hessen in 1902 (plate 33). Its centre is a rich yellow but it is otherwise identical to 'Duarte de Oliveira'.

'Earl of Eldon' [Coppin, 1872]. This is one of the most beautiful coppery orange Tea-Noisettes. The flowers are not large (about 7 cm across) and only lightly double, but they are carried in small clusters in great abundance on a vigorous plant which grows quite quickly to 5 m. The colour is really very striking, especially when sunlight shines through the petals. The flowers also have a good tea scent.

'Gribaldo Nicola' [Soupert & Notting, 1890]. 'Bouquet d'Or' × 'La Sylphide'. This beautiful early-flowering and strongly remontant rose has flowers which are large even by today's standards (11–12 cm). They have a hint of cream at the centre, and the backs of the outer petals sometimes have red spots on them, but otherwise are pure white. The plant has large round leaves and grows fairly vigorously to about 3 m.

'La Biche' [Toullier, 1832]. 'La Biche' combines many of the virtues of the Teas and the Noisettes. The flowers are medium sized (7–9 cm across), very full, and open out flat. They come in large clusters almost continually. They are white, with a hint of mother-of-pearl in the centre at first, and strongly scented with a mixture of damask and tea. The leaves are dark, like a China rose. Although fairly vigorous, this cultivar grows only to about 2.5 m.

'L'Abondance' [Moreau-Robert, 1887]. The Noisette influence is uppermost in this rose, which carries thirty or forty flowers in a cluster. They are medium sized (5–6 cm), double, pure white (slightly pink in the bud), and carried with the abundance their name suggests. The plant grows to about 3 m and repeats well.

'Lamarque' [Maréchal, 1830]. This has the same parentage, 'Blush Noisette' × 'Parks' Yellow', as 'Desprez à Fleurs Jaunes' but is a much better rose (plate 35). It is noted for its great vigour. Established plants put on 6 m of growth a year and are capable of much more: a plant at New Orleans was said to be 26 m long after seventeen years (*Journal des Roses* 1883, 67). The flowers are medium sized (7–8 cm), bright creamy white (pure white at the edges, cream at the centre), very double, quilled, and quartered; they open flat and have a light tea scent. It is "a profuse and continuous bloomer, demanding no attention" according the Anglo-American rosarian Francis E. Lester (1942), who also described it as a "rank grower." The leaves are a fresh bright green, and it has few prickles.

'Maréchal Niel' [Pradel jeune; distributed by Eugène Verdier, 1863]. Seedling of 'Chromatella' (either selfed or crossed with 'Isabella Gray'). This rose was immediately recognised as something quite exceptional and the most yellow of all Tea roses (plate 36). It was also extremely strongly scented (of tea, but some said of raspberries), floriferous, and vigorous, with large, pale green leaves. A plant of 'Maréchal Niel' planted at Whitby in Yorkshire in 1865 carried more than three thousand blooms in 1885. The colour is variable, paler in warm climates, richest in cool ones like England, where its huge, elegant, pendulous flowers tend to ball. Two white forms of 'Maréchal Niel' appeared during the 1890s, one from Hungary called 'Franz Degen Junior' and the other from Russia, still grown at Sangerhausen, named 'Alupka'.

'Marie Dermar' [Geschwind, 1889]. The small to medium-sized flowers (5 cm) are well shaped, pale yellow or cream, and carried in small, open, airy clusters of about five to seven. The plant is very prickly but grows to about 3.5 m. 'Marie Dermar' is always listed as a Tea-Noisette, specifically as a seedling of 'Louise d'Arzens', but the slender, crimson new growth may suggest a trace of *Rosa arvensis*, too.

'Multiflore de Vaumarcus' [Menet, 1875]. This is an increasingly popular Noisette which is rather bushy in habit, but reaching up to 2.5 m. The flowers are small to medium sized, pale pink, very double, strongly scented, and continuously produced.

'Perle des Blanches' [Lacharme, 1872]. This is yet another of Lacharme's seedlings of 'Mlle Blanche Laffitte'. The flowers are pure white and 5–7 cm across and open from a slightly pinkish bud (the outer petals have crimson tips) to reveal a very full, slightly cabbagey shape and a mass of short petals. The flowers have a rich sweet scent, with a hint of tea, and are borne in rather tight clusters of up to ten flowers on a stiff, upright, remontant plant which grows to about 3 m. 'Perle des Blanches' is a very attractive rose which flowers best in dry weather.

'Solfatare' syn. 'Solfaterre', 'Augusta' [Boyeau, 1843]. 'Lamarque' seedling. This rose is a fine Tea-Noisette with beautiful buff yellow flowers which are fully double (although the long petals are somewhat loose and thin) and cupped at first, but quickly open out flat. The flowers are about 9 cm across, have a delicate tea scent, and come in small clusters, typically three or five at a time. The plant makes vigorous red new growths and reaches about 3–4 m. It is fairly prickly, but remontant.

'Sombreuil' syn. 'Mlle de Sombreuil', 'Colonial White' [Robert, 1850]. This is a very popular and comparatively hardy Tea-Noisette whose beautiful medium to large flowers (9–10 cm) open out flat to reveal a mass of quilled petals and, occasionally, a green eye (plate 37). The flowers are creamy white, with a hint of pale pink at the centre, and are held fairly upright in small clusters (sometimes singly). The petals are rather soft, so this cultivar performs best in dry, warm weather, but the flowers are well scented and the plant grows fairly vigorously to 3–4 m.

The 'Gloire de Dijon' Line

Among the delicate Tea roses, 'Gloire de Dijon' made a sudden arrival in 1851. No Tea was so vigorous and tough. Its fame spread quickly and it won first prize at the Dijon Show in June 1852 and a Gold Medal at the Paris Exhibition twelve months later. Soon every nurseryman in France offered it for sale. The happy man who raised this rose of roses was a florist in Dijon named Jacotot. He grew Tea roses for cutting and sowed seeds of his better varieties as a way of increasing his stocks. Jacotot could not recall its provenance but, some seventy years later, his granddaughter stated that her family believed 'Souvenir de la Malmaison' to be the pollen parent of 'Gloire de Dijon' and a vigorous climbing yellow Tea the seed-bearer—the usual nominee is 'Desprez à Fleurs Jaunes'.

'Gloire de Dijon' [Jacotot, 1853]. The flowers of this important rose are about 10 cm across (occasionally more) and open out fairly flat to show a mass of irregularly quartered petals; the outline of the flowers is also somewhat irregular. Their colour is buff yellow, fading to pale yellow, but tinged at first with salmon in the centre, especially on the outer tips of the petals. The flowers are strongly scented and last well when cut for the house, but they dislike rain. The flowering comes early and continues late—perpetually in warm climates. The plant grows to about 5 m and should not be pruned hard; the leggy growths need to be bent down so that they break at the axils and produce flowering spurs all along their length.

'Gloire de Dijon' had its faults. Chief among them was the lanky straggly growth which rendered it bare at the base. Nor was 'Gloire de Dijon' popular with exhibitors. The dour English cleric Andrew Foster-Melliar claimed that there was very little beauty of colour or form to a florist's eye in the well-known "Glory Die-John." But 'Gloire de Dijon' also had its defenders. The lankiness, for instance, was easily masked by complimentary planting round the base of the plant, observed a correspondent of *The Gardener's Chronicle* in 1888, who thus proposed what we would consider a very modern solution to the problem.

The great quality of 'Gloire de Dijon' was its hardiness. In North America it was tough enough to thrive in southern Pennsylvania and along the Atlantic coast as far north as Narragansett Bay. A poll of German rose growers in 1888 revealed that 'Gloire de Dijon' was overwhelmingly considered the hardiest of all Tea roses. It also had the virtue of perpetual flowering. 'Gloire de Dijon' really came into its own in tropical and subtropical climates, however, where roses with a strong need for winter dormancy are a failure. Indeed, for more than a hundred years, until the winds of change blew away the European overseas empires, horticultural journals frequently reported from outlandish corners of the world—Ceylon, Réunion, Mozambique, and Curaçao—that 'Gloire de Dijon' was one of the most widely grown and reliable of varieties. More than a century later, Graham Stuart Thomas (1994, 159) confirmed that it was still "the most popular and satisfactory of all old climbing roses, an epoch-making rose."

'Gloire de Dijon' was extensively used for breeding in the fifty years or so after its introduction. The Belgian rosarian Max Singer claimed in 1885 that he could name a hundred varieties which were raised from it, including, in his opinion, rather too many mediocrities. The first horticulturist to breed extensively from 'Gloire de Dijon' was Antoine Levet (1818–1891); fortunately, it was a reliable seed-setter. Levet's aim was to combine its hardiness and perpetual flowering habit with larger flowers and, above all, to introduce new colours from white to deepest crimson. He created a breed of hardy, perpetual flowering climbers, the 'Gloire de Dijon' race, which dominated the market for climbing roses until the appearance of the first Multiflora and Wichurana Ramblers at the turn of the twentieth century.

Levet introduced sixteen new climbers. Because he was rigorous in his selection, they show a significant sequence of improvement. Nevertheless, there is always a limit to the number of cultivars which the market can sustain; Levet's later hybrids, although undoubtedly superior, were ultimately not such commercial successes as his earlier introductions. Many a breeder discovers that the novelty of his first hybrids counts for more than the excellence of his mature work.

Levet introduced his first 'Gloire de Dijon' seedling early in 1869 and named it 'Belle Lyonnaise'. It bore large, sweet-scented, lemon yellow flowers that faded to cream and white. 'Belle Lyonnaise' shared its parent's vigour, hardiness, and freedom of flower. It is still one of the earliest and latest to flower at the English national collection at Mottisfont Abbey. A contemporary grower commented, "One is always sure of some of its huge, solid blooms till November."

Later in 1869 Levet issued 'Mme Trifle' and 'Mme Levet'. 'Mme Trifle' had the colouring of 'Gloire de Dijon' but larger flowers, with thicker, firmer petals and greater resistance to balling, whereas 'Mme Levet' (now extinct) had a tinge of violet in its neatly cupped salmon yellow flowers. Both roses equalled 'Gloire de Dijon' in vigour and hardiness. They were followed in 1870 by 'Mme Émilie Dupuy' and 'Mme Bérard', an energetic climber whose parentage ('Gloire de Dijon' × 'Mme Falcot') shows in its elegantly pointed buds and reflexed petals. 'Mme Bérard' also had flowers of salmon and yellow that were altogether brighter and fresher than 'Gloire de Dijon'. Its strong scent, hardiness, and floriferousness presaged a long commercial life span, some thirty or forty years of popularity around the world.

Its excellence ensured that 'Mme Bérard' too was used for further breeding. Perhaps its most significant descendant was 'Gottfried Keller', the first yellow Hybrid Tea, raised by a German amateur called Dr Müller in 1894, some six years before the Frenchman Joseph Pernet-Ducher introduced 'Soleil d'Or'. The breeding of 'Gottfried Keller' is complicated: (['Mme Bérard' × *Rosa foetida* 'Persiana'] × ['Pierre Notting' × 'Mme Bérard']) × *R. foetida* 'Persiana', but the point to note is that the 'Gloire de Dijon' line played a crucial part in the development of hardy yellow bush roses.

Other 'Gloire de Dijon' hybrids followed 'Mme Bérard'. By the mid-1870s, the 'Gloire de Dijon' race was firmly established as a separate section in nurserymen's catalogues, and horticultural journals were full of articles which sought to identify what they had in common and which were the best cultivars. All were agreed, however, that the greatest advance in rose breeding would be a hardy, perpetual-flowering climber with crimson flowers—a red-flowered 'Gloire de Dijon'. To universal acclaim, Antoine Levet duly introduced such a seedling in 1878, as 'Reine Marie Henriette', raised by crossing 'Mme Bérard' with the Hybrid Perpetual 'Général Jacqueminot'.

'Reine Marie Henriette' had large, cupped, double flowers with somewhat wavy inner petals. It was a vivid cherry red when it first opened, variously described as "fiery", "glowing with life", and "most desirable to look upon." 'Reine Marie Henriette' grew with vigour and flowered both early and in great abundance, so that "a building covered with this rose presents an unbroken surface of colour." To our modern eyes 'Reine Marie Henriette' resembles nothing so much as a crimson Hybrid Tea, but that does not detract from the measure of Levet's achievement in introducing the first large-flowered, everblooming, red climbing rose.

Levet continued to improve his 'Gloire de Dijon' line. By 1880, however, the market had had its fill of Levet's hardy Climbing Tea roses and was content to enjoy three of the best: the creamy 'Belle Lyonnaise', the bright salmon yellow 'Mme Bérard', and the crimson 'Reine Marie Henriette'. All have remained widely available from nurseries in such places as California, Australia, and Egypt since they were first introduced.

'Belle Lyonnaise' [Levet, 1869]. 'Gloire de Dijon' × an unnamed Tea rose. The flowers usually open pale yellow and fade to white. The rose is paler when grown in a glasshouse, and sometimes there is a hint of pink on the backs of the petals. The flowers are about 10–11 cm, full, somewhat loosely quartered (but better formed than 'Gloire de Dijon'), and lightly scented. They tend to be borne singly and are good for cutting. The plant has large prickles and grows vigorously to about 5 m.

'Mlle Mathilde Lenaerts' [Levet, 1879]. This beautiful, scented seedling of 'Gloire de Dijon' is deep pink (with a white base), very full and quartered, and very much the Malmaison shape (plate 38). The petals are slightly paler towards their edges and some have white flecks in them, too. This cultivar is the latest of Levet's 'Gloire de Dijon' hybrids to have survived; all others introduced after 1878 are extinct.

'Mme Bérard' [Levet, 1870]. Levet's contemporaries considered this cross with 'Mme Falcot' an improvement over its better-known parent 'Gloire de Dijon' (plate 39). This rose is brighter with slightly fewer petals and without such a muddled centre. The buds are long and elegant, like a Hybrid Tea, and open out cleanly to a medium to large flower (10–11 cm), with outer petals that eventually reflex. They are deep buff yellow, with apricot pink undersides, and fade to cream when the flowers are fully open. They are scented and last well when cut. All in all, 'Mme Bérard' is an excellent rose. A pale sport was introduced in 1897 as 'René Denis' by Denis of Grisy-Suisnes and as 'Eugène Bourgeois' by Bourgeois of Villecresnes; neither survives.

'Mme Émilie Dupuy' [Levet, 1870]. This hybrid of 'Mme Falcot' × 'Gloire de Dijon' has large, buff lemon flowers, which fade to cream and white and are lightly scented. I have seen it only at L'Haÿ-les-Roses, where it suffers from mildew.

'Mme Trifle' [Levet, 1869]. Early reports on this seedling were very favourable, although all agreed that it was very similar to 'Gloire de Dijon'. The plants now grown in France as 'Mme Trifle' (all of which originated from L'Haÿ-les-Roses) are so close to 'Gloire de Dijon' that they are difficult to distinguish. The flowers are 9–10 cm across, rather full and flat with muddled centres, and well scented. The colour is pure buff, with no hint of pink or yellow, and the flowers fade uniformly to cream. The plant is fairly vigorous, with handsome broad leaves, and grows to about 3 m. 'Mme Trifle' repeats well.

'Reine Marie Henriette' [Levet, 1878]. 'Mme Bérard' × 'Général Jacqueminot'. This red 'Gloire de Dijon' is at best pale crimson or bright dark pink and fades to magenta, but there was little to match it for colour until the first crimson Hybrid Teas arrived in the 1900s. The petal-backs are transparent silvery pink, an attractive contrast to the dark upper sides. The buds are very large and plump, although elegantly pointed. They hang down on weak stalks. The lightly scented flowers are large (10–11 cm) and shapely, not quite fully double, and loveliest at the half-open stage. The plant has deep green leaves and thick green wood and grows to about 4 m but is best tied down so that it flowers all along the long stems. It roots easily from cuttings. 'Reine Marie Henriette' has two main weaknesses. First, it is susceptible blackspot, mildew, and rust. Second, its petals are soft and prone to damp off in cool weather, although superb in warm, dry climates like California. A striped sport was introduced by Thiriat in 1902 as 'Mme Driout'; it is identical in every respect to 'Reine Marie Henriette', except for the colour, which is predominantly pink, with pale crimson stripes. It is extremely attractive when it flowers well.

The Guillot Family

Jean-Baptiste Guillot (1803–1882) started his nursery in Lyon in 1829. He did not try his hand at breeding roses for some years; his first cultivar, a red Bourbon rose called 'Lamartine', came out in 1842. Guillot did, however, raise one unusual hybrid called 'Triomphe de la Guillotière', bred from *Rosa roxburghii*.

His son Jean-Baptiste André Guillot (1827–1893) became known as Guillot fils. He started work with his father when he was only fourteen, but broke away to start his own firm in 1852. Guillot fils had the good fortune to introduce both the first Hybrid Tea, 'La France', in 1867 and the first Polyantha rose, 'Pâquerette', in 1875. Tea roses were his main interest, and he is best remembered for introducing 'Catherine Mermet' in 1869 and 'Mme de Watteville' in 1883; neither of them is a climber. Guillot fils brought his own son Pierre into partnership in 1884, and their introductions include 'Gloire Lyonnaise' and 'Mme Laurette de Messimy'. Pierre Guillot took over completely in 1892 and bred mainly Chinas and Hybrid Teas. None of the Guillots set out to breed climbing roses, but they have bequeathed us half a dozen very pleasant Tea-Noisettes:

'Étoile de Lyon' [Guillot fils, 1881]. This is undoubtedly a rose which demands a warm, dry climate where, all through the year, its large, elegant, full buds open out into medium-sized (8–10 cm), tea-scented flowers (plate 40). Their colour is palest peach yellow fading to ivory white, but the centre is darker—a sort of pinkish apricot at first—and the backs are always paler. 'Étoile de Lyon' also has nicely reflexed petals, lots of leaves, crimson stems, dense growth, and moderate vigour, growing to 2.5–3.0 m.

'François Crousse' [Pierre Guillot, 1901]. This rose is probably a descendent of 'Gloire de Dijon', whose habit, remontancy, and hardiness it shares. However, the flowers are a particularly bright shade of dark pink or pale crimson, medium to large (10 cm), scented, full, and somewhat globular when they first open. The plant is of moderate vigour and grows to about 2.5 m.

'Marie Accarie' syn. 'Marie Accary' [Guillot fils, 1872]. This Noisette has recently been reintroduced by Jean-Pierre Guillot. Its flowers are medium sized, creamy white, fading to pure white, with mother-of-pearl at the centre, and carried in clusters.

'Mme Falcot' [Guillot fils, 1858]. Reputedly a 'Safrano' seedling, 'Mme Falcot' was an important parent of Teas and Hybrid Teas in the nineteenth century. It was grown under glass for the cut-flower trade, but makes a short climber or pillar rose in warm climates.

The flower opens from a plump but elegant bud to reveal a mass of petals, which are mother-of-pearl at the edges and buff yellow at the centre, fading to fawn. The flowers are medium sized (about 7 cm across), deliciously tea scented, and usually borne singly. The new growth is a wonderful rich red.

'Pavillon de Prégny' [Guillot père, 1863]. Although listed as a Noisette, the rose now grown as 'Pavillon de Prégny' has more than a trace of Hybrid Perpetual in its appearance. It opens from small, cropped buds like those of 'Cramoisi Picoté' to large (10–11 cm), flat, crimson flowers with masses of short petals and a sweetish scent. The leaves are small but the plant makes dense growth, with short internodes, which creates a leafy effect.

'Triomphe de Guillot Fils' [Guillot fils, 1861]. This beautiful Tea rose has recently been reintroduced by Jean-Pierre Guillot. Its flowers are medium to large (9 cm), double, lightly scented, apricot pink at the centre and fading almost to white at the edges, with paler streaks running through the petals. It grows to about 3 m.

The Schwartz Family

Joseph Schwartz was born at Bourgoin in 1846. He so impressed his employer when he was apprenticed to Guillot père that in 1871 he was able to take over his master's business. Schwartz bred mainly Hybrid Perpetuals, Teas, and Bourbons, but several climbing roses too, including the rose for which he is best remembered, 'Mme Alfred Carrière'. Schwartz was created a Chevalier of the Ordre du Mérite Agricole in 1884, but he died the following year—of overwork, it was said. His widow kept the business going and herself introduced a number of climbing roses, including the beautiful 'Dr Rouges'.

'Dr Rouges' [Vve Schwartz, 1894]. This beautiful rose should be better known. The flowers are of an exceptionally bright coral crimson, with a hint of peach at the base, and open to a spiky shape (the petals are very reflexed, like a cactus dahlia), about 8 cm in diameter, with a good tea scent. They make a striking contrast to the beetroot new leaves. The plant grows to 2.5–3.0 m and is almost always in flower.

'Gaston Chandon' [Schwartz, 1885]. This 'Gloire de Dijon' hybrid still grows at Sangerhausen. The flowers are buff yellow fading to white, with pink edges and a paler pink overlay, medium sized, fully double, and strongly remontant.

'Mme Alfred Carrière' [Schwartz, 1879]. This famous old climber was described as "worthless" when it first came out; forty years later, the National Rose Society of Great Britain recommended it as "still the best white hardy climber." It is one of the earliest to flower and is seldom without flowers. The buds are mother-of-pearl pink, as are the flowers when they first open, especially in cool weather, although they fade eventually to white. They are borne in small clusters and are fully double, about 10 cm across, with muddled centres and a wonderful sweet scent. The plant has bright green leaves on slender, pale green stems with only a few prickles. It is one of the hardiest of the Tea-Noisettes, growing to 5 m, more in a warm climate or up a wall, such as the famous example on the tower at Sissinghurst Castle, which reaches 7–8 m.

'Mme Auguste Perrin' [Schwartz, 1878]. This Noisette hybrid has a passing resemblance to the Bourbon roses. The flowers are rose pink, paler towards the centre and on the backs of the petals, and very full. Sometimes they form a button eye. They are medium sized (about 7 cm), damask scented, and very attractive. I have seen 'Mme Auguste Perrin' only at Sangerhausen.

'Reine Maria Pia' [Schwartz, 1880]. Another hybrid of 'Gloire de Dijon', this is a fairly hardy Climbing Tea rose, bearing its flowers singly or in small clusters (plate 41). They are medium to large (9–10 cm), full, and rather globular, with long, soft petals, which are rich pink on their upper sides and pale silvery pink on the undersides. The colour is more intense towards the centre of the flower, where it is almost crimson at first. The plant grows vigorously to about 5 m. This attractive rose ought to be more widely grown.

'Souvenir de Lucie' [Vve Schwartz, 1893]. 'Fellemberg' × 'Ernestine de Barante'. This looks most like a China rose. Its small crimson buds open out to flat, semi-double, flowers about 5 cm across. They are cerise pink, paler on the undersides, and borne in small clusters. The leaves are small and glossy, and the plant scrambles fairly vigorously to about 3 m. There are two cultivars grown under this name in Europe; the one at L'Haÿ-les-Roses fits the old descriptions exactly.

Pernet, Ducher, and Pernet-Ducher

Two Lyons nurseries came together in the person of Joseph Pernet-Ducher, who went on to accomplish much more in his own name. Claude Ducher (1820–1874) began his nursery in 1845. After his death, the firm was run by his widow as Veuve Ducher. The Duchers were principally interested in raising Teas and Noisettes. Mme Ducher's greatest introduction is probably the Polyantha 'Mlle Cécile Brunner'. The Duchers' monuments among climbing roses are 'Bouquet d'Or' [Ducher, 1872], 'Rêve d'Or' [Ducher, 1869], and its seedling 'William Allen Richardson' [Vve Ducher, 1878].

Jean Pernet (1832–1896) founded his nursery in 1856, but was never one of the leading horticulturists of Lyon. His best-known introduction is probably the silvery pink Hybrid Perpetual 'Baronne Adolphe de Rothschild'. His son Joseph was born in 1858 and apprenticed at the age of twelve to a minor rose grower and breeder called Alégatière. Then he went to work for Veuve Ducher, who appointed him foreman in 1880. Joseph Pernet married her daughter Marie Ducher in 1881, took over the management of the Ducher nursery, and thereafter called himself Joseph Pernet-Ducher. Pernet-Ducher was keenly interested in the possibility of raising new roses through controlled pollination and by experimenting with unusual parents to breed new combinations. He bred only a couple of Tea-Noisettes, 'Beauté Inconstante' [1892] and 'Billard et Barré' [1898], as byproducts of his work on developing hardy yellow garden roses. His great contribution to our garden roses was to breed yellow and orange Hybrid Teas, all descended from crosses he made with *Rosa foetida* 'Persiana'.

Plate 1. A pergola of roses in the nineteenth-century garden of Insel Mainau, Baden.

Plate 2. *Rosa* 'Albertine' on the wall of an inn at Hindon, Wiltshire.

Plate 3. *Rosa* 'Nanette' is one of many old climbing roses preserved at the Europas Rosarium, Sangerhausen.

Plate 4. *Rosa* 'Paul's Himalayan Musk' flourishes at Regent's Park, London.

Plate 5. *Rosa* 'The Garland' at Roseto di Cavriglia, Arezzo.

Plate 6. The spectacular large clusters of *Rosa filipes* at L'Haÿ-les-Roses, Paris.

Plate 7. *Rosa* 'Lykkefund' in David Austin's garden, Albrighton, Shropshire.

Plate 8. *Rosa* 'Kew Rambler' at Roseto di Cavriglia, Arezzo.

Plate 9. *Rosa banksiae* grown from wild-collected seed flowering profusely at Quarryhill in the Sonoma Valley, California.

Plate 10. *Rosa* 'Mermaid' in the Royal National Rose Society's gardens near St Albans.

Plate 11. *Rosa* 'Anemonenrose' at Mottisfont Abbey, Hampshire.

Plate 12. *Rosa* 'Belle Blanca', the white-flowered sport of 'Belle Portugaise', is planted on one side of an archway at the Huntington Botanical Gardens, San Marino, California.

Plate 13. *Rosa* 'Montecito' climbs to the top of a 30-m tree at the Huntington Botanical Gardens, San Marino, California.

Plate 14. *Rosa* 'Emmanuela de Mouchy' at L'Haÿ-les-Roses, Paris.

Plate 15. *Rosa* 'Kitty Kininmonth' in the Alister Clark rose garden at Carrick Hill, Adelaide.

Plate 16. The white-flowered form of *Rosa chinensis* var. *spontanea* grown from an Erskine, Flieder, Howick, and McNamara collection flourishes at Quarryhill in the Sonoma Valley, California.

Plate 17. *Rosa* 'Bennet's Seedling' at L'Haÿ-les-Roses, Paris.

Plate 18. *Rosa* 'Venusta Pendula', an old Arvensis Hybrid, at Wilhelmshöhe, Kassel.

Plate 19. *Rosa sempervirens* growing wild in the hedgerows near Roseto di Cavriglia, Arezzo.

Plate 20. *Rosa* 'Adélaïde d'Orléans' at Mottisfont Abbey, Hampshire.

Plate 21. *Rosa* 'Flore' in Peter Beales's garden at Attleborough, Norfolk.

Plate 22. *Rosa* 'Baltimore Belle' at the Europas Rosarium, Sangerhausen, Sachsen-Anhalt.

Plate 23. *Rosa* 'Erinnerung an Brod' at Wilhelmshöhe, Kassel, which has a good collection of Geschwind's roses.

Plate 24. *Rosa* 'Himmelsauge' in the author's garden.

Plate 25. *Rosa* 'Asta von Parpart' at the Europas Rosarium, Sangerhausen, Sachsen-Anhalt.

Plate 26. The splendid *Rosa* 'Futtaker Schlingrose' flourishes at the Europas Rosarium, Sanger-hausen, Sachsen-Anhalt.

Plate 27. *Rosa* 'Geschwind's Schönste' at the Roseto di Cavriglia, Arezzo.

Plate 28. Its Alba ancestry is clearly seen in *Rosa* 'Aennchen von Tharau', growing at Wilhelms-höhe, Kassel.

Plate 29. *Rosa* 'Griseldis' at the Europas Rosarium, Sangerhausen, Sachsen-Anhalt.

Plate 30. *Rosa* 'Long John Silver' at the Roseto di Cavriglia, Arezzo.

Plate 31. *Rosa* 'Mme Sancy de Parabère' in a good year at Mottisfont Abbey, Hampshire.

Plate 32. The mystery Noisette *Rosa* 'Belle Vichysoise' has been preserved at the Europas Rosarium, Sangerhausen, Sachsen-Anhalt.

Plate 33. *Rosa* 'Gruß an Friedberg' makes a fine display at the Europas Rosarium, Sangerhausen, Sachsen-Anhalt.

Plate 34. The early Noisette rose *Rosa* 'Bougainville' at Roseto di Cavriglia, Arezzo.

Plate 35. *Rosa* 'Lamarque' covers the office buildings at Jon Nieuwsteeg's Nursery in the Yarra Valley, Victoria.

Plate 36. A flower of *Rosa* 'Maréchal Niel' fully expanded at the Roseto di Cavriglia, Arezzo.

Plate 37. *Rosa* 'Sombreuil' at Ross Roses, Willunga, South Australia.

Plate 38. *Rosa* 'Mlle Mathilde Lenaerts' is one of several Levet hybrids preserved at L'Haÿ-les-Roses, Paris.

Plate 39. *Rosa* 'Mme Bérard' in the author's garden.

Plate 40. *Rosa* 'Étoile de Lyon' at San Jose Heritage Rose Garden in California.

Plate 41. *Rosa* 'Reine Maria Pia' at L'Haÿ-les-Roses, Paris.

Plate 42. *Rosa* 'William Allen Richardson' at L'Haÿ-les-Roses, Paris.

Plate 43. *Rosa* 'Lady Waterlow' against a wall at Mottisfont Abbey, Hampshire.

Plate 44. *Rosa* 'Duchesse d'Auerstædt' on a wall at Mottisfont Abbey, Hampshire.

Plate 45. *Rosa* 'Noëlla Nabonnand' at San Jose Heritage Rose Garden in California.

Plate 46. *Rosa* 'Papillon' at the Roseto di Cavriglia, Arezzo.

Plate 47. *Rosa* 'Crépuscule' flowers most abundantly in warm climates, as here at Thorne Park, Clare, South Australia.

Plate 48. *Rosa* 'Crépuscule' has deeper colouring in cool climates, as here at Mottisfont Abbey, Hampshire.

Plate 49. This plant of *Rosa* 'Paul's Lemon Pillar' in David Ruston's garden at Renmark, South Australia, has been grafted on 'Dr Huey' and the stock has suckered.

Plate 50. Wild-collected stock of *Rosa multiflora* at the Europas Rosarium, Sangerhausen, Sachsen-Anhalt.

Plate 51. *Rosa multiflora* 'Carnea' in Regent's Park, London.

Plate 52. *Rosa* 'Dawson' at L'Haÿ-les-Roses, Paris.

Plate 53. The early-flowering *Rosa* 'Gruß an Zabern' at Westfalenpark, Dortmund.

Plate 54. *Rosa* 'Trier' is a handsome climber in David Ruston's garden at Renmark, South Australia.

Plate 55. *Rosa* 'Thalia' at L'Haÿ-les-Roses, Paris.

Plate 56. *Rosa* 'Perle von Britz' at the Europas Rosarium, Sangerhausen, Sachsen-Anhalt.

Plate 57. *Rosa* 'Wartburg' at Roseto di Cavriglia, Arezzo.

Plate 58. *Rosa* 'Tausendschön' shows its colours in the Austrian national rose garden at Baden bei Wien.

Plate 59. *Rosa* 'Goldfinch' in the author's garden.

Plate 60. *Rosa* 'Charlotte Mackensen' is one of many rarities at the Europas Rosarium, Sanger-hausen, Sachsen-Anhalt.

Plate 61. *Rosa* 'Psyche' at Longleat House, Wiltshire.

Plate 62. *Rosa* 'Paul's Scarlet Climber' wound round a metal cone at L'Haÿ-les-Roses, Paris.

Plate 63. There are several plants of *Rosa* 'Paulette Bentall' at the Europas Rosarium, Sangerhausen, Sachsen-Anhalt.

Plate 64. *Rosa* 'Phyllis Bide', often a disappointing colour, shows its best here in André Eve's garden, Pithiviers, France.

Plate 65. *Rosa* 'Rambling Rector' in the author's garden.

Plate 66. *Rosa* 'Emerickrose' in a good year at the Europas Rosarium, Sangerhausen, Sachsen-Anhalt.

Plate 67. *Rosa* 'Maria Liesa' is the best known of Bruder Alfons's roses, seen here in André Eve's garden, Pithiviers, France.

Plate 68. This plant of *Rosa* 'Kde Domov Můj' at the Europas Rosarium, Sangerhausen, Sachsen-Anhalt, is fairly similar to 'Debutante'.

Plate 69. The arching specimen of *Rosa* 'Bloomfield Courage' in David Ruston's garden at Renmark is the most famous rose plant in Australia.

Plate 70. The beautiful repeat-flowering *Rosa* 'Frau Eva Schubert' at Longleat House, Wiltshire.

Plate 72. *Rosa* 'Améthyste' at L'Haÿ-les-Roses, Paris.

Plate 71. *Rosa* 'Turner's Crimson Rambler' at L'Haÿ-les-Roses, Paris.

Plate 73. *Rosa* 'Bleu Magenta', of mysterious origins, growing here at Hunt's Court, Gloucestershire.

Plate 74. *Rosa* 'Mosel' at Wilhelmshöhe, Kassel.

Plate 75. *Rosa* 'Rosemarie Viaud' at Gerlev, near Copenhagen.

Plate 76. *Rosa* 'White Dorothy' at les Chemins de la Rose, Doué-la-Fontaine.

Plate 77. *Rosa* 'Jessica', now seldom seen, is spectacular at the Roseto di Cavriglia, Arezzo.

Plate 78. *Rosa* 'Minnehaha' at Roseto di Cavriglia, Arezzo.

Plate 79. *Rosa* 'Bonfire' at Roseto di Cavriglia, Arezzo.

Plate 80. *Rosa* 'Ghislaine de Féligonde' in the Jardins de Valloires, Somme.

Plate 82. *Rosa* 'Emile Nérini' at the Europas Rosarium, Sangerhausen, Sachsen-Anhalt.

Plate 81. *Rosa* 'Paul Noël' at Insel Mainau, Baden.

Plate 84. *Rosa* 'Flower of Fairfield' at the Europas Rosarium, Sangerhausen, Sachsen-Anhalt.

Plate 83. *Rosa* 'Dorcas' at the Europas Rosarium, Sangerhausen, Sachsen-Anhalt.

Plate 85. *Rosa* 'Fragezeichen' is a cross between 'Dorothy Perkins' and a Hybrid Perpetual, as can be seen in this plant grown at the Roseto di Cavriglia, Arezzo.

Plate 86. There is just a hint of a reversion to *Rosa* 'Mrs F. W. Flight' in this picture of *Rosa* 'White Flight' at the Roseto di Cavriglia, Arezzo.

Plate 87. *Rosa* 'Mrs F. W. Flight' at les Chemins de la Rose, Doué-la-Fontaine.

Plate 88. *Rosa* 'Lyon Rambler' has a central position at the Roseto di Cavriglia, Arezzo.

Plate 89. *Rosa* 'Selandia' at Gerlev, near Copenhagen.

Plate 90. *Rosa* 'Strombergzauber' at Insel Mainau, Baden.

Plate 91. *Rosa* 'Super Dorothy' at Westfalenpark, Dortmund.

Plate 92. *Rosa* 'Super Excelsa' at Westfalenpark, Dortmund.

Plate 93. *Rosa* 'William C. Egan' at the Roseto di Cavriglia, Arezzo.

Plate 94. *Rosa* 'Alida Lovett' at L'Haÿ-les-Roses, Paris.

Plate 95. *Rosa* 'Breeze Hill' at the Europas Rosarium, Sangerhausen, Sachsen-Anhalt.

Plate 96. *Rosa* 'Glenn Dale' at Westfalenpark, Dortmund.

Plate 97. *Rosa* 'May Queen' at Ross Roses, Willunga, South Australia.

Plate 99. *Rosa* 'Albertine' in the author's garden.

Plate 98. *Rosa* 'Christine Wright' at the Europas Rosarium, Sangerhausen, Sachsen-Anhalt.

Plate 100. *Rosa* 'Alexandre Girault' in Peter Beales's garden at Attleborough, Norfolk.

Plate 101. *Rosa* 'François Foucard' is a good colour at Roseto di Cavriglia, Arezzo.

Plate 102. *Rosa* 'Alexandre Tremouillet' is one of many rare Barbier hybrids at L'Haÿ-les-Roses, Paris.

Plate 103. *Rosa* 'Jacotte', seen here at L'Haÿ-les-Roses, Paris, has always been more popular in New England than its native France.

Plate 104. *Rosa* 'Primevère' at L'Haÿ-les-Roses, Paris.

Plate 105. *Rosa* 'Paul Ploton' at Roseto di Cavriglia, Arezzo.

Plate 106. *Rosa* 'Aviateur Blériot' at L'Haÿ-les-Roses, Paris.

Plate 107. *Rosa* 'Général Tétard' in the author's garden.

Plate 108. *Rosa* 'Mme Alice Garnier' at the Roseto di Cavriglia, Arezzo.

Plate 110. *Rosa* 'Souvenir de J. Mermet' at the Europas Rosarium, Sangerhausen, Sachsen-Anhalt.

Plate 109. *Rosa* 'Mme Portier-Durel' is one of many old ramblers found, identified, and conserved at the Roseto di Cavriglia, Arezzo.

Plate 112. *Rosa* 'Fräulein Oktavia Hesse', here growing at the Roseto di Cavriglia, Arezzo, is one of the hardiest of the white Wichuranas.

Plate 111. The little-known *Rosa* 'Vîcomtesse de Chabannes' is a handsome rambler at the Europas Rosarium, Sangerhausen, Sachsen-Anhalt.

Plate 113. *Rosa* 'Easlea's Golden Rambler' in Regent's Park, London.

Plate 114. *Rosa* 'Emily Gray' in Regent's Park, London.

Plate 115. *Rosa* 'Lucy', seen here in a private garden in Wiltshire, has recently been reintroduced to commerce.

Plate 116. Too many first-rate ramblers such as *Rosa* 'Nanette' now grow only at the Europas Rosarium, Sangerhausen, Sachsen-Anhalt.

Plate 117. *Rosa* 'Snowflake' at Roseto di Cavriglia, Arezzo.

Plate 118. *Rosa* 'Thelma' at L'Haÿ-les-Roses, Paris.

Plate 119. *Rosa* 'Blaze' in the Gönneranlage in Baden-Baden.

Plate 120. *Rosa* 'Heidekönigin' is a true rambler at Westfalenpark, Dortmund.

Plate 121. *Rosa* 'Scorcher' in David Ruston's garden at Renmark, South Australia.

Plate 122. *Rosa* 'Victory', an underestimated rose, at the Europas Rosarium, Sangerhausen, Sachsen-Anhalt.

Plate 123. *Rosa* 'Elegance' at the Royal National Rose Society's gardens near St Albans.

Plate 124. *Rosa* 'New Dawn' in the deserted Czechoslovak national rose garden at Olomouc.

Plate 126. *Rosa* 'Morning Jewel' at the Royal National Rose Society's gardens near St Albans.

Plate 125. *Rosa* 'Aloha' at Rosemoor, Devon.

Plate 127. *Rosa* 'Pink Perpétue' in the Royal Horticultural Society's garden at Wisley, Surrey.

Plate 128. *Rosa* 'Rhonda' at the Roseto di Cavriglia, Arezzo.

Plate 129. *Rosa* 'Max Graf' at the Roseto di Cavriglia, Arezzo. It is hard to believe that this is the only parent of 'Kordesii'.

Plate 131. *Rosa* 'Ilse Krohn Superior', seen here at Longleat House, Wiltshire, is one of the best modern white climbers.

Plate 130. *Rosa* 'Kordesii' flowers superbly at Westfalenpark, Dortmund.

Plate 132. *Rosa* 'Morgengruß' at the Roseto di Cavriglia, Arezzo.

Plate 133. *Rosa* 'Norwich Pink' at Bagatelle, Paris.

Plate 135. *Rosa* 'Rote Flamme' at Westfalenpark, Dortmund.

Plate 134. *Rosa* 'Rosarium Uetersen' is unbelievably floriferous in the rose garden at Rosendorf Seppenrade, Nordrhein-Westfalen.

Plate 136. *Rosa* 'Zweibrücken' at Insel Mainau, Baden.

Plate 137. *Rosa* 'Climbing Mrs Herbert Stevens' at Mottisfont Abbey, Hampshire.

Plate 138. *Rosa* 'Climbing Captain Hayward' grown against a wall at Mottisfont Abbey, Hampshire.

Plate 139. *Rosa* 'Climbing Pompon de Paris' is a mass of colour at the San Jose Heritage Rose Garden in California.

Plate 140. *Rosa* 'Climbing Pride of Reigate' is a speciality of the Europas Rosarium, Sangerhausen, Sachsen-Anhalt.

Plate 141. *Rosa* 'Climbing Souvenir de la Malmaison', seen here at Hughes Park in the Clare Valley, South Australia, has even larger flowers than the bush form.

Plate 142. *Rosa* 'Climbing Ena Harkness', always popular in England, grows here at the Royal National Rose Society's gardens near St Albans.

Plate 143. *Rosa* 'Climbing Frau Karl Druschki' at Bagatelle, Paris.

Plate 144. *Rosa* 'Climbing Josephine Bruce' looking rather pale in David Ruston's garden at Renmark, South Australia.

Plate 145. *Rosa* 'Climbing La France' at L'Haÿ-les-Roses, Paris.

Plate 146. *Rosa* 'Climbing Landora' at Parc de la Tête d'Or, Lyon.

Plate 147. *Rosa* 'Climbing Mme Edouard Herriot' on a cottage wall in Wiltshire.

Plate 149. *Rosa* 'Climbing Lady Forteviot' in Gregg Lowery's private garden, Sebastopol, California.

Plate 148. *Rosa* 'Climbing Peace' flowers well in hot gardens like David Ruston's at Renmark, South Australia.

Plate 150. *Rosa* 'Climbing Silver Jubilee' at the Royal National Rose Society's gardens near St Albans.

Plate 151. *Rosa* 'Climbing Snowbird' on an arch at the Huntington Botanical Gardens, San Marino, California.

Plate 152. *Rosa* 'Grimpant Alain', seen here at the Europas Rosarium, Sangerhausen, Sachsen-Anhalt, is one of the better Climbing Floribundas.

Plate 153. *Rosa* 'Climbing Allgold' at Bagatelle, Paris.

Plate 154. *Rosa* 'Auguste Kordes', a climbing form of 'Joseph Guy', at the Europas Rosarium, Sanger-hausen, Sachsen-Anhalt.

Plate 155. *Rosa* 'Grimpant Edith de Martinelli', seen here at Bagatelle, Paris, is spectacular in its first flowering.

Plate 156. *Rosa* 'Climbing Iceberg' at the Royal National Rose Society's gardens near St Albans.

Plate 157. *Rosa* 'Grimpant Lilli Marleen' in David Ruston's garden at Renmark, South Australia.

Plate 158. *Rosa* 'Climbing Rimosa' at Bagatelle, Paris.

Plate 159. *Rosa* 'Climbing Masquerade' shows its colours in David Ruston's garden at Renmark, South Australia.

Plate 160. *Rosa* 'Climbing Winifred Coulter' is one of the sights of the rose gardens at the Huntington Botanical Gardens, San Marino, California.

Plate 161. *Rosa* 'Climbing Woburn Abbey' looks stunning in David Ruston's garden at Renmark, South Australia.

Plate 162. *Rosa* 'Climbing Frau Astrid Späth' at the Europas Rosarium, Sangerhausen, Sachsen-Anhalt.

Plate 163. *Rosa* 'Climbing Moulin Rouge' in David Ruston's garden at Renmark, South Australia.

Plate 164. *Rosa* 'Chaplin's Pink Companion' at the Royal National Rose Society's gardens near St Albans.

Plate 165. *Rosa* 'Cupid' looking unusually attractive in Peter Beales's garden at Attleborough, Norfolk.

Plate 166. *Rosa* 'Soleil d'Orient' at Roseto di Cavriglia, Arezzo.

Plate 167. *Rosa* 'Daydream' in David Ruston's garden at Renmark, South Australia.

Plate 169. The little-known *Rosa* 'Glarona', growing here at the Europas Rosarium, Sangerhausen, Sachsen-Anhalt, deserves to be more widely grown.

Plate 168. *Rosa* 'Ringlet', seen here at the Royal Botanic Gardens, Melbourne, is hardy enough to survive unprotected at the Europas Rosarium, Sangerhausen, Sachsen-Anhalt.

Plate 171. *Rosa* 'Mady' grows still at the Europas Rosarium, Sangerhausen, Sachsen-Anhalt, where it combines the hardiness of the Hybrid Perpetuals with the floral beauty of the Teas.

Plate 170. When well grown, as here at L'Haÿ-les-Roses, Paris, nothing surpasses the beauty of *Rosa* 'Lorenzo Pahissa'.

Plate 172. *Rosa* 'Réveil Dijonnais', seen here at Bagatelle, Paris, was an experimental hybrid in its day, and its colour still provokes comment.

Plate 173. *Rosa* 'Dreaming Spires' is one of the best early-flowering climbers at the Royal National Rose Society's gardens near St Albans.

Plate 174. *Rosa* 'Fourth of July', growing here in a public park in downtown Los Angeles, is the best of the new striped climbers.

Plate 175. *Rosa* 'Goldfassade' growing near the chapel at Insel Mainau, Baden.

Plate 176. *Rosa* 'Heinrich Blanc', seen here at Insel Mainau, Baden, is very beautiful in bud.

Plate 177. *Rosa* 'Ludvik Večeřa' makes a good display at the Europas Rosarium, Sangerhausen, Sachsen-Anhalt.

Plate 178. *Rosa* 'Meg' is a short-lived beauty in David Ruston's garden at Renmark, South Australia.

Plate 180. *Rosa* 'Rosenfest' flowers profusely at the Europas Rosarium, Sangerhausen, Sachsen-Anhalt.

Plate 179. *Rosa* 'Red Flare' is popular in North America, although this photograph was taken at the Europas Rosarium, Sangerhausen, Sachsen-Anhalt.

Plate 182. *Rosa* 'Odette Joyeux' at L'Haÿ-les-Roses, Paris.

Plate 181. *Rosa* 'Schloß Dryberg' is a good bright yellow at the Europas Rosarium, Sangerhausen, Sachsen-Anhalt.

Plate 183. *Rosa* 'Intervilles' at L'Haÿ-les-Roses, Paris.

Plate 184. *Rosa* 'Cassandre' at the rose garden at Saverne, Alsace.

Plate 185. *Rosa* 'Fugue' in David Ruston's garden at Renmark, South Australia.

Plate 186. *Rosa* 'Looping' at the Roseto di Cavriglia, Arezzo.

Plate 187. The seldom-seen *Rosa* 'Declic' is an impressive sight early in the season at Bagatelle, Paris.

Plate 188. *Rosa* 'Altissimo' against a wall at the Huntington Botanical Gardens, San Marino, California.

Plate 189. *Rosa* 'Tarzan' at L'Haÿ-les-Roses, Paris.

Plate 191. *Rosa* 'Shirpa' at Bagatelle, Paris.

Plate 190. *Rosa* 'Zénith' at the Roseto di Cavriglia, Arezzo.

Plate 193. *Rosa* 'Gruß an Heidelberg', seen here at the Roseto di Cavriglia, Arezzo, has proved an important parent of modern climbers.

Plate 192. *Rosa* 'Royal Sunset' at the Roseto di Cavriglia, Arezzo.

Plate 195. *Rosa* 'Morgensonne' 88' at Westfalen-park, Dortmund.

Plate 194. *Rosa* 'Harlekin', growing here at the Descanso Gardens in Los Angeles, is the best of the bicolor climbers.

Plate 196. *Rosa* 'Direktor Benschop', seen here at Bagatelle, Paris, profusely flowers once per year.

Plate 197. *Rosa* 'Lawinia' is one of the most florif-erous of climbers at Westfalenpark, Dortmund.

Plate 198. *Rosa* 'Santa Catalina' wound around a cone at Bagatelle in Paris; it is still a popular rose in France.

Plate 199. A row of climbers in the international trials at the Royal National Rose Society's gardens near St Albans. Are these the climbing roses of tomorrow?

Plate 200. *Rosa* 'Alexandre Girault' flowers spectacularly along the trelliswork in the centre of the rosery at L'Haÿ-les-Roses, Paris.

'Albert la Blotais' syn. 'Climbing Albert la Blotais' [Pernet, 1887]. 'Gloire de Dijon' × 'Général Jacqueminot'. Breeders made many crosses between these two most famous roses of the late nineteenth century. Pernet's cultivar became known as 'Climbing Albert la Blotais' to distinguish it from Moreau et Robert's Hybrid Perpetual of 1881. Both are grown at Sangerhausen still. Pernet's rose is a deep pink or light red, with a muddled centre that recalls 'Gloire de Dijon' and a very rich scent that comes from 'Général Jacqueminot'. The flowers are fairly large (11 cm) and open out flat and full. It grows to about 3 m and repeats all through the season.

'Beauté Inconstante' syn. 'Beauté de Lyon' [Pernet-Ducher, 1892]. 'Safrano' × 'Earl of Eldon'. The name of this rose refers to the extraordinary variability of its colouring: the medium to large (9–10 cm) flowers are sometimes red, sometimes yellow, sometimes creamy white, and usually a combination of all three. It also fades as it ages. The shape too is irregular, usually semi-double with a mass of twisting petaloids. The plant is upright, rigid, prickly, and vigorous with gleaming green foliage, reaching about 4 m.

'Billard et Barré' [Pernet-Ducher, 1898]. 'Mlle Alice Furon' × 'Duchesse d'Auerstædt'. This is one of the most beautiful of Tea roses; it has medium to large flowers (9 cm), which are held erect, full of petals, and strongly tea scented. Their colour is deep buff at the centre of the flowers, with the outer edges of the petals cream or white, not the golden yellow of old descriptions. The leaves are dark for a Tea rose, and the plant grows to about 3 m.

'Bouquet d'Or' [Ducher, 1872]. The medium to large flowers (9 cm) are tea scented, double, and open out flat to a mass of rather broad petals. The colour is pure buff yellow, with a very occasional hint of pink, and a tendency to fade at the edges. Its distinctive characteristic is the way all the petals reflex along their edges, while keeping a crease down their middles. The leaves are typical of the Tea roses, and the plant grows to about 4 m.

'Jean Ducher' [Ducher, 1873]. The flowers of this stout Tea rose are generally borne singly. The buds are elegant in a tubby sort of way and pale cream, apart from occasional streaks of red. When they open out, the medium to large (8–9 cm), nearly double flowers are pale creamy pink with a buff yellow wash, and strongly scented of tea. It is a good perpetual-flowerer, but sensitive to rain and therefore best in hot, dry climates.

'Mme Louis Henry' [Vve Ducher, 1879]. This Tea-Noisette has medium-sized (7 cm) flowers in clusters of up to about ten flowers, which are pure white and double, with the stamens showing at the centre. It is a reliable repeat-flowering plant, rather prickly, and with light green leaves. It grows to about 3 m, but I have seen it only in France, at L'Haÿ-les-Roses and in the Jardin des Plantes at Lyon. 'Mme Louis Henry' should be tried in the United States and Australia.

'Monsieur Désir' [Pernet père, 1888]. A seedling of 'Gloire de Dijon' × a crimson Hybrid Perpetual. This Tea-type climber has pale crimson or dark pink flowers, which are medium sized (8 cm), almost full, well-held, and strongly scented. However, they are usually produced from split buds and open out irregularly. It is not as good as 'Climbing Albert la Blotais', which Pernet introduced the previous year.

'Rêve d'Or' [Ducher, 1869]. Allegedly a seedling of 'Mme Schultz', a Tea-Noisette. 'Rêve d'Or' appears buff yellow but its flowers are pale yellow at the edges, and darker in the middle with a hint of apricot from the pinker tones of the backs of the petals. It fades only slightly to pale buff, and the petals too reflex as they age. The flowers have a good tea scent and usually appear in clusters (of up to twelve), although sometimes singly. The plant has deep green, glossy foliage which is tinted red when young and is very vigorous, growing quickly upwards. It is also one of the hardier Noisettes (the original plant survived the hard winter of 1879–80 at Lyon), and there are few better roses for quickly covering a large space in a warm climate. Instantly popular, 'Rêve d'Or' also proved an important seed parent.

'Triomphe des Noisettes' [Pernet père, 1887]. 'Général Jacqueminot' × 'Ophirie'. This vigorous pillar rose has medium to large flowers (9–10 cm) which open bright dark pink and fade to medium pink. They are fully double and often have a quartered centre as well as a moderate scent. They are borne in clusters on a fast-growing plant which repeats well.

'William Allen Richardson' [Vve Ducher, 1878]. A seedling (*not* a sport) of 'Rêve d'Or'. The buds are deep orange apricot and open rather slowly into beautiful, small flowers whose central petals are deep orange or apricot yellow while the outer ones turn quickly to cream or white (plate 42). The flowers are exquisite when half open (it was a famous buttonhole rose), but flat and rather irregular later. They have a fairly strong scent of tea and are carried in small to medium-sized clusters. 'William Allen Richardson' flowers freely and early, and repeats all through the year in hot climates, although the flowers bleach quickly in bright sunlight. That said, it remains one of the finest continuous blooming climbers for the American South. The foliage is dark glossy green and is sometimes subject to blackspot. The plant grows vigorously to about 6 m. Like its parent 'Rêve d'Or', it proved a fecund seed parent.

Jean-Alexandre Bernaix

Jean-Alexandre Bernaix founded his nursery in Villeurbane in 1860 and, by the 1890s it was the largest in Lyon. Although Lyon was at that time the capital of the world's rose industry, Bernaix did not start to specialise in roses until 1886. All his thirty or so new introductions were bred between then and 1897. His Tea-Noisettes are among the most exciting ever introduced; there is not a single dud among them, and the greatest— 'Baronne Henriette de Snoy', 'Claire Jacquier', 'Duchesse d'Auerstædt', and 'Souvenir de Mme Léonie Viennot'—are still among the best of all climbers for warm climates. His nursery was taken over first by his son F. Bernaix and later by F. Boujard.

'Baronne Henriette de Snoy' [Bernaix, 1897]. 'Gloire de Dijon' × 'Mme Lombard'. The flowers of this excellent rose are medium to large (9–10 cm) and open out flat. The short wide petals are creamy pink, darker towards the outside, with crimson blotches on the buds and the backs of the outer petals. The flowers come in open bunches of up to five, which are produced in succession over a long time. They have a slight scent. The plant is free-flowering, reliably remontant, and grows to 4 m in a hot climate. Two distinctive and charming characteristics are its stout purple stems and beetroot new growths.

'Claire Jacquier' syn. 'Mlle Claire Jacquier' [Bernaix, 1888]. The small (3 cm), semi-double flowers open pale yellow with a hint of buff, but quickly fade to cream and white as they open to show their stamens. They have a musky scent and are borne in clusters of five to ten; they are also very attractive to bees. 'Claire Jacquier' is a lushly leafy plant, with glittering leaves and dark stems. It grows vigorously to 5 m—twice that on a wall. There are a few late flowers, but not every year.

'Comtesse de Galard-Béarn' [Bernaix, 1893]. This Tea-Noisette was originally described as yellow, and a plate in *Journal des Roses* in 1902 confirms this. The only plants that I have seen, at San Jose Heritage Rose Garden in California, are very like that old plate but with pink flowers, not yellow. Everything else tallies: the flowers are 7–9 cm in diameter, strongly tea scented, very full of short petals which have slightly darker undersides. Sometimes it opens out to an imbricated shape; other times it opens out fully. The colour varies and parts of the flower (especially the centre) are usually pinker than others. But it is definitely pink and not yellow, so I question if it is correctly named.

'Duchesse d'Auerstædt' syn. 'Mme la Duchesse d'Auerstædt' [Bernaix, 1888]. This open-pollinated seedling of 'Rêve d'Or' has larger flowers than its parent and they are pure yellow (plate 44). There is just a hint of apricot at the centre of the flowers, which are generally borne singly on long stems and nodding stalks. They are about 11 cm across, very full, usually quartered, and deliciously tea scented. Because the flowers dislike rain, 'Duchesse d'Auerstædt' does best in warm, dry climates like the American South, where it reaches 6 m and rivals 'Maréchal Niel' for its colour. The new growth is particularly elegant and soft; the bloomy stems and purple colour set off the flowers well. 'Duchesse d'Auerstædt' flowers continuously.

'E. Veyrat Hermanos' syn. 'Pillar of Gold' [Bernaix, 1895]. This Climbing Tea rose opens from beautiful long pointed buds to large (9–10 cm) flowers with reflexed petals and a strong tea scent. It is a rose of many colours—a fully open flower is a glorious mixture of pinks, creams, crimsons, and apricots. They are usually borne in small clusters of three to five flowers and repeat well, although they are susceptible to cold and damp weather. The plant is moderately vigorous but eventually grows to about 5 m high.

'Souvenir de Mme Joseph Métral' syn. 'Mme J. Métral' [Bernaix, 1887]. 'Mme Bérard' × 'Eugen Fürst'. The medium to large (9–10 cm), rather full flowers with masses of small petals are plain dark pink and slightly darker, almost cerise, on their backs. It is said to be sweetly scented, but the only plant I have seen of it, at L'Haÿ-les-Roses, was scentless. It repeats well and grows to about 3 m.

'Souvenir de Mme Léonie Viennot' [Bernaix, 1898]. This is the best known of Bernaix's Teas, still widely grown and sold. Its flowers have almost a modern look. The flowers are fairly large (10–11 cm), open flat and very full with recurved petals like a paeony. They are deep peachy pink at first, but turn pinker and paler as they age. The outer petals fade to pale pink and the backs are silvery pink. The flowers are strongly tea scented and set off by the dark green, rather corrugated leaves, which have long leaflets and red midribs. Its first flowering comes early, but it flowers continually in warm climates and grows densely to about 3 m.

Drögemüller

Pastor Heinrich Drögemüller of Neuhaus-Elbe was a well-regarded amateur rosarian at the end of the nineteenth century. He bred eleven roses between 1886 and 1896, of which five have survived at Sangerhausen. All his hybrids are crosses of 'Gloire de Dijon' except for 'Kaiser Wilhelm der Siegreiche', a seedling of 'Mme Bérard'. They were introduced by Schultheis—then, as now, one of the greatest German rose nurseries. Drögemüller tended to choose Hybrid Perpetuals as pollen parents, in the hope that they would impart extra hardiness. He also liked to give them patriotic names when his seedlings were released.

'Emin Pascha' [Drögemüller, 1894]. 'Gloire de Dijon' × 'Louis van Houtte'. The pollen parent is a crimson Hybrid Perpetual: 'Emin Pascha' has a good crop of large (11 cm), deep pink, fully double flowers on a plant which repeat-flowers in autumn and grows fairly vigorously to about 3.5 m.

'Fürst Bismarck' [Drögemüller, 1886]. This cultivar is probably a selfed 'Gloire de Dijon' seedling; their colouring is similar, but 'Fürst Bismarck' flowers more abundantly. The Tea rose genes show clearly in its nodding flowers. It has a fruity scent but a tendency for the flowers to ball in damp climates.

'Fürstin Bismarck' [Drögemüller, 1887]. 'Gloire de Dijon' × 'Comtesse d'Oxford'. The flowers show their hybrid origin: they open dark pink and fade to medium pink like the Hybrid Perpetual 'Comtesse d'Oxford', but have the scent and shape of 'Gloire de Dijon' with a muddled centre. 'Fürstin Bismarck' repeats well and grows to about 3 m.

'Kaiserin Friedrich' [Drögemüller, 1889]. 'Gloire de Dijon' × 'Perle des Jardins'. This rose flourishes in hot climates, and *The Gardener's Chronicle* (1892) recommended it for British Guyana. It closely resembles 'Gloire de Dijon'. The colour is variable, although the flowers generally have pale yellow petals towards the outside and white towards the centre; all are tipped with pink, like 'Marie van Houtte'. 'Kaiserin Friedrich' repeats well and is strongly scented, but only of moderate vigour, growing to 2.5–3.0 m.

'Kaiser Wilhelm der Siegreiche' [Drögemüller, 1887]. 'Mme Bérard' × 'Perle des Jardins'. This cross has a reputation for greater hardiness than either of its parents. Pretty at all stages, the flowers are fairly large (10 cm), very full, well scented, and borne singly or in small clusters. The outer petals are pale cream, fading to white, whereas the inner petals are rather more yellow. The petals also have pink edges. The plant grows to about 3 m.

Nabonnand

Gilbert Nabonnand moved from Lyon to Golfe-Juan in 1864 and flourished. As the Riviera expanded into the world's smartest international winter resort, Nabonnand built up the largest nursery in the south of France. Fully grown specimen palm trees, agaves, and unusual plants (often new to cultivation) were some of its specialities. Nabonnand also designed and planted a large number of gardens for the fashionable rich along the Côte d'Azur. When he retired in 1885, he handed over his nursery to his two sons Paul (a famous breeder of palms) and Clément.

The Nabonnands were prolific, perhaps overprolific, breeders of Tea roses and Tea-Noisettes. Every year they issued a dozen or so new cultivars, few of which were real improvements on what had gone before, and named them after the fashionable people of the season. Many of their hybrids were seedlings of 'Gloire de Dijon' which had rather globular flowers with muddled, quartered, or imbricated centres. The Nabonnands were loud in their praise of these creations, and eventually they did introduce two really great Tea-Noisettes in 'Lady Waterlow' and 'Noëlla Nabonnand', but there were many more than the market could absorb. Only eleven are still in cultivation, most of them precariously, while an additional thirty-five or so are probably extinct, to say nothing of the scores of bush Tea roses which the Nabonnands produced with up-market names year after year to flatter their rich cosmopolitan customers.

'Comtesse de Noghera' [Nabonnand, 1902]. This rose's elegant buds open into beautiful, apple-scented flowers with rather a modern look. They are pale buff, merging to cream at the edges, but with a pink flush at the centre that comes from the backs of the petals. The effect is exquisitely delicate, yet this is quite a tough rose and, unlike most Teas, the flower-stalks are fairly sturdy, so the flower does not droop much. The plant grows vigorously to 3.0–3.5 m.

'Comtesse Georges de Roquette Brisson' [Nabonnand, 1884]. There is a pink Hybrid Perpetual of this name, introduced by Lévêque in 1899, but Nabonnand's Tea Noisette is pale yellow, fading to cream, and with pink hints at the centre of the flower. It grows still at L'Haÿ-les-Roses.

'Lady Waterlow' [Nabonnand, 1902]. 'La France de '89' × 'Mme Marie Lavalley'. This ravishing rose represents the culmination of nineteenth-century rose breeding and suggests how the history of climbing roses might have developed if these late Tea-Noisettes had not been overtaken by the fashion for Multifloras and Wichuranas (plate 43). Its buds are as elegant as any Tea or Hybrid Tea. The flowers are large (about 11 cm), lightly filled, and deliciously scented. When the red buds open, the flowers are palest pink with a slight yellow flush and bright crimson edges to the petals. But the colours fade and merge when they are fully open to give an overall impression of rose pink. 'Lady Waterlow' is seldom without flowers and grows fairly vigorously to 4–5 m.

'Lily Metschersky' [Nabonnand, 1878]. This cultivar was introduced as the first purplish red Noisette, but it fades quickly to a mauve pink. The scentless flowers are full, small (about 5 cm), and usually carried in clusters of up to ten. The plant has dark wood and many large prickles. It grows with moderate vigour to about 3 m and repeats well throughout the season.

'Marguerite Desrayeux' [Nabonnand, 1906]. 'Mme Alfred Carrière' × 'Mme Marie Lavalley'. This Tea-Noisette has shapely buds which open out to medium to large (9–10 cm), rather full, tea-scented flowers in small clusters. Their colour is a mixture of peachy pink and white, but the petals are soft and the buds tend to ball. The plant has large leaves and is almost thornless; it grows to about 3 m.

'Mme Rose Romarin' [Nabonnand, 1888]. 'Papillon' × 'Chromatella'. Intended to combine the shape of 'Papillon' with the brilliant colouring of 'Chromatella', 'Mme Rose Romarin' more closely resembles the former. It makes an elegant, high-peaked, dark pink bud which opens out to a much paler flower, pink towards the outside, especially on the edges of the petals, and creamy buff inside, although Nabonnand described it as "bright red with copper tints." 'Mme Rose Romarin' is very full, scented, remontant, and vigorous, although it reaches no more than about 2.5 m.

'Monsieur Rosier' [Nabonnand, 1887]. Allegedly a 'Mlle Mathilde Lenaerts' seedling, this is a very stiff, upright, and vigorous climber with pink flowers right at the top. The flowers are medium to large (9–10 cm), with muddled centres and have a hint of yellow in the centre. The plant will grow as much as 6–8 m.

'Nardy' [Nabonnand, 1888]. This was introduced as an improved 'Gloire de Dijon' with larger flowers. They open buff yellow, with an occasional hint of pink, but soon fade to creamy white and are susceptible to mildew. They are full, fairly well scented, and borne on long stems. The plant has large leaves and broad, slightly glaucous leaflets; it grows to 3–4 m.

'Noëlla Nabonnand' [Nabonnand, 1901]. 'Reine Marie Henriette' × 'Bardou Job'. This is the best-known and most widely grown of all Nabonnand's roses (plate 45). Like 'Lady Waterlow', it represents the culmination of nearly a century of breeding roses to be large flowered, hardy, and reliably remontant. Even by today's standards, the flowers are very large, as much as 15–16 cm across when the tall, elegant buds open out to their large, floppy, loosely petalled flowers. Their colouring is not unlike 'Reine Marie Henriette', bright purplish crimson with much paler pink undersides (white at the base), but the influence of 'Bardou Job' gives the crimson a special brilliance peculiar to the China roses. The flowers of 'Noëlla Nabonnand' are, moreover, very strongly scented. The leaves have a glaucous hue and the plant grows to 4–5 m. It makes a spectacular sight in spring, especially in a dry climates, with a few flowers all through the season. It does not suffer from mildew or balling like 'Reine Marie Henriette', but the long petals spoil in wind and rain.

'Papillon' [Nabonnand, 1879]. The inner petals of this attractive and unusual Noisette reflex their edges so abruptly that a plant in full bloom resembles a swarming multitude of butterflies—hence its name. The flowers are coral, but fade to coppery pink and rose pink, whereas the backs of the petals are pink and fade almost to white (plate 46). They are medium sized (about 6 cm), semi-double, only lightly scented, but abundantly borne in medium-sized clusters. 'Papillon' spoils in the rain, so it performs best in warm, dry climates, where it flowers repeatedly and makes a leafy, twiggy bush which climbs to 3–5 m.

'Reine Olga de Würtemberg' [Nabonnand, 1881]. This climber was highly regarded when it first came out for its semi-double, medium-sized (9 cm), brilliant cherry red flowers and its repeat-flowering habit. The flowers are graceful and cheerful when they first open, but then turn a dull crimson and lose their shape. The plant grows vigorously to about 4 m.

Decline and Fall: The Last of the Tea-Noisettes

By the end of the nineteenth century, the Tea-Noisettes were the most popular of climbing roses, and there was a certain nostalgia for the passing of the early Noisettes, which had so many virtues. The English nurseryman A. W. Paul (1907), for example, declared that "There is one class of older roses whose gradual disappearance, I think, is to be deplored from the present standpoint of rose-growing, and that is the stronger-growing hardy Noisette roses which are so valuable as autumn-blooming climbing roses." But, in the spirit of his age, Paul felt compelled to add that, despite this decline, he did believe in progress.

The reason that the old Noisettes lost out was simply that their successors, the Tea-Noisettes, had bigger flowers. Size mattered. Ever-larger flowers are the perennial aim of every plant breeder, whatever the genus. But the last quarter of the nineteenth century also saw a surge of interest in growing roses competitively, so that for many garden owners and their gardeners it was the size and shape of a rose on a competition bench which counted for more than such qualities as its scent or abundance. It was in the 1890s and 1900s too that the first Hybrid Teas came into their own, so that by 1910 they were not only the dominant type of garden rose but also the preferred choice for exhibition. They had all the virtues of the Tea-Noisettes, but took up less space; Hybrid Teas were also more compact, more productive, and hardier. This left the Tea-Noisettes vulnerable to market competition from the wave of new Wichurana Ramblers which swept across the gardening world between 1900 and 1910 and displaced them almost overnight. The Wichuranas had the Tea-Noisettes beaten on hardiness, vigour, habit, abundance, weather resistance, and sheer flower-power. There was no real rearguard action—only a few second-rate breeders such as Chauvry and Viaud-Bruant continued to produce new cultivars into the 1910s. But so completely had fashion taken to the Wichuranas that these last Tea-Noisettes faded immediately from memory.

It was some years before people realised the magnitude of their loss. By the middle of the twentieth century, Domenico Aicardi, an underestimated rosarian, was much regretting the disappearance of the old Climbing Teas and Noisettes "which are inexorably vanishing, without being replaced, except by climbing sports, which are not the same thing at all" (Aicardi 1951, 37–38). He added that "it is an absolute iniquity that an inheritance of such value should disappear," and he attributed its decline to a mania for hardiness. He also pinpointed the cause: domination of the rose industry by breeders from cooler climates. One of the consequences of the changes which took place in the trade in the 1890s and 1900s was that its centre of gravity moved from such places as Lyon and Golfe-Juan to the United Kingdom, Germany, and New England.

The market was dominated by rose books by English writers who regarded Teas and Noisettes as difficult to grow and flower, which also contributed to their decline in popularity. Some may never have known more than a handful of cultivars, but these experts were read and studied by garden owners in warm and tropical parts of the world as if everything applied to their own gardens, where the true problems of cultivation were heat and drought for which the Teas and Noisettes are uniquely adapted. Now the economic and horticultural centres of gravity have moved towards those warmer areas like California, where the perpetual-flowering Tea roses do best, while those with a strong need for winter dormancy and summer rain are a failure. In warmer parts of the world it is the Teas, the Noisettes, and their hybrids, the Tea-Noisettes, which are the mainstay of the rose garden, where they flower in every month of the year and especially freely in spring. Thus, the remaining Tea-Noisettes listed below do not just represent the culmination of years of breeding and interbreeding to bring this race of roses to the summit of their capabilities, they also point to the direction in which new breeders might progress if they pick up the challenge and develop the race anew.

'Alister Stella Gray' syn. 'Golden Rambler' [A. Gray, introduced by G. Paul, 1895]. 'William Allen Richardson' × 'Mme Pierre Guillot'. Although bred in England, this rose grows better still in a warm, dry climate where its soft petals can open out unspoiled by drizzle. The flowers are small to medium sized (6–7 cm across), opening deep buff, fading to cream and white, and deliciously sweet scented. Most open loosely and somewhat untidily. The small, neat, dense, glossy foliage is sometimes susceptible to mildew. The flowers come in small clusters in the first flowering but as many as thirty-five on the vigorous new growths which flower in autumn. Like 'Aimée Vibert', and indeed many of the Noisettes, 'Alister Stella Gray' may be grown either as a climber reaching up to 4–5 m or as a 2-m shrub or hedge.

'Amélie Gravereaux' [Gravereaux, 1903]. ('Général Jacqueminot' × 'Maréchal Niel') × 'Conrad Ferdinand Meyer'. Jules Gravereaux was very interested in the possibilities of using *Rosa rugosa* to breed new qualities into garden roses. When crossed with the diploid Teas the resultant hybrids were often vigorous enough to be classed as climbers. Such is 'Amélie Gravereaux'. It has large (10 cm), loosely semi-double to double, bright crimson flowers which fade to a purplish tint and are intensely sweet scented. It makes a lanky bush with extremely prickly stems which are best tied in to break and flower all along their length.

'Beauté de l'Europe' [Gonod, 1881]. Seedling of 'Gloire de Dijon' (or 'Mme Bérard', according to the records at L'Haÿ-les-Roses). It resembles 'Gloire de Dijon' (or 'Mme Bérard', according to Geschwind [1884]) in its peach yellow flowers edged with pink or crimson. They are scented and fully double and hang down under their own weight on long flower-stalks. When open they sometimes show a quartered centre and appear larger than many 'Gloire de Dijon' descendants. The plant is moderately vigorous, with only a few prickles, and shares the family weakness for mildew. Some of the later flowers are exceptionally large and beautiful.

'Carmen' [Dubreuil, 1888]. This Climbing Tea belongs to the 'Gloire de Dijon' group, but more closely resembles its parent 'Souvenir de la Malmaison' in its pale creamy pink flowers. There is also hint of buff in the flower when it first opens. 'Carmen' still grows at L'Haÿ-les-Roses.

'Cherub' [Clark, introduced by Brundrett, 1923]. 'Claire Jacquier' seedling. The single-flowered pink-and-white Multiflora Rambler which currently does duty for this cultivar in Australian gardens and nurseries is not the original cultivar, which was semi-double, pinkish yellow, and remontant, "somewhat like 'Phyllis Bide'" (Stevens 1933).

'Crépuscule' [Dubreuil, 1904]. This wonderful Tea-Noisette "is of such rare loveliness and gentle charm as to deserve re-enthronement among our best Tea roses of today" wrote the Anglo-American Francis E. Lester (1942). Its medium-sized (8–9 cm), semi-double flowers are carried in small clusters but with extraordinary abundance. They open a deep rich copper, fading to butterscotch and buff at the edges, before reflexing their petals and paling yet further as they age (plates 47, 48). The sweet musky scent is as rich and free as the flowering itself. The leaves and young stems are limp and crimson as they expand, which provides a beautiful contrast to the flowers. The colour is particularly intense in cool climates, but the plant grows better in warm ones, where it is never out of flower. The soft petals spoil in rain and fade in sun. It grows slowly to about 2.5 m.

'Dr Domingo Pereira' [de Magalhaes, 1925]. I have not seen this late-raised Tea-Noisette which, so far as I know, grows only at Sangerhausen. It is said to have pale lilac pink Tea flowers (with a hint of yellow in the centre) which are large, double, and scented. The plant is by all accounts very vigorous and repeats well.

'Elie Beauvillain' [Beauvillain, 1887]. 'Gloire de Dijon' × 'Ophirie'. One of the handsomest Tea-Noisettes, 'Elie Beauvillain' has big arching clusters of large (9–10 cm across), tea-scented, double flowers which open out to reveal muddled centres, buff towards the outside and pink towards the centre (especially on the petal edges). Then the buff fades to cream and the pink intensifies to crimson, so that the fully blown flowers appear deep pink at a distance. The plant has rather long leaflets, lots of large prickles, a tendency to mildew (not too bad in dry climates) and a vigorous habit; it grows to about 4 m.

'Étendard de Jeanne d'Arc' [Armand Garçon, introduced by Margottin, 1883]. Alleged 'Gloire de Dijon' seedling. This rose is a shrubby white climber that might just be described as cream when it first opens. The flowers are medium sized (9–10 cm), well scented, and double. It grows to about 3 m.

'Louis Barbier' [Barbier, 1909]. 'Mme Bérard' × *Rosa foetida* 'Bicolor'. This interesting cross produced an early-flowering climber or lanky bush with medium-sized (7 cm), semi-double flowers that open copper and salmon and fade to various shades of pink. The colouring is more pronounced on the undersides. The flowers come in small clusters (typically five at a time) on a once-flowering bush with the warm brown wood and scrawny leaves of *R. foetida*. 'Louis Barbier' grows to 2–3 m.

'Marie Robert' [Cochet, 1893]. 'Isabella Gray' seedling. This rose opens an attractive warm pink outside and pale peach within, which makes for a delicate contrast, but then fades quickly to translucent mother-of-pearl. The flowers are scentless and hang down on weak pedicels. That said, it flowers fairly well and repeats all through the season; the plant grows to about 3 m.

'Meteor' [Geschwind, 1887]. Geschwind always considered this a Noisette rose, even though it is bright crimson and unusually hardy. It resembles more closely a step on the road towards 'Gruß an Teplitz'. The flowers are strongly scented, very double, medium sized (7 cm), with outer petals that are incurved around rather a messy centre. The plant has dense, healthy foliage, with slightly overlapping leaflets. It flowers early, repeats well, and grows to about 2–3 m.

'Milkmaid' [Clark, 1925; introduced by Brundrett, 1925]. Reputedly a fairly inferior 'Crépuscule' seedling. The flowers are small (5 cm), semi-double, and borne in medium-sized clusters. Their colour is cream at first with a hint of buff within, which soon fades to white. It has a delicious scent—part musky, part sweet—and is very attractive to bees. The leaves are dark and the slender stems reddish on their sunny sides. The plant is very vigorous and grows to 6–7 m.

'Mlle Marie Gaze' [Godard, 1892]. This run-of-the-mill Tea-Noisette from a not-very-distinguished breeder still grows at L'Haÿ-les-Roses. The flowers are a peachy yellow, fading to white at the edge of the petals, medium sized (7 cm), and tea scented. It has weak stems, so that the flowers hang down in small clusters. The plant grows to about 3 m.

'Mme Auguste Choutet' [Godard, 1902]. 'William Allen Richardson' × 'Kaiserin Auguste Viktoria'. This is a Tea-Noisette, with medium-sized (7–9 cm) semi-double flowers in small clusters (usually three to seven flowers) on long stems. They are yellowish buff with mother-of-pearl edges, although the colour is deeper on the petal-backs. The new growth is a beautiful bloomy red, and the flowers have a delicious strong scent of tea. The plant is of moderate vigour and grows to about 2.5 m.

'Mme Chabanne' [Liabaud, 1896]. This creamy white Tea rose from an undistin-guished breeder still grows at L'Haÿ-les-Roses, but I have not seen it in flower. Appar-ently it has long pointed buds and full-petalled, medium-sized flowers.

'Mme Creux' [Godard, 1890]. Probably a seedling of 'Gloire de Dijon'. The petals are apricot buff on the upper side and pink on the backs, which makes for interesting contrasts when the very large (13–15 cm), fat flowers open out. They are strongly scented of tea and hang down under their own weight. The plant is of moderate vigour and somewhat susceptible to blackspot. It grows to about 3 m.

'Mme Gaston Anouilh' [Chauvry, 1899]. This Tea-Noisette has pale buff yellow flowers, fading to cream, although the buds and the backs of the petal-tips are lightly tinged with pink. It has a good tea scent. The flowers are fairly full, and the plant grows to about 3 m at Sangerhausen.

'Mme Jules Gravereaux' [Soupert & Notting, 1900]. 'Rêve d'Or' × 'Viscountess Folkestone'. The large flowers (10 cm) open from very long pointed buds. They are palest pink, with a hint of buff towards the centre and a rich tea scent. The bush is fairly hardy, as Teas go, but does best in hot, dry climates, where it will reach 4 m.

'Mme Léon Constantin' [Bonnaire, 1908]. The flowers are silvery pink, with just a hint of salmon in the centre and rose pink underneath. They are fairly large (10 cm), but tend to open from split buds, which gives their outline an unattractive shape. This rose flowers well and continuously, but the soft petals make this more suitable for warm, dry climates. Jules Gravereaux thought well of it at L'Haÿ-les-Roses.

'Mme Martignier' [Dubreuil, 1903]. This Tea-Noisette has that mixture of pink and yellow in its flowers which suggests descent from 'Gloire de Dijon'. They are small to medium sized and open bright cinnamon orange, but quickly fade. The undersides of the petals are always paler. 'Mme Martignier' is well scented and grows to about 3 m.

'Neervelt' [Verschuren, 1910]. 'Gloire de Dijon' × 'Princesse de Béarn'. This rose has the brightest flowers of any of the offspring of 'Gloire de Dijon'. They are a glowing crimson (later purple) with paler backs, richly scented, fully double, medium sized (9 cm), and usually produced singly. The plant is moderately vigorous, reliably remontant, and grows to about 3 m, but it flowers sparingly.

'Oscar Chauvry' [Chauvry, 1900]. Seedling of 'Mme Elise Heyman', a buff pink bushy Tea rose. This is another of those pale, somewhat mother-of-pearl Tea roses which grow tall enough (2.5 m) to be considered as climbers. The flowers are medium to large (8–10 cm), scented, and carried in rather tight clusters of up to seven. The bush is very prickly and looks as if it has a trace of Bourbon in it.

'Paul's Lemon Pillar' [G. Paul, 1915]. 'Frau Karl Druschki' × 'Maréchal Niel'. Although widely considered the epitome of the Hybrid Tea type of climber, the parentage of 'Paul's Lemon Pillar' places it closer to the Tea-Noisettes (plate 49). It is also less hardy than most Hybrid Teas. Nor is it lemon yellow, for it opens cream and fades to white, but to this day many rosarians consider it the most beautiful and most elegant of all white roses of any class. The flowers are large (12–13 cm), high pointed, long lasting, and sweetly scented, with reflexing petals which are rather soft and liable to spoil in rain. They are carried on long, strong stems and backed by large leaves. The plant is lanky and vigorous and covers itself in flowers, but never repeats. Although bred in England, 'Paul's Lemon Pillar' performs much better in warm, dry climates.

'Princess May' [W. Paul, 1892]. This rose is pure pale pink, slightly darker on the undersides of the petals than the upper. The influence of 'Gloire de Dijon' is nevertheless seen in the muddled (sometimes quartered) shape of the flowers. These are large (10 cm), double, globular, scented, and borne singly or in small clusters on a moderately vigorous, remontant bush which grows to about 3 m and has few prickles. So far as I know, it now grows only at Sangerhausen.

'Waltham Climber No 1' and 'Waltham Climber No 2' [W. Paul, 1885]. Both these climbers (along with 'Waltham Climber No 3', now extinct) were bred from 'Gloire de Dijon'. They are really very similar to each other. Both have bright crimson flowers which fade to dark pink and are very full, medium-sized (No 2 is slightly larger than No 1), scented, and borne either singly or in clusters of two to four flowers. They have a lax habit of growth, nearly thornless stems, and broad leaves and grow vigorously to 3–4 m at L'Haÿ-les-Roses, which is the only garden where they survive.

Rosa multiflora

The Species and Its Early Forms

Rosa multiflora was first described by the Swedish botanist Carl Peter Thunberg (1743–1828), as a result of his visit to Japan in 1775–76. The epithet *multiflora* refers to the sheer number of flowers which the plant produces. It is an important species in the history of the rose, because *R. multiflora* is the ancestor of every modern Polyantha and Floribunda rose. Its significance for the development of climbing roses lies in the large number of Multiflora Ramblers which were bred from it in the period 1890–1930.

    Rosa multiflora in its purest form is a native of northern Japan and parts of Korea. Varieties, probably of hybrid origin, are found in southern Japan, China, Taiwan, and into the Philippines. Western botanists have tended to treat *R. multiflora* as a preeminently Japanese plant, but recent research and fieldwork are leading them to revise that assessment. Nor is enough known about the history of the species and its forms in cultivation in Japan and China. Certainly, the Japanese have long held it in high regard as an ornamental plant—it has featured in Japanese florals for several centuries, and there is a fine collection of historic *R. multiflora* cultivars at Hirakata Park near Osaka.

    Thunberg and his companions were little better than prisoners at the Dutch trading station in Deshima. Their botanising was largely confined to the dried-up plants they found by picking through the hay that was brought into the city as fodder, and to the plants they saw cultivated in the gardens around them, which were often horticultural selections, hybrids, or exotics. The forms of *Rosa multiflora* which Thunberg and other early botanists introduced from Japan were garden cultivars. The first to arrive in Europe was the double-flowered 'Carnea', which Thomas Evans took to England in 1804, whence Boursault imported it into France. When it was first offered for sale in Philadelphia, the price was twenty dollars for a single plant. Philipp von Siebold later brought a form back to Holland from Japan which he called *R. polyantha*. Its flowers were pinkish yellow, double, and scented; they came in clusters of up to one hundred and grew vigorously to a height of 2 m. Siebold was also the first Westerner to find the single-flowered type with white petals, although it was not introduced to Europe (France) until about 1860. *Rosa multiflora* is one of the most beautiful of all wild roses, a staggering sight when every graceful branch is wreathed with quantities of blossom. In 1895 the English plantsman Canon Henry Ellacombe commented that *R. multiflora* was "rightly so named for, though the flowers individually are small, the trusses of flowers are wonderful," adding that in one cluster he had counted more than six hundred flowers (Ellacombe 1982, 120).

Rosa multiflora grows naturally over a very wide area. It does well in extreme heat and cold and is able to grow in both dry and wet conditions. Not surprisingly, therefore, *R. multiflora* was widely promoted in the mid-twentieth century in parts of the United States as a landscape and hedging plant, to prevent erosion and to consolidate embankments. It was even used as a crash-barrier on the central reservation of highways. No one anticipated the ecological consequences. *Rosa multiflora* took to life in continental North America with the same enthusiasm that every new American citizen has for his adopted country. It survived, indeed flourished, on heavy soils or light, poor ground or fertile, in eroded gullies or on more favourable land, in a tangle of competing grass or where soil was cleanly cultivated. Within twenty years, some states had declared *R. multiflora* a "noxious weed."

Both in Europe and North America, *Rosa multiflora* is much used as a stock for grafting garden roses. It roots very quickly from hardwood cuttings lined out in an open field: indeed, in nature, the lower branches root where they touch the soil. The cuttings are ready for budding sooner than 'Manettii' or *R. canina* stocks and produce plants of exceptional vigour. In its native Japan *R. multiflora* remains the only understock for roses.

Rosa multiflora Thunberg ex Murray [= *R. polyantha* Siebold & Zuccarini, not Roessig]. A strong-growing, wide-spreading shrub or climber, with long arching or trailing stems which grow out each year from the main body of the plant (plate 50). A free-standing bush is usually about 2 m wide and 3 m high, but it will reach 5 m if given the opportunity to climb. The branches are glabrous and moderately armed with small, stout, decurved prickles. The flowers are borne in large, upright, conical, branching panicles of about 15 cm and appear in the early or middle part of the summer—late spring in hot climates. Individually, they are 2.5–3.0 cm and usually white, with a conspicuous bunch of golden stamens in the centre which tend to shed their pollen and turn brown long before the petals drop. The petals may be cream, as well as white, or occasionally pink. Sometimes the bud is pink, but the flower opens white, before pink tinges appear all over the petals again as the flower fades. The petals vary in size and shape, but are generally about 1 cm long, sometimes narrow, but sometimes broad enough to overlap with each other. They tend to have a distinct notch at the apex and to recurve as they age. The scent is fairly strong and musky. The sepals are shorter than the petals, even in the bud, and glandular-bristly on the back. The pedicels and receptacles are hairy, and the pedicels are sometimes also glandular. The foliage is most attractive. The leaves are deciduous, typically 10–15 cm long but more if the plant is growing vigorously. There are usually seven or nine leaflets, each 3–5 cm long, obovate or elliptic, acute, acuminate or obtuse at the apex, and cuneate at the base. They are hairless above and sometimes beneath, but more commonly downy beneath. The margins are simply toothed. The stipules are ciliate, or deeply and conspicuously laciniated. (This genetic characteristic is very dominant, so that these finely serrated stipules are almost always seen in hybrids of *R. multiflora*.) The hips are about 0.7 cm, red, oval to round, with the sepals fallen away; they usually last through the autumn and a fair time into winter. Although small, they look very attractive in their large clusters.

Rosa multiflora var. *cathayensis* (Rehder & Wilson). This is the typical wild *R. multiflora* of Hubei, Gansu, Yunnan, and Sichuan. The flowers are larger than the type (about 4 cm), bright rosy pink, fading to pale pink, and borne in somewhat flat corymbs. *Rosa multiflora* var. *adenochaeta* is similar; it opens deep bright pink and fades to rose pink with a white base to the petals. Both varieties are probably the result of introgression with *R. chinensis*.

Rosa multiflora 'Carnea'. This robust and popular cultivar was the first to be introduced to Europe and North America (plate 51). The attractive flowers are fully double, pearly pink fading to white, about 4 cm, and strongly scented. The petals recurve rather charmingly and the central petals are always slighter darker than the outer ones. There seem to be a number of clones in cultivation under this name.

Rosa multiflora 'Platyphylla' syn. 'Grevillei', 'Seven Sisters'. John Loudon (1844) gave an exuberant description of a specimen of this rose in the Goldsworth Nursery: "The variety of colour produced by the buds at first opening was not less astonishing than their number. White, light blush, deeper blush, light red, darker red, scarlet and purple flowers all appeared in the same corymb, and the production of these seven colours at once is said to be the reason why this rose is known as the Seven Sisters Rose." In fact, the flowers open dark pink (dark enough on occasions to appear as red or purple) and fade to white. 'Platyphylla' is thought to be an old Chinese garden rose which was introduced from Japan to England by Charles Greville in the early 1800s. It is likely, however, that the clone currently in cultivation as 'Platyphylla' was grown from seeds imported from Japan and acquired by Philippe Noisette from a London market gardener in 1817. One curious attribute is its foliage: the leaves and leaflets are both large, whereas the leaflets are distinctly wrinkled. It too has affinities with *R. chinensis*.

Rosa multiflora 'Watsoniana'. This cultivar has large panicles of very small flowers (0.75 cm across) which are white, pink-tipped, and have very narrow petals. But it is the foliage which is so distinctive—the leaves are wavy and look as if they are suffering from leaf-curl, although the distortion is actually caused by a viral infection. The leaflets are reduced to long, narrow, clawlike segments and the leaf-stalks are often twisted or waved. The nodes too are very close to one another, so that the overall impression is of a mass of foliage. 'Watsoniana' is very prone to mildew, and the combination of this fungal disease with a viral infection of the leaves gives the cultivar a white bloom which is not unattractive. Certainly, the Japanese consider it pleasing.

'Iwara' [= *Rosa ×iwara* (Regel) Siebold] [Siebold, 1832]. This is a natural hybrid between *R. multiflora* and *R. rugosa* which grows on the shores of Hokkaido and northern Honshu. The cultivar grown at Sangerhausen has white flowers which are on the small side (only 3 cm) and come in clusters of five to fifteen.

Early European and American Hybrids of *Rosa multiflora*

The first Multiflora roses to reach Europe and North America were selections or hybrids with other diploid roses from the Far East. Because the species, its forms, and almost all its hybrids set copious quantities of fertile seed, a great number of seedlings are mentioned in the horticultural literature of the first half of the nineteenth century. Henry Crapo's 1848 catalogue declared that "the Multiflora roses are all pretty," although he added that many of them were rather tender in New Bedford, Massachusetts, whereas modern collections of the true wild species have proved quite hardy throughout New England and much of the Midwest. Imported seed was often sourced from garden forms and was extremely variable, as was seed from the original plants introduced into Europe. In 1878 Pierre Guillot wrote that he had sowed the seed of "a Japanese Polyantha," and found great variation among its seedlings: single, semi-double, and fully double forms of yellow, white, or pink. His bewilderment was shared by many—the following year, the French rosarian, Jean Sisley, asserted that *Rosa multiflora* did not even exist in the wild in Japan, but only as garden varieties.

Few of the early seedlings raised in Europe or North America found their way into commerce, and fewer still have survived into modern times. One of the earliest European hybrids 'De La Grifferaie' was widely employed as a hardy rootstock, especially in England, during the latter half of the nineteenth century. A popular thornless selection in the twentieth century was 'Clarke's Multiflora'; another, with a hint of *Rosa wichurana* in its ancestry, is variously known as 'I. X. L.' or 'Coolidge'. 'De La Grifferaie' had an extraordinary career as a rose. It was a cross between East and West, between an unknown form of *R. multiflora* and a hybrid of *R. gallica*. The rugose leaflets suggest that 'Platyphylla' may have been one parent, with its remarkable hardiness coming from its Gallica parent.

> 'De La Grifferaie' [Vibert, 1845]. This is considered to be *Rosa multiflora* 'Platyphylla' × a Gallica rose, because of its highly dissected stipules and crimson colour. The flowers open pale crimson but fade through degrees of pinkness almost to white. However, they fade unevenly, so that parts of an individual flower may be darker or paler than others, and sometimes the petals have paler stripes on them, too. The flowers are medium sized (about 8 cm), full, round and flat like a Gallica, and fairly well scented. 'De La Grifferaie' flowers only once, with ten to fifteen flowers in a cluster. The foliage too resembles a Gallica rose, with large, round, rugose, matt green leaflets. The strong stems are almost thornless, but have a few reddish brown bristles and occasional long prickles; they grow to about 3 m. 'De La Grifferaie' was often used as a rootstock, especially in France and England, where its hardiness, adaptability, and tendency to sucker all ensured that it survived in old gardens long after the scion it supported had faded away. It makes a good free-standing shrub at the back of a mixed border, where its lanky growths arch over with flowers in high summer and mix well with other soft-toned plants.

'Olivet' [Vigneron fils, 1892]. Geschwind's 'De La Grifferaie' hybrids inspired several French nurserymen to try breeding with this cultivar. Vigneron's 'Olivet', bred from 'De La Grifferaie' × 'Mme Baron Veillard', is still grown and available from at least one French nursery. This attractive, vigorous, crimson or dark pink rambler shows little sign of its *Rosa multiflora* ancestry. Its flowers are about 10–11 cm (large for its period), full, and flat. 'Olivet' grows to at least 4 m.

'Russelliana' syn. 'Russeliana', 'Russell's Cottage Rose' [Cormack & Sinclair, pre-1826]. The parents of this early hybrid are not known, but it is clearly related both to 'Platyphylla' and to 'De La Grifferaie'. The earliest mention I have found of 'Russelliana' is in *Jardinier Amateur* (1826). Henry Crapo's 1848 catalogue sums up its attractions wonderfully well: "Vivid purplish crimson and white, variegated, changeable, beautiful." To which one should add that the flowers are medium sized (5–7 cm), very double, and flat like most old Gallica roses. 'Russelliana' is very floriferous, but has little scent. The fimbriated stipules indicate its *Rosa multiflora* ancestry, although the matt leaves are more like a Damask's. It grows vigorously to as much as 6 m and has proved almost as hardy as 'De La Grifferaie'.

'Tricolore' [Robert et Moreau, 1863]. Probably a 'De La Grifferaie' hybrid. The flowers open rich bright pink and fade to the shade sometimes called "silvery pink" and sometimes "lilac pink." The base of the petals is white, and white stripes occasionally stretch up into the pink parts above. The petal edges are rather ragged, which gives the flower a distinctive charm, and the flowers are medium sized (7 cm) and double. They are borne in clusters of five to twenty-five on a hardy, once-flowering plant which grows to about 3 m. This climber should not be confused with any of the Gallica roses with the same name.

There has always been much confusion between Polyanthas and Multifloras. This dates back to an early taxonomic heresy, when *Rosa multiflora* was renamed *R. polyantha* by von Siebold and Zuccarini in 1844. The renaming was incorrect, and quickly reversed, but in 1888 the great Belgian botanist François Crépin expressed concern that the term "Polyantha" was applied to a new group of hybrids derived from *R. multiflora × indica*. These were the dwarf, repeat-flowering derivatives of *R. multiflora* now universally, and properly, called "Polyantha roses." In 1902 Gertrude Jekyll added to the confusion by suggesting that the name "Polyantha" should be used "only for the rambling kinds that retain the free-growing character of the type" and by calling the smaller bushy sorts "Pompon" roses, which by good fortune never caught on. By that time, the group of roses largely derived from crosses between *R. multiflora* and Teas or Hybrid Teas had become known as "Multiflora Ramblers."

It is often thought that the race of Multiflora Ramblers, which increased so quickly towards the end of the nineteenth century, owed its identity and homogeneity to the use of a single cultivar to breed them, 'Turner's Crimson Rambler'. There is no doubting the importance of 'Turner's Crimson Rambler' (see chapter 8), but it is a complex hybrid with more than a trace of *Rosa wichurana* in its ancestry, and that latter species has often dominated the hybrids bred from it. This chapter examines the pure hybrids of *R. multi-*

flora whose development galloped apace after the introduction of 'Pâquerette' by Pierre Guillot of Lyons in 1875. 'Pâquerette' was a revelation. It appeared to be, and *was*, a form of the vigorous climbing species *R. multiflora*, but barely 50 cm high and flowering without interruption all year round. French nurserymen crossed it with Teas and Hybrid Teas to widen to the colour range and many of these crosses turned out to be once-flowering climbers: the Multiflora Ramblers had arrived.

The Multiflora Ramblers tend to have four drawbacks. First, their flowers are often too close together. This is most clearly seen in such introductions as 'Euphrosyne' [Schmitt/Lambert, 1896] and 'Queen Alexandra' [Pemberton, 1915], whose pedicels are too short, so that the clusters look congested and, in wet weather, often decay. Second—and this fault is common to all Synstylae roses and their primary hybrids—their stamens (often an attractive part of the composition) shed their pollen and turn from yellow to brown early on, long before the petals drop. The flowers, so full of promise when the golden anthers glow against the newly opened petals, lose their charm as those anthers turn brown and wither. Third, the Multiflora Ramblers seem not to take easily to yellows; efforts to breed a pure bright yellow Multiflora Rambler end in wishy-washy shades which promise bright yellow roses in bud, but soon fade to cream or white. Nothing could be more disappointing than such so-called yellow ramblers as 'Goldfinch' [George Paul, 1907] and 'Oriole' [Peter Lambert, 1912]. Fourth, the Multiflora Ramblers have a reputation for contracting mildew which, although it never seems to harm the plant, covers the receptacles and pedicels with an unsightly white mould to the dismay of garden owners.

Many of the Multiflora Ramblers described in this chapter were a by-product of breeding Polyantha roses. For some breeders, the raising of ramblers and Polyanthas went hand-in-hand: Hermann Kiese and Jan Böhm, for example, were enthusiastic introducers of Multiflora Hybrids great and small and have left a wonderful record of their productivity in the Rosarium at Sangerhausen. Polyanthas have a tendency every so often to produce climbing sports, which are separately listed and described in chapter 12. On this basis it is fair to claim that a complete account of Multiflora Ramblers cannot be given without proper reference to the Climbing Polyanthas. The following early Multiflora cultivars are still grown.

'Coccinea' [Van Houtte, pre-1865]. This old hybrid is still grown at L'Haÿ-les-Roses. The round, fat buds open to flowers of a good medium pink, fading to palest pink with a hint of mauve. They are very full, with slightly reflexed petals, and carried in clusters of up to thirty. The leaves suggest Hybrid Perpetual ancestry.

'Daniel Lacombe' [Allard, 1885]. A Polyantha × 'Margarita'. This very important rose ('Leuchtstern', 'Rubin', and 'Tausendschön' are all seedlings of it) has passed on its health and thornlessness to many of its descendants. The flowers are small to medium-sized (5–6 cm), very fully double, flat, and pale pink, fading to pale mother-of-pearl and white. They are borne early in the season in great profusion in large, upright, long-stemmed rather congested clusters of up to sixty flowers, with a few later flowers in autumn. The thornless stems are beautiful when they arch over under the weight of flowers all along their length; the plant grows very vigorously to as much as 6–7 m in height. 'Daniel Lacombe' makes an excellent and highly desirable rambler. It is still occasionally seen in old gardens, flowering for many weeks.

'La Prosérpine' [Ketten Bros., 1897]. 'Georges Schwartz' × 'Duchesse Marie Salviati'. There is a climber of this name, attributed to Ketten, at L'Haÿ-les-Roses, which has dark pink flowers in short clusters which fade to pale pink and almost to white at the edges of the petals. However, Ketten's catalogue for 1897–98 describes it as a bushy Polyantha, not a climber, so I am inclined to conclude that the L'Haÿ-les-Roses plant is wrongly named.

'Max Singer' syn. 'Rosiériste Max Singer' [Lacharme, 1885]. Origin unknown, possibly a Polyantha × 'Général Jacqueminot'. The flowers are light crimson, paling to pink, fully double, medium sized (7–8 cm), slightly cup shaped, with a distinct tea scent. They are borne singly or in small clusters on a vigorous plant with few prickles that grows to about 2.5 m.

'Mme Auguste Rodrigues' [Chauvry, 1897]. 'Souvenir de Nemours' × 'Max Singer', that is, a Bourbon crossed with a Polyantha. This once-flowering rambler has large (9 cm), full, globular, pink flowers with a silvery underside to the petals, usually in small corymbs.

Jackson Dawson and His Multiflora Hybrids

Jackson Thornton Dawson was the first American to breed new climbing roses from the wild *Rosa multiflora* and the first person in the world to raise hybrids from *R. wichurana*. Few people realise just what a pioneer he was, because many of his hybrids were introduced by nurseries without any acknowledgement of his part in their raising. Dawson was superintendent of the Arnold Arboretum for more than forty years. He felt that it was essential for Americans to create an American race of roses which were suited, above all, to the bitter winters of New England. With this in mind he started to hybridise in the early 1880s, by crossing *R. multiflora* with the bone-hardy crimson Hybrid Perpetual 'Général Jacqueminot'. The resultant seedlings were all triploid, which held up further progress until he apparently succeeded in backcrossing one of them to 'Général Jacqueminot' to produce the climber called 'Dawson' or 'Dawsoniana' in 1888. This is a stupendously hardy rambler whose merits were recognised by the award of a silver medal in 1894 by the Massachusetts Horticultural Society. Dawson used it to breed additional climbers, but soon turned his attention instead to other species, most especially to raising hybrids of *R. wichurana*.

'Apple Blossom' [Dawson, c. 1890; introduced by Stark Bros., 1932]. 'Dawson' × a 'Dawson' seedling. The flowers are semi-double, pink with a white centre, fading to nearly white. They come in small clusters with distinctly ruffled petals, which give character to the whole plant. The flowers do not drop their petals until very late, so the clusters become far too congested, and the petals rot off in wet weather. The plant looks best when it starts into bloom—the first flowers are then set off by pink unopened buds and the green sepals of yet later flowers poking through the clusters.

'Dawson' syn. 'Dawsoniana' [Dawson, 1888]. Reputedly (*Rosa multiflora* × 'Général Jacqueminot') × 'Général Jacqueminot'. The small (3 cm), semi-double flowers are bright pale crimson (fading to pink) with white centres, borne very early in the season in clusters of ten to twenty on a tremendously vigorous plant (plate 52). The flowers are curiously scented: "peppery" is one description, although I prefer "strong, musky, and delicious." 'Dawson' is a tough performer; it is unaffected by cold, disease, or neglect, daintier than 'Apple Blossom' and almost as floriferous. It flowers only once, but is often the earliest of all roses to flower—earlier, for example, than most of the Boursault roses.

'Royal Cluster' [Conard & Jones Co, 1899]. This too was raised by Jackson Dawson, by crossing the China rose 'Hermosa' with his own 'Dawson', although it was not much of an improvement on either parent. It has small (4 cm), semi-double, white flowers, tinged with pink.

The Rush of New Multiflora Hybrids, 1900–1920

It is now time to look in detail at the work of the two leading breeders of Multiflora Ramblers: Peter Lambert and Hermann Kiese, both German. The German Rose Society, now the most successful in Europe, was not founded until 1883, when French nurserymen were still the leading breeders and growers of roses. The founding fathers of the Verein Deutscher Rosenfreunde included Heinrich Schultheis of Steinfurth, Johann Lambert of Trier, Heinrich Drögemüller of Neuhaus-Elbe, and, above all, Friedrich Harms from Hamburg. Harms was a nurseryman who grew about 20,000 roses per annum, a substantial undertaking at the time. There were no professional rose breeders in Germany in 1883, when such men as Jean-Baptiste Guillot and Paul Nabonnand in France and Henry Bennett and William Paul in England were developing new classes of roses and conquering new markets. Rudolph Geschwind had set down his ideas on rose breeding in *Die Hybridation und Sämlingszucht der Rosen* in 1863, but the breeding of new German roses was a hobby for such amateurs as Dr Krüger of Freiburg and Dr Müller of Weingarten. When Peter Lambert began hybridising in the late 1880s, his success gave such a boost to rose growing in Germany that we must give him most of the credit for establishing the German rose industry in the years leading up to World War I.

Peter Lambert of Trier

Peter Lambert was born in 1859, the third generation of a well-established partnership of nurserymen in Trier. He trained at the Prussian school of horticulture at Potsdam and then gained work experience at nurseries in France and England, before settling down with the family firm of Lambert & Reiter. His first new rose hybrids were introduced in 1889: a thornless deep pink China hybrid called 'Moselblümchen' and a yellow Tea rose named 'Rheingold'. The following year he introduced a white Hybrid Tea which established his reputation as a rose breeder of international standing. 'Kaiserin Auguste Viktoria' was an immediate best-seller all over the world and proved itself a fertile parent. Lambert left the family firm in 1891 and started his own rose nursery at Trier; his business flourished and expanded until he employed more than seventy workers.

Lambert's career as a breeder spanned more than fifty years. He worked widely with different classes of roses, and his achievements include the vigorous Hybrid Tea 'Frau Karl Druschki' [1901], the *Rosa rugosa* cross 'Schneezwerg' [1912], the Bourbon × China rose 'Adam Messerich' [1920], and the Hybrid Musk 'Mozart' [1936]. He sought good health, hardiness, vigour, and freedom of flower in all roses and was quick to acquire other breeders' roses of merit. Lambert saw the potential of 'Turner's Crimson Rambler' and imported it into Germany even before it went on sale officially in England. His last introduction was 'Aloysia Kaiser' in 1939, the year of his death, but Lambert's garden in the walls of the old Benedictine abbey in Trier and his collection of roses, including the original plant of 'Frau Karl Druschki', were all destroyed during World War II.

His first climbers were derived from three vigorous once-flowering Multiflora Ramblers he bought in from J. B. Schmitt of Bischweiler (now Bischwiller) in Alsace, and introduced as the Three Graces in 1895: 'Aglaia', 'Euphrosyne', and 'Thalia'. Their offspring yielded vigorous once-flowering climbers like the beautiful pink rambler 'Helene' [1897]. Exciting new combinations of genes began to appear in the next generation, beginning in 1899 with the dwarf Polyantha roses 'Léonie Lamesch' (the name of his future wife) and 'Eugénie Lamesch'. Rosarians were again surprised that the union of strong-growing climbing cultivars should result in progeny of dwarf habit. Gregor Mendel's *Versuche über Pflanzenhybriden* was not published until 1901; it made an enormous impact on rose breeders all over the world, especially in Germany, where Mendel's findings were articulated and debated at great length in the horticultural press.

Lambert's breakthrough in breeding new types of climbers came with 'Thalia Remontant' in 1901. It was the first remontant rose derived principally from *Rosa multiflora* which was not a dwarf Polyantha, and it was variously described as a large bush, a moderate climber, or a semi-climber. 'Thalia Remontant' was followed in 1905 by a truly outstanding long-flowering rose with mother-of-pearl flowers fading to white which Lambert called 'Trier' in honour of his hometown. The vigorous, free-flowering, and remontant semi-climber was here to stay. Lambert's success in developing *R. multiflora* hybrids into a distinctive new class of large repeat-flowering shrubs and climbers with wonderfully handsome leaves and deliciously strong scent led to their being named after him—the Lambertianas.

Because of the Teas and Noisettes in their ancestry, many Lambertianas are not completely hardy in central and eastern Europe: 'Gneisenau', for example, has never been reliably hardy in cold winters at the great experimental gardens at Weihenstephan run by the Technical University of Munich. Nevertheless, the Lambertianas remain popular in such diverse parts of the world as Denmark and California, although surprisingly little known in England, where the home-grown 'Phyllis Bide' [Bide, 1926] is commonly thought to be the only Multiflora Rambler which repeats.

Lambert was a great educator. He joined the German Rose Society in 1885 and was editor of the *Rosen-Zeitung* from 1890 to 1911, openly sharing his discoveries with his readership. He was also an early conservationist. In 1897 he wrote of the need to found a garden in which old roses could be collected and conserved, a living museum which would preserve cultivars from extinction. This led to the foundation of the German National Rosarium at Sangerhausen in 1904, which Lambert actively promoted. He was instrumental in securing Conrad Straßheim's collection of rose species for the Rosarium and he supported the important rose collections at Zweibrücken and Zabern (now Saverne); in 1914, for example, he sent some 160 different cultivars to Zweibrücken, some of which survive to this day. But the defeat and humiliation of World War I weighed heavily on him, as indeed it did on many Germans of his generation, and he found the 1920s a difficult time to earn a living. His natural curiosity faded, and he failed to keep pace with the innovations of younger rose breeders. His attempts to breed a yellow Lambertiana, for example, by crossing 'Chamisso' with the yellow Hybrid Tea 'Mrs Aaron Ward', were not a success. Thereafter, he stuck increasingly to his own breeding lines and seldom took in new genes from other breeders' breakthroughs. Strangest of all was Lambert's growing conviction in the 1930s that a great renaissance of enthusiasm for Hybrid Perpetual roses was just about to happen. The following is a list of climbers and semi-climbers bred by Lambert which are still in cultivation.

'Adrian Reverchon' [Lambert, 1909]. This was once well-described as a remontant 'Leuchtstern'. The flowers are medium pink fading almost to white (always with a white middle), small to medium sized (5–6 cm), semi-single, and plentifully borne in large loose clusters. The plant grows to about 3 m and is a useful autumn flowerer. 'Adrian Reverchon' is still grown at Sangerhausen and other European gardens.

'Aglaia' syn. 'Yellow Rambler' [Schmitt, introduced by Lambert, 1896]. *Rosa multiflora* × 'Rêve d'Or'. More than a hundred years on, 'Aglaia' is still a good early-flowering rambler. The flowers are semi-double to double, cupped, pale yellow fading to white, with a fairly strong musky scent and there may be as many as a hundred of them in a rather tight cluster, although it is seldom remontant. The fresh bright green leaves and greenish brown young wood are a good foil, and it has few prickles, but grows vigorously to 5 m. 'Aglaia' is the best of the Three Graces for its foliage, scent, comparatively large flowers, and floriferousness; she also opens a few days earlier than her sisters.

'Arndt' [Lambert, 1913]. 'Helene' × 'Gustav Grünerwald'. 'Arndt' grows vigorously to about 2.5 m and has orange pink buds which open to small (4–5 cm), semi-double, rich pink (fading to rose pink), well-scented flowers, with conspicuously glandular pedicels in erect, rather tight clusters of ten and twenty. These are complemented by handsome, glistening, dark new leaves and appear recurrently throughout the summer and autumn. It is one of the best Lambertianas and fairly popular still.

'Chamisso' [Lambert, 1922]. 'Geheimrat Dr Mittweg' × 'Tip Top'. This semi-climber descends from 'Trier' on both sides. It carries small to medium-sized (5–6 cm), semi-double, moderately scented flowers. These open mother-of-pearl and fade to white, but retain a creamy centre and a pink flush on the backs of the petals. The young leaves are bronze red—a good foil to the large, open clusters of flowers. Its growth is vigorous, to about 2.5 m, and it blooms remontantly; the autumn flowers are often finer and carried in larger sprays than the summer flowers. 'Chamisso' is still quite commonly found in European rose collections.

'Euphrosyne' syn. 'Euphrosine' [Schmitt, introduced by Lambert, 1896]. 'Mignonette' seedling. This cultivar is one of Lambert's Three Graces. The small (3–4 cm) flowers, little more than single, are best when newly opened and clear, pale pink, but they soon fade to white and have a tendency later to develop ugly pink blotches. The bright yellow stamens soon turn brown and wither. The flowers come in large, rather congested clusters of up to fifty and have a fair scent. The plant grows vigorously to 4 m, flowers only once, and is prone to mildew.

'Frau A. von Brauer' [Lambert, 1912]. 'Farquhar' × 'Schneewittchen'. This beautiful late-flowering white rambler inherits some characteristics of *Rosa wichurana* from its 'Farquhar' ancestry. It is extremely hardy and disease resistant and was once much planted for hedging because its habit of growth is very dense. The flowers are small (3–4 cm), very double, and pure white, but turn slightly pink just before dropping their petals, which they hold for several weeks. I find it very strongly scented, although not everyone agrees. It grows to 3–4 m and is as good a rose as its sister-seedling 'Freifrau von Marschall', but it is seldom seen now except in historic collections.

'Frau Helene Videnz' syn. 'Helene Videnz' [Lambert, 1904]. 'Euphrosyne' × 'Princess Alice de Monaco'. This has dense clusters of small (3–4 cm), semi-double to double, pale salmon pink flowers, which change quickly to pure pink and then fade to white and are attractively cupped in shape. The clusters carry anything from twenty-five to seventy-five flowers, which have a delicious strong musky scent. The plant grows vigorously to 3 m and has few prickles. Although no longer in commerce, it is still quite commonly found in European gardens and in its overall appearance is reminiscent of the better-known 'Debutante'.

'Freifrau von Marschall' [Lambert, 1912]. 'Farquhar' × 'Schneewittchen'. This sister-seedling of 'Frau A. von Brauer' is still fairly well established in the trade. The flowers are small (3–4 cm), double, and deep marshmallow pink, fading to soft pink and white; they remain fresh for a long time, even after cutting. The flowers are borne in midseason in large, tight clusters on a vigorous bush which can reach 3 m in height. The lush foliage is bright green and hides a fair quantity of large prickles.

'Gneisenau' [Lambert, 1924]. Allegedly ('Schneelicht' × 'Killarney') × 'Veilchenblau'. This beautiful semi-climber flowers mid to late season and shows little sign of the influence of its purple-flowered pollen parent, although the buds are at least pale pink. Its flowers are by far the largest of the Lambertiana roses, about 8 cm, and resemble the Pemberton Hybrid Musks. They are semi-double, cupped, pure white, with yellow stamens in the centre, and well scented. The clusters of five to fifteen flowers are set off by handsome dark leaves and long stems which grow to about 2.5 m high. Its leafy growth, bushy habit, and numerous large prickles make it an excellent Multiflora for hedges.

'Goethe' [Lambert, 1911]. 'Goethe' is a once-flowering, shrubby climber, whose heavily mossed buds, stems, and sepals make a fine contrast to the small (4 cm), semi-double, open, deep pink or pale crimson flowers (with white flashes on some of the petals), which are fairly sweetly scented. The flowers do not, in my experience, suffer from mildew to the same degree as the other mossy climbers 'Le Poilu' and 'Wichmoss'. 'Goethe' is a very hardy cultivar and the leaves have a bluish cast. The plant as a whole is extremely prickly. The prickles appear as moss on the buds and pedicels and then emerge as true prickles on the stems; they are long and slender, and create an attractive pink haze on the outline of the new growths. Lambert never wrote about this unusual rose. I am puzzled by this omission, particularly because it lies well outside Lambert's normal breeding lines. It fits the descriptions exactly of a Moss rose bred by Rudolph Geschwind and memorably described in *Rosen-Zeitung* (1901) as having a circle of brown mossy buds just like a small bird's nest. Is it too much to suggest that Lambert, who introduced a number of Geschwind's roses without acknowledging their origin, might also have sneaked this unusual hybrid into commerce shortly after Geschwind died in 1910?

'Gruß an Zabern' [Lambert, 1903]. 'Euphrosyne' × 'Mme Ocker Ferencz'. This is one of the greatest Multiflora Ramblers of all time (plate 53). Lambert recognised its merits from the start and prophesied that it would put all previous white climbers in the shade because of its free and very early flowering, size of cluster, scent, and cheerful demeanour. The flowers are pure white, small to medium sized (3.0–4.5 cm), well filled, and come in thick flat clusters of twenty to sixty. They have a strong sweet-spicy scent, a mixture of musk and damask. The stems are very prickly and grow vigorously to 4–5 m. 'Gruß an Zabern' is also very hardy and resistant to late frost damage. It is still widely available today, and deservedly so.

'Heideröslein' [Lambert, 1932]. 'Chamisso' × 'Amalie de Greiff'. This was the best of Lambert's attempts to produce a remontant yellow Lambertiana. The buds are bright yellowish salmon pink, but the flowers soon fade from sulphur yellow almost to white. They are small or medium sized (4–5 cm), single, and scented. They come in clusters of ten to thirty. It makes a rounded bush about 2 m high—more, if trained as a climber. The cut flowers last a week in water.

'Heine' [Lambert, 1912]. Allegedly 'Trier' × 'Frau Karl Druschki'. 'Heine' has small (no more than 2.5–3.0 cm), pure white, double flowers borne in congested clusters of up to fifty. However, they are semi-double and set off by dark red stamens and reflexed petals which give the flowers a distinctive outline. The bush is remontant, hardy, and grows vigorously to about 2 m. 'Heine' is seldom seen now, although still grown in several gardens in Germany.

'Heinrich Conrad Söth' [Lambert, 1919]. Allegedly 'Geheimrat Dr Mittweg' × *Rosa foetida* 'Bicolor'; probably a selfed seedling of 'Geheimrat Dr Mittweg'. The unsophisticated single flowers open dark pink but soon fade to pale pink, with a white centre. The stamens too soon change from yellow to brown. The individual flowers are small (3 cm), but they come in broad upright pyramidal clusters of ten to seventy, on long, strong stems, and have a fair scent. The plant is very floriferous and makes a good effect in the garden. The foliage is large, glossy, and pale, with conspicuous veins and fimbriated stipules, and the bush grows fairly vigorously to 2 m, repeating well in the autumn. It is said to be hardy and is still fairly common in European nurseries.

'Helene' syn. 'Hélène' [Lambert, 1897]. Lambert wrote that 'Helene' (named for his sister) was bred from (Hybrid Tea × 'Aglaia') × 'Turner's Crimson Rambler', but I doubt if these crosses were possible between his acquisition of 'Aglaia' in 1894 and the launch of 'Helene' three years later, so it is more likely to be a straight 'Aglaia' × 'Turner's Crimson Rambler' cross. Usually described as lilac pink, in my experience 'Helene' is an ordinary pink, with a white ground. The moderately scented flowers are single, with perhaps a few extra petals (enough to call it semi-double on occasions), and open from deep pink buds. They come in clusters of up to ten—more, if the plant is growing vigorously. The bush is almost thornless, flowers once and early, and grows to 4 m.

'Hoffman von Fallersleben' [Lambert, 1917]. 'Geheimrat Dr Mittweg' × 'Tip Top'. This rose has apricot yellow flowers with the tinges of pink and peach which are associated with Tea roses; indeed, they sometimes open quite deep pink, although they usually fade to white and have the unfortunate habit of holding the petals even after they have turned to brown. The flowers are about 4 cm, come in small clusters of five to twenty, and have a good scent. It is a vigorous grower, reaching 2 m high and wide as a shrub, but more as a climber. 'Hoffman von Fallersleben' sometimes repeats. The leaves are very beautiful: healthy, glossy, and with red rachis—very Multiflora. It is beginning to be listed by nurserymen rather more widely now.

'Kommerzienrat W. Rautenstrauch' [Lambert, 1909]. Reportedly 'Léonie Lamesch' × *Rosa foetida* 'Bicolor'. I suspect the pollen parent was a repeat-flowering Pernetiana rose, because this rose is reported to be remontant. It has small, rather congested clusters (ten to twenty blooms) of pink flowers tinged with pale yellow, especially towards the centre, and fading to white, although the undersides of the petals are whitish at all times. The flowers are medium sized (5–6 cm), semi-double, open, and lightly scented of musk. It grows fairly vigorously (and nearly thornlessly) to 2.0–2.5 m and is still quite common in historic rose collections.

'Marie Henriette Gräfin Chotek' syn. 'Gräfin Marie Henriette Chotek' [Lambert, 1911]. 'Farquhar' × 'Richmond'. This rose may have more *Rosa wichurana* than *R. multiflora* in its makeup, but the overall effect is definitely of a Multiflora Rambler. The flowers are a good bright crimson and hold their colour well. They are scentless, but fairly large, double, and borne in large clusters. 'Marie Henriette Gräfin Chotek' flowers freely over a long period, but there is no second flowering in autumn. It grows vigorously to about 3 m and is very hardy. It is still available from several nurseries and is grown in old gardens.

'Oriole' [Lambert, 1912]. 'Aglaia' seedling. Yellowish pink buds open to small (3–4 cm), creamy white flowers, which are double, rounded, and incurved in shape. They come in rather tight bunches of up to seventy flowers and are moderately scented. The shiny dark green foliage is a good foil and the plant is said to be mildew-free; it grows fairly vigorously to 3–4 m. 'Oriole' has never enjoyed the popularity of the French and English yellow ramblers and, in my opinion, is markedly inferior to 'Goldfinch'. The flowers of 'Oriole' are too cupped, too crowded, too short-stemmed, and too susceptible to rain damage.

'Paul Kadolozigue' [Lambert, pre-1912]. The flowers open crimson and fade to lilac pink. They are about 3.5–4.0 cm, come in clusters of ten to twenty, and have a scent which is a mixture of damask and musk. It has beautiful pale green Multiflora leaves; in fact,. the overall impression is that it is *very* Multiflora Rambler, with few prickles and a fairly vigorous habit, but it grows only at Sangerhausen, where roses are tied and pruned to short poles.

'Peter Rosegger' [Lambert, 1914]. 'Geheimrat Dr Mittweg' × 'Tip Top'. This Lambertiana has coral buds which open to pale pink flowers that soon fade to white. They are medium sized (5–6 cm), double, rosette shaped, strongly musk scented, and borne in clusters of five to fifteen. The foliage is dark; the plant grows vigorously as a climber and flowers repeatedly. I have seen it at Sangerhausen, but nowhere else.

'Rudolf von Benningsen' [Lambert, 1932]. ('Geheimrat Dr Mittweg' × 'Souvenir de Paul Neyron') × 'Joanna Hill'. This bushy repeat-flowering climber was named after a German parliamentarian who died in 1902. The pink flowers have broad petals with pale yellow edges and are fairly double; they come in loose clusters of five to twenty.

'Thalia' [Schmitt, introduced by Lambert, 1895]. 'Thalia' is one of Lambert's Three Graces bred from the white Polyantha 'Pâquerette', and is very much a strong-growing, early-flowering Multiflora Rambler (plate 55). It has huge clusters of small (3 cm), flat, semi-double white flowers (slightly pink in the bud) with a distinct scent. They are borne in large umbels, as many as a hundred in a cluster, but typically thirty to fifty. The stems have few prickles, but bright green leaves. The plant grows vigorously to 3 m, although it flowers only once. 'Thalia' is hardy, still widely available, and can look very elegant when trained over a fence or pergola. It is a particular feature of the rose garden at L'Haÿ-les-Roses.

'Thalia Remontant' [Lambert, 1901]. 'Thalia' seedling × 'Mme Laurette Messimy'. This is a forerunner of the Lambertiana race, with clusters of very small (2.5–3.0 cm), pure white, semi-single flowers, which open out flat and are borne in clusters of ten to fifty, more or less intermittently all summer. It grows to 3 m. Its only merit is its strong musky scent, but it is still quite widely grown, somewhat unaccountably.

'Trier' [Lambert, 1904]. Reportedly 'Aglaia' × 'Mrs R. G. Sharman-Crawford', although chromosome analysis has established that 'Trier' was probably a selfed seedling of 'Aglaia' or an accidental hybrid with a Noisette. It has pale yellowish pink buds which open to reveal beautiful ivory white flowers, slightly fuller than single (plate 54). They are borne in large, loose clusters of perhaps thirty to fifty flowers in the first flowering but double that number when the late summer growths bear their flowers in enormous airy corymbs. The flowers are set off by dark glossy green leaves with red midribs. There are a few, decurved red prickles and a rich scent of sweetness and musk. 'Trier' is surprisingly hardy; a note in *Rosen-Zeitung* claimed that a plant survived temperatures of −26°C in Upper Silesia in the winter of 1927–28. German photographs taken in the 1910s clearly show it trained up a wall to a height of 3 m or more, convincing me that this founder of the Pemberton Musks may fairly be described as a climbing rose, or at least as a semi-climber, although it has never made more than a 2 m bush in my own garden. Most of the plants sold in Europe as 'Trier' are actually 'Moonlight' [Pemberton, 1913].

Chapter 7

HERMANN KIESE OF VIESELBACH

Hermann Kiese was one of the most successful rose breeders of the early twentieth century, second in importance in Germany only to Peter Lambert. His work with *Rosa multiflora* has given us some of the finest ramblers ever bred and, in 'Tausendschön', one of the greatest garden roses of all time.

Kiese was born in 1865 near Frankenstein in Silesia, now Zabkowice Šlaskie, close to the Polish border with the Czech Republic. His most formative experiences were the visits he made in 1883–84 to Schultheis of Steinfurth (then, as now, one of the leading German rose nurseries) and to the pioneer German rose breeder Harms near Hamburg. The training and knowledge he gained during these years allowed Kiese, in 1887, to take up a position as foreman with J. C. Schmidt at Erfurt, where he remained for twenty-one years. One of his earliest seedlings, issued in 1895, was a vigorous crimson Hybrid Perpetual bred from 'Général Jacqueminot' × 'Princesse de Béarn' and named 'Venus'. (My wife, Brigid, reintroduced 'Venus' to England some years ago from Sangerhausen and planted it in a central position in the Marquess of Bath's Rose Labyrinth at Longleat in Wiltshire.)

In March 1908 Kiese set himself up in partnership as a rose grower and rose breeder in a old fruit orchard at Vieselbach, a few kilometres east of Erfurt on the Weimar road. Here he remained until his premature death in 1923. Kiese was a great supporter of the German National Rosarium at Sangerhausen, and never refused a request for roses to plant in public parks and gardens—an expensive undertaking, but one which brought him renown. Contemporaries knew him as a stalwart supporter of the rose trade; his exhibits were one of the most reliable features of the horticultural shows of their day, packed with luxuriant specimens of popular roses and his own novelties. Kiese also proved himself a competent journalist: he edited the *Rosen-Zeitung* between 1911 and 1919 and contributed more than fifty articles to its pages over the years.

Kiese made the development of thornless Multiflora Ramblers the central plank of his breeding, but his interests were extremely wide ranging and extended to Polyanthas, Hybrid Teas, and hybrids of more unusual origins. He had a particular flair, an important gift in any successful breeder, for recognising potential winners while they were still at the seedling stage. Kiese won the prize of three thousand German marks to breed and introduce a Hybrid Tea worthy to carry the name of 'Otto von Bismarck'. He tried to breed Climbing Moss roses but found most of the climbing seedlings lacked conspicuous mossiness. Kiese sought to develop new and better understocks. One result was the handsome red shrub rose, bred from a cross between *Rosa canina* and 'Général Jacqueminot' and still much used for landscaping, known as 'Kiese', although correctly 'Kiese's Unterlage'.

Kiese's first three ramblers were issued in 1899: 'Leuchtstern', 'Rubin', and 'Weißer Herumstreicher'. All were bred from the thornless 'Daniel Lacombe', which thus became the foundation of his breeding lines. 'Leuchtstern' was popular in England, whereas 'Rubin' (a better rose) is still to be found in some European gardens, but 'Weißer Herumstreicher' (meaning "white run-around") appears to have been lost to cultivation. Kiese's best-known rose, the incomparable 'Tausendschön' [1906], was also bred from 'Daniel Lacombe' and passed on its gene for thornlessness to its descendants. It was followed in 1908 by the ever-popular 'Veilchenblau', which became the originator of a small group of purple-flowered ramblers, many of which are widely grown today in gardens all over the world. Kiese's first repeat-flowering climber was 'Magda Wichmann' [1911]. Now extinct, it was probably surpassed in any event by three ramblers which only flower once but have remained firmly in cultivation: 'Eisenach' [1909], 'Wartburg' [1910], and 'Hakeburg' [1912]. 'Wartburg' and 'Eisenach' were planted against the castle walls of the Wartburg and grew to 5 m in the outer courtyard. Kiese's later ramblers have not fared so well. His business was badly hit by World War I. His last rambler, 'Andenken an Gartendirektor Siebert' [1923], issued in the year of his death, is now itself extinct, a sad finale to a career which has left such a legacy of enjoyment for later generations of rose lovers.

'Andenken an Breslau' [Kiese, 1913]. Kiese bred very few Wichurana Hybrids. The brilliant carmine cerise flowers of this rose appear very late in the season, are 5–6 cm and very double, and come in large clusters. These are enhanced by typical *Rosa wichurana* leaves and robust, vigorous growth. 'Andenken an Breslau' is still grown at Sangerhausen.

'Andreas Höfer' [Kiese, 1910]. 'Tausendschön' seedling. Early descriptions (including Kiese's) insist that it carries small, brilliant, double, blood red flowers, but the plants which grow at Sangerhausen under this name (and nowhere else, that I know of) have flowers which start deep pink and fade almost to white. The rest of Kiese's description fits well enough: the flowers come in clusters of up to thirty, the leaves are bright green, the stems are thornless, and the plants grow vigorously to 3 m.

'Blumen Dankert' [Kiese, introduced by Schmidt, 1904]. One of Kiese's hardy Multi-flora Ramblers, with small (3.5 cm), fully double, neat, imbricated flowers, and fifteen to forty of them in thick clusters. They open pale crimson or deepest pink and fade only a little, to medium pink, but have no scent. The stems carry some prickles and have a vigorous upright habit of growth to about 3 m.

'Eisenach' [Kiese, 1909]. *Rosa wichurana* hybrid. 'Eisenach' is not one of Kiese's best roses. The flowers are single, dull red, and borne in large, rather congested clusters. On the other hand, it flowers heavily for a long time (with sometimes a few later blooms) and it grows vigorously.

'Hakeburg' syn. 'Hackeburg' [Kiese, 1912]. Possibly a 'Tausendschön' seedling. This is an excellent Multiflora Rambler—hardy, almost thornless, and very floriferous. It bears enormous, rather tight clusters of flowers (each about 4 cm) which open bright pink and pale slightly to a delicate shade of lilac pink that manages to look fresh even as it fades, with conspicuous yellow stamens. The general effect is of rose pink abundance. The flowers carry a light musky scent. 'Hakeburg' is still seen in collections in Europe and available from nurseries there.

'Leuchtstern' [Kiese, introduced by Schmidt, 1899]. Supposedly 'Daniel Lacombe' × 'Turner's Crimson Rambler'. The flowers are small (3–4 cm), single, deep pink with a white centre, and scentless. They come in large clusters (typically ten to thirty) on a hardy plant which is quite floriferous, but the flowers are overcrowded and the overall effect is dull. Gertrude Jekyll called it "a charming pillar rose" in *Roses for English Gardens*, although there was little to compare it with in 1902 when she was writing. The plant flowers early and remains in flower for a long time; it is also less susceptible to mildew and rust than some of its contemporaries.

'Lisbeth von Kamecke' [Kiese, 1910]. 'Veilchenblau' × 'Katharina Zeimet'. Rose breeders know that the way to develop an unusual colour break is to cross it with a white cultivar, because white is usually recessive to all other colours. Kiese must therefore have hoped that this cross would give rise to interesting purple roses and prove a further step on the road to creating a truly blue rose. 'Lisbeth von Kamecke' is at best a pale lilac pink, although a very attractive and unusual colour. The flowers are about 3 cm, lightly double, in large clusters, and are set off by dainty bright green leaves. It is still grown in such collections as Sangerhausen.

'Perle von Britz' [Kiese, 1910]. 'Tausendschön' seedling. This is a very vigorous, almost thornless Multiflora Rambler with pale green leaves and very large panicles (thirty to fifty flowers) of beautiful semi-double flowers (plate 56). They are pearly pink, fading to white, and have a mild musky scent. The flowers are small to medium sized (about 3 cm) and elegantly held in loose, open clusters. 'Perle von Britz' has for long survived only in old gardens, but it has recently been reintroduced to commerce.

'Rubin' [Kiese, introduced by Schmidt, 1899]. 'Daniel Lacombe' × 'Fellemberg'. 'Rubin' was released at the same time as 'Leuchtstern' and is a much better rose. The flowers are a bright deep crimson, with occasional white flecks which recall its China parents, as do the brown stems. The flowers are full, medium sized (4–5 cm), and come in nicely open clusters of ten to thirty in one midseason flowering. The plant grows vigorously to about 3–4 m. It is said to be susceptible to mildew, although I have not found this.

'Rudelsburg' [Kiese, 1919]. This once-flowering Multiflora Rambler has small to medium-sized (3–4 cm), semi-double flowers which open out flat, violet crimson at first but fading to plum pink and slate grey. They come in large clusters of up to fifty flowers, typically about twenty-five, and have a slight scent. The plant grows vigorously to 3–4 m and has long, strong, thornless stems.

'Tausendschön' [Kiese, introduced by Schmidt, 1906]. 'Daniel Lacombe' × 'Weißer Herumstreicher'. This rose alone is enough to guarantee Kiese an honoured place in the history of the rose. He used it to breed additional roses and passed on its thornlessness to many of its descendants. 'Tausendschön' is one of the hardiest climbing roses and is widely available all over the world (plate 58). Its flowers are medium sized (6 cm), double, with distinctively ruffled petals when they open out. The name's "thousand beauties" are the shades of colour which the flowers display: tints of white, pale pink, rose, and cream. They are deep rose pink when they open and fade to paler pink, although the centre petals open creamy and usually remain that shade throughout the long flowering period. The flowers come in large, strong-stemmed clusters (twenty to forty flowers) and have a slight musky scent. The soft green disease-resistant leaves are a good foil to the gentle hues of the flowers, and the smooth stems are pliable and easy to train.

Growth is vigorous; most authorities say 3–4 m, but I have seen specimens as much as 7 m tall.

'Tausendschön' was an instant success and widely grown. It produced several colour sports, none as good as the original, and a pair of dwarf repeat-flowering sports, too. 'White Tausendschön' syn. 'White Merveille' [W. Paul & Son, 1913] was a straightforward sport with pure white flowers and an occasional pink tint, but otherwise similar to 'Tausendschön'. In 1909 another white sport occurred in Kiese's own nursery which he called 'Weiße Tausendschön'; it opened from a pale yellow bud into a mother-of-pearl flower which faded to white with no hint of pink. Kiese held back 'Weiße Tausendschön' when Paul's introduction appeared, but he was eventually persuaded to introduce it by Gräfin von Chotek, who considered it superior to Paul's form. The two forms are somewhat mixed in the trade now, but I am inclined to agree that Paul's 'White Tausendschön' is marred by its pink flecks. Kiese's 'Weiße Tausendschön' acquires a greenish tinge as it ages. Jan Böhm released an ivory white (and strongly scented) sport of 'Tausendschön' in 1925 called 'Mána Böhmová' but, by that time, the other sports were well established, so 'Mána Böhmová' is rarely seen. As sometimes happens, its name was also an obstacle to commercial success. 'Mána Böhmová' was, however, considered an improvement on both 'White Tausendschön' and 'Weiße Tausendschön', for its larger clusters and larger individual blooms, which remain pure ivory white as they age. 'Roserie' [Witterstätter, 1917] is a pure pink sport whose flowers, instead of paling, darken quickly to cherry crimson. The 'Rote Tausendschön' referred to in *Rosen-Zeitung* in 1919 was not a sport but a seedling of 'Tausendschön' and was never introduced commercially. The amateur rose grower Louis Walter from Saverne introduced a 'Red Tausendschön' sport in 1931, but that genuine mutation of 'Tausendschön' is now extinct. The rose grown at Sangerhausen under the name 'Dunkelrote Tausendschön' [M. Vogel, 1942] is a seedling with scentless, bright pale crimson flowers (smaller than its parents', about 5 cm) borne in small clusters of about ten flowers. 'Indispensable' [Klyn, 1947] was introduced as a pink-flowered semi-climbing sport of 'Roserie'. And doubtless there have been other sports of 'Roserie' which have not been named or introduced commercially.

'Tausendschön' also sported to create a dwarf repeat-flowering form—in effect, a Polyantha. This has always been an unusual phenomenon among roses, which are much more likely to mutate from a dwarf repeat-flowering bush into a vigorous once-flowering climber. 'Echo' syn. 'Baby Tausendschön' [Lambert, 1914] was for many years one of the most popular dwarf bedding roses, similar in every respect to its parent except for its stature and repeat flowering. It too produced a white sport, another dwarf-growing Polyantha, 'Eva Teschendorff' [Teschendorff, 1923]. 'Eva Teschendorff' then sported back to a climbing form not once, but twice: 'Climbing Eva Teschendorff' [A. Op de Beeck fils, 1926], and 'Climbing Eva Teschendorff' [Teschendorff, 1932]. There are thus five white forms of 'Tausendschön' still in cultivation: 'White Tausendschön',

'Weiße Tausendschön', 'Mána Böhmová', 'Climbing Eva Teschendorff', and 'Eva Teschendorff'.

'Wartburg' [Kiese, 1910]. 'Tausendschön' seedling. This beautiful Multiflora Rambler has the distinctively fimbriated stipules of the species (plate 57). The flowers are small (3–4 cm) and double, with petals whose habit of twisting and reflexing gives much charm to the open bloom. Deep pink at first, they eventually fade to lilac pink, but keep their distinctive overall hue throughout. They also hold their shape well, so that the clusters of fifteen to fifty flowers radiate an appearance of neatness. The flowers have a slight musky scent and are set off by the large, light green leaves and the wonderful, succulent, thornless growth which so characterises the 'Tausendschön' race. 'Wartburg' grows vigorously to 4–5 m, sending out shoots at least 3 m long every year, and is said to be hardier even than 'Tausendschön'. It is one of my favourite once-flowering ramblers, for its sheer abundance and long flowering season.

William Paul and George Paul

William Paul (1823–1905) is the best-known member of this distinguished family of nurserymen. He was a horticultural polymath whose interests extended far beyond roses. His first and best-known book, *The Rose Garden*, was first published in 1848 when he was barely twenty-five and eventually went through eleven editions—the last, posthumously, in 1910. William Paul's father, Adam Paul, founded a nursery at Cheshunt, Hertfordshire, in 1806. On their father's death in 1847, his two sons George and William carried on the business as A. Paul & Sons at Cheshunt until 1860, when they dissolved the partnership and divided the nurseries. George Paul continued in business at Cheshunt as Paul & Son, while William founded William Paul & Son of Paul's Nursery at Waltham Cross, about a mile away from his brother. The "Son" in William Paul & Son was Arthur William Paul, who was himself a distinguished writer on roses and a breeder, too. George Paul was succeeded by *his* son, George Laing Paul; both traded as George Paul & Son (of Cheshunt). George Laing Paul raised such hybrids as 'Goldfinch' and 'Psyche'. William Paul and Arthur William Paul employed Walter Easlea as their hybridiser. It was Easlea who raised the popular Pernetiana rose 'Juliet' in 1910. But by 1915, Easlea had established himself independently at Leigh-on-Sea on a career of rose growing and rose breeding which would culminate in the beautiful 'Easlea's Golden Rambler'. In 1922, William Paul & Son was bought by its foreman, a man named Chaplin, who brought his six brothers into partnership and renamed the firm Chaplin Bros. Their father, W. E. Chaplin, remained as head of the firm until well into his eighties.

Both parts of the Paul family bred roses—and the same sorts of roses, too, not just such Multiflora Ramblers as 'Goldfinch' and 'Buttercup', but also Wichurana Ramblers (which, for convenience, are included in this chapter, although the Chaplin hybrids are in chapter 9) and such other roses as 'Paul's Lemon Pillar' which are described elsewhere in this book. And both branches used their name Paul as a prefix to rose names, to create a brand image, so that each benefited from the competition between them and the publicity given to either.

'Buttercup' [W. Paul, 1908]. The youthful beauty of this early-flowering rose is not sustained. The light orange buds open to cheerful bright yellow single flowers with narrow petals which do not overlap and briefly have the exact colour of the common European buttercup *Ranunculus acris*. The colour soon fades through lemon and cream to a dirty white. Its leaves are small, neat, dark green and glossy, suggesting some *Rosa wichurana* in its ancestry. 'Buttercup' has comparatively few prickles and grows fairly vigorously to about 3 m. It is still offered by a few nurseries, but should not be confused with other roses that share the name.

'Coralie' [W. Paul, 1919]. 'Hiawatha' × 'Lyon Rose'. The rich coral pink flowers of this strong-growing Wichurana resemble a modern Floribunda. The flowers are scented, medium sized (6–7 cm), and almost double; they lose the yellow tints as they open and change to a good deep pink. A well-grown specimen is very impressive in full flower. The leaves are deep glossy green but a little susceptible to blackspot. The plant grows to about 4 m. It is still available from several nurseries.

'Elsie' [W. Paul, 1910]. Still grown occasionally, this late-flowering Wichurana Rambler has long-lasting, small to medium-sized (4 cm), double flowers which open flat and are carried in great profusion in clusters of ten to thirty. They open bright cherry crimson and fade to a good rose pink, always a little paler at the edges with a few white flecks. They are scentless. The foliage is bright glossy green and disease resistant, and the plant grows vigorously to as much as 5 m.

'Goldfinch' [G. Paul, 1907]. Possibly a 'Helene' seedling. The flowers are quite small (only 4 cm), but abundantly borne, in clusters of up to twenty-five (plate 59). The apricot buds open out to rich yellow flowers, but pale quickly to white, especially in hot sunny weather. The flowers are semi-double with deep yellow stamens and a moderate, rather fruity scent. 'Goldfinch' can suffer from blackspot and mildew, but these never seem to have any effect on its vigour, floriferousness, and ability to flower well, year in, year out. The leaflets are small, glossy, and turn up at the edges, and the wood is nearly thornless. The plant grows vigorously to about 3 m high, but it also makes a handsome shrub, 2 m high and often 4 m across. Although hardy, 'Goldfinch' is rather susceptible to damage by late frosts. It is widely grown, perhaps because it is easily raised from hardwood cuttings, and often found in old gardens.

'Kathleen' [W. Paul, 1908]. 'Crimson Rambler' × 'Félicité-Perpétue'. This somewhat experimental cross has pale pink, single flowers (and white centres) in large clusters that are borne rather late in the season. This rose is interesting rather than exciting.

'Lucens Erecta' [W. Paul, 1921]. This cultivar, presumably bred from *Rosa lucens*, an old name for *R. longicuspis*, is available again from one or two European nurseries. Original descriptions indicate a once-flowering, vigorous climber with small to medium-sized flowers which are blush pink, semi-double, and abundantly produced. The leaves are dark glossy green and fairly disease resistant.

'Oriflamme' [G. Paul, 1914]. This charming rose looks much more like a Wichurana

Rambler with its prostrate habit, red stems, and neat, dark, glossy leaves. The flowers are rich peachy buff at first, with an overlay of pink on the petals and a yellow base, but lose their yellow tone and fade to pink and creamy white. They are semi-double and open out attractively, are medium sized (5 cm across), and have a strong musky scent. They are borne in small clusters (typically three to twelve) on a very vigorous plant.

'Paul's Carmine Pillar' syn. 'Carmine Pillar' [G. Paul, 1895]. This handsome climber is seldom seen today, which is a pity, because it is hardy and flowers very early, if fleetingly. It has been variously classed as a Multiflora Rambler and a Hybrid Perpetual but it fits in best here. The flowers are large (8–10 cm), scented, single, bright pale crimson, and come in clusters of five to twenty-five. The foliage is rich green, and the plant grows vigorously to about 3 m.

'Paul's Scarlet Climber' [W. Paul, 1915]. This very hardy, cheerful rambler is extremely popular in North America and Europe. It took over from 'Excelsa' as everyone's favourite red climber. The flower is not exactly scarlet—it may have a hint of that harsh uncompromising colour on opening, but then loses its vividness and turns to cherry red (plate 62). The flowers are well formed, medium sized (6–7 cm), semi-double, slightly scented, and borne in tremendous profusion in medium-sized clusters all through summer and early autumn. Sometimes there are a few later flowers. The flowers are quite unaffected by heat or rain. 'Paul's Scarlet Climber' is only moderately vigorous, typically 3 m high, but can be seen growing to a much greater height trained round a tall metal cone at L'Haÿ-les-Roses. Richard Vogel, the curator of Sangerhausen, declared in 1923 that "none of the many climbers in our rosarium gives me so much joy as this gloriously coloured rose."

'Psyche' [W. Paul, 1899]. 'Turner's Crimson Rambler' × 'Golden Fairy'. The attractive flowers open medium pink, slightly paler on the outside of the petals, and fade just a little over succeeding days (plate 61). They are sweet scented, small to medium sized (5 cm), full, with a button eye, and last a long time. The large clusters of thirty to fifty start rather late in the season and open in succession over a long period, so they never appear congested. The foliage is handsome, bright green in the Multiflora manner, and the plant grows quickly to at least 4 m.

'Purple East' [W. Paul, 1901]. 'Turner's Crimson Rambler' × 'Beauté Inconstante'. Despite the name, this Multiflora Rambler is not at all purple—the flowers are light crimson, and fade to deep pink. They are semi-double, small to medium sized (4 cm), and come in rather tight clusters, starting very early in the season and lasting a long time, although without any second flowering. Two other distinguishing features are the very glandular pedicels and the very prickly stems. 'Purple East' grows vigorously to about 3 m.

'Queen of the Musks' [W. Paul, 1913]. The plant grown under this name is a vigorous bushy climber, reaching some 2.5 m, and carrying large, open clusters of about thirty flowers. These are semi-single and open pink but fade quickly to white, although the outsides of the petals are a darker pink and the clusters are attractively set off by coral red buds. The plant is remontant and has a tendency to produce lots of small bristly prickles on some of the thicker flowering stems. 'Queen of the Musks' does not appear in William Paul's catalogue of 1913–14, so its identity needs to be confirmed.

'Repens Alba' [G. Paul, 1904]. This is probably the correct name for the rose we grow as *Rosa ×paulii*, a hybrid of *R. rugosa* f. *alba* × *R. wichurana*. It is a modest trailing rose with small clusters of single white flowers which appear intermittently throughout the summer and autumn. It is widely planted in western Europe as a hardy ground-covering landscape rose.

'Shower of Gold' [G. Paul, 1910]. 'Jersey Beauty' × 'Instituteur Sirdey'. Although hailed as a valuable addition to the yellow climbers, this is another of those early ramblers whose yellow colouring passes quickly, fading through cream to white as the flowers open. They are, however, fairly large (7–8 cm), fully double, rosette shaped (at first, but later blowsy), and borne in small clusters, five to fifteen together. This rose flowers early, but does not repeat, and the blooms are scentless. The foliage is excellent, a beautiful coppery colour and very glossy; it is a good foil for the flowers, like the bronze green new wood. The plant has a trailing habit and grows vigorously to about 4 m, but is sensitive to late frosts.

'Tea Rambler' syn. 'Paul's Tea Rambler' [W. Paul, 1904]. 'Turner's Crimson Rambler' × a Tea rose. This is a rose of great delicacy and beauty. Its elegantly pointed buds, each like a miniature Hybrid Tea, open out to reveal flat, medium-sized (4–5 cm) flowers with loosely double centres. Their colour is coppery pink, but they fade to pure shell pink, and the petals are always darker on their backs, which creates attractive contrasts within the open flower. The flowers are sweetly scented and come in clusters of three to fifteen. They are well set off by the lush growth, fat stems, soft new leaves, and bright green older leaves with a distinct red edging. The plant will reach 5 m.

'The Beacon' [W. Paul, 1922]. Launched as a Wichurana Hybrid, this shows traces of Multiflora, even to the extent of carrying mildew on its pedicels—a sure taxonomic indicator of *Rosa multiflora* in the bloodlines. The scentless flowers are single, medium sized (about 5 cm), very bright crimson with white centres, and resemble an early Floribunda. They are rather tightly but abundantly borne in fairly large clusters. The plant is hardy, prickly, and moderately vigorous, growing to about 3 m.

'The Lion' [G. Paul, 1901]. 'Turner's Crimson Rambler' × 'Beauté Inconstante'. The single flowers open brilliant crimson with a white centre, but fade to a duller shade. They open flat, and are only medium sized at first (about 7 cm), but they grow until they reach about 10 cm before dropping their petals. They come in small clusters of three to twenty, but are scentless. The plant grows vigorously but is not tall, 2.0–2.5 m at most.

'The Wallflower' syn. 'Wallflower' [G. Paul, 1901]. 'Turner's Crimson Rambler' × 'Beauté Inconstante'. This is the best of the three Multiflora Ramblers ('Purple East', 'The Lion', and 'The Wallflower') bred from the same parents and issued together. The medium-sized (4–5 cm), semi-double flowers open clear crimson and change to deep pink, but always with a few white flecks and flashes at the base of the petals. They are flat, well scented, and nicely held, in broad open sprays of up to fifteen flowers. 'The Wallflower' flowers late. Its leaves are quite broad and were once considered particularly healthy, although there are later reports of occasional mildew. It is an excellent old cultivar, somewhat in advance of its times, and unfairly overlooked nowadays. At L'Haÿ-les-Roses it looks very fine pegged down annually to maximise its flowers along the whole length of its stems. Its light green wood has only an occasional large prickle and, left to scramble, it grows vigorously to about 2.5 m.

'Waltham Bride' [W. Paul, 1904]. Although not a match for other early-flowering ramblers, its small (3–4 cm), snow white, scented, semi-double flowers in clusters of five to twenty-five are fairly attractive. It is almost completely thornless and grows vigorously to about 4 m. Although not in commerce for many years, it survives in some of the older rose collections in Europe.

Ludwig Walter of Zabern

Ludwig Walter founded the Verein Elsässer Rosenfreunde at Zabern in Alsace in 1898 and helped to establish the rosarium there in 1900. Walter was not a professional rose grower or nurseryman, just an enthusiastic amateur; he worked all his life for the postal service. Like all Alsatians of his generation, he witnessed many changes of nationality in the history of his native town. We find him writing in fluent German, as Ludwig Walter from Zabern, to the *Rosen-Zeitung* in the summer of 1918 and in fluent French, as Louis Walter from Saverne, to *Les amis de la Rose* in the following year. He remained at the helm of the La Société des Amis des Roses d'Alsace until his death during World War II, when the society was, of course, once again known as the Verein Elsässer Rosenfreunde. Walter's rose breeding was a minor interest, and only 'Madeleine Selzer' has established itself in commerce; it remains one of the loveliest of all midsummer roses. Here is a full list of his eight surviving climbing roses, all palest pink or white:

'Baronin Anna von Lüttwitz' [Walter, 1909]. 'Euphrosyne' × 'Rösel Dach'. The attractive, well-filled, double, pale pink flowers hang down under their own weight when they open out. The clusters are large, typically fifteen to fifty flowers, which gives an impression of great profusion although the individual flowers are only about 3.5 cm. Unfortunately, they fade quickly to white and do not disintegrate cleanly. Nevertheless, this is still a pleasant, once-flowering cultivar, with a musky scent and bright green leaves, which grows extremely vigorously to at least 6 m.

'Fernande Krier' [Walter, 1925]. This attractive 'Excelsa' sport has all the same characteristics except for colour, usually described as peachy pink but actually paler, closer to mother-of-pearl, and fading to white. It tends to revert, so that often individual flowers or clusters are a dark bright red, but 'Fernande Krier' enjoys a daintiness which 'Excelsa' lacks.

'Frau Georg von Simson' [Walter, 1909]. 'Helene' × 'Rösel Dach'. This attractive Multiflora Rambler opens light pink but fades to white. The flowers are medium sized (5–6 cm), full, and come in clusters of up to thirty; they have a strong, musky scent. The plant flowers once, is thornless, and grows vigorously to 3 m.

'Gräfin Ada von Bredow' [Walter, 1909]. 'Thalia' × 'Rösel Dach'. The plant at Sangerhausen is more of a Wichurana Rambler than the published parentage would suggest. The semi-double flowers are small (2.0–2.5 cm) and carried in large, rather congested clusters, early in the season. They open mother-of-pearl but quickly fade to white and have a musky scent.

'Ida Klemm' [Walter, 1906]. 'Ida Klemm' is a white-flowered sport of 'Turner's Crimson Rambler', with all the virtues of that cultivar: vigour, hardiness, and quantities of large clusters growing profusely on long strong stems. It is now almost forgotten, except in such collections as Sangerhausen and L'Haÿ-les-Roses. The specimen at Sangerhausen is rather earlier flowering than 'Turner's Crimson Rambler' and carries slightly congested clusters of pure white flowers (about 3.5 across) and typically with ten to fifteen flowers in a cluster. When the flowers die they tend to hang on and turn brown.

'Jeanne Richert' [Walter, 1929]. 'Léontine Gervais' seedling. The colour is said to be creamy white at the edges and yellowish red at the centre, but the flowers on the plants at Sangerhausen are white, with a hint of pale salmon pink when they open and not very distinguished. The flowers are lightly scented, about 4 cm, and fairly double, and come in clusters of ten to thirty. The plant grows vigorously to 3–4 m. The stems are prickly and the foliage is glossy, in the Wichurana style.

'Madeleine Selzer' [Walter, 1926]. Reputedly 'Tausendschön' × 'Mrs Aaron Ward'. This is one of the most beautiful of all Multiflora Ramblers. Despite Walter's claims, it is more likely to be a either a selfed seedling of 'Tausendschön' (because there is no trace of Hybrid Tea in it) or a cross Walter made between 'Tausendschön' and 'Gruß an Zabern' which he wrote about in *Rosen-Zeitung* in 1918. Nevertheless Walter introduced it as a "yellow 'Tausendschön'," which would be exciting if it were true, but most certainly is not. The deliciously scented flowers are pale cream, fading to bright white, very fully double, and medium sized (5–6 cm), in spacious clusters of up to twenty flowers. The neat, recurved petals are rather delicate and thin, which means that it is not a good rose in a soft climate. However, 'Madeleine Selzer' is also very hardy, which makes it suitable for continental climates where the flowers open out spectacularly. The bright green foliage is a great foil for the flowers; the leaves are big, broad, and plentiful and borne on supple thornless stems, although there are small barbs on the back of the leaves. It flowers only once, but grows vigorously to 3–4 m.

'Marie Dietrich' [Walter, 1928]. 'Léontine Gervais' × 'Eugénie Lamesch'. This is a Wichurana Rambler with the small glossy leaves that are typical of such roses. The buds are small and crimson; the flowers are small to medium sized (4.0–5.5 cm), semi-double, mother-of-pearl, but fading quickly to white, while retaining a few crimson splashes on the backs of the outer petals. The flowers have an agreeable scent of musk and sweetness and are borne in small clusters of ten to twenty. The plant grows vigorously to about 4 m.

Miscellaneous Early Multiflora Ramblers

Any rapid development in a cultivated genus is usually the work of an energetic and committed professional nurseryman. One has only to study the Barbier ramblers or the Kordesii climbers to understand how, within as little as ten years, it is possible for a breeder to develop a distinctive new strain which remains popular for many years to come. After that first major advance, however, come the copycats, the amateurs, the johnny-come-latelies, and the happy finders of chance seedlings. The dribble of further introductions continues, on and off, forever. And thus it has been with *Rosa multiflora*. The pioneering work of Jackson, Lambert, and Kiese brought the Multiflora Ramblers to the position of prominence which they still enjoy. Some of the later hybrids undoubtedly represent advances on what has gone before, but others add little or nothing to the sum of horticultural human happiness. What follows is a mixed bag.

'Andrée Vanderschrick' [Buatois, 1935]. This Multiflora Rambler is no improvement on what was already available thirty years earlier. The flowers are small (3–4 cm), double, white and slightly scented. It grows vigorously to about 4–5 m, but flowers only once.

'Blanche Frowein' [Leenders, 1915]. This is more of a Lambertiana than a Multiflora, because it is not overvigorous but fully remontant. The flowers are deep golden yellow at first, but fade to cream; they are sweetly scented, medium sized (5–6 cm), and double. The plant grows to about 2 m.

'Bonnie Prince' [Cook, 1924]. 'White Tausendschön' seedling. This was bred in 1916 by an amateur in Boston, Massachusetts, and introduced by the Portland Rose Society in Oregon in 1924. It has long graceful clusters of snow-white flowers which are loosely petalled, open, and frilled, although they never reflex completely. They come in loose clusters of eight to twenty and have a fine, sweet scent. The plant is very vigorous, and grows to 6 m; it has thick leaves and no prickles. It is also notably early flowering.

'Cato' [Gratama, 1904]. The flowers open deep pink and fade to a pale lilac pink. They are small to medium sized (5 cm) and double, while also opening out to show their stamens. They have a very strong musky scent. The overall effect is of a pink rose of the 'Debutante' type, with vigorous growth and small clusters of ten to twenty-five flowers.

'Charlotte Mackensen' [M. Vogel, 1938]. The flowers are medium to large (7–8 cm) and open rich reddish crimson, but fade to dark pink, with paler undersides (plate 60). They are double, with their short petals neatly arranged (almost imbricated) around the central stamens. The flowers are scentless and held on short pedicels in rather tight clusters; the overall effect is slightly uneven. The stems are rather prickly.

'Crimson Grandiflora' [Ghys, 1911]. This is one of the last Multifloras to flower. It has crimson purple flowers which are about 6 cm and fairly double, in clusters of twenty to fifty. It grows vigorously to about 3 m.

'de Candolle' [A. Robichon, 1912]. 'Eugénie Lamesch' seedling. 'de Candolle' has a most unusual mixture of colours—the overall impression is of salmon pink (darker and more salmon-coloured when the flowers first open, but paler and pinker later on), but the flowers are actually cream or pink, with very dark patches and markings of mulberry red, dark copper, coral, and yellow, and always darker on the outside than the inside. They are double, medium sized, completely scentless, and borne in small clusters of ten to thirty. The shiny leaves suggest *Rosa wichurana* in the ancestry. It is a vigorous grower, to 3–4 m high.

'Electra' [Veitch, 1900]. *Rosa multiflora* × 'William Allen Richardson'. The flowers open pale yellow or cream, but turn to white. They are double or semi-double, small to medium sized, and carried in small clusters. They have a pronounced musky scent. The leaves are a bright rich green with rather broad leaflets, and the plant grows vigorously to 3–4 m. 'Electra' is very charming when in full flower—more's the pity that it is no longer available commercially.

'Eléonore Berkeley' [breeder unknown]. Supposedly *Rosa multiflora* × 'Mme Luizet'. In commerce since 1900, 'Eléonore Berkeley' is a slightly mauve, pale pink and still sold in Europe.

'Fiamma Nera' [possibly Yugoslavia, 1938]. This mystery rose is a very fine white-flowered Multiflora Rambler with a hint of yellow in the centre when it first opens. The flowers are medium sized (5 cm), semi-double and carried in clusters of ten to thirty on a very vigorous plant which will reach at least 5 m. It is very floriferous—a beautiful sight in full flower.

'Frau Käte Schmid' syn. 'Käte Schmid' [Vogel, introduced by Kordes, 1931]. 'Fragezeichen' × 'Tausendschön'. The flowers are very slightly scented, double, medium to large (7 cm), and bright pink fading to silvery pink (slightly darker on the backs of the petals). They are cup shaped at first, but then open out flat with short petals, and stand up well to rain. They are profusely carried on long stems in small clusters (typically five to ten flowers) against a background of lush, pale green leaves. The plant has large, healthy, glossy, Wichurana leaves and grows very vigorously to 3–4 m.

'Gardeniaeflora' [Benary, introduced by Schmitt, 1901]. This is a dull, musk-scented Multiflora with large clusters of small (2.5–3.0 cm), semi-double, white flowers. It flowers early and grows to about 3 m.

'G. F. Veronica' [Demitrovisi (or Demitrowski), date unknown]. This Multiflora Rambler has peachy pink buds and small (3–4 cm) semi-double flowers which open buff yellow and fade to white. It has a fairly good scent, a mixture of musk and sweetness. The flowers are borne in clusters of five to twenty and are popular with bees. I have seen this rose only at Sangerhausen.

'Gruß von Tannenhof' [Friedrich, 1913]. This is a pure Multiflora Rambler, with large clusters (up to forty flowers) of small (3 cm), double, bright white flowers with a fair scent. It is very floriferous, hardy, and vigorous, growing to at least 4 m.

'Karl Schneider' [Max Vogel, 1934]. ('Fragezeichen' × 'American Pillar') × 'Professor C. S. Sargent'. The original description refers to this rose as salmon red and lightly double, but the plant at Sangerhausen is rose pink (fading to silvery pink) and very full. The rest of the description tallies: the flowers are medium to large (9 cm) and sweetly scented, open out flat, and are borne singly or in small clusters. Cabbagey buds and round leaflets suggest Bourbon ancestry. The plant is long-flowering and floriferous and grows vigorously to about 3 m. 'Karl Schneider' is remarkably attractive and ought to be more widely grown.

'Le Droit Humain' [Vilin, 1907]. This rose has pale crimson buds which open to medium pink; 6- to 7-cm, fully double flowers with deep rose pink undersides; glandular pedicels; and little scent. The flowers are borne in fairly small clusters, normally of five to ten flowers, but enough to bend the flower-stalks under their weight. The leaves are neat, fairly typical of Multiflora Ramblers, and show a slight tendency to mildew. I know of this rambler only at Sangerhausen.

'Miss Flora Mitten' [Lawrenson, 1913]. Reputedly *Rosa wichurana* × *R. canina*, the rose still grown as 'Miss Flora Mitten' at Sangerhausen is a Multiflora Rambler, although it agrees in all its other details with the original descriptions. The flowers are single, sweet rose pink, about 6 cm, and borne four to ten in a cluster on rather bristly flower-stalks. It is a lanky, gawky, upright grower and moderately vigorous.

'Neige d'Avril' [Robichon, 1908]. This charming rose is still valuable because it flowers very early in the season and lasts a long time in bloom. The medium-sized (4–5 cm) flowers are semi-double and open out to show their golden stamens. They are borne in large, pyramidal clusters on a vigorous, thornless plant which grows to about 3 m. 'Neige d'Avril' was particularly highly regarded by Dr J. Horace McFarland.

'Nymphe' [Türke, 1910]. 'Mignonette' × 'Maréchal Niel'. The result of this interesting cross is not unlike a Floribunda climber. The flowers are white, with pale yellow centres (most attractive), medium sized (6 cm), double, and borne in small clusters. They have a good scent of vanilla. It is said to be remontant, although that is not my experience, and grows vigorously to 3–4 m high. Türke was a professional painter of flowers at the famous Meissen porcelain factory and one of the founders of the rosarium at Sangerhausen. The rose still grows there.

'Paulette Bentall' [Bentall, 1916]. This impressive crimson Multiflora was bred by Joseph Pemberton's gardener. The flowers are a good purplish red, with white flashes to the base of their petals, fairly double, and carried in very large, widely spaced clusters, typically of thirty to sixty flowers (plate 63). The plant is very late flowering but characterised above all by its extreme vigour and lush fat growths. This rose is still grown at Sangerhausen.

'Pearl' [Turner, 1915]. 'Pearl' is a late-flowering Multiflora Rambler, with the healthy green foliage and fringed stipules which are such a dominant feature of the race. It carries large panicles of small to medium-sized (5 cm), single, pearly pink flowers which fade quickly to white. The overall effect is rather dim and dull, especially because the flowers are too close together in the bunches, although the new stems are a striking purple.

'Perle des Neiges' [Dubreuil, 1902]. This remontant rambler, one of the earliest ever bred, is again available in commerce. Its flowers are small to medium sized, semi-double, brilliant white, and produced in clusters of fifteen to thirty over a long season. It grows to about 2.5 m.

'Phyllis Bide' [Bide, 1923]. 'Perle d'Or' × 'Gloire de Dijon'. This perpetual-flowering Multiflora has the pink, salmon, and gold colouring of the 'Gloire de Dijon' tribe. It carries long, loose clusters of small (3 cm) flowers in great profusion (plate 64). They are nearly double, slightly scented, and open pale gold, tipped with pink, but fade quickly, so that they soon look washed out and white, especially when exposed to full sun. The stamens also turn quickly from yellow to brown. The first flowering is abundant, and the plant remains almost continuously in flower until early winter. The wiry stems build up to a 2-m bush, but it may reach 4 m on an arch or wall. The leaves are small, like a Polyantha, but attractive, neat, and fairly resistant to disease. 'Phyllis Bide' has always divided opinion between those who consider it "a charming little everblooming climber, particularly [good] early in the morning because of its cheerful daintiness" and those who know that it is "a piffling thing which takes up the room for a good rose" (*American Rose Annual* 1927, 141–142). I am decidedly in the latter camp.

'Rambling Rector' [Daisy Hill, 1912]. This foundling is almost certainly an older rose renamed. I have compared it with all other white Multifloras introduced before 1912, without yet finding a match. The flowers are pale creamy white, soon turning to pure white, small (4 cm), semi-double, with golden stamens which are very attractive at first, but turn quickly to brown as the flower ages (plate 65). The flowers have a musky scent and come in large, well-spaced clusters of ten to fifty roses. It grows vigorously to about 4 m and is fairly hardy. The pale green leaves and new growths are also very attractive. 'Rambling Rector' is popular in England because of the name. There is considerable confusion in the trade between this rose and 'Seagull'.

'Roby' [P. Guillot, 1912]. 'Léonie Lamesch' × 'Leuchtstern'. 'Roby' is not listed by nurseries, but is commonly found in gardens throughout mainland Europe. The buds are deep pink or crimson, but the flowers are best described as white with pink margins. They are about 6–7 cm, large for a single-flowered Multiflora Hybrid, with just a few extra petals, and rather tightly held in clusters of twenty to fifty. The scent is fairly good, a mixture of sweetness and musk. The plant is somewhat prickly, not hardy in the coldest zones, and grows to about 4 m.

'Seagull' [Pritchard, 1907]. The flowers are small (about 3 cm), pure white, and lightly semi-double; they open from pink-tinged buds to reveal their golden stamens. The petals are notched and waved in a typically Multiflora manner which makes the flower seem more substantial than it really is. The strongly musk-scented flowers are extravagantly carried in large, upright panicles: 'Seagull' must be one of the most floriferous of all ramblers, a wonderful sight when covered in billowing masses of flowers. It grows vigorously to about 4 m high and has large prickles.

'Steyl Rambler' [Leenders, 1915]. This is a vigorous, 3-m, once-flowering Multiflora Rambler which bears its flowers in clusters of up to thirty. They are small to medium sized (3–4 cm), full, and bright vermilion, not unlike the Polyantha 'Orléans Rose'.

'Summer Snow' syn. 'Climbing Summer Snow' [Couteau, 1936]. This 'Tausendschön' seedling has semi-double flowers, which are small to medium sized (5–6 cm), pure white, scentless, and thin petalled. Although they seem to bruise in the rain, they are very attractive, most abundantly produced, and can be quite breathtaking in dry weather. The plant is very vigorous, grows to 5 m, and produces a few later flowers. The thick medium green foliage is a wonderful foil to its beauty.

The Reverend Joseph Pemberton

In its early years, the National Rose Society of Great Britain (like other national rose societies) tended to be run by well-to-do amateurs. Among them was a sprinkling of Anglican clergymen. Joseph Pemberton was a keen rosarian, a successful exhibitor, an acknowledged expert on roses, and later president of the society, which he first joined a few months after it was founded in December 1877. Meanwhile, he devoted more than thirty years of his life to his religious duties. Not until retirement loomed in 1914 could he turn his energies to the pleasures of rose breeding. Pemberton was born in

1852 at the family house at Havering-atte-Bower in Essex. It was called The Round House, and here he lived with his sister Florence until his death in 1926. Theirs was a comfortable life, with more than a hectare of garden to explore as children and to enjoy as adults.

When he turned his hand to breeding new roses, Pemberton sought not to raise bigger and better Hybrid Teas, the sort that won him prizes at the National Rose Society's shows, but turned instead to the memory of "Grandmother's roses," the tough old-fashioned garden cultivars which had seemed so full of scent and beauty to him as a boy. The cornerstone of his hybridisation was 'Trier', the same sweet-scented and floriferous semi-climber that Peter Lambert had bred and built upon in his own quest for perpetual-flowering shrub roses and climbers. Pemberton's method was to cross 'Trier' with a large-flowered Hybrid Tea; the shrubs which followed were easy to grow, free-flowering, and sweetly scented. Scent mattered enormously to Pemberton. He maintained that roses had four types of fragrance: the musk, which is delicate and refined, suggestive of heather and lime blossom, and the only one of the four to diffuse itself freely into the air; the damask, heavy, strong, and pleasant; the tea, not as definite or dominant as the damask; and the fruit, which came with 'Persian Yellow', suggestive in one rose of apricot, in another of pineapple.

At first Pemberton called his new roses Hybrid Teas. He soon realised, however, that he would have to distinguish them from the classic large-flowered Hybrid Teas and was persuaded by the National Rose Society to call them Hybrid Musks instead. The strict definition of a Hybrid Musk is therefore a cross between 'Trier' and a Hybrid Tea. However, the name was later also applied to other breeders' shrub roses of rather different ancestry, including some of Peter Lambert's and Louis Lens's introductions. This has led to considerable confusion.

Pemberton's Hybrid Musks are perpetual-flowering and sweetly scented shrubs which grow up to 2 m high. Although some are grown as pillar roses in hot climates, they cannot really be called climbing roses. On the other hand, their affinity to Floribundas can plainly be seen. Both were bred from crosses between Multifloras and Hybrid Teas—the Musks from the semi-climbers and the Floribundas from Polyanthas. The difference is one not of substance but of scale.

Not all Pemberton's Musk seedlings turned out to be shrubs. They also exhibited a Mendelian proportion of tall, once-flowering ramblers and, although he did not value them highly, Pemberton was persuaded to allow a handful to be released as climbing roses. The following are still grown in specialist gardens, and some of them are offered by nurserymen. Although none enjoys the currency or the popularity of Pemberton's shrub roses, all should be better known than they are.

'Havering Rambler' [Pemberton, 1920]. 'Turner's Crimson Rambler' seedling. The small (3–4 cm), lightly scented flowers are medium pink ("almond-blossom" pink, Pemberton wrote), fading slightly and always paler towards the base of the petals, and semi-double; they open out neatly to show their stamens. They are profusely carried in large, open clusters of up to thirty flowers on long stems, and the plant grows vigorously to 3–4 m.

'Pemberton's White Rambler' [Pemberton, 1914]. This is an excellent Multiflora with large, long, airy clusters of typically five to fifteen small (3–4 cm), very double, pure white, rosette-shaped flowers with a strong musky scent. It blooms only once, but with great generosity, and will grow to 4–5 m. The glossy leaves suggest a trace of *Rosa wichurana* in its ancestry and the stems have large prickles.

'Queen Alexandra' [Pemberton, 1915]. This is an undistinguished Multiflora Rambler with large, overcrowded clusters (typically twenty to sixty blooms) of small (2–3 cm) single flowers; they are bright pink at first but fade to rose pink and produce a musky scent. The plant has bright green leaves.

'Rivers' Musk' [Pemberton, 1925]. This is another dull Multiflora. Its flowers start pink, but turn to dirty white; they are small (3 cm), double, musk scented, and borne in clusters of twenty to fifty. They come on a moderately vigorous but very hardy plant which grows to about 3 m and has rather rugose leaves. I have seen 'Rivers' Musk' at Sangerhausen, but nowhere else.

'Sea Spray' [Pemberton, 1923]. The flowers of this vigorous Multiflora Rambler open out from fat buds to fully double, slightly cupped, pale pink rosettes which turn to white. They have a musky scent and come in small, tight clusters (typically of ten flowers) on a bristly plant with bright green leaves which grows vigorously to 3–4 m. It is a useful rose, because it flowers prolifically and late, and its period of bloom is a long one.

'Star of Persia' [Pemberton, 1919]. 'Trier' × *Rosa foetida*. This is an early-flowering, vigorous climber, reaching about 2.5 m, with medium-sized (3.5–4.5 cm), single or semi-double, bright unfading yellow flowers (with reddish gold stamens) in loose clusters of three to eight flowers. The scent is foetid and the foliage somewhat susceptible to black-spot, but the plant is very hardy and the flowers do not fade to white as so many yellow Multiflora Hybrids do. Certainly 'Star of Persia' stands comparison well with the two climbing hybrids of *R. foetida* released by Pernet-Ducher in the 1920s, 'Le Rêve' and 'Lawrence Johnston'. 'Star of Persia' has slightly smaller flowers than either of these, but it keeps its colour better.

Bruder Alfons Brümmer

Like Gregor Mendel, Bruder Alfons Brümmer was an Augustinian monk. He was born in 1874 at Bieringen in Württemburg and christened Franz Karl Brümmer; Alfons was the name he professed when he took his final vows in 1896. Much of his life as a monk was spent at the order's monasteries at Germershausen, in the Eichsfeld region, and Würzburg (where he was the gardener-monk). Alfons loved roses and was an enthusiastic member of the German Rose Society, insofar as his religious duties permitted. He also wrote occasional articles and notes for *Rosen-Zeitung* in the 1920s and 1930s. From time to time he tried his hand at crossing roses, and on other occasions he sowed open-pollinated seeds and lined out the progeny in his garden.

Most of Bruder Alfons's roses have been preserved at Sangerhausen. With the honourable exception of 'Maria Liesa' and 'Gruß an Germershausen', which are spectacularly profuse in flowering, they are an unmemorable assortment of inferior seedlings: small-flowered Multiflora Hybrids. Only 'Maria Liesa' is still available in commerce, and widely so; their main claim to fame, one suspects, is the curiosity value of being raised by an Augustinian monk. Bruder Alfons died at the Augustinian monastery at Münnerstadt near Bad Kissingen in 1946. One of his brother monks, now an old man, said recently that Bruder Alfons was generally thought by other members of the order to spend too much time in the garden and not enough at prayer.

'Agnes und Bertha' [Brümmer, 1926]. 'Tausendschön' × 'Dorothy Perkins'. The dark pink buds open to small (2.5–3.0 cm), semi-double, white flowers with a hint of mother-of-pearl when they first open. The pink on the outside of the unopened buds shows off the open flowers nicely; they are carried in large clusters of twenty to fifty flowers. This rose is very floriferous for a short time, strongly scented, and grows vigorously to 4–5 m.

'Blanda Egreta' [Brümmer, 1926]. 'Tausendschön' seedling. This is a dull rambler with very small (2 cm), medium pink flowers which fade to pale pink. The leaves are bright green and lush, the stems are almost thornless, and the plant grows fairly vigorously to about 3 m.

'Eichsfeldia' [Brümmer, 1925]. The creamy white, simple flowers are small (3–4 cm), single, and come in small clusters of five to fifteen flowers. The buds and the backs of the petals when they first open are palest pink. The flowers have a musky scent, which is not very pleasant. The glossy leaves and red stems suggest that this seedling is closer to *Rosa wichurana* than *R. multiflora*. It is not very vigorous, perhaps about 3 m high.

'Elisabeth' [Brümmer, 1926]. 'Wartburg' seedling. The flowers are pale pink, fading to white, small (3.0–3.5 cm), double, in small clusters of five to fifteen, and have a light musky scent. They have rather soft petals which do not stand up well to rain. The leaves are bright green, suggesting some *Rosa wichurana* ancestry, and the plant throws up long, vigorous, near-thornless growths to about 5 m.

'Emerickrose' [Brümmer, 1922]. Allegedly a 'Tausendschön' seedling. The Sangerhausen plant is a late-flowering Wichurana Rambler with clusters of ten to fifty flowers (plate 66). The flowers are briefly pale pink with a yellow base, but fade quickly to a uniform white. They are double, small (about 5 cm), and fairly well scented, with a mixture of sweetness and musk. The overall effect is quite attractive when it is in flower, and the bush is said to be very hardy. It grows to 3–4 m.

'Evodia' [Brümmer, 1925]. It is difficult to praise this undistinguished Multiflora Rambler. Its slightly scented, double, flowers are white, with a hint of pink, and are borne in loose pendulous clusters of ten to thirty blooms on a near-thornless plant which grows to about 3 m. The leaves are little glossier than one would expect of a pure Multiflora Hybrid.

'Gruß an Breinegg' [Brümmer, 1925]. Very much a Multiflora, this simple single rose opens deep pink but quickly fades to pale pink and almost to white. The flowers, which are fairly insignificant in themselves, are set off by attractive puffs of yellow stamens.

They come in clusters of ten to thirty, backed by rather bristly stems and masses of bright green foliage. The plant grows vigorously to at least 4 m, probably more.

'Gruß an Germershausen' [Brümmer, 1926]. This Multiflora Rambler is a spectacular sight in full flower, not unlike the better-known 'Maria Liesa', but a little more crimson. It has small (2–3 cm), lightly scented, single flowers with white centres; they come in very large clusters and make a conspicuous display. The leaves are bright medium green with a trace of *Rosa wichurana* in their breeding, but this rose's parentage is not recorded. 'Gruß an Germershausen' suffers a little from mildew, but its dense growth means that it is absolutely covered in flowers, and it is very attractive to bees.

'Hildeputchen' [Brümmer, 1922]. Reputedly an 'Eisenach' seedling. The flowers are small (2–3 cm), single, and open light crimson or bright pink, but quickly fade to palest pink. They have a light scent. The leaves suggest that *Rosa wichurana* played a part in this cultivar's breeding.

'Maria Liesa' syn. 'Maria Lisa' [Brümmer, 1925; introduced by Liebau, 1936]. This is the best by far of Bruder Alfons's roses. The individual flowers are small (2.5–3.0 cm), single, pink, with a white centre and conspicuous yellow stamens, but they have an openness which is very charming (plate 67). They are also very popular with bees and generously borne, in large clusters of up to eighty flowers, over a long period. 'Maria Liesa' is very hardy and a notably late flowerer in cool climates, but a midseason performer where it is warmer. The plant grows vigorously to 3–4 m and is almost thornless. The tough dark leaves and the loose panicles suggest some *Rosa wichurana* in its makeup.

'Prior M. Oberthau' [Brümmer, 1923]. This rose is better than most of Bruder Alfons's seedlings. The flowers open rich deep pink (with a hint of purple) but soon fade to medium pink and then to pale pink, and the petals at all times have white flashes at their bases. The flowers are small (3.5 cm), double, and flat and come in short clusters of ten to twenty-five blooms with a light musky scent. It is once flowering, with typically lush Multiflora leaves and growth, and has few prickles.

Jan Böhm of Blatná

Jan Böhm was a Czech who built up one of the largest nurseries in central Europe during the years between the two world wars. In 1919, he bought a plot of land near the small town of Blatná in southern Bohemia (famous for its carp lakes) and began growing ornamental shrubs and trees. Roses soon became his most popular line, and Böhm was fortunate to discover a number of mutations among his roses, which he then issued as new cultivars. His first was an ivory white sport of 'Tausendschön' which he sent out in 1925 attached to the name of his daughter 'Mána Böhmová'. Then he started to hybridise and raised about a hundred cultivars in almost every group and section of the genus *Rosa*, including the sumptuous Hybrid Perpetual 'Eliska Krásnohorská' and some excellent Polyantha roses, for instance, the dark crimson 'Čsl. Červeny Kríz' and the pink 'Ta Naše Písnička Česká', both of which deserve reintroduction. His last rose was introduced as 'Mir' (meaning "peace") in 1950, but Böhm was an old man by then, and his nursery was not the type of endeavour to flourish under the Communist economic system, when all large enterprises were controlled and managed by the state. His most widely grown introduction is probably 'Demokracie', which Americans incorrectly call 'Blaze Superior'.

Böhm also introduced the hybrids of several amateur rose breeders. The most successful was Dr Gustav Brada, an industrial chemist from Zdice in Bohemia who had settled at Piešt'any in Slovakia and died in 1937. Brada was well regarded in the world of German roses and often contributed articles on breeding to *Rosen-Zeitung*. I have included his roses here with Böhm's because all were introduced by his fellow-Czech.

Many of Böhm's roses were rather old-fashioned by the time they were introduced. Such cultivars as 'Srdce Evropy' and 'Symbol Míru' were no improvement on roses which had been in commerce for as much as twenty or thirty years. And there is sometimes a suspicion that Böhm was not above reintroducing an old rose under a new name. In 'Demokracie', however, Böhm has given us one of the greatest pillar roses of all time.

'Anči Böhmová' [Böhm, 1929]. This 'Marietta Silva Taroucová' sport has all the qualities of that popular Multiflora Rambler, but is lighter and brighter in colour. The gently scented, small or medium-sized (5–6 cm), semi-double or double flowers have ruffled, bright pink petals with a white base and are borne in small clusters (typically five to ten blooms) on a vigorous, wiry, almost thornless plant with beautiful medium green Multiflora leaves.

'Blatenská Královna' syn. 'Königin von Blatna' [Böhm, 1937]. This rose survives at Sangerhausen as a Wichurana Rambler with medium-sized (5–6 cm), full, dark pink flowers. The flowers hang down under the weight of petals, which are soft and somewhat liable to rain damage.

'Demokracie' syn. 'Blaze Superior' [Böhm, 1935]. This modern climber is by far the most widely grown of Böhm's roses. I imagine that it is a seedling of 'Blaze', although I have not seen this confirmed. 'Demokracie' has larger, fewer, deeper-coloured flowers than 'Blaze' itself; the flowers are medium to large (8 cm) and of a more intense colour than the rich red of 'Blaze'. The flowers are fully double, round, and borne in great profusion, singly or in clusters of half a dozen blooms, with some recurrent flowering. It is a fairly vigorous grower and, like 'Blaze', quite scentless.

'Dr Zamenhof' [Brada, introduced by Böhm, 1935]. This Wichurana Rambler has exceptionally large (12–14 cm) flowers, although their shape is a little too loose for extravagant praise. The flowers are crimson red, fading only slightly with age, and very strongly and sweetly scented. They are borne in small clusters on a fairly vigorous plant.

'Jitřenka' [Böhm, 1933]. The semi-double, musk-scented flowers open rich pink and fade to pale pink, with white at the base of the petals. They are about 4 cm and come in long, lax clusters of ten to thirty blooms; the shape of these clusters suggests a measure of *Rosa wichurana* in the background. The flowers have long pedicels which give the sprays a light and airy look. The plant is healthy, with long fat stems; it will reach at least 5 m.

'Kde Domov Můj' [Böhm, 1935]. The flowers are a good deep pink with paler centres and fade to rose pink with a hint of lilac (plate 68). They are about 4 cm, semi-double to double, lightly but sweetly scented, and borne in rather dense clusters of ten to twenty blooms. The plant is very vigorous and floriferous, so that a plant in full flower is a beautiful apparition. The healthy bright green leaves are reminiscent (as are the flowers) of the better-known 'Debutante'.

'Matka Vlast' [Böhm, 1934]. 'Dorothy Perkins' sport. The flowers are pink, striped with red and white. In all other characteristics, this rose is identical to 'Dorothy Perkins'.

'Památník Komenského' [Bojan, introduced by Böhm, 1936]. Early records describe this as a vigorous, floriferous, and early-flowering Multiflora Rambler with medium-sized, salmon pink, scented flowers. The plant which now grows under this name at Sangerhausen is a midseason crimson Wichurana Hybrid with fairly large (8 cm), pendulous flowers individually borne on long, weak, slender stems. They are bright crimson, with paler backs to the petals.

'Poëma' [Brada, introduced by Böhm, 1933]. 'Tausendschön' × 'Farbenkönigin'. Apart from 'Demokracie', this is the only climber introduced by Böhm which is still available in commerce. The flowers are small to medium sized (4–5 cm), semi-double, flat, and bright pink at first, but fading to white, with a large white centre. They are borne in small upright clusters of ten to twenty. 'Poëma' is remontant and will grow, with little encouragement, to at least 6 m.

'Slavia' [Brada, introduced by Böhm, 1934]. 'Tausendschön' seedling. This Multiflora Rambler is a semi-climber or pillar rose, whose pink buds open to small (about 4 cm across), fully double, creamy white flowers which are strongly scented. They are borne in small clusters (typically two to ten blooms) throughout the summer and autumn.

'Srdce Evropy' [Böhm, 1937]. This has dainty, medium-sized (4.5–5.0 cm), deep pink (or light crimson), single flowers which pale slightly as they age. They have a white patch at the base of the petals, with a white centre which contrasts with the yellow stamens. The flowers are borne in very large clusters of thirty to sixty flowers and have a light sweet scent. The glittering glossy foliage indicates its Wichurana heritage, but the stems are unusually prickly. 'Srdce Evropy' is not an especially distinctive cultivar, although a useful late-flowering and prolific shrub for the wild garden.

'Svatopluk Čech' [Brada, introduced by Böhm, 1936]. The Multiflora Rambler which grows under this name at Sangerhausen has pale buff buds; it opens palest pink and turns quickly to white, with perhaps a hint of apricot at the centre. The flowers are small (3.0–3.5 cm) and lightly double and have a good musky scent; they are borne in rather tight clusters of four to twelve blooms. The glossy leaves suggest some *Rosa wichurana* in its ancestry.

'Symbol Míru' [Böhm, 1937]. This is a handsome Wichurana Rambler, very much like 'François Foucard'. It has an attractive, medium-sized flower (6–8 cm), with a mass of petals which are lemon yellow at first but fade quickly to white, keeping a hint of lemon at the centre. They then develop pink blotches as they age and die. The outer petals recurve attractively, whereas the middle ones are quilled. The flowers have a fairly good scent and are borne on very long stems either singly or in small clusters (up to seven flowers). 'Symbol Míru' makes a very vigorous plant and will grow to 6–7 m.

Chapter 7

Captain Thomas of Beverly Hills

At his garden in Philadelphia, George C. Thomas Jr. built up one of the world's largest private rose collections in the years immediately before and after World War I. He had planted almost every cultivar available when, somewhat to his contemporaries' surprise, he moved to a new 80-hectare ranch at Beverly Hills in California. Here he planted a commercial avocado orchard and turned from Multifloras to breeding Noisettes. Thomas was one of the inner circle of wealthy enthusiasts who supported the American Rose Society in its great expansion of the 1920s, but certain aspects of his life and work remain clothed in mystery. It is said, for example, that his wife burned all his roses, books, and manuscripts the day after he died. However, some of Thomas's earlier climbing, hardy, ever-blooming roses, dating from his days on the East Coast, are still in cultivation. I describe four of these roses below.

'Bishop Darlington' [Thomas, 1926]. 'Aviateur Blériot' × 'Moonlight'. This semi-climber resembles most closely a lightly filled Tea rose, although much hardier. The flowers are fairly large (10–11 cm), semi-double, with long petals and an elegant bud, but slightly untidy when opened out. They are creamy buff, paler at the edges, and rich coppery yellow at the base. The blooms are prolifically carried in small clusters on a lax shrub which will grow to 2.5 m. This hybrid is widely available worldwide.

'Bloomfield Courage' [Thomas, 1925]. Although it is only slightly remontant, Thomas saw this rose as a step on the road to breeding repeat-flowering Wichuranas (plate 69). The flowers are small (3 cm), scentless, single, dark velvety crimson, with a vivid white centre and yellow stamens. They come in large (fifteen to forty), loose clusters in immense profusion rather early in the season on a plant of extraordinary vigour, followed by small red hips. The plant has few prickles and requires little pruning.

'Dr Huey' [Thomas, 1914]. 'Ethel' × 'Gruß an Teplitz'. 'Dr Huey' is a first-class, red Wichurana, extensively used as an understock (as 'Shafter'). It is very vigorous, nearly thornless, and a good rooter, but should also be grown for its own beauty. The flowers are small (5 cm) and lightly semi-double; their fiery, unfading, rich crimson is intensified by the yellow stamens. The flowers come in small clusters (five to ten) and do not drop their petals cleanly when they die. 'Dr Huey' grows to at least 7 m and has rich green foliage.

'W. Freeland Kendrick' syn. 'Bloomfield Endurance' [Thomas, introduced by Bobbink & Atkins, 1920]. 'Aviateur Blériot' × 'Mme Caroline Testout'. More Wichurana Rambler than Multiflora, this is a very attractive and distinctive ever-blooming semi-climber or sprawling shrub with small clusters of sweetly scented, fully double flowers, of a good size (about 8–9 cm). They open mother-of-pearl and fade to white, with a hint of pink at the centre. The foliage is large, dark, and bronze green (with reddish flower stems) and the plant grows to 2.0–2.5 m.

Modern Cultivars of *Rosa multiflora*

Multiflora Ramblers continued to turn up as new introductions in nursery catalogues long after horticultural fashion had moved first towards Climbing Hybrid Teas and later towards perpetual-flowering modern climbers. Some are chance seedlings which garden owners have preserved, admired, propagated, given to friends, sold to visitors, and eventually caused to be introduced on a larger scale. Others are a by-product of some serious reworking of neglected cultivars in search of new advances: Louis Lens's wonderful 'Pleine de Grâce' would be a good example. I have had to leave out a few cultivars of confused or uncertain origin, which have a strong following within a limited area, but are foundlings with no clear history or identity—hence no 'Pretty Polly' (popular in South Australia) or 'Hadspen Eleanor' (which has its supporters in southern England). And it should be noted that Louis Lens used *Rosa multiflora* var. *adenochaeta* extensively to breed a remarkable new race of shrubs and semi-climbers, including 'Paganini' and 'Magie d'Orient'.

'Alfred Dietrich' [Mertens, 1980]. This is a carmine red modern Multiflora Rambler, with white stripes, a slight scent, and fully double flowers. I have seen it only at Sangerhausen, but it is also available from at least one nursery in Germany.

'Andenken an Alma de l'Aigle' [Kordes, 1948]. This is a semi-climbing, vigorous Hybrid Musk, with large (9 cm), full, scented, pink flowers in clusters. It is still fairly widely available from nurseries.

'Bobbie James' [Sunningdale, 1961]. This is quite the most sumptuous and generous of the small-flowered white ramblers. Its neat, 4.5-cm, semi-single flowers in large, tight corymbs recall cherry blossoms. The plant is very vigorous (reaching 7 m) and richly furnished with large, bright green, glossy leaves, but the flowers are carried in such abundance that the foliage is smothered by a froth of white. The flowers have bright yellow stamens and a strong musky scent. More than one rose is in cultivation under this name.

'Brigitte de Landsvreugd' [Mertens, 1988]. Although little improvement on the older Multiflora Ramblers, this cultivar has small (3 cm), semi-double, white flowers in large clusters on a hardy and vigorous plant.

'Erato' [Tantau, 1937]. ('Ophelia' × *Rosa multiflora*) × 'Florex'. 'Erato' came out with two other Multiflora Ramblers, 'Euterpe' and 'Indra', each with the same parentage. 'Erato' has small (3 cm), dark pink, lightly scented, semi-double flowers which fade to pale pink and have crinkly petals which give them a particular charm. They come in clusters of up to thirty on long stems and the plant grows vigorously to about 5 m high.

'Euterpe' [Tantau, 1937]. ('Ophelia' × *Rosa multiflora*) × 'Florex'. This Tantau rambler has open, semi-double, light yellow flowers in long-stemmed clusters and a slight scent. The foliage is attractively glossy and it makes a vigorous climber. Neither 'Euterpe' nor 'Erato' is in commerce now, although they are sometimes seen in European rose gardens.

'Frau Eva Schubert' syn. 'Gela Tepelmann' [Tepelmann, 1937]. The flowers of this remontant Lambertiana are a bright marshmallow pink when they first open, but fade to pale pink and eventually to white (plate 70). Unfortunately, the flowers also turn to brown and do not drop their petals as they die but, apart from this defect, 'Frau Eva Schubert' is an excellent rose. The lightly scented flowers come in tight clusters and are fully double but the petals do not reflex, so the flowers appear never to open out fully. It is particularly good in dry warm climates and is a reliable repeat flowerer.

'Gardejäger Gratzfeld' [Gratzfeld, 1939]. This rose most resembles a climbing sport of a Polyantha or early Floribunda. The flowers are bright pale crimson, medium sized (about 6 cm), lightly double, almost scentless, and borne on long stems in small clusters, occasionally singly.

'Gladsome' [Clark, 1937]. It is slightly surprising that Alister Clark, who bred such wonderful roses for the Australian climate, should also be credited with this rather ordinary and undistinguished rambler. The flowers are small (3 cm), single, pink with a white centre, musk scented, and carried in large clusters. 'Gladsome' flowers only once, rather late in the season, and makes a sprawling shrub or pillar. Its best feature is its beautiful light green Multiflora foliage.

'Gruß an Hannover' [Lahmann, 1938]. This has medium-sized (6 cm), double, orange pink flowers on a vigorous, upright plant which grows to about 4 m. It still grows in several German rose collections, for instance, Sangerhausen and Westfalenpark.

'Indra' [Tantau, 1937]. ('Ophelia' × *Rosa multiflora*) × 'Florex'. This is the only one of Tantau's Multiflora Ramblers still in commerce. Its medium-sized flowers (6–8 cm) are semi-double, open, slightly scented, and rose pink. As with the other cultivars, the flowers are carried in small clusters on long arching stems which are designer-made for cutting. The leaves are slightly greyish, glossy, and borne on slender stems. It is free-flowering and very vigorous, growing to about 4 m. 'Indra' is one of the best of the Floribunda-type climbers from the 1930s.

'Maytime' [Maney, introduced by Iowa State College, 1953]. *Rosa maximowicziana* var. *pilosa* × 'Betty Uprichard'. (*Rosa maximowicziana* is a close relation of *R. multiflora*.) Professor Maney bred for hardiness, which 'Maytime' has in good measure. The buds are red, but the flowers open mother-of-pearl and fade to white. They are single, fairly large, and borne in clusters. The plant reaches at least 6 m. This is the only one of Maney's hybrids still in commerce.

'Morning Light' syn. HARlecho [Harkness, 1994]. 'Liverpool Echo' seedling. Harkness issued this rose in New Zealand, where it did well in trials, but not elsewhere. The lightly scented flowers are elegantly shaped like a Hybrid Tea, creamy pink, and borne in large clusters. The leaves are handsome and pale green.

'Pleine de Grâce' syn. LENgra [Lens, 1984]. 'Ballerina' × *Rosa filipes*. The flowers of this remarkable hybrid are medium sized (4–5 cm) and single, but they are borne in large clusters of twenty to fifty in such amazing profusion that a specimen in full flower presents a sheet of glittering white during its one flowering. The flowers also have a strong musky scent. The plant makes a tall shrub (3 m high) or lax climber (5 m up a tree). Although perhaps not as good as 'Polyantha Grandiflora', it is much hardier, and Lens used it to breed a whole race of charming shrub roses.

'Red Moss Rambler' [Moore, 1988]. This medium red hybrid from Ralph Moore is presumably a by-product of his breeding of miniature roses. I have not seen it, even in California, although it is listed by two nurseries there.

'Unique' [Evans, 1928]. This rose is a shrubby semi-climber of the Lambertiana type, but with medium-sized (4–5 cm), double flowers, which are coral pink with darker markings and come in small clusters. It is fully remontant, has typical pale green Multiflora leaves, and grows to about 2.5 m. 'Unique' is still offered by a few nurseries in Europe.

'Wind Chimes' [Lester Rose Gardens, pre-1949]. This was probably a casual seedling raised by Francis Lester from a Hybrid Musk. It has small to medium-sized, pink flowers in large clusters and a very strong scent. It grows vigorously to 5–6 m and remains fairly popular, especially in the United States.

The 'Turner's Crimson Rambler' Race

The arrival of 'Turner's Crimson Rambler', followed five years later by the first Wichurana Hybrids, quite revolutionised the development of climbing and rambling roses. It also contributed substantially to the development of Polyantha roses: almost every famous Polyantha bred between 1900 and 1920 owes its charm to it. In 1902 Gertrude Jekyll summed up its impact: 'Turner's Crimson Rambler' "took the garden world by storm, for its easy cultivation, great speed of growth, and its masses of showy crimson bloom."

'Turner's Crimson Rambler' was a garden rose from China, where its name 'Shi Tzmei' means "Ten Sisters." In 1878 it was introduced to Europe from Japan, where it was known and grown as 'Soukara-Ibara'. It was part of a consignment of Japanese plants which was sent to the distinguished plantsman Thomas Jenner of Easter Duddingston in Midlothian. The sender was another Scot, R. Smith, who was professor of engineering at Tokyo University. The rose was said to be very common in the environs of the port of Nagasaki, where it was used to make garden hedges. Jenner named it 'The Engineer' in his friend's honour, and in 1889 gave stock to John Gilbert, the owner of a small nursery in Lincoln. In July 1890 Gilbert took it to London to show the Royal Horticultural Society, in the hope that the society might give it an Award of Merit. Somewhat surprisingly, 'The Engineer' did not meet with universal approbation; only thirteen members of the Floral Committee voted it an award, and four voted against. Lacking resources for large-scale propagation, Gilbert then passed his stock to Arthur Turner of the Royal Nursery, Slough, who sent it out in 1892 as 'Turner's Crimson Rambler'. So immediate and sensational was its success that Queen Victoria visited Turner's nursery to see the plants for herself. Ellwanger & Barry grew it in pots under glass in New York for sale at Easter; some of the clusters were as large as hydrangea heads (*Journal des Roses* 1897, 41–42). In 1898 a specimen was reported to have as many as 32,000 flowers on it (*Journal des Roses* 1898, 145).

'Turner's Crimson Rambler' syn. 'Crimson Rambler'. This is an important rose which bears vast quantities of rather small (3.5–4.0 cm), lively crimson, semi-double to double flowers late in the season (plate 71). The flowers are scentless and hang down in large, loose clusters, typically of twenty flowers, but sometimes twice as many. They appear over a long season but do not repeat. The plant is very vigorous, with pale green wood and very glossy leaves, and grows to about 5 m. A sport with variegated leaves was reported (*Journal des Roses* 1898, 128) and a pink one introduced as 'Turner's Pink Rambler' in 1911; both are extinct. A white-flowered sport, 'Ida Klemm', was described in chapter 7.

'Turner's Crimson Rambler' combines *Rosa multiflora*, *R. wichurana*, and *R. chinensis* in its makeup. Like many descendants of *R. multiflora*, 'Turner's Crimson Rambler' has fimbriated stipules, but the glossy leaves, long loose clusters, and late-flowering habit come from *R. wichurana*. It is a combination which many of its descendants share.

'Turner's Crimson Rambler' did indeed take the gardening world by storm. Its floriferousness was astounding, and the flowers remained on the plant for many days without losing their brightness. Its glossy green foliage was retained during the winter and made it almost evergreen. People were also impressed by its hardiness down to −20°C, provided that the cold did not endure too long. It was not completely hardy, for example, in such parts of central Europe as the Silesian foothills (*Rosen-Zeitung* 1899), and people noticed early on that it was subject to mildew. 'Turner's Crimson Rambler' had one other lasting effect. The English-speaking world did not know, at first, just what name to give these new, vigorous roses—the Multifloras, the Wichuranas, and the hybrids of 'Turner's Crimson Rambler'—which appeared in such quantities during the 1890s and 1900s. Eventually they settled on the name of ramblers, and it was 'Turner's Crimson Rambler' which fixed the trend.

'Turner's Crimson Rambler' is a prolific seed-setter and a large number of seedlings raised from open-pollinated seed were named and introduced in the twenty years after its introduction in Europe and the United States. Many of the so-called hybrids of 'Turner's Crimson Rambler' were actually selfed seedlings. Some were decidedly inferior to their parent, but almost all have wonderful vigorous growth, glossy foliage, and the habit of flowering late in the season. They also tend to have the same small flower size, profusion, and fullness, although not every cultivar combines all these characteristics. Most have the distinctively fimbriated stipules of *Rosa multiflora*, although not all: 'Andenken an Breslau', among others, does not. Unfortunately, the tendency to mildew also persists in many.

Because of the sheer numbers and importance of these descendants, I think it helps to place them together as a separate group of hybrids, the 'Turner's Crimson Rambler' race. I will examine particular strains, for instance, the blue ramblers and the 'Dorothy Perkins' lines, and look at the work of such important individual breeders as Michael Walsh of Massachusetts and Eugène Turbat of Orléans.

The Blue Roses

I decided to put all the blue roses together in one section of this chapter, not just because it makes for easier analysis of what they share and how they differ, but because I hoped that the exercise might enable me to make a tentative identification of the mysterious 'Bleu Magenta'. All we know about this most richly purplish blue of roses is that it came from L'Haÿ-les-Roses in the 1950s as a rose without a name. I came to the conclusion that it was probably 'Mme E. Rocque', a rose bred from 'Veilchenblau' × 'Reine des Violettes' and introduced in 1918 by Lottin, a not-very-important nurseryman from Avranches on the Normandy-Brittany border. The description seemed to fit 'Bleu Magenta' exactly. The large, flat flowers and their shape and shadings as they open and fade are very similar to 'Reine des Violettes', whose contribution is also seen in the foliage of 'Bleu Magenta', quite different from other 'Veilchenblau' seedlings. Convinced that 'Mme E. Rocque' was the true identity of the foundling known as 'Bleu Magenta', I asked the scholarly French rosarian François Joyaux, who is also vice president of the Friends of the Rose Garden at L'Haÿ-les-Roses, whether he would kindly check the records to discover whether they had any trace of 'Mme E. Rocque'. Back came the firm, authoritative answer—No. He had checked the card indices and it had never been grown at L'Haÿ-les-Roses. So we are no closer to putting a true name to this most beautiful of all the blue ramblers.

'Veilchenblau' is generally regarded as the founder of a group of purple roses. It would be more correct to give the credit to its parents, Geschwind's remarkable Setigera Hybrid 'Erinnerung an Brod' and 'Turner's Crimson Rambler', because almost all the blue ramblers are known to have one or other in their ancestry. That said, 'Veilchenblau' was itself a fecund parent of blue roses and the one to which all were invariably compared. As a group they tend to open dark purple or dark crimson and become paler, ending up some shade of mauve, lilac, or grey. They then hold onto their petals instead of dropping them cleanly. More often than not, 'Veilchenblau' also passes on its thornlessness and its rather long leaflets.

The possibility of breeding blue roses has divided rose lovers from the earliest days. The English rose breeder Jack Harkness summed up the positive attitude we should adopt to horticultural novelty: "Those who are repelled by the so-called blue roses might well start their conversion with 'Veilchenblau'." My own belief is unambiguous: it is important to appreciate the achievements of the past while keeping an open mind about the future.

'Améthyste' [Nonin, 1911]. This is often described as a sport of 'Non Plus Ultra', but Henri Nonin (the son of the breeder) referred to it as a seedling. Nonin père called it "steel blue," but it is a crimson purple rose, with lots of white flashes to the petals (plate 72). The flowers are best enjoyed for their overall effect and appear rather scrappy close up. When they first open, the flowers are neat and attractive, but soon become loose petalled and pale, and fail to shatter until rather late. They are fuller than 'Veilchenblau', appear later, and come in fairly large, distinctly upright panicles. Quite vigorous, 'Améthyste' will grow to 4 m.

'Aurélien Igoult' [Igoult, introduced by Viaud-Bruant, 1924]. 'Veilchenblau' seedling. This Multiflora was said to have bluish violet flowers with reddish markings, but the plant now grown at Sangerhausen (and nowhere else) under this name has flowers which open mother-of-pearl and fade to white.

'Bleu Magenta' [Unknown, 1910s.]. The name of this cultivar is provisional; it is probably an old variety renamed. The individual flowers open dark pink or crimson, change first to purple, then to violet, and finally to slate blue, but the overall effect is of a dark and rich crimson purple (plate 73). Some of the petals have white flecks across them. The flowers are among the largest of the blue roses (6–7 cm), very full, and open out flat. They come in medium-sized clusters, rather too densely packed. The wood is nearly thornless, which suggests 'Veilchenblau' as one of its ancestors, but the leaves are very different from other blue roses, being smaller, denser, and more serrated than the others. The plant will grow to at least 4 m; it looks particularly fine on the circular trellis at Mottisfont Abbey in Hampshire, where it grows alternating with 'Debutante'.

'Donau' [Praskač, 1913]. 'Erinnerung an Brod' × 'Wichuraiana Rubra'. This cultivar is rather similar to 'Veilchenblau'. It is exceptionally vigorous and grows quickly to at least 6 m tall. The name suggests blueness; the flowers are crimson at first, but turn quickly to purple and then to lilac, with paler centres and lots of white stripes in their petals. They are about 5 cm across, semi-double, and open out to show their stamens. The scent is said to resemble lily-of-the-valley. There are up to thirty flowers in a cluster. The wood is pliable, with few prickles and bright green leaves. Its only drawback is a tendency to attract mildew, which suggests rather more *Rosa multiflora* in its composition than its raiser admitted.

'Gartenstadt Liegnitz' [Lambert, 1910]. This undistinguished semi-rambler now exists only in such old collections as Sangerhausen. The scentless, semi-double flowers open bright crimson and fade to purplish mauve pink, almost lilac. They are medium sized (5–6 cm), with long petals, and come in clusters of up to twenty, but do not repeat in the autumn. The leafy bush grows to 2.0–2.5 m.

'I. X. L.' syn. 'Coolidge' [Coolidge, 1925]. 'Tausendschön' × 'Veilchenblau'. This rose is still quite widely used as an understock, especially by American nurseries. The flowers are crimson (with a white centre), double, small (3–4 cm), slightly scented of musk, and borne in small clusters. It has the thornlessness of its parents and extraordinary vigour. The English rosarian T. C. Mansfield (1946) wrote that it had "the doubtful characteristic of throwing up long straight stems of terrifying thickness"—hence its value as a stock.

'Mosel' [Lambert, 1920]. 'Mme Norbert Levavasseur' × 'Trier'. 'Mosel' is one of the prettiest of the blue roses, although not the strongest coloured (plate 74). The flowers are very double, nicely formed rosettes, sometimes with an attractive button eye; they are also quite large for a Multiflora Rambler, up to 6 cm across. Their colour changes nearly as much as 'Platyphylla', the 'Seven Sisters' rose, passing from crimson to purple, lilac, and almost to white, always slightly paler on the backs of the petals and towards the centre of the flower. The flowers come in large, rather open clusters of fifteen to thirty and have a light scent. The plant has beautiful bright green leaves and bristly stems. It grows to 2.0–2.5 m and is occasionally remontant.

'Mosellied' [Lambert, 1932]. ('Geheimrat Dr Mittweg' × 'Tip Top') × ('Chamisso' × 'Parkzierde'). 'Mosellied' is not as elegant as 'Mosel', but it is much more strongly scented (of musk) and repeats well in the autumn. The small flowers (4 cm) are single, reddish purple or dark pink with a white eye and a nice circle of golden stamens, all of different length, which gives them a wispy look. The flowers fade to mauve pink and are held erect in upright clusters of about twenty or thirty. The wood is thornless and the dark green foliage particularly fine. 'Mosellied' makes a broad, dense bush and grows to about 2.5 m high.

'Purpurtraum' [Kayser & Seibert, 1922]. 'Excelsa' seedling. Despite the name, this rose is no more than dark crimson (bright and rich), with a white eye. It resembles its parent closely, but is only semi-double. The flowers are small (3 cm) and scentless in clusters of fifteen to fifty. The leaves are small and glossy, and it grows vigorously to 3–4 m. This rose makes a cheerful contribution to the garden, flowering rather earlier than most of the 'Excelsa' types.

'Rosemarie Viaud' syn. 'Rosemary Viaud' [Igoult, introduced by Viaud-Bruant, 1924]. 'Veilchenblau' seedling. This is bluer than its parent, starting violet purple but quickly fading to a distinctive shade of Parma violet, with conspicuous white flecks in its petals (plate 75). The flowers are small (3 cm), double, rosette-like, and completely scentless, although they come in large clusters on a vigorous thornless plant which grows to 4–5 m. It has the family weakness for mildew, particularly on the pedicels.

'Schloß Friedenstein' [J. C. Schmidt, 1915]. 'Veilchenblau' × 'Mme Norbert Levavasseur'. This rose was correctly launched as a darker version of 'Veilchenblau'; it is also more double. The small (3–4 cm), scentless flowers are a very good colour at all stages; they open as violet purple, but soon fade to plum and then to lilac and Parma violet. The backs of the petals are always paler. In other respects 'Schloß Friedenstein' closely resembles other seedlings of 'Veilchenblau', especially 'Rosemarie Viaud'. Yet its flowers have a beauty which marks it as one of the best.

'Veilchenblau' syn. 'Bleu-Violet' [Kiese, introduced by Schmidt, 1908]. 'Turner's Crimson Rambler' × 'Erinnerung an Brod'. 'Veilchenblau' is the mother of all the best blue roses, the best known, and the most widely grown. Indeed, it remains the measure to which all other purple ramblers are compared. It is very hardy in such places as central Europe, but it also grows well in hot climates such as Queensland and tolerates quite a lot of shade. Its popularity is no doubt due in part to its unusual colouring, but also to the fact that it roots so easily from cuttings. The flowers are small (3.5 cm), semi-double, and borne in large clusters in great profusion. The buds are purplish pink, open to a purplish crimson, then change to dark bluish violet. Later, especially in hot weather or in open positions, the flowers continue to fade until they acquire an attractive lilac grey hue. The centre of the flower is always white, and the white streaks sometimes extend right to the petal-tips. The sweet scent is variously described as reminiscent of lily-of-the-valley or apples. 'Veilchenblau' is once flowering and bears good crops of small orange hips in autumn. The plant grows very vigorously, throwing out long succulent wands which are almost thornless with large, glossy, fresh green leaves; it will make 5 m within a few years, sometimes more. It flowers comparatively early and is very popular with bees.

'Violette' syn. 'Violetta' [Turbat, 1921]. This rose is noticeably darker—more purple and less mauve—than 'Veilchenblau', although even the most violet of petals is soft lilac on the back. When not growing well, the flowers sometimes ball or come out pink. The flowers are small (3 cm), semi-double, and slightly cupped, with a very light musky scent. They come in large clusters of up to thirty flowers. The growth is long and almost thornless, and the foliage has the bright pale green lustre of many Multiflora Ramblers. The plant grows fairly quickly to 3–4 m.

'Vltava' [Böhm, 1936]. 'Veilchenblau' seedling. The flowers are very attractive, medium-sized (4–5 cm), and very double, and they eventually reflex like a pompon to reveal a white centre. They are deep violet at first, but purplish red and dusky Parma violet later, although completely scentless. They are borne in small clusters on a very vigorous climber which reaches 4–5 m and carries slightly puckered, glossy leaves.

The Tribe of 'Dorothy Perkins'

'Dorothy Perkins' was the rose that made the ramblers famous. "She has thrown her wands of light pink beauty across ten thousand doorways in eastern America," wrote Dr J. Horace McFarland in 1936. Like so many ramblers, 'Dorothy Perkins' roots very easily from cuttings and was passed from garden to garden, so that in no time whole villages and neighbourhoods were decked out in this one rose. So popular indeed did it become that fashion-conscious garden owners soon moved away from it, declaring that 'Dorothy Perkins' was wearisome and unrefined and that there were many much better rambling roses whose qualities were eclipsed by the sheer volume of 'Dorothy Perkins' in other people's gardens.

It is ironic that this most successful of the seedlings of 'Turner's Crimson Rambler' should have been brought into this world with a false declaration of parentage. Jackson & Perkins described 'Dorothy Perkins' as a seedling of *Rosa wichurana* crossed by the pink Hybrid Perpetual 'Mme Gabrielle Luizet', but the similarity to 'Turner's Crimson Rambler' was noted immediately. There was a lively correspondence in many horticultural journals (especially in France) which pointed out that crosses between *R. wichurana* and Hybrid Perpetuals had produced very different roses with much larger flowers and concluded that the similarity of 'Dorothy Perkins' to 'Turner's Crimson Rambler' was more than a coincidence. In fact, very few seedlings of 'Turner's Crimson Rambler' or 'Dorothy Perkins' were bred from Hybrid Perpetuals or Hybrid Teas; genuine hybrids of such descent (for instance, 'Fragezeichen' or 'Johanna Röpke') have much larger flowers than any of the 'Dorothy Perkins' tribe. It is best to think of 'Dorothy Perkins' as the pink counterpart to 'Turner's Crimson Rambler'.

'Dorothy Perkins' [Jackson & Perkins, 1901]. The flowers are small (4.5–5.0 cm), double, and rosette shaped with crinkly petals that are bright medium pink, but slightly paler on the undersides and towards the centre of the flower. They also fade a little with age, with the individual flowers remaining on the plant for a long time. The flowers are moderately scented and carried in large, pendulous clusters of twenty to forty, open and airy at first but increasingly full and even congested as more flowers open. The leaves are small, glossy, and liable to mildew if grown against a wall, but the disease is less of a problem on open structures like fences. The plant grows to at least 5 m. This late-flowering rambler is spectacular in full flower and sometimes has a few flowers right through until winter. It was named after the young daughter of a director of Jackson & Perkins.

'Dorothy Perkins' threw up a large number of colour sports in the ten years or so after it was introduced. Best known was 'Lady Godiva', discovered by George Paul in 1907 and put out by him the following year. The flowers are pale blush pink with a deeper centre and exquisitely attractive. It was followed by 'Christian Curle' [Cocker & Sons, 1910] and 'Dorothy Dennison' [Dennison, 1909], which were so like 'Lady Godiva' that they were said to be practically identical with it. A dark pink or pale crimson sport of 'Dorothy Perkins', now extinct, was introduced as 'Elizabeth Ziegler' [Pierson, 1917]. Jan Böhm put out 'Makta Vlast' as a red-and-white striped version of 'Dorothy Perkins' in 1934, but the rose now grown under that name at Sangerhausen is a straight Wichurana Hybrid. A white form was introduced as 'White Dorothy' by Cant in 1908 (plate 76) and is identical to 'Dorothy Perkins' in everything except colour. It has a tendency to produce an occasional pink or partly pink flower, which sets off the rest of the clusters very attractively. 'White Dorothy' is also very similar to 'Mrs Littleton Dewhurst' [Pearson, 1911], which is actually a white sport not of 'Dorothy Perkins' but of 'Lady Gay'. 'Lady Gay' [Walsh, 1905] was from the beginning hopelessly confused with 'Dorothy Perkins'; more than one clone of each is still sold commercially.

Michael Walsh: 'Excelsa' and Others

Michael Walsh (1848–1922) was an Englishman, born near Chester, who emigrated to the United States when he was twenty and sought employment as a gardener in private service. He eventually settled in Woods Hole, Massachusetts, where he acquired land of his own, but his rose breeding was never a commercial undertaking. In the 1916 *American Rose Annual* he wrote: "Roses were my first love and I still cherish them and am happy in growing and experimenting with them."

All Walsh's climbers were introduced over a period of twenty years quite late on in his life, starting with 'Sweetheart' [1899] and ending with 'Nokomis' [1918]. I calculate that he introduced a total of forty ramblers, of which eighteen are extinct, although some may yet be found again. Two recent reintroductions are 'America' [1915] and 'Summer Joy' [1911], both of which were unavailable commercially for many years. Many of the others survive only at Sangerhausen in Germany.

G. A. Stevens (1933) of the American Rose Society dismissed Walsh's life work as "innumerable hardy climbers which produced small flowers in giant clusters." Yet the same society, more than twenty years earlier, had recognised Walsh's achievement by awarding him a gold medal for 'Mrs M. H. Walsh' (now extinct) and, in 1914, the Hubbard Gold Medal for 'Excelsa'. Walsh's roses were late flowering, vigorous, fairly healthy, profuse in their flower, with handsome, glossy foliage and, occasionally, more flowers in the autumn. And they were popular, especially in New England.

Walsh was always very vague about the parentage of his hybrids. Those that are given are rather far-fetched. I do not believe that 'Minnehaha' is bred from 'Paul Neyron' or that 'Lady Gay' came from *Rosa wichurana* × 'Bardou Job'. Many are said simply to be crosses between *R. wichurana* and 'Turner's Crimson Rambler'. My own belief is that, when they are subjected to genetic analysis, many will be found to be selfed seedlings of 'Turner's Crimson Rambler'.

'America' [Walsh, 1915]. Supposedly *Rosa wichurana* × 'Turner's Crimson Rambler'. This rose has small (3.0–3.5 cm), single, pale pink flowers which fade to white; they are borne in large clusters on a vigorous plant with dark green, glossy leaves.

'Arcadia' [Walsh, 1913]. Supposedly *Rosa wichurana* × 'Turner's Crimson Rambler'. This is a very late-flowering rambler with small clusters (five to fifteen flowers) of small flowers (3 cm) which open bright pale crimson and fade to a rather ordinary pink. They are very double, with their petals tightly packed into a rosette, and have little or no scent.

'Babette' syn. 'Babette Rambler' [Walsh, 1906]. This rose bears very dark scarlet or crimson flowers, paling to pink at the edges, rather late in the season. They are semi-double, scentless, small (4 cm), and carried in large clusters (typically ten to thirty flowers). It is very vigorous, climbing to 4–5 m, and has glossy leaves, but flowers only once. Still at Sangerhausen, it is also available from one nursery in Switzerland.

'Bonnie Belle' [Walsh, 1911]. The plant grown under this name at Sangerhausen and Westfalenpark in Dortmund is an exceptionally vigorous, very late-flowering rambler with the glossy leaves and fimbriated stipules of the 'Turner's Crimson Rambler' class. It has small flowers (5 cm) which are bright pink at the centre, paler at edges, and borne in clusters of ten to fifty. They are scentless and very full—sometimes with a button eye, a quilled centre, and slightly paler undersides, which give rise to nice contrasts. But some of the older descriptions insist that this rose is single.

'Carissima' [Walsh, 1904]. This is one of the most charming of Walsh's seedlings. It is late flowering, with long airy sprays and gleaming, dark green leaves. The flowers are small (4 cm), pale pink (slightly deeper towards the centre), and very full, but they open flat and neat, with lots of small petaloids and sometimes a button eye. They are lightly scented and come in large quantities in small to medium-sized clusters, typically of about eight flowers. The plant grows vigorously to about 5 m.

'Cinderella' [Walsh, 1909]. Of all the 'Turner's Crimson Rambler' tribe, this is probably the latest to flower. It more closely resembles a darker version of 'Dorothy Perkins', with small (4 cm), medium pink, double flowers with a mass of small petals in clusters of twenty to thirty. The plant has dark Wichurana leaves and grows vigorously to about 4 m. 'Cinderella' survives in a few European gardens.

'Coquina' [Walsh, 1909]. This very late-flowering descendant of 'Turner's Crimson Rambler' is definitely not one of Walsh's better introductions. The flowers are medium pink with a white centre, but fade and then go brown. The single, barely scented flowers are borne in large clusters on a very vigorous plant which has handsome glossy green leaves and quickly reaches 5 m.

'Debutante' [Walsh, 1901]. This is a very good rambler indeed, although I question its alleged parentage of *Rosa wichurana* × 'Baronne Adolphe de Rothschild'. The flowers are a beautiful clear rose pink when they open and fade to creamy pink with a hint of lilac in hot weather. They are profusely borne in long, small clusters so that the whole plant seems to cascade with flowers. The flowers are lightly scented and fully double. The outer petals fold back so that the full-blown flower forms an irregular ball of reflexed petals. They are produced midseason on a vigorous, slender plant which grows quickly to 5 m. The leaves are neat, dark and glossy—very Wichurana.

'Delight' [Walsh, 1904]. Delight is a misnomer. The single or nearly single flowers open a fairly dark pink, although not as rich as 'Hiawatha', and fade quite quickly. The large, long-stemmed clusters flower very late in the season. The plant grows vigorously to 5–6 m and has the usual small, glossy Wichurana foliage.

'Evangeline' [Walsh, 1906]. Allegedly *Rosa wichurana* × 'Turner's Crimson Rambler'. If dumb prettiness were all one sought, 'Evangeline' would be everyone's favourite rambler. It bears a myriad of simple, single flowers which are pink around the edges and white at the centre; they stay on for far too long, turn white, then brown, and eventually make the clusters look congested. The flowers are small (4.5 cm), scented, and have a distinctive notch which gives them their characteristic demeanour. The clusters are large and long-stemmed. 'Evangeline' is in every way a vigorous plant, growing to as much as 6–7 m and starting to flower at midseason. The hips are an attractive vermilion in autumn.

'Excelsa' syn. 'Red Dorothy Perkins' [Walsh, 1909]. Supposedly *Rosa wichurana* × 'Turner's Crimson Rambler'. This is Walsh's most famous rambler, introduced as an improved, healthier version of 'Turner's Crimson Rambler'. But 'Turner's Crimson Rambler' is a better colour (redder, less crimson) and does not turn blue in the sun. As for mildew, there is nothing to choose between them. 'Red Dorothy Perkins' is a fair description. The flowers are fairly double, bright glowing crimson with white streaks towards the centre, small (3 cm), and daintily held in large sprays of ten to thirty. It flowers late, but very freely, and is very hardy. The foliage is medium green, small, tough, and glossy, with prickly stems. It grows to about 5 m. A red-and-white striped sport was introduced as 'Harlequin' by Cant in 1935 and still grows at Sangerhausen. The pale pink sport 'Fernande Krier' was described in chapter 7.

'Hiawatha' [Walsh, 1904]. This seedling of 'Turner's Crimson Rambler' is probably the best known of its type—the old-fashioned, scentless, single-flowered, bright crimson-and-white, once-flowering rambler. It was very popular when first launched, and rightly so. The single flowers are small (4.5 cm) and cheerful, with a particular glow which comes from the yellow stamens and bold white circle at the centre, but this disappears when the anthers turn quickly to brown; the flowers too fade to pink. They are extrava-gantly carried, late in the season, in large clusters (fifteen to thirty-five at a time) on a very vigorous, hardy plant which grows to about 5 m. The foliage is the usual thick, glossy, dark green Wichurana type.

'Jessica' [Walsh, 1909]. 'Jessica' is an excellent rose, which should be better known. The flowers are medium sized (7–9 cm), very sweetly scented, and full of quilled petals; the blooms open pale pink (mother-of-pearl at the edges) and fade almost to white (plate 77). They hang down nicely, are well spaced, and come in succession over a long season with a few late flowers in autumn. They are carried singly or in small clusters (three to five flowers) in great profusion on a vigorous, prickly plant which grows to about 3–4 m with fairly typical, dark, shiny green leaves.

'Lady Gay' [Walsh, 1905]. Alas, this rose was so similar to 'Dorothy Perkins' that few could distinguish them and now it is uncertain which of the clones in cultivation is the real 'Lady Gay'. All agree that 'Lady Gay' is almost scentless, flowers late, and carries its flowers in large clusters. It was said to have been bred from *Rosa wichurana* × 'Bardou Job', a crimson China rose, sometimes classed among the early Hybrid Teas. But, from the start, *Rosen-Zeitung* (e.g., 1905, 11) maintained that 'Lady Gay' was a seedling of 'Turner's Crimson Rambler'.

'La Fiamma' [Walsh, 1909]. Supposedly *Rosa wichurana* × 'Turner's Crimson Rambler'. This rose is a red-and-white 'Hiawatha' look-alike. The old descriptions call it "flame" but it is a dull, light red which fades to pink. The small flowers (3 cm) come in medium-sized clusters (usually five to twenty flowers) on a vigorous, prickly plant which grows to about 4 m. It has small, glossy, bright green leaves.

'Minnehaha' [Walsh, 1904]. Supposedly *Rosa wichurana* × 'Paul Neyron'. This rose is always described by reference to 'Dorothy Perkins' but, the old authorities disagree about the differences. Some suggest 'Minnehaha' has thicker, sturdier stems and a more upright cluster of flowers. Everyone agrees that it is one of the best ramblers, makes a good standard, and flowers rather late in the season (plate 78). A sport named 'Shalimar' was introduced by Burrell in 1914; it has cream-coloured flowers with pink edges and still grows at Sangerhausen.

'Paradise' syn. 'Paradise Rambler' [Walsh, 1907]. It is the conformation of the petals which distinguishes this single-flowered, pink-and-white rambler; they are notched, wavy, quilled, and twisted in a particularly charming manner. The flowers are medium sized (6–7 cm), lightly scented, and carried in large clusters. Otherwise, 'Paradise' is an undistinguished rambler, flowering late but only once, and growing vigorously to about 5 m.

'Summer Joy' [Walsh, 1911]. I have not seen this cultivar, which was recently reintroduced by a New Hampshire nursery. Contemporary descriptions mention double flowers which open dark pink from white buds and a very vigorous plant.

'Sweetheart' [Walsh, 1899]. Supposedly *Rosa wichurana* × 'Bridesmaid'. This rose has typical small glossy Wichurana leaves, dense foliage and long, flexible growths. The flowers are small to medium sized (5–6 cm), medium pink with white flecks, paler towards the base and back of the petal with yellow anthers and pink or white petaloids in the centre. It is quite strongly scented, with ten to fifteen flowers in a cluster. The plant is hardy, middle to late flowering, and grows vigorously to 3–4 m.

'Troubadour' [Walsh, 1910]. The lightly double flowers have occasional white streaks, which emphasise their very handsome crimson colouring. They are scentless, small to medium sized (5–6 cm), and freely borne in open clusters of ten to twenty-five. The plant grows vigorously to 3–4 m.

'Wedding Bells' [Walsh, 1906]. This descendant of 'Turner's Crimson Rambler' is not one of Walsh's best ramblers. It is quite dainty, but undistinguished, and it holds onto its brown, dead flowers. The flowers are small (3 cm), very double, and open out flat and imbricated. They start deep pink and fade to silvery pink (the contrast is attractive when there are ten to twenty-five flowers in a cluster) and are scentless. The plant has bright green leaves and grows vigorously to 3 m.

Soupert & Notting

At the start of the twentieth century, Soupert & Notting of Luxemburg could claim to be the most renowned firm of rose growers in Europe. The company was founded in 1855 by Pierre Notting, who died in 1895, and his brother-in-law Jean Soupert, who died in 1910. It had a truly international clientele and published separate catalogues in German, English, French, and Italian. Its list of customers reads like a European social register. Soupert & Notting bred a few Tea-Noisettes in the 1880s and 1890s, but decided in the early 1900s that they should try to produce some new, hardy, floriferous ramblers like everyone else. All of their ramblers have lots of little flowers in big clusters and, with the possible exception of 'Hugo Maweroff', are fairly undistinguished.

'Bagatelle' [Soupert & Notting, 1908]. 'Turner's Crimson Rambler' × 'Mignonette'. This has attractive pinkish white, semi-double flowers in large, long-stemmed clusters. They are quite small (4 cm) but carried in great profusion. The plant has bright green leaves and grows vigorously to 3–4 m. The overall effect is slightly reminiscent of 'Blush Rambler' and 'Mrs F. W. Flight'.

'Bordeaux' [Soupert & Notting, 1907]. 'Turner's Crimson Rambler' × 'Blanche Rebatel'. The flowers are semi-double to double, about 3.5 cm across, with a light sweet scent. They are dark pink with a slight purplish tint, flecked with white towards the base and white undersides to the petals. The plant has the bright green leaves of many Multiflora Ramblers and rather glandular stems. It flowers only once, in medium-sized, rather erect clusters, but the blooms last for a long time.

'Hugo Maweroff' [Soupert & Notting, 1910]. 'Turner's Crimson Rambler' × 'Mrs W. H. Cutbush' (a Polyantha). The best of the Soupert & Notting ramblers gives an overall impression of cheerfulness. The semi-double flowers are pale crimson at first, with paler edges, a white centre, and paler backs to the petals. The flowers are lightly scented, 5 cm across, and freely carried in medium-sized clusters. It has large, pale green leaves and grows vigorously to 3–4 m.

'Laure Soupert' [Soupert & Notting, 1927]. 'Tausendschön' × 'George Elger' (a yellow Polyantha). I am not sure why this Multiflora Rambler was released so long after all the other Soupert & Notting ramblers—it was certainly outdated by 1927. The flowers are small (3 cm), double, creamy white and fade quickly to pure white; they die badly, keeping their dead petals even when they have turned to brown. The flowers have a strong musky scent and come in small to medium-sized clusters all through summer and autumn. The plant has small leaves and lots of them, but is not very vigorous, perhaps 2 m high.

'Stella' [Soupert & Notting, 1906]. 'Turner's Crimson Rambler' seedling. This commonplace Multiflora Rambler has small (3–4 cm), single, lightly scented flowers which are pale crimson with a white centre. They come in small clusters (five to ten flowers) on a fairly floriferous, vigorous, plant that climbs to 3–4 m and has lots of little hips in autumn.

Turbat

E. Turbat & Cie. of Olivet near Orléans was one of the largest European wholesalers of general nursery stock in the first part of the twentieth century. Rose breeding was only a very small part of its activities and limited to the production of new Polyantha roses and ramblers, most of them bred from 'Turner's Crimson Rambler' or its descendants. Some were developed for pot culture, including 'Marie Gouchault', which was widely distributed in the United States as a forcing rose. Turbat produced about 500,000 roses a year on their 40 ha, until the new U.S. quarantine laws, introduced to protect and encourage American growers, cut this to 150,000. Turbat introduced some thirty-five ramblers, of which rather more than usual have disappeared from cultivation. Of those which survive, nine have been preserved only at Sangerhausen. Turbat also introduced a number of roses bred by amateurs and semi-professionals, including Rémy Tanne from Rouen, who sent no fewer than twenty-six Wichurana seedlings to the Bagatelle trials in 1911–12.

'Ardon' [Turbat, 1925]. This cheerful climber grows only at Sangerhausen. The flowers are small to medium sized (5–6 cm), double, flat, bright crimson at first with flecks of white at the base of the petals, but fading much more than usual; the older flowers are no more than light pink. The flowers are borne in small, open sprays on a fairly vigorous, nearly thornless plant with glossy Wichurana leaves which grows to about 2.5–3.0 m.

'Beauté Orléanaise' [Turbat, 1919]. This is one of the prettiest and daintiest of ramblers. The flowers are only about 4 cm, but very neat, very double, and often nicely quartered. Although the buds are salmon red, the flowers open white, stay white, and look like miniature versions of the Damask rose 'Mme Zoëtmans' against small, dark, glossy leaves. They are almost scentless, but elegantly borne in long open sprays of five to fifteen flowers. The plant grows vigorously to 3–4 m.

'Bonfire' [Turbat, 1928]. 'Turner's Crimson Rambler' seedling. The small to medium-sized (4–5 cm), reddish crimson flowers form a perfect rosette with paler undersides to the petals, which make a very attractive contrast (plate 79). They are borne in medium-sized clusters on a very vigorous, strong-growing plant which will reach 5–6 m with dense, bright green Wichurana foliage.

'Clematis' [Turbat, 1924]. The flowers are very small (2 cm), scentless, very deep crimson, and shaped like the European *Clematis viticella*. They are carried in loose, pendant clusters of ten to twenty-five. The plant has small Wichurana leaves and grows to about 3 m.

'Daisy Brasileir' syn. 'Daisy Brazileir' [Turbat, 1917]. The flowers are small (3 cm), single, and a very vivid dark purplish red, with white at the base of the petals and some scent. The flowers glow intensely when they first open. They come in tight clusters of about thirty flowers, followed by orange red hips in autumn. The bush is sturdy, erect, prickly, and hardy and grows vigorously to 3–4 m. I consider this one of the best single-flowered red-and-white ramblers; I wish someone would reintroduce it to commerce from Sangerhausen.

'Fernand Rabier' [Turbat, 1918]. 'Delight' seedling. This is darker than 'Excelsa' and brighter than 'Turner's Crimson Rambler', with neat, small (3.0–3.5 cm), semi-double flowers of deep glowing red. The lightly scented flowers are carried in erect, long-stemmed clusters (good for cutting) of about twenty to thirty, on a hardy, vigorous plant which grows to 3–4 m.

'Fernand Tanne' [Tanne, introduced by Turbat, 1920]. The flowers of this attractive rose (very similar to 'Albéric Barbier' and 'François Foucard') have buff yellow centres when they open, then fade through buff pink to white. They are medium sized (7 cm), very full, roughly quartered, and tea scented. 'Fernand Tanne' flowers early, but holds its brown petals when it fades. The flowers come in clusters of five to twelve on a very vigorous plant with small glossy leaves. It grows to about 5 m and has a scattering of flowers later in the season.

'Gaston Lesieur' [Turbat, 1915]. This Wichurana Hybrid is one of the 'Excelsa' types and still grows at Sangerhausen. The bright red flowers are double, small to medium sized, and flat and appear rather late in the season in long airy clusters of ten to fifteen. The plant is very vigorous, with glossy leaves; it grows to 4–5 m.

'Ghislaine de Féligonde' [Turbat, 1916]. 'Goldfinch' seedling. This popular rose can also be grown as a large bush. The flowers open apricot with a yellow base from orange buds, then fade to peach, pink, and white (plate 80). Colour and intensity vary considerably from year to year. It flowers heavily over a long period and repeats in autumn, when the flowers are pinker. The well-scented flowers are held in good, long, upright clusters of about ten. The plant has few prickles, but often carries a mass of bristly crimson prickles on the flowering shoots and stems. 'Ghislaine de Féligonde' is hardier than many Multi-floras, with handsome leaves. It grows to about 4 m as a climber and half that as a shrub. Turbat was surprised when this rose won an award at the Bagatelle trials in 1916. However, the award could not be made final until the variety was named. At that moment Turbat, having heard the story of a heroic woman who had rescued her wounded husband from between the battle lines, called his rose 'Ghislaine de Féligonde' (Nicolas 1930).

'Hélène Granger' [Granger, introduced by Turbat, 1910]. 'Tea Rambler' × 'Aglaia'. This hybrid was introduced as an unfading yellow rose with coppery centres and pink edges. In fact, it fades so quickly to cream and white that the overall impression is of mother-of-pearl or white. The flowers are small (4.0–4.5 cm), double, lightly scented, and attractively carried in airy open clusters of ten to fifteen. The plant has large, bright green leaves and grows vigorously to about 4 m.

'La Fraîcheur' syn. 'Fraîcheur' [Turbat, 1921]. Best summed up as a 'Dorothy Perkins' type and very late-flowering, this is a very attractive climber which flowers most abundantly but only once. The flowers are quite a dark pink, with paler edges, in cool weather, but softer from the start when it is hot. They are fairly small (4 cm), double, and lightly (but sweetly) scented. The clusters are long and upright with fifteen to twenty flowers. The plant is vigorous, with reddish wood and little dark green leaves, and grows to 4–5 m.

'Louis Sauvage' [Turbat, 1914]. Another unsuccessful contender for the title of *the* dark red rambler, 'Louis Sauvage' has small (3 cm) crimson flowers, which are fairly full, flat, and scentless. There are five to fifteen in an upright cluster, whose open flowers hang down under their weight. The plant has rather a lot of prickles with medium green leaves and grows vigorously to 3–4 m.

'Marie Gouchault' [Turbat, 1927]. Turbat introduced this as a good forcing rose because it is comparatively early flowering and less prone to mildew than many of its cousins. The flowers are small (4.5 cm), scentless, but last well, and most abundantly produced. They are a good dark pink, with a white base. The blooms are much paler on the back of the petals and this gives rise to some attractive contrasts of colour and shadow within the very full flowers. The flowers come in fairly long, upright clusters of about twenty and occasionally repeat in autumn. The plant has lovely lush, dense foliage; the leaves are medium green, with fimbriated stipules, but with the glossiness of *Rosa wichurana*. It is nearly thornless and grows to 3–4 m.

'Marie-Jeanne' [Turbat, 1913]. This is a shrubby, remontant climber whose flowers open a very attractive pearly pink and fade to white. They are small (4 cm), round, and rather full, with a musky scent. They come in clusters of about twenty on a vigorous, thornless bush which grows to 3 m as a climber or 2 m as a loose shrub. The foliage is dense, with bright green Multiflora-type leaves.

'Papa Gouchault' [Turbat, 1922]. 'Rubin' seedling. Although early flowering and bred for forcing, this rose is no improvement on 'Turner's Crimson Rambler' as a garden plant. The flowers are small (3 cm), scentless, bright crimson, very double, and well held in large clusters of up to thirty. Grown under glass the flowers are more scarlet. The long-stemmed clusters are good for cutting. The plant has bright green leaves, few prickles, and grows vigorously, although stiffly, to about 4 m.

'Papa Rouillard' [Turbat, 1923]. Allegedly bred from 'Léontine Gervais'. This late-flowering rambler has small (3–4 cm), very double flowers with crimped petals and an attractive shape. They are pale crimson outside and deep pink inside and they come in long panicles (about fifteen flowers) with distinctly glandular pedicels. The plant is almost thornless. It has rich green glossy leaves and grows vigorously to 3–4 m. 'Papa Rouillard' flowers exuberantly, but only once.

'Paul Noël' [Tanne, introduced by Turbat, 1913]. *Rosa wichurana* × 'Mme Bartélémy Levet' or (more probably) *R. wichurana* × 'Monsieur Tillier'. The flowers are medium sized (6 cm), salmon pink, but fade to medium pink; they are very full of neatly imbricated quill-shaped petals splaying out from a button-shaped eye (plate 81). They come early, in small clusters (typically of four to eight flowers) and repeat intermittently. The scent is moderate. The leaves are small, tough, and quite dark (very typical of a Wichurana Rambler), and the plant grows loosely to about 4 m. 'Paul Noël' is popular as a high-grafted standard because of its weeping habit.

'Printemps Fleuri' [Turbat, 1922]. 'Étoile Luisante' seedling. This is another 'Excelsa' look-alike, with small to medium-sized (3 cm), dark crimson purple, double flowers in clusters of five to fifteen, which fade to pale crimson. Occasionally the colour is more purple and fades to magenta or pink. Turbat thought the colour and early flowering were enough to distinguish it, but it is too similar to many other ramblers with hordes of dark scentless flowers. The plant is vigorous and grows to about 3.5 m.

'Solarium' [Turbat, 1925]. This rambler has bright vermilion red flowers, an unusual colour among Wichuranas, with the typical white centre and yellow stamens of a single-flowered cultivar. The flowers are medium sized (6 cm) and come in clusters of about fifteen. The plant grows vigorously to about 4 m. It survives only at Sangerhausen and, indirectly, through the genes it passed on to its famous offspring 'Raubritter' [Kordes, 1936].

'Source d'Or' [Turbat, 1912]. This is one of Turbat's best roses. It opens deep yellow, sometimes golden, sometimes more apricot, and is very attractive because the flower is full and neat, with a button eye. It then fades quickly through buff, cream, and white, keeping a contrast between the pale edges and the darker centre. The medium-sized (5–6 cm) flowers come early in small clusters (three to eight) and hang down attractively. They have a strong musky scent. The plant grows strongly to about 3–4 m with bright, glossy leaves and is said to be among the hardiest of yellow Wichuranas.

Nonin in the 1910s and 1920s

A. Nonin et fils are perhaps best remembered for the Polyantha rose 'Joseph Guy', known in the United States as 'Lafayette'. The company introduced 'Joseph Guy' in 1919 and gave our ancestors a foretaste of the Floribundas. The climbing form is one of the most floriferous and spectacular of all climbers when it first flowers. Auguste Nonin (1856–1936) was a great breeder of popular garden plants who introduced new carnations, dahlias, and chrysanthemums as well as roses. He exhibited his novelties widely and published a catalogue which was for many years considered the most comprehensive in France. Breeding Polyanthas was his main interest, and many of the climbers listed here were by-products of that pursuit. Most of the Nonin ramblers have 'Turner's Crimson Rambler' or 'Dorothy Perkins' in their ancestry, but the published pedigrees are perhaps rather more open to challenge than usual.

'Caroubier' [Nonin, 1912]. Allegedly 'Hiawatha' × *Rosa multiflora*. This rose is like a watered-down version of 'Hiawatha' with single or lightly semi-double flowers, which have a pale crimson edge and a white centre. However, the colour fades quickly to pink, and the overall impression is of a perfectly ordinary pink Multiflora Rambler. It has a musky scent and somewhat incurved petals, but it does produce flowers on and off right through to the autumn.

'Châtillon Rambler' [Nonin, 1913]. 'Dorothy Perkins' × 'Turner's Crimson Rambler'. This was introduced as an earlier-flowering substitute for 'Dorothy Perkins' with better colour and larger clusters, but it soon proved the latest of all to flower. The flowers are small (3 cm), semi-double, cupped, pale pink, and fairly scentless. The leaves mildew, but the plant grows very vigorously to about 6 m.

'Emile Nérini' [Nonin, 1911]. 'Turner's Crimson Rambler' × 'Dorothy Perkins'. Wilhelm Kordes (1928) described this as "an undeservedly neglected beauty." It is very vigorous, grows to about 5 m, and has few prickles and foliage which is large and more disease-free than many (plate 82). The large (5 cm) flowers come in rather rounded clusters. They are lightly double, with three or four rows of petals and attractive golden stamens. Their colour is a glowing cherry pink, with only the slightest fading, and a white patch towards the base of the petals.

'Île de France' syn. 'Adoration' [Nonin, 1922]. Open-pollinated seedling of 'American Pillar'. This rose was introduced as a semi-double form of 'American Pillar'; it is not unlike 'Général Tétard' [Pajotin-Chédane, 1918], but not as good. The flowers are rather variable in colour. At their best a vivid, dark cerise, they often open dull dark pink, although the conspicuous white patch at the centre and the yellow stamens do provide a lively contrast. It also has large white flecks which cut right through from the base to the edge of the petal. The flowers are small (4–5 cm), musk scented, and carried in medium or large clusters (twenty to forty). The foliage is large, healthy, dark, and tough. The plant has many prickles and climbs to 4–5 m.

'Luciole' [Nonin, 1923]. 'Hiawatha' seedling. I have not seen this rose, although it was until recently available from several European nurseries. It is said to be a bright red-and-white single-flowered Wichurana, much like 'Hiawatha', with many small flowers in large clusters.

'Madeleine Lemaire' [Nonin, 1917]. 'Mrs F. W. Flight' seedling. This is not a very distinguished rose. The scentless flowers are small to medium sized (5–6 cm), little more than single, deep pink with a white centre, and carried in dense congested clusters of five to twenty. The plant grows lushly and vigorously to 4–5 m and is very hardy.

'Mme Auguste Nonin' [Nonin, 1912]. 'Dorothy Perkins' × 'Blush Rambler'. This is one of Nonin's best roses, closer to 'Blush Rambler' than 'Dorothy Perkins', with very attractive pale pink flowers, which have a white centre and hold their colour well. They are about 4.5 cm across, more than semi-double, and carried in fairly large clusters of twenty to thirty. The blooms are nicely set off by shiny medium green leaves. They also have a light musky scent. The plant is vigorous, prickly, and late flowering; it grows to 5–6 m.

'Mme Jenny' [Nonin, 1925]. 'Dorothy Perkins' seedling. The flowers are small (4 cm), cupped, coral pink at first, and fade to silvery pink. They are fully double, lightly but sweetly scented, and come in clusters of five to fifteen. The growth is rather stiff and upright, with dark green foliage. It flowers very late, but freely, and grows very vigorously to 3–4 m.

'Normandie' [Nonin, 1929]. This is yet another late-blooming Wichurana of the 'Dorothy Perkins' line with medium-sized clusters of small flowers (4 cm) which open salmon pink and fade to pale pink. The flowers are double, scentless, and borne in clusters of ten to twenty on a vigorous plant which grows to about 3–4 m.

'Petit Louis' [Nonin, 1912]. 'Dorothy Perkins' seedling. Nonin's son Henri considered this one of his father's best hybrids (*Rosenjahrbuch des Vereins Deutscher Rosenfreunde* 1963, 208). The flowers open quite a dark pink and fade to a pale shade with traces of white. They are very double, small (3.5 cm), lightly scented, late flowering, and carried in medium-sized clusters. The plant grows densely, with small, neat foliage, and has a tendency to mildew.

'Petit René' [Nonin, 1925]. This rose looks like a seedling of 'Turner's Crimson Rambler' or 'Excelsa'; the small (3.5 cm), very full, lightly scented, dark crimson flowers are typical of the offspring of both. The petals are rather reflexed and the flowers come in open sprays of five to thirty. It flowers only once, starting late and continuing for a long period. The plant is vigorous and grows to 3–4 m.

Praskač in the 1910s and 1920s

We have already encountered the Praskač Nursery: Franz Praskač bred the blue rose 'Donau'. He was the most eminent central European nurseryman of his day, and the firm he founded at Tulln, near Vienna, is still the market leader in Austria today. He introduced only a handful of roses, but two of them, 'Gruß an Freundorf' and 'Regierungsrat Rottenberger', are very good indeed. All are exceptionally hardy and deserve to be more widely grown outside the German-speaking areas of central Europe.

'Exquisite' [Praskač, 1926]. 'Dorothy Perkins' × 'Rubin'. The tiny (2–3 cm) pearly pink flowers often do not open properly. When they do, they have neatly imbricated petals around fully double flowers, well set off by red stalks and red sepals. They come in large clusters on a fairly vigorous plant which grows to 3–4 m.

'Gruß an Freundorf' [Praskač, 1913]. *Rosa wichurana* 'Rubra' × 'Turner's Crimson Rambler'. This good dark red rambler has small to medium-sized (4–5 cm), rather puckered, semi-double flowers which are deep crimson with white flashes and stripes running right the length of their petals. Bright yellow stamens and a strong scent are also attractive features. The colour darkens as it ages, eventually assuming a maroon black intensity. The flowers are freely carried in long panicles set off by small, glossy leaves. The prickly plant grows vigorously to 3–4 m and is notably late flowering. Tests at Weihenstefan near Munich confirm it as one of the hardiest of ramblers.

'Perle vom Wienerwald' [Praskač, 1913]. 'Helene' × 'Turner's Crimson Rambler'. This is a very attractive Multiflora Rambler, with masses of small (4–5 cm), semi-double, soft pink flowers, paler towards the edges, in medium to large clusters (twenty to thirty flowers). The leaves are bright medium green and the nearly thornless plant grows vigorously to 3–4 m.

'Regierungsrat Rottenberger' [Praskač, 1926]. 'Fragezeichen' × 'Tausendschön'. "Under this awful name may lie hidden a beautiful rose but the world will never know it" wrote Steve Stevens in 1933. The truth is that 'Regierungsrat Rottenberger' is a Multiflora Rambler of supreme elegance and beauty. The flowers are 4–5 cm in size and open out flat to reveal that rarest of qualities among roses, a perfectly circular outline. Their colour is a rich medium pink which fades to pale pink towards the edges, but the very edge of the petals is finely delineated by darker pigmentation. The backs of the petals are slightly darker, too. The flowers come in large clusters of twenty to thirty and have a strong musky scent. The plant has lush green leaves and grows very vigorously to 3–4 m.

Miscelleanous Descendants of 'Turner's Crimson Rambler'

Many nurserymen tried their hand at raising seedlings of 'Turner's Crimson Rambler' and 'Dorothy Perkins'. So popular were such roses when they first came out that few could resist the opportunity to introduce at least one or two seedlings. Many of those introductions were worthless. The breeders who crossed 'Turner's Crimson Rambler' or 'Dorothy Perkins' with Hybrid Teas began to make progress towards the large-flowered, repeat-flowering modern climbing roses that we take for granted. 'Fragezeichen' and 'Johanna Röpke', for example, represent a substantial improvement on the puerile prettiness of the 'Dorothy Perkins' tribe. By 1930, a number of breeders were developing climbing roses to match the early Floribunda roses which were then emerging from crosses between the Polyanthas (closely related to the ramblers) and the Hybrid Teas. Of necessity, the following are rather a mixed batch, but they include a number of first-rate roses. I would never choose to be without 'Mrs F. W. Flight', 'Fragezeichen', and 'Johanna Röpke' in my own garden.

'Aristide Briand' [Penny, 1928]. 'Yseult Guillot' seedling. The attractive, very double, flowers open pale crimson, but fade through pink to dull white, always paler on the undersides. They are abundantly borne in clusters of eight to fifteen on a vigorous and very hardy plant which grows to about 3 m. It produces some later flowers after the first show.

'Bocca Negra' [Dubreuil, 1910]. The lilac pink flowers vary in size (3.5–5.0 cm) and are very neatly semi-double, opening sometimes crimson, with a white patch at the base of the petals. They come in clusters of five to twenty and have a pronounced musky scent. The plant is extremely vigorous, with beautiful dark green leaves.

'Bouquet Rose' [Theunis, 1912]. 'Turner's Crimson Rambler' × 'Ernst Grandpierre'. The small flowers (3–4 cm) open pink and double, like 'Dorothy Perkins', and fade to white. They have a musky scent and are borne in medium-sized clusters of ten to twenty flowers. This is a dull rose.

'Carolina Budde' [Leenders, 1913]. 'Turner's Crimson Rambler' × 'Léonie Lamesch'. The flowers are scentless, medium sized (about 6 cm), fully double, and open a good rich crimson but fade to a bluish red. The leaves have inherited the shiny sheen of 'Turner's Crimson Rambler', but the flowers suggest a Bourbon or Hybrid Perpetual pollen parent rather than 'Léonie Lamesch'.

'České Praci čest' [Večeřa, c. 1970]. This is a 'Turner's Crimson Rambler' type of rambler: deep pink, late flowering, very floriferous, and very vigorous with noticeably large prickles. It must have seemed very old-fashioned when it was first introduced. The name means "Honour to Czech Labour" and, incredibly, was a common greeting in communist years.

'Coronation' [Turner, 1911]. This is rather a scruffy small-flowered rambler of the 'Dorothy Perkins' type, with semi-double, bright pale crimson flowers, spattered and flaked with white flashes. It is a strong, late-flowering plant and very hardy.

'Crimson Shower' [Norman, introduced by Harkness, 1951]. This rose was briefly popular in England, largely because Albert Norman bred two excellent bush roses, 'Ena Harkness' and 'Frensham'. The flowers are small (3 cm), reddish crimson (slightly paler on the backs of the petals), scentless, semi-double, and abundantly carried in attractive, loose, pendulous clusters. It flowers very late and grows vigorously to about 3–4 m. The foliage is small, dark, and glossy.

'Dorcas' [English, 1922]. The flowers are small (3 cm), medium pink with a hint of coral, lightly double, late flowering, and borne in long clusters of twenty to fifty (plate 83). The plant grows moderately vigorously to about 3 m. The Wichurana leaves are small and not too glossy. English introduced a sport with variegated leaves called 'Achievement' in 1925. Because it scorches in the wind, it fares better under glass.

'Dr Reymond' [Mermet, 1907]. Alleged seedling of 'Turner's Crimson Rambler'. This rose is a white Multiflora, very early flowering, vigorous, and prickly. All the old accounts describe the flowers as "large" with a hint of green in their colouring; on the contrary, they are small (no larger than 3 cm in diameter) and pure white. They are fairly double and borne in upright, pyramidal clusters of five to twenty flowers. The plant is hardy and vigorous, growing to 4 m.

'Ethel' [Turner, 1912]. Open-pollinated 'Dorothy Perkins' seedling. This rose produces fairly large clusters (twenty to forty flowers) of medium pink (fading to light pink), semi-double flowers late in the season. The petals are slightly crinkled and incurved, with deeper pink patches on their upper sides and paler undersides. The flowers have a slightly sweet musky scent, glossy leaves, and a long flowering period. The plant is vigorous, and grows to about 5 m. In parts of Europe 'Princess Marie' and 'Belvedere' are mistakenly distributed as this cultivar.

'Flower of Fairfield' syn. 'Immerblühende Turner's Crimson Rambler' [Ludorf, 1908]. Although introduced as an ever-blooming version of 'Turner's Crimson Rambler', only a few flowers appear later, but 'Flower of Fairfield' makes a good show in midseason (plate 84). The flowers are vivid crimson, small (2.5–3.0 cm), fairly double, scentless, and come on a moderately vigorous plant with bright green leaves which grows to about 3 m.

'Fragezeichen' [Böttner, 1910]. 'Dorothy Perkins' × 'Marie Baumann'. This is a truly wonderful rose, with rather a modern look (plate 85). From the start, its large flowers attracted much comment (Rudolf Geschwind's niece described them as "pink coffee-saucers") and the foliage too was completely different from 'Dorothy Perkins'. The flowers are deep pink with paler shadings, medium sized (8 cm), semi-double to double, scentless, and carried in clusters of five to ten over a long flowering period. The plant is vigorous, hardy, with large glossy leaves (occasionally susceptible to mildew and black-spot) and grows to 4–5 m.

'Frau Lina Straßheim' [Straßheim, 1906]. 'Turner's Crimson Rambler' seedling. This very attractive rose has masses of small (3.5 cm), semi-double flowers in midseason. They are salmon pink at first and eventually fade to a somewhat wishy-washy pink; the petal-edges are always paler but the overall impression is bright rose pink. The dark pedicels and sepals contrast attractively with the flowers. They are borne in clusters of five to fifteen flowers. The plant is prickly, hardy, and grows vigorously to 3–4 m.

'Grevinde Sylvia Knuth' [Poulsen, 1913]. This rare survivor of Poulsen's earliest rose-breeding days has small (3 cm), white, double flowers with yellow centres which fade quickly to cream and white. They come in small clusters, typically eight to ten flowers. The plant is fairly compact, with glossy leaves that show the influence of *Rosa wichurana* and narrow leaflets.

'Großherzogin Eléonore von Hessen' [Straßheim, 1906]. This is not as good as 'Frau Lina Straßheim'. It has small (3.0–3.5 cm), scentless, semi-double flowers in erect clusters of five to fifteen. They are deep reddish purple fading to crimson, with a few white flecks. The leaves are rich and green, of the Multiflora type, and the plant grows vigorously to 3–4 m.

'Hiawatha Remontant' syn. 'Hiawatha Recurrent' [Sauvageot, 1931]. 'Hiawatha' × 'Mme Norbert Levavasseur'. This rose is superficially very like 'Hiawatha', with small (3.5 cm), single, bright crimson, white-eyed flowers in round, medium-sized clusters and small glossy leaves. It is, however, genuinely repeat flowering and produces a good quantity of flowers in autumn. The bush is less vigorous than its parents (growing to 3 m) and the flowers have a slight musky scent.

'Jean Girin' [Girin, 1910]. This cultivar has small (3.5–4.0 cm), scentless, bright pink flowers (which fade to pale pink) borne in long, loose, pendulous clusters of ten to twenty. The flowers are very double indeed and particularly gracefully spaced in their long sprays. It is said to produce a few flowers in autumn and is very vigorous.

'Johanna Röpke' [Tantau, 1931]. 'Dorothy Perkins' × 'Ophelia'. This is a textbook example of how to produce a beautiful and novel type of rose by crossing the best of two very distinct races. 'Johanna Röpke' resembles a modern Floribunda is some ways, and yet it is a rose of style and delicacy. Its semi-double flowers open medium pink, show their centres, and fade slightly. They are medium sized (7–9 cm, occasionally larger) and sweetly scented. The blooms are gracefully carried in small clusters (three to eight) on short laterals which break the whole way along the long, arching, and completely thorn-less stems. 'Johanna Röpke' grows fairly quickly to 3–4 m, but is occasionally susceptible to blackspot.

'Le Mexique' [Schwartz, 1912]. 'Dorothy Perkins' × 'Marie Pavie'. Most of the old descriptions say that the flowers of 'Le Mexique' are pale pink, but the plants grown at Sangerhausen under this name open bright pale crimson and fade first to dark pink and then to pale pink. They have paler undersides at all times.

'Lyon Rambler' [Dubreuil, 1909]. 'Turner's Crimson Rambler' seedling. This splen-did rose is an exceptionally vigorous plant, reaching 7–8 m. The dark pink flowers often have broad white flecks in them and are very abundantly carried in particularly large, long panicles of up to forty, late in the season (plate 88). They contrast nicely with the beauti-ful, healthy, glossy, slightly crinkly, dark green foliage.

'Malva Rambler' [Puyravaud, 1908]. This cultivar has small (3 cm), semi-double, lightly scented flowers which open medium pink and fade to pale mauve pink. It is a vigorous plant, which reaches 3–4 m and flowers in midseason.

'Marietta Silva Taroucová' [Tarouca, 1925]. 'Colibri' × 'Turner's Crimson Rambler' (or vice versa). 'Marietta Silva Taroucová' was introduced by Zeman, the head gardener at the Tarouca Castle of Průhonice, near Prague; he described the rose as "glowing dark pink, with darker stripes, large, three-quarters full, and shell shaped." It has nearly single flowers which open deep pink with a white centre and golden stamens and petals which tend to crinkle and reflex unevenly. However, the flowers soon change to an unattractive shade of muddy pink, and eventually to white, before turning dirty brown. The flowers seem never to drop, and the clusters get ever more congested as the season progresses. In short, its early promise is lost in ugly old age. The very lightly scented flowers come in midseason in small clusters (five to twenty) carried abundantly on a very hardy plant which grows to about 3 m. The bright green leaves are susceptible to mildew.

'Mary Hicks' [Hicks, 1927]. This rose was introduced as an improved 'Excelsa'; the market, however, did not agree. The flowers are small (3.0–3.5 cm), semi-double, and bright pale crimson. They have a light scent. The foliage is a good, bright green, but subject to mildew. The plant grows fairly vigorously to 3–4 m.

'Merveille de la Brie'. The provenance of this vigorous rambler is unknown. It produces small (3–4 cm), semi-double flowers in loose, pendulous, medium-sized clusters. The flowers are bright crimson with a small white patch towards the centre, numerous conspicuous white flecks, and dark yellow stamens when they first open. It grows very vigorously to at least 5 m.

'Mme François Royet' [Royet, 1914]. 'Turner's Crimson Rambler' × 'Général Jacqueminot'. It is a pity that more hybrids were not bred between members of the 'Turner's Crimson Rambler' tribe and Hybrid Perpetuals or Hybrid Teas. The flowers of 'Mme François Royet' are medium sized (6–7 cm), cupped, crimson (bright at first, dull later), and rather too tightly held in small clusters. They have a distinctive scent and equally distinctive deeply toothed leaflets. The foliage is broad, large, and dense with very prickly stems. The whole plant is somewhat susceptible to mildew.

'Mrs F. W. Flight' [Flight, introduced by Cutbush, 1906]. 'Turner's Crimson Rambler' × 'The Garland'. This is an immensely vigorous rambler, which just stops short of coarseness (plate 87). The flowers are semi-double and quite small (4.5 cm); they open dark pink and fade to pale pink. However, the rose is best enjoyed from a distance for its overall effect, which is of pure radiant pink. The flowers are carried in large, round clusters of thirty to fifty and in very great quantities so that, when it is in full bloom, there is no rose so exuberantly floriferous. 'Mrs F. W. Flight' has pale green, lush Multiflora foliage and grows to 4–5 m. A pure white sport was introduced by Rochford in 1916 as 'White Flight' (and later by Koster in 1923; plate 86). It has creamy pink buds and is one of the most arresting sights in a rose garden when in full flower. Its flowers turn rather a greenish grey when they fade. A twig or two occasionally reverts to the pink 'Mrs F. W. Flight', and the plant looks all the better for the contrast. 'White Flight' circulates in parts of Europe under the erroneous name of 'Astra Desmond'.

'Newport Fairy' syn. 'Newport Rambler' [Gardner, 1908]. This putative hybrid between *Rosa wichurana* and 'Turner's Crimson Rambler' is a very dull rose indeed. It has small (3 cm), single, pink-and-white flowers in large clusters of fifteen to twenty-five. They open dark pink and fade to pale pink. There is nothing about the flowers, leaves (ordinary, medium green, glossy), or habit (fairly vigorous, to 5 m) to merit its popularity among U.S. nurserymen today.

'Prinzessin Ludwig von Bayern' [Brög, 1911]. 'Turner's Crimson Rambler' seedling. This rose is another worthless introduction. The flowers are small (3.5 cm), bright pink (with paler undersides), and scentless. They appear late in the season in clusters of ten to twenty. The leaves are pale green and rather crinkly. The plant grows to about 3 m.

'Robinette' [Moore, 1943]. 'Hiawatha' × self. I have not seen this vigorous, once-flowering rambler, which Ralph Moore bred early in his career, but it is said to have small, single, red-and-white flowers in large clusters and, apart from having a strong scent, to be fairly similar to 'Hiawatha'.

'Selandia' [Poulsen, 1913]. 'Mme Norbert Levavasseur' × 'Dorothy Perkins'. This attractive 'Dorothy Perkins' type of rambler has rich pink flowers fading to rose pink, livened by paler undersides (plate 89). They are about 4 cm across and are borne on long panicles, typically of twenty to forty flowers. The glossy leaves have fimbriated stipules, and the plant grows to about 3 m.

'Souvenir de l'Exposition de Bordeaux' [Puyravaud, 1905]. Allegedly 'Turner's Crimson Rambler' × 'Simon de St Jean'. This has medium-sized (5–6 cm), pale pink, semi-double flowers in small, loose clusters. The blooms are really only shell pink, with slightly darker patches on the upper sides of the petals and a paler centre. The plant is vigorous and extremely floriferous, but does not repeat. It grows to about 4–5 m and may show a tendency to mildew and blackspot later in the year.

'Souvenir de Paul Raudnitz' [Cochet-Cochet, 1909]. This is a typical seedling of the 'Turner's Crimson Rambler' type, except for its colour, which is mother-of-pearl, fading to white. The flowers are small (3–4 cm), neatly double, often imbricated, and borne in loose clusters of ten to twenty. The plant is quite bushy and twiggy and has a few flowers in the autumn, but it does not start its main flowering until late into the season. It grows to about 3 m.

The Hetzel Renaissance

When Karl Hetzel began to hybridise roses in the mid-1950s, he lived in a small apartment in Stuttgart. He grew all his mother plants in window-boxes. Every day he or his wife would move them from one side of the apartment to the other, and back again, so that the plants received as much sunlight as possible. Thirty years later, back in his home village of Oberderdingen, between Heilbronn and Bruchsal in Baden, he rented a 0.8-ha nursery with two small glasshouses. His first aim had been to breed garden roses that were mildew-free and thornless: 'Karl Höchst' is his best-known thornless Floribunda and 'Kronprinzessin Viktoria' his most widely grown Hybrid Tea. But Hetzel also pondered the 'Dorothy Perkins' roses, whose tendency to mildew he regretted. By crossing these old once-flowering ramblers and other roses (probably Polyanthas), he was able to develop several repeat-flowering ramblers of the 'Dorothy Perkins' and 'Excelsa' type. These have been introduced as 'Super Dorothy', 'Super Excelsa', 'Super Fairy', and 'Hermann Schmidt'. They are less vigorous than the original ramblers, but very hardy, and their lax habit renders them particularly suitable as weeping standards.

'Heinfels' syn. 'Super Sparkle' [Hetzel, 1994]. The flowers of this repeat-flowering rambler are cherry scarlet, double, almost scentless, quite small (4–5 cm), and carried in large clusters of up to forty. They come repeatedly and are accompanied by handsome, dark green, semi-glossy foliage. The plant is not as lax as most of Hetzel's ramblers, but grows to about 3 m.

'Hermann Schmidt' [Hetzel, 1986]. This rose is crimson or cherry red, with a white centre, and semi-double, not unlike a fuller form of 'American Pillar'. The flowers are small (4–5 cm) and come in clusters of twenty to forty. They are very strongly and sweetly scented. The plant grows to about 3 m and repeats well. I consider it a better rose than 'Super Excelsa'.

'Strombergzauber' syn. 'Super Elfin' [Hetzel, 1996]. This rose is among those modern climbers which closely resemble Climbing Floribundas. The flowers are orange scarlet, 6 cm in diameter, and lightly double (plate 90). They come in medium-sized clusters which are rather congested and have little scent. The leaves are glossy and medium green, and the plant has thicker wood than most climbers. It grows to about 3 m, but is not one of Hetzel's best hybrids.

'Super Dorothy' [Hetzel, 1986]. 'Super Dorothy' is darker than 'Dorothy Perkins' but a good medium to deep pink, with flowers in characteristic long sprays (plate 91). They are 4–5 cm and open deep pink, although the parts which are directly exposed to sunlight bleach in the sun and turn almost white. The backs of the petals are always paler. The flowers are almost scentless and come in large clusters, typically of twenty to sixty. The leaves are small and glossy, and the plant has some prickles. It grows to 2.5–3.0 m. I consider it the best of Hetzel's rambler hybrids.

'Super Excelsa' [Hetzel, 1986]. 'Super Excelsa' produces very large clusters of carmine crimson flowers with white stripes (plate 92). The petals fade to a more purple colour as they age and have paler undersides. The flowers are about 3.5 cm across, fully double, and are said to be slightly fragrant. The plant has only average vigour, but produces its flowers repeatedly all through summer and autumn. It grows to 2.5–3.0 m.

'Super Fairy' [Hetzel, 1992]. The most vigorous, by far, of Hetzel's hybrids, 'Super Fairy' will grow to 4–5 m. The flowers are a delicate, soft pink, fully double, small (3.0–3.5 cm), only lightly scented, and carried in long clusters like 'The Fairy', with up to thirty in a spray. It repeats consistently until winter. The leaves are medium green, glossy, and disease resistant.

CHAPTER 9

The Wichurana Hybrids

Rosa wichurana

The Wichurana Ramblers are the world's most popular climbing roses. All are descended from a trailing evergreen rose first collected by Max Ernst Wichura in 1859. It is one of the ironies of horticultural nomenclature that the man after whom these famous ramblers are named had no interest in roses. Wichura was a government lawyer attached to the Prussian diplomatic mission to China and Japan in 1859–60. (He died of carbon monoxide poisoning in 1866.) During this mission, Wichura collected plants on behalf of the Berlin Botanic Garden. Among the herbarium specimens he brought back was the type specimen of what was later to be called *Rosa wichurana* by the great Belgian rose taxonomist, François Crépin.

Crépin first described *Rosa wichurana* in 1886; it was a split from *R. luciae*, which Crépin himself had described and named in 1871. This has led to much subsequent confusion. Because *R. luciae* would have precedence over *R. wichurana*, some authors have insisted that the former species was the progenitor of the Wichurana Ramblers, which should be renamed in consequence. However, Crépin himself was adamant that typical *R. luciae* had not been introduced into Europe when the earliest Wichurana Hybrids were being bred. Moreover, the Wichurana Ramblers have been known under that name (or, incorrectly, as "Wichuraiana" Ramblers) for more than a century now.

> *Rosa wichurana* Crépin. *Rosa luciae* Crépin (1871), in part, not Crépin (1886); *R. luciae* var. *wichuraiana* (Crépin) Koidz. A shrub with stems that are usually procumbent and trailing, rising only 25 cm above the ground, but sending out new growths as much as 4 m long in a season. It is naturally evergreen, and the glabrous, unbranched shoots are armed at irregular intervals with occasional strong, curved prickles. The flowering shoots are shorter, branched, and more slender. The leaves are 5–10 cm long, with five to nine leaflets (typically nine); the leaf-stalks are glabrous, and each is armed underneath with two small, hooked barbs. Leaflets are elliptic, broadly ovate, or rounded; 2–4 cm long; coarsely toothed; deep shiny green on both surfaces; obtuse; and glabrous except occa-

153

sionally on the midrib beneath. The margins are simply toothed. Bracts are absent; stipules are broad and toothed; the receptacle is sometimes glandular. There are typically six to ten flowers borne in loose panicles. Flowers are single, strongly scented (of white clover), 3–5 cm in diameter, pure white, and produced rather late in the season and continuing intermittently until autumn. Pedicels are glabrous. Sepals are 1 cm long, entire or with a few lateral lobes, often downy or slightly glandular on the back, reflexed, and they fall after flowering. Styles are united into a hairy exserted column. Fruits are orange red to dark red, ovoid or spherical, 1–2 cm across and ripen in early autumn. *Rosa luciae* differs by having thinner leaves (darker but less glossy), five to seven leaflets (never nine), a larger terminal leaflet, and fewer teeth on the stipules. The flowers are smaller, never exceeding 3 cm. Ohwi (1965) recognised four naturally occurring varieties. *Rosa sambucina* Kodz is also close to *R. wichurana* but easily distinguished by its long narrow leaflets, long pedicels, and early flowering.

Rosa wichurana is a native of eastern China, Korea, southern Japan (Honshu, Shikoku, and Kyushu), Okinawa, and Taiwan. It is most common in sunny locations in exposed coastal regions but is also found in pastures and on mountains. The Japanese do not hold it in any regard (the long trailing branches do not conform to their aesthetic sensibilities), but it is well worth growing for its own sake. *Rosa wichurana* flowers when most wild roses have finished, spreads quickly, rooting and forming tufts and thickets as it progresses. It can scarcely be bettered as a ground-cover plant, and the same is true of its offspring, for example, 'Immensee' (syn. 'Grouse'). Its tough, dark, glittering leaves are a delight all the year round and have proved to be a dominant gene when put to hybridisation; many of our modern bush roses owe their handsome shiny foliage to their distant descent from *R. wichurana*. There are a number of cultivated forms and botanical varieties. Best known is 'Variegata', whose leaflets are creamy white (with pink tips when young) and suffer from exposure to sun, wind, and drought. It is so strongly variegated that it has very little vigour. Several other forms of *R. wichurana* are available in commerce, including a double white and a thornless one.

Rosa wichurana was for many years widely known as *R. wichuraiana*. This breaches the rules for Latin terminations set out in the *International Code of Botanical Nomenclature* (Greuter et al. 1994, Recommendation 60C.1 and Article 60.11). It matters not that the original spelling was different: "The use of a termination contrary to [the rules] is treated as an error to be corrected." Thus, Herr Regierungsrat Wichura should be commemorated as *wichurana* and not as *wichuraiana*.

There are conflicting accounts about when *Rosa wichurana* was first introduced into cultivation in the West. The American hybridist Michael Walsh wrote that it was introduced to European horticulture in 1873 and to North America in 1891. The Ketten brothers of Luxemburg claimed that *R. wichurana* flowered for the first time in the Botanic Garden in Brussels in 1888.

The Wichurana Hybrids

The honour of being the first to hybridise *Rosa wichurana* belongs to two Americans, Jackson Dawson and Walter Van Fleet. Their successes in the 1890s were soon followed by the famous series of hybrids bred by Barbier of France. One hundred years later, Van Fleet and Barbier remain the leading breeders, with some thirteen and thirty-four cultivars, respectively, still grown today. No other breeders raised Wichurana Ramblers on such a scale, and hybridists in Germany and England were slow to copy them. But by the outbreak of World War I in 1914, the Wichurana Ramblers had transformed everyone's vision of what a climbing rose should be and do. The reasons for this popularity are easily explained when we consider their qualities. No one has summed them up so fully and exactly as Dr A. H. Williams, president of the National Rose Society of Great Britain, writing for the society's 1913 *Rose Annual*. It is a long quotation, but merits slow and careful reading:

> The Wichurana roses are possessed of an astonishing exuberant vitality; they are hardy; they thrive in almost any soil or situation and under any sort of treatment; their growth, while extraordinarily rapid and rampant, is clean and graceful; their flexible stems lend themselves to be trained readily in any way desired. Their beautiful foliage shows, in the different varieties, almost every shade of bright glossy green; it covers the plants from the roots to the tips of the stems; in many of the varieties it is evergreen; in many it is mildew-proof, and in none is it exceedingly liable to any pest. The flowers are produced in splendid profusion from all parts of the plant; and although in most of the varieties the chief burst of bloom lasts for only a month or six weeks, if we take the family as a whole we get a very long season. The flowers themselves may be either single or double, large or small, produced singly or in magnificent clusters. Some are most beautiful in the bud, others when fully blown. Many are delicately or sweetly perfumed. In one variety or another we have almost every shade from white to pink, from rose to crimson, from cream to orange, or beautiful combinations of these colours. In most cases the blooms withstand well the vagaries of the weather.

It was difficult in the early 1900s to sort the new Wichurana Ramblers into distinct categories. In the event, three main types of hybrid were acknowledged. First, there were the late-flowering, small-flowered ramblers bred from 'Turner's Crimson Rambler' and showing the influence of *Rosa multiflora*; these are described in chapter 8. The second category most closely resembles the species. These cultivars have large clusters of small flowers, single or double, which open late in the season. The foliage is generally small and very glossy, and the plant throws up numerous long, slender, flexible stems from the base each year. These are the canes which will bear the best flowers next year. The third group comprises ramblers of the 'Albéric Barbier' type, bred by crossing *R. wichurana* with Tea roses and Hybrid Teas: large flowers, but fewer of them. These were sometimes known as "Barbier types." The clusters may also be large, but are often less dense, more airy, and looser. They tend to open early in the season. These plants build up a more rigid framework of branches but may eventually cover a large area. Good flowering clusters may be expected not only from the one-year-old stems but also from the previous year's laterals. In the 1930s and 1940s, observers came to add a fourth group—ramblers with little *R. wichurana* left in them. These are climbers like 'Paul's Scarlet Climber' and the descendants of 'New Dawn'. Their growth is moderate, with even fewer basal shoots and few laterals. The flowering season is long, and the flower clusters may come from laterals which are several years old.

The Wichurana Ramblers had an immediate and far-reaching effect on garden design. In the 1900s and 1910s, garden designers came up with some original ideas for displaying them to advantage. Wichuranas are made for festoons, garlands, arches, and floral cascades—they require pillars, pergolas, walls and weepers to show them off. The taste for formal gardens engendered by the Arts and Crafts movement was reinforced by a need to accommodate these new rambling roses. In France and Germany Wichurana Ramblers were grown widely as tall weeping standards, draped over a semicircular metal crinoline. Sometimes they were trained into more extraordinary shapes—butterflies, baskets, and even aeroplanes.

The Wichuranas differed in their habit of growth and thus in their individual usefulness for specific purposes. The contemporary wisdom was that trelliswork required the slender flexible stems of 'Alexandre Girault', 'Aviateur Blériot', 'François Juranville', 'Fräulein Oktavia Hesse', 'Jules Levacher' and 'Valentin Beaulieu'. The famous trellises at L'Haÿ-les-Roses are still entirely covered by sweeping growths of 'Alexandre Girault'. Walls and pillars were easier to cover with cultivars of more rigid growth: 'Albéric Barbier', 'Christine Wright', 'Diabolo', 'Gardenia', 'Gerbe Rose', 'Léontine Gervais', and 'Purity'. Thick-stemmed, rigid growers were best as free-standing shrubs: 'Diabolo', 'Gerbe Rose', and, later, 'Albertine'. Screens were best covered by cultivars with dense and persistent or evergreen foliage: 'Albéric Barbier', 'Jersey Beauty', 'Jules Levacher', 'Paul Ploton', and ' Purity'.

No sooner had Wichurana Ramblers swept across the world of gardening fashion on a wave of irresistible success and popularity, than the inevitable reaction set in. People began to find fault with them. There were too many of them. They were too vigorous. Their flowers were too large. Their flowers were too small. They did not flourish in hot climates. They were not hardy in a New England winter. Yet, the truth was that there were suitable Wichurana Rambler cultivars for almost every requirement and taste.

The Wichurana Ramblers were certainly numerous, perhaps too numerous. Many nurserymen tried their hand at sowing a few open-pollinated seeds of Wichurana Ramblers and then introduced the best. Some 110 cultivars were introduced in the years before World War I, without taking account of the descendants of 'Turner's Crimson Rambler' described in chapter 8. A keen rose lover might accommodate 200 or more different Hybrid Teas in a small garden, but Wichuranas need space, so that even the grandest of gardens seldom grew more than a representative selection. Yet, among the cultivars which languish unsung and half-forgotten in European rose gardens are a wealth of good climbers that deserve to be admired again more widely.

It was soon discovered that the Wichurana Hybrids were not the best choice for Mediterranean or hotter climates because their growth cycle needs a period of winter dormancy. Those like 'Paul's Scarlet Climber' with a high proportion of other genes do best. Nor are they always hardy in such climates as New England or central Europe. *Rosa wichurana*'s reputation for coming through cold winters rests upon its natural habit of creeping along the ground, where its growths are often protected by snow or other shrubs. 'Albéric Barbier' and 'Albertine' are considered hardy anywhere within the British Isles, but neither is reliable at Munich or Prague, where 'Fräulein Oktavia Hesse' and 'Alida Lovett' do duty for them. There was also great suspicion of any Wichurana Rambler with yellow flowers. Yellowness was thought of as a sure sign of low resistance to cold because it derived from the tender Tea roses. By the 1920s, however, the first yellow roses descended from the bone-hardy *R. foetida* began to appear, and such breeders as the Brownells in New Jersey made the development of improved hardy yellow climbers one of the keystones of their breeding programme. Large flowers were also associated with winter-kill. The American Steve Stevens wrote in 1933 that a "sign of tenderness is *large* flowers. Those which most closely resemble the original species are likely to be the hardiest." By then, however, breeders had succeeded with such cultivars as 'Mrs Arthur Curtiss James' and 'Primevère' in imbuing large-flowered yellow roses with considerable hardiness even in New England. Indeed, the flowers were so large and the plants so stiff that they ceased to be true Wichurana Ramblers. Dr A. H. Williams had noticed the trend as early as 1913: "the flowers above all have changed. They are individual and enormous. Is this good? Is this bad? Do not our charming Wichurana Hybrids run the risk of losing their beauty and their charm, that is to say the flexibility of their growths and their dainty corymbs?"

I have treated 'New Dawn' as the last of the line or, rather, as the first of the modern climbers. 'New Dawn' was a repeat-flowering sport of the large-flowered 'Dr W. Van Fleet' and was used to breed many of the shorter climbers of the mid-twentieth century. It gave rise to a race of its own, which is examined in chapter 10.

Wichurana Ramblers in the United States

JACKSON DAWSON

When Jackson Dawson was head gardener at the Arnold Arboretum in the 1890s, he started to breed from *Rosa wichurana*. His earliest surviving seedling is 'William C. Egan', the result of a cross with 'Général Jacqueminot' which Dawson exhibited to the Massachusetts Horticultural Society in 1896. It has large clusters of double, creamy pink flowers resembling a scaled-down 'Souvenir de la Malmaison' and the bright glossy foliage which was to become the key indicator of *R. wichurana* among its hybrid descendants. Other parents for Dawson's Wichurana Hybrids were the Polyantha 'Clothilde Soupert' [Soupert & Notting, 1890] and the sumptuous Hybrid Tea 'Mrs W. J. Grant' [Dickson, 1895]. Dawson also made many crosses between *R. wichurana* and the late-flowering 'Turner's Crimson Rambler'; best known and most popular was 'Farquhar', a bright pink rose which resembles a carnation. Then Dawson turned to crossing *R. wichurana* with *R. rugosa* to give rise to 'Lady Duncan', an extremely hardy ground-cover rose which may be identical with 'Max Graf', the founder of the Kordesii Climbers.

'Farquhar' syn. 'The Farquhar Rose' [Dawson, 1903]. *Rosa wichurana* × 'Turner's Crimson Rambler'. 'Farquhar' has small (3.0–3.5 cm), double, pale pink flowers (with a hint of salmon, like 'Dorothy Perkins'), borne in large clusters. The flowers fade eventually to white and are slightly scented. The plant is vigorous, grows to 6 m, with shiny green leaves and rather long prickles. It sometimes gets blackspot.

'Lady Duncan' [Dawson, 1900]. *Rosa wichurana* × *rugosa*. I have not been able to compare this with 'Max Graf', but the photograph in the *American Rose Annual* for 1924 seems different. The old descriptions say that its "carnation pink" flowers are single and 7–8 cm in diameter, have golden stamens, and do not repeat. They are borne in clusters of one to four and contrast nicely with the glossy foliage. The floppy habit of growth is a compromise between the upright form of one parent and the trailing habit of the other. All authorities agree that 'Lady Duncan' is very hardy.

'Sargent' [Dawson, 1912]. (*Rosa wichurana* × 'Turner's Crimson Rambler') × 'Baronne Adolphe de Rothschild'. Dawson considered 'Sargent' his finest production. It had "semi-double flowers borne in huge clusters [which] vary from pale pink to creamy white, like apple-blossom, very beautiful and fragrant" (Snyder 1953). "Huge" meant clusters of about fifty flowers. It grows to about 6 m. The plant at Sangerhausen is closer to *R. multiflora* than to *R. wichurana*—pale medium pink, scentless, with terminal clusters of three to ten flowers and a tendency to blackspot. Its leaves resemble those of 'Baronne Adolphe de Rothschild', being round and slightly corrugated. I believe it is probably correctly named.

'William C. Egan' [Dawson, introduced by Hoopes, 1900]. *Rosa wichurana* × 'Général Jacqueminot'. This early cross remained popular for as much as fifty years. It is a medium-sized (7–8 cm), once-flowering Wichurana, with very full flowers which are the same creamy pink and quartered shape as 'Souvenir de la Malmaison' (plate 93). They are strongly scented and come in small tight clusters, typically five to seven. The plant is moderately vigorous to about 3 m, with long prickles, and has a slight tendency to blackspot.

M. H. Horvath and W. A. Manda

Michael Horvath first saw *Rosa wichurana* when he was working for the Newport Nursery Company at Newport, Rhode Island, in 1892 or 1893. Years later, he remembered having been struck by its beautiful, lustrous, shiny foliage. He thought it was too bad that such wonderful growth and foliage should be topped by the meager little flowers it bore. Horvath decided that it would make a good subject to experiment on, and proceeded to pollinate some of its flowers. He had only two rose cultivars handy from which to get pollen, the Polyantha 'Mignonette' and the hardy old China rose 'Climbing James Sprunt'. 'Manda's Triumph' and 'Universal Favorite' resulted from the pollen of the Polyantha and 'Pink Roamer' and 'South Orange Perfection' from 'Climbing James Sprunt'. When the American Rose Society ran its first flower show in 1897, Horvath exhibited some fourteen new roses. Their impact was sensational: Horvath was lauded by the horticultural press; his four named cultivars were introduced by Manda & Pitcher of South Orange, New Jersey, in 1898 and 1899; and the production of Wichurana Hybrids on the East Coast got off to a roaring start. Manda himself then turned to breeding Wichuranas. He tended to use Tea roses, so his introductions were not always hardy in a New England winter. Below are the hybrids which he introduced, whether of Horvath's raising or his own.

'Gardenia' [Manda, 1898]. *Rosa wichurana* × 'Perle des Jardins'. The first large-flowered Wichurana Rambler is still one of the most widely grown. Its flowers open a fine buff yellow, but fade quickly to cream and milky white, with a hint of pale yellow at the centre. The flowers are about 6–7 cm across, quartered, sometimes cupped, and borne on short stems in small clusters. They resemble a gardenia, although with a mild and musky scent. The flowers appear early, last well, and continue a few at a time, through until autumn. 'Gardenia' is a tremendously vigorous grower, with lots of small, dark green, glossy leaves and red new growths. This cultivar is very handsome, but not reliably hardy in cold areas.

'Jersey Beauty' [Manda, 1898]. *Rosa wichurana* × 'Perle des Jardins'. A simple beauty; the flowers are 6 cm across, single, cream fading quickly to white, with fine golden stamens and often a hint of pink or red on the backs of the petals. The clusters have three to five flowers and the flowers are short lived. They start early, continue intermittently, and are followed by a heavy crop of large, showy hips. The healthy foliage is dark glossy green, with red new growths, and quite evergreen. 'Jersey Beauty' is a rampant grower to some 8 m, with fine, flexible stems, valuable for draping around arches and pillars.

'Manda's Triumph' [Horvath, c. 1893; introduced by Manda, 1898]. Reputedly *Rosa wichurana* × 'Ma Pâquerette'. The flowers are sweetly scented, small (4.5–5.0 cm), pure white, very double, and imbricated. They appear late and put on a smaller second flowering in autumn. Old authorities say the clusters have fifty to one hundred flowers, but ten to fifteen is more normal in my experience. The foliage is disappointing (neither copious, nor disease resistant), but the plant grows vigorously to 4–5 m.

'Pink Pearl' [Manda, 1901]. *Rosa wichurana* × 'Meteor'. This rose has fairly large (6–7 cm), scented, double flowers in small clusters, which open from crimson buds to pale pink flowers, often slightly darker at the centre. It is not among the best early Wichuranas, but interesting for its comparative size and hardiness. It still survives in such collections as L'Haÿ-les-Roses.

'Pink Roamer' syn. 'Manda's Pink Roamer' [Horvath, c. 1893; introduced by Manda, 1898]. *Rosa wichurana* × 'Climbing James Sprunt'. This unexciting early hybrid has airy clusters of single, crimson or deep pink flowers, which fade to pale mauve pink, with a white base to the petals, a conspicuous exserted style, and a nice brush of stamens. They are 3.0–3.5 cm across and have a moderate scent. 'Pink Roamer' has small leaves, vigorous growth (to 3–4 m), and a lax leafy habit. The plant is hardy, with attractive little hips in autumn, but little of ornamental value.

'South Orange Perfection' [Horvath, c. 1893; introduced by Manda, 1898]. *Rosa wichurana* × 'Climbing James Sprunt'. As with the rest of Manda's first Horvath hybrids, this has greater historic interest than horticultural value. The flowers are small (3 cm), double, and nicely imbricated; they open pale pink but fade quickly to white. They are lightly scented and borne in clusters of about twenty flowers. This rose grows fairly vigorously to about 3 m but has a reputation for tenderness, although it survives in the relatively protected garden at L'Haÿ-les-Roses.

'Universal Favorite' syn. 'Manda's Universal Favorite' [Horvath, c. 1893; introduced by Manda, 1898]. *Rosa wichurana* × 'Pâquerette'. This rose has tiny double flowers, barely 2.5 cm in diameter, and reflexed petals like little pompon daisies. They open pale pink, fade almost to white, have a fairly strong scent, and are borne in large clusters. The plant is vigorous, with a somewhat trailing habit and typical bright green *R. wichurana* foliage.

'White Star' [Manda, 1901]. 'Jersey Beauty' × 'Manda's Triumph'. A rose of this name is still grown at L'Haÿ-les-Roses. It has small (3.0–3.5 cm), white flowers in clusters of about thirty and grows to about 3 m.

Dr Walter Van Fleet

Walter Van Fleet embodied the American conviction that men can improve upon God's handiwork and leave the world a better place. He and his contemporaries Dr J. Horace McFarland and Robert Pyle took charge of the American Rose Society in the 1910s and turned it from a trade association for East Coast florists into a national crusade for the appreciation of roses as garden plants. They were conviction rosarians. Dr Van Fleet dreamed of breeding dooryard roses of such hardiness that they could stand with the lilacs and spiraeas among all the other hardy shrubs of American homes and gardens. In addition to vigour and hardiness, he also sought good appearance when out of bloom. For much of the 1920s the three most popular climbing roses in the United States were all raised by Van Fleet; in order of popularity, they were 'Dr W. Van Fleet', 'Silver Moon', and 'American Pillar'.

Van Fleet was brought up on a farm near Watsontown, Pennsylvania, studied medicine at Harvard University, and practised as a doctor. But there was a streak of idealism and enthusiasm which governed his life, and in the early 1890s he went as a medical doctor to serve the Ruskin Colony in Tennessee. This colony was a socialist utopia, run by a small group of people who sought to establish a cooperative commonwealth and to transform mankind. Theirs was a radical vision, a mixture of courage, naivety, and recklessness. The community attracted individuals who were inspired by such different philosophies as anarchism, Christian socialism, free love, and a desire for female emancipation—it would be interesting to know which particular thread of idealism attracted Van Fleet. After the inevitable collapse of the colony, he came north again, but not to practise medicine. He was already an experienced amateur plant breeder and had raised money for Ruskin by running an avant-garde floristry enterprise. Thus began his true life's work as a plant breeder for the Department of Agriculture at Bell Station, between Baltimore and Washington, D.C. Here Van Fleet bred strawberries, gooseberries, maize, tomatoes, peppers, cannas, gladioli, pelargoniums, honeysuckle—and roses.

It was climbing roses which Van Fleet loved most. When he moved down to Ruskin in the early 1890s, he took with him a cross which he had made between *Rosa wichurana* and the yellow Tea rose 'Safrano'. There he crossed it with pollen from 'Souvenir du Président Carnot', a pale pink Hybrid Tea, and gave the name 'Daybreak' to the best of the resultant seedlings. In 1901 he sold 'Daybreak' to the New York florist Peter Henderson for seventy-five dollars and, as was his custom, kept a plant for himself. This was fortunate because, through a series of mishaps and mismanagement, Henderson lost his entire stock. After several years, Van Fleet wrote to ask Hendersons when they were going to introduce his seedling. They confessed their misfortunes, whereupon Van Fleet supplied fresh budwood, for which they paid him an additional royalty. When the rose was eventually introduced in 1910, Henderson named it, despite his protestations, not 'Daybreak', but 'Dr W. Van Fleet'.

No one could ask for a finer rose to commemorate his name. The American rosarian G. A. Stevens (1933) summed up its importance more than twenty years later: "I approach this rose with awe and humility. Its influence has been stupendous. Its introduction broke the garden's thraldom to innumerable, fussy little cluster-flowered ramblers which bore us to distraction with their infantile prettiness and indistinguishable differences. Here was an heroic rose, of noble size and perfect form, borne on a rampant plant, first of the new race of climbers. Its value and importance to rose-growers in cold climates can hardly be estimated."

Van Fleet was a highly experimental breeder who used a wide choice of species and cultivars for his hybridisation. Typical of his method was the way Van Fleet successfully brought such species as *Rosa soulieana*, *R. moyesii*, and *R. laevigata* into his breeding lines. 'American Pillar' was derived from a seedling of *R. wichurana* × *setigera*. That said, the published parentages of some of Van Fleet's roses are open to question. Such sumptuous beauties as 'Mary Lovett' and 'Mary Wallace' are unlikely straight seedlings of the species *R. wichurana*; the presence of so much Hybrid Tea in their makeup suggests that their seed parents were first-generation seedlings of the species. Van Fleet never wavered in his aim to create the ideal rose—a garden form with the health of the best rose species, hardy under ordinary garden culture, and a continuous bloomer.

'Alida Lovett' [Van Fleet, c. 1905; introduced by Lovett, 1917]. *Rosa wichurana* × 'Souvenir du Président Carnot'. This underestimated climber has coral pink buds which open into pure pink flowers and fade to mother-of-pearl (plate 94). The outsides of the petals are slightly darker than the insides. The medium-sized flowers (7–8 cm) have short petals and open flat. They are strongly scented and come in clusters of three to ten. The plant is hardy and vigorous, making strong, upright growth to about 3–4 m. 'Alida Lovett' makes a good hedge.

'American Pillar' [Van Fleet, 1902]. (*Rosa wichurana* × *setigera*) × Hybrid Perpetual. This astute cross produced a hardy climber of astonishing vigour which flowers in mid-season with wonderful exuberance. The flowers come in clusters of five to twenty and are single, 5–6 cm across; they are a distinctive bright glowing crimson with a white centre and conspicuous golden stamens. In hot weather the colour is paler. The leaves are large, healthy, glossy, and dark green, changing to purplish red before they fall. The plant also bears a fine crop of brilliant red hips. The growth is rather rigid, with upright stems that tend to go bare at the base unless they are trained horizontally. They reach 3–4 m in a year but start to die back after three or four years. 'American Pillar' makes an impenetrable hedging plant. No climber is easier to grow, and it is exceptionally easy to propagate from cuttings. With so many advantages, and such an attractive name, 'American Pillar' has always been very popular.

'Bess Lovett' [Van Fleet, 1905; introduced by Lovett, 1917]. *Rosa wichurana* × 'Souvenir du Président Carnot'. Seldom seen now, even in North America, and often incorrectly named, 'Bess Lovett' has medium to large (7–8 cm) flowers which are double, open, well-formed, loosely cup shaped, fairly well scented, and clear brilliant crimson (brighter than 'American Pillar'). They are borne in clusters of five to twenty during the long, abundant flowering season. The leaves are deep shiny green, and the plant is vigorous and grows strongly. It climbs to about 5 m and is fairly hardy in even the coldest climates.

'Birdie Blye' [Van Fleet, introduced by Conard & Jones, 1904]. 'Helene' × 'Bon Silène'. This is not a Wichurana Rambler, but the first Lambertiana to be bred in North America, a repeat-flowering semi-climbing Multiflora. The flowers come in small clusters and open from dark carmine buds. They are medium sized (7–8 cm) but seem larger, very double, cupped, and soft dark pink, with a hint of magenta. Later the tips of the petals fade to pale pink, contrasting with the deeper colours at the centre. The petals have a satiny surface and recurve at the tips. It has a distinct, light scent. The bush is moderately vigorous, with pale leaves and stems which are covered in lots of little prickles. It will grow to 2 m against a wall in cool climates, but to twice that height in warmer areas.

'Breeze Hill' [Van Fleet, introduced by the American Rose Society, 1926]. Reputedly *Rosa wichurana* × 'Beauté de Lyon'. The small, hard, matt rounded foliage is so unlike other Wichurana Hybrids that this may be a lost seedling of 'Dr W. Van Fleet' with *R. soulieana* in its ancestry. It is arguably the best of Van Fleet's roses, remarkable for the size and beauty of its very double flowers, which are borne singly or in small clusters in mid-season and occasionally thereafter (plate 95). The flowers are about 8 cm across and a wonderful colour. As they age, the outer petals turn from buff to cream (and finally to white in hot weather), but the centre is a warm apricot, flushed with pale salmon and creamy pink. This colour, contrasted with the paler edges, gives 'Breeze Hill' its distinctive loveliness. The flowers are cup shaped and remain half closed for a long time, but eventually open out to a quilled and quartered centre. 'Breeze Hill' is said to have a scent of green apples. The plant is bushy, prickly, and thick-stemmed; it grows slowly to 4–5 m.

'Dr W. Van Fleet' [Van Fleet, introduced by Henderson, 1910]. (*Rosa wichurana* × 'Safrano') × 'Souvenir du Président Carnot'. This is "an heroic rose" and, through its perpetual flowering sport 'New Dawn', the ancestor of many of the most popular climbing roses of today. The buds are elegant, with long petals, which open to cup-shaped, full flowers whose wavy petals add to their delicacy. This delicacy is illusory, however; the petals stand up remarkably well to wet weather. The flowers are variously described as "soft," "delicate," "flesh-tinted," or "peachy pink" and show more colour towards the centre. They are surprisingly large (some 10 cm across), strongly scented, and abundantly produced on long, strong stems—a good cutting rose. The flowers last about a month in midseason, with sporadic blooms later, followed by red hips in autumn and winter. The handsome shiny polished foliage is strongly resistant to disease. Growth is vigorous—the plant easily reaches 5 m. It is hardy in much of inland North America and central Europe.

'Glenn Dale' [Van Fleet, introduced by the American Rose Society, 1927]. *Rosa wichurana* × 'Isabella Sprunt'. This charming, hardy, white rambler has flowers which resemble a perfect small Hybrid Tea (plate 96). The small lemon yellow buds open into surprisingly large (7–8 cm) flowers, which are cream at first, then pure ivory white. They are semi-double, borne in clusters of five to ten on long strong stems, good for cutting. The blooms have a musky scent. The dark green Hybrid Tea–type foliage is fairly disease resistant. The plant is not overvigorous, perhaps 3 m tall, more against a wall or in a warm climate.

'Heart of Gold' [Van Fleet; introduced by the American Rose Society, 1926]. *Rosa wichurana* × *moyesii* or possibly *Rosa* (*wichurana* × *setigera*) × *moyesii*. This intelligent attempt to bring new genes into climbing roses produced a disappointing result. The dull dark crimson blooms discolour to an unattractive purple and the gold stamens brown quickly. The flowers are single, 4–5 cm in diameter, quite strongly scented, and come in clusters of five to fifteen. The leaves are rich green and glossy. It makes a bushy climber or shrub, 2.5–3.0 m high, and is very hardy.

'Mary Lovett' [Van Fleet, introduced by Lovett, 1915]. Allegedly *Rosa wichurana* × 'Kaiserin Auguste Viktoria'. This beautiful rambler produces quantities of medium to large (7–8 cm), very double, scented, snow white flowers rather late in the season. They are freely borne, typically twelve to twenty in a cluster, with a few flowers later in the year. The individual flowers open out to show a very attractive, full centre, but they do not shatter cleanly. This cultivar grows vigorously, to at least 5 m if allowed.

'Mary Wallace' [Van Fleet, introduced by the American Rose Society, 1924]. Allegedly *Rosa wichurana* × a pink Hybrid Tea. The buds are long and pointed, like a Hybrid Tea. The flowers are semi-double, bright rose pink, slightly paler at the edge of the reflexed petals, and among the largest of the Wichurana Ramblers (8 cm). The blooms have a moderate scent and are borne on long stems but tend to hang on to their petals, which spoils the overall effect. The foliage is large, thick, glossy, rich green, and fairly disease resistant. The plant grows to about 4–5 m and is hardy, except in the coldest places.

'May Queen' [Van Fleet, introduced by Conard & Jones, 1898]. *Rosa wichurana* × 'Mrs de Graw'. 'May Queen' is an early to midseason rambler, with masses of medium to large (7–8 cm), pure pink flowers, which open from light red buds (plate 97). They are very full and roughly quartered, with an irregular outline. The outer petals fade, but seem to glow more brightly than the darker ones in the centre. The flowers are borne in small to medium-sized clusters on slender stalks which hang down under the sheer weight of the petals. They have an unusual fruity scent and rather elongated capsules like a Damask rose. The shiny foliage is somewhat rounded. The plant grows vigorously to 8 m. It does best in a dry climate.

'Philadelphia' syn. 'Philadelphia Rambler' [Van Fleet, 1904]. 'Turner's Crimson Rambler' × 'Victor Hugo'. 'Philadelphia' was introduced as an improved 'Turner's Crimson Rambler', more scarlet, but no less dark; it is one of the few really deep red roses which glow brilliantly. The undersides of the petals are pinker. The flowers are very full, tightly packed with short neat petals, and about 4 cm in diameter. They are borne in clusters of ten to twenty but are scentless. 'Philadelphia' is immensely floriferous in midseason. The foliage shows the influence of *Rosa multiflora* and the stems are prickly. It grows vigorously to about 4 m.

'Ruby Queen' [Van Fleet, introduced by Conard & Jones, 1899]. Supposedly *Rosa wichurana* × 'Cramoisi Supérieur'. The flowers are dark pink or pale crimson with a white eye, like a loosely semi-double form of 'American Beauty', but the petals have silvery pink undersides. The small to medium-sized (4–5 cm) flowers are at first held upright, but later hang down gracefully. The clusters have ten to fifteen flowers. They appear early and have a slight scent. The semi-evergreen foliage is dense, small, bright green, and glossy and the plant produces strong, fairly upright, prickly stems, which grow 2–3 m in a season.

'Silver Moon' [Van Fleet, introduced by Henderson, 1910]. *Rosa wichurana* × 'Devoniensis'. This is still one of the finest white-flowered ramblers for a mild climate. The lightly semi-double flowers open pure white from long, elegant, creamy buds, with a broad boss of long golden stamens. The petals are enormous, and the flowers themselves can be as much as 11 cm across. They are borne in small clusters on long stems, have a good musky scent, and flower in midseason. 'Silver Moon' flowers sparsely in cool climates, but is very free-blooming and reliable in warmer ones. The leaves are nearly evergreen, disease-free, very glossy, large, and bronze green at first but dark green later. It is a very vigorous grower which can reach 10 m. DNA studies have shown that 'Silver Moon' is not a hybrid of *R. laevigata*, as once believed.

Hoopes, Bro., & Thomas Co.

This nursery of West Chester near Philadelphia was an unusual company in its heyday. Its leading light was the botanist-nurseryman Josiah Hoopes, an expert on ornamental trees, especially conifers. Jackson Dawson's early experiments at the Arnold Arboretum inspired him to try breeding Wichurana Ramblers himself. In 1898 Hoopes instructed one of his assistants, James A. Farrell, to fertilise *Rosa wichurana* with pollen from several Teas and Hybrid Teas. The first batch of first-generation crosses was undistinguished; only 'Professor C. S. Sargent' is still in cultivation, although the plant grown under this name does not entirely match the original descriptions. In the second generation of crosses, however, some excellent roses emerged. Farrell crossed an unnamed seedling which he had bred from *R. wichurana* × 'Marion Dingee', but never introduced, with such popular bush roses as 'American Beauty' and 'Mme Caroline Testout'. The result of using the Hybrid Perpetual 'American Beauty' was the rose he introduced as 'Climbing American Beauty' (a rather misleading name, because it was a seedling of 'American Beauty', not a sport). But Hoopes was operating on a very small scale. He made only one cross with 'Mme Caroline Testout' which gave rise to four seedlings. One he discarded because it had too many petals and would not open properly; a second he intended to introduce under the name 'Columbia', but did not do so; and the remaining two were introduced and have become well known as the pink 'Christine Wright' and white 'Purity'. After that, he bred no more roses.

'Christine Wright' [Hoopes, 1909]. (*Rosa wichurana* × 'Marion Dingee') × 'Mme Caroline Testout'. The flowers are 7–9 cm in diameter, fairly double, and open out to show a muddled arrangement of petals and a heart of yellow stamens (plate 98). The flowers are bright pink, then fade to pale silver pink. The outer petals are usually paler than the inner ones. The flowers are generously produced, singly and in clusters of up to eight. The light scent is a mixture of sweet damask and musk. 'Christine Wright' flowers early for a Wichurana, with occasional blooms later. The leathery leaves are fairly resistant to blackspot. It makes a strong, upright, prickly rambler or pillar rose, growing to about 3 m high.

'Climbing American Beauty' [Hoopes, 1909]. (*Rosa wichurana* × 'Marion Dingee') × 'American Beauty'. Although originally described as crimson, the flowers give an impression of pinkness, opening deep pink (paler on the undersides) and fading to medium pink. They are 7–8 cm across, have a good damask scent, and are borne in small clusters on long stems. The leaves are dense and glossy; the plant grows vigorously to 5 m. Unfortunately, the fading flowers turn an unpleasant bluish brown and do not drop their petals cleanly. They need to be dead-headed before they spoil the overall effect.

'Professor C. S. Sargent' [Hoopes, 1903]. *Rosa wichurana* × 'Souvenir d'Auguste Métral'. Old records describe this rose as opening apricot yellow and fading to buff and cream. The plants surviving at Sangerhausen differ by having coral buds which open to yellowish pink double flowers and end up pale pink. The petals are deeper pink on their backs and are about 5–6 cm across, coming in rather small clusters, typically of up to ten flowers. The leaves are large and pale (the original descriptions mention small leaves), and the flowers have glandular pedicels indicating *R. multiflora* ancestry. The plant is hardy, vigorous, and early flowering.

'Purity' [Hoopes, 1917]. (*Rosa wichurana* × 'Marion Dingee') × 'Mme Caroline Testout'. This is a hardy, vigorous climber of exceptional beauty when its large (8–10 cm) white flowers are set off by rich bronze green foliage. The flowers are only semi-double, elegantly cupped, with long white petals and a strong sweet scent. They are produced in small loose clusters early in the season with a smattering again in the autumn. The dark green foliage is glossy and dense. The plant gets some blackspot, with no ill results. The stems are well armed with handsome large prickles. It grows to about 5 m but becomes rather bare at the base. 'Purity' is a great personal favourite of mine.

Wichurana Ramblers in France

THE BARBIER FAMILY

The Barbier roses, introduced over a period of more than thirty years, are the single most impressive corpus of Wichurana Ramblers ever produced—indeed, they represent one of the greatest individual contributions towards the advancement of the climbing rose.

Barbier et Cie. was founded in 1875 and grew fast by a process of expansion and amalgamation. The Barbiers were always general nurserymen, with a good reputation in the trade for their fruit trees, but never noted as rose specialists, even though a Monsieur Barbier was Président de la Commission Permanente des Roses de la Société Horticole du Loiret as early as 1879. They seem never to have promoted themselves as major rose breeders or rose growers, and by 1966 their list of climbing roses included only three roses of their own raising—the ever-popular 'Albéric Barbier', 'Albertine', and 'François Juranville'.

René Barbier was the hybridist. He imported *Rosa wichurana* from the United States in the 1890s, although he may have worked with one of the early American hybrids, for instance, 'Jersey Beauty'. It is said that his first cross produced ten seeds, of which five germinated and grew to become 'Albéric Barbier', 'Elisa Robichon', 'François Foucard', 'Paul Transon', and 'René Barbier'. He reported his successes in *Journal des Roses*: "[These] varieties constitute a new group. They are the result of pollinating *R. Wichuraiana* [sic] with different Teas and Noisettes. These roses have inherited the remarkable vigour of their mother, its glossy foliage and rampant growth. The long flexible branches often put on three or four metres in growth, which makes them suitable climbing roses to train up trees, adorn pergolas, and make hedges. Top-grafted, they make magnificent weeping specimens completely covered with flowers." It is interesting that Barbier should have emphasised the uses to which this new race of roses could be put, rather than extolling their floral qualities, because his introductions represented a significant improvement on the flowers bred by American hybridists. They were generally larger and more floriferous, with a wider range of colours and a tendency to flower on and off throughout the summer and autumn, in addition to their first, spectacular flowering early in the season.

Most of the Barbier hybrids were bred by crossing the species (or a first-generation hybrid) with a Tea rose. Crosses with 'Souvenir de Catherine Guillot', a fashionable Tea rose, alone accounted for seven of their introductions: 'Adélaïde Moullé', 'Alexandre Tremouillet', 'Edmond Proust', 'Jean Guichard', 'Léontine Gervais', 'Pinson', and 'Valentin Beaulieu'. Barbier also experimented with some unusual crosses, including *Rosa moyesii*, 'Harison's Yellow', and *R. foetida*.

Almost all the climbing roses bred by Barbier are still in existence, thanks to conservation work at L'Haÿ-les-Roses and Sangerhausen. They are a quintessence of what a Wichurana Rambler should be: vigorous, flexible, floriferous, and healthy. Some are not hardy in the coldest climates, but such cultivars as 'Jacotte' and 'Primevère' can confidently be recommended in central Europe and the American Midwest. Not all remain as widely known and grown as they deserve to be. The list that follows is a roll-call of the longest and possibly the greatest series of climbing roses ever to have come from a single breeder.

'Albéric Barbier' [Barbier, 1900]. *Rosa wichurana* × 'Shirley Hibberd'. This famous white rambler has the colour and form of a Tea rose. Its buds are a rich apricot yellow and open to creamy white flowers flushed with a hint of buff yellow towards the centre. They are fully double, about 8 cm across, and quartered, with distinctly pointed petals, but prettier en masse than individually when mature. The flowers are borne singly or in small clusters and are produced in great profusion early in the season with occasional flowers until late autumn. They are strongly scented with a mixture of fruitiness and sweetness, like fine German wine, according to Hugh Johnson, the English garden and wine writer. Its foliage is very beautiful: dark, dense, firm, glossy green with red petioles, almost evergreen, and healthy. 'Albéric Barbier' grows vigorously, putting on 3 m a year, and is capable of reaching 8 m up a tree. Its prickles are fairly large and numerous. It remains the best all-rounder for mild climates.

'Albertine' [Barbier, 1921]. Allegedly *Rosa wichurana* × 'Mrs Arthur Robert Waddell'. This is one of the most popular climbing roses. It is not really hardy in central Europe or New England, but is widely grown, sometimes ubiquitously, in France, England, Australia, and New Zealand. The coral buds open to medium-sized (7–9 cm), semi-double flowers which are salmon pink, shaded with yellow when fresh, paling to pale pink as they age, and with brighter, darker, coppery undersides at all times (plate 99). The colour blends well with other roses. The flowers are carried in small clusters (three to seven flowers) with extraordinary exuberance in midseason and occasionally until autumn. Their strong, sweet scent carries in the air. The leaves are glossy, dark green, bronze when young, and susceptible to mildew later in the year but not damaged by it. The plant is thick-set, with somewhat rigid stems and lots of large prickles, and it roots easily from cuttings. 'Albertine' makes a good free-standing shrub. Its ultimate height as a climber is about 5 m.

'Alexandre Girault' [Barbier, 1909]. *Rosa wichurana* × 'Papa Gontier'. The colour of the flowers is variable: crimson pink, with a hint of yellow towards the centre and nearly white backs to the petals (plate 100). The crimson pink fades, acquiring a lilac tinge with age. The flowers are medium sized (about 6–7 cm across), fairly full, with a loose arrangement of small petals in the centre. They are produced in profusion on long stems in small, elegant, pendulous clusters, which cut well but are practically scentless. The flowers come early and occasionally again in autumn. The foliage is light, glossy green, and free from mildew. It is a vigorous but lanky grower, with slender, flexible stems that respond particularly well to training. Better known in Europe than North America, 'Alexandre Girault' covers the trellising behind the central pool at L'Haÿ-les-Roses, where it grows to at least 10 m.

'Alexandre Tremouillet' syn. 'Alexandre Trimouillet' [Barbier, 1903]. *Rosa wichurana* × 'Souvenir de Catherine Guillot'. This attractive rose is best described as a mother-of-pearl version of 'Albéric Barbier'. The flowers are peachy pink, fading to pearl, about 8–9 cm in diameter, and open out flat and fully double (plate 102). The centre retains its peachy pink while the outer petals are paler, which gives the flowers their distinctive character; they often have a button eye, too. They are borne singly or in small, loose, open clusters (typically three or five flowers) but have little scent. 'Alexandre Tremouillet' flowers among the second earlies, with occasional flowers later. The foliage is dark and glossy, the stems fairly prickly, and the plant itself vigorous, growing to about 4 m.

'Auguste Gervais' [Barbier, 1918]. *Rosa wichurana* × 'Le Progrès'. This popular rose has large flowers (10–12 cm), more than semi-double, apricot pink, and fading to cream, although the undersides and the centre always retain richer tints than the outer petals, especially in cool climates. Elegant in bud, 'Auguste Gervais' opens to a flat, old-fashioned centre. The flowers are fairly well scented and are borne midseason, then occasionally until autumn. They come in medium-sized clusters, nicely spaced with little overlap, and about ten flowers in a cluster. The plant grows very vigorously to about 6 m.

'Casimir Moullé' [Barbier, 1910]. Allegedly *Rosa wichurana* × 'Mme Norbert Levavasseur'. The flowers are small (about 4.5 cm across) and freely borne in long clusters reminiscent of the 'Turner's Crimson Rambler' race. They are purplish pink, with much paler backs to the petals and, because the flowers are flat, imbricated, and very double, this gives them a charming two-effect. 'Casimir Moullé' flowers later than other Barbier hybrids, but does not repeat. The leaves are brilliant green and glossy, and the plant grows vigorously to 3–4 m.

'Coupe d'Or' [Barbier, 1930]. 'Jacotte' seedling. This beautiful rambler survives without protection at Sangerhausen, but was not listed by any nurseryman for many years. The flowers are medium sized (about 7 cm across) and open bright buttercup yellow, but fade to cream and white as they open, giving a charming contrast between the yellow centre of the flower and paler outer petals. The flowers are very full and usually open out to display a button centre and a green eye. They are borne singly or in clusters of up to seven and are strongly scented—a mixture of lemon and sweet damask. The leaves are dark green, glossy, and tough, with crimson rachis. The new growth is likewise crimson, slender, and pliable.

'Cramoisi Simple' [Barbier, 1902]. Allegedly 'Wichurana Rubra' × 'Turner's Crimson Rambler'. This rose now grows only at L'Haÿ-les-Roses. Descriptions of the now-extinct 'Wichurana Rubra' published in 1901 and 1902 read very like the only original surviving description of 'Cramoisi Simple'. This suggests that either they are sister-seedlings or synonyms—one and the same plant. The flowers are single, about 4 cm in diameter, and dark pink (fading to pale pink) with a white eye. They are carried in large upright panicles, typically twenty to forty in a cluster, and have a slight musky scent. The leaves are glossy but pale green with laciniate stipules. 'Cramoisi Simple' has large prickles and makes a vigorous upright rambler, up to 5 m in height.

'Désiré Bergera' [Barbier, 1909]. *Rosa wichurana* × 'Aurore'. There are two different Wichurana Ramblers in cultivation under this name: one at L'Haÿ-les-Roses, with large panicles of small (3.0–3.5 cm) pink flowers, and one at Cavriglia, with medium-sized (5–6 cm) apricot flowers in small clusters. Early descriptions all refer to medium-sized flowers of coppery pink, coppery yellow, or salmon pink, which suggests the specimen at Cavriglia is correct. The flowers are full, sometimes quartered, and sweetly scented. The colour is stronger in the centre, fading towards the edge, which makes a very attractive contrast. The flowers are borne singly or in small clusters, abundantly and early. The leaves are small, dark, glossy, and dense, with bronze young growth. It is a fairly strong grower and will reach 5 m.

'Edgar Andreu' [Barbier, 1912]. *Rosa wichurana* × 'Cramoisi Supérieur'. The semi-double, medium-sized flowers (7 cm) open crimson and fade to dark pink, although the backs of the petals are always paler. The petals have conspicuous white flashes which run through them and, together with the stamens, intensify the colour when the flowers open. The flowers are borne in clusters of five to ten, rather late in the season, and the leaves are small, dark and shiny. 'Edgar Andreu' survives only at Sangerhausen.

'Edmond Proust' [Barbier, 1902 or 1903]. *Rosa wichurana* × 'Souvenir de Catherine Guillot'. The charm of this cultivar lies in the individual flowers, which is perhaps just as well, because it is a niggardly bloomer. The edges are palest pink or white, contrasting abruptly with the deep strawberry pink centre. The fully double flowers are 5–6 cm across and open to a muddled centre full of soft petals. They are carried in small clusters of three to twelve flowers with a slight scent. The plant grows vigorously to about 4 m.

'Elisa Robichon' [Barbier, 1901]. *Rosa wichurana* × 'L'Idéal'. René Barbier had a high regard for this cultivar. The flowers are lightly musk scented, semi-double, about 4–5 cm across, and open to show their stamens. Although the effect from a distance is of a creamy white mass (set off by wonderfully dark, glittering leaves) the flowers have the subtle colouring of their Noisette parent, with hints of buff, pink, lilac, pale salmon, and mother-of-pearl. They are carried in clusters of five to ten with a tremendous burst at the first flowering and then intermittently until autumn. The plant is slender and vigorous, reaching 4–5 m.

'Emile Fortépaule' [Barbier, 1902]. *Rosa wichurana* × 'Souvenir de Catherine Guillot'. The flowers are small to medium-sized (5 cm) and open cream coloured, with a hint of lemon or buff in the centre, but quickly fade to white. They are fairly double and somewhat irregularly arranged, but prolifically borne in medium-sized clusters, typically of five to ten flowers. The shiny, medium green leaves are a good foil for the flowers, and the somewhat prickly plant grows to 4–5 m.

'Ferdinand Roussel' [Barbier, 1904]. Allegedly *Rosa wichurana* × 'Luciole'. The flowers are small (3–4 cm), very double, and a vinous purplish red, bright when the flowers open and duller, more cherry crimson, later. The white bases of the petals only show when the flowers open out flat, but they intensify the colour. The flowers have a neat green eye and come in medium-sized clusters of five to fifteen, rather late in the season. The foliage is very fine—dark and lustrous. The growth is slender, and the plant grows vigorously to about 4 m.

'François Foucard' [Barbier, 1901]. *Rosa wichurana* × 'L'Idéal'. René Barbier regarded this as one of his finest Wichuranas. At its best, it has a supremely beautiful flower, deep lemon yellow at first, slightly paler at the edges, about 5–6 cm across, and with neatly quartered and imbricated petals (plate 101). It flowers particularly early and continues into autumn. The flowers have rather disorganised, semi-double centres and fade very quickly from yellow to white, giving a creamy white impression. They do, however, have a light musky scent, and the plant grows very vigorously to about 5 m. It is also fairly resistant to mildew and blackspot.

'François Guillot' [Barbier, 1905]. *Rosa wichurana* × 'Mme Laurette Messimy'. The flowers are among the largest seen on ramblers (8–10 cm). The long, elegant buds are cream coloured, but the flowers open pure white and are little more than semi-double, with a beautiful rounded shape, like milky hemispheres. They have a moderate scent and are carried singly or in small clusters, seldom more than four at a time. It is not the most floriferous of ramblers, but the individual flowers are supremely beautiful. The leaves are a good foil: dark bronze green, and glossy. The plant is vigorous, open, lax, and healthy, quickly making 5 m, perhaps more.

'François Juranville' [Barbier, 1906]. *Rosa wichurana* × 'Mme Laurette Messimy'. The combination of coppery pink flowers, dark foliage, and vigorous graceful growth is still unbeaten, especially in a cool climate. The flowers are medium sized (7 cm), loosely double, quilled, and occasionally quartered; they fade to medium pink but hold their attractive shape throughout. They have a fruity scent and are copiously carried either singly or in small clusters of up to seven. The dark, glossy foliage is small, tough, and only susceptible to mildew if grown against a wall. The growths are long, slender, flexible, pendulous, and a wonderful dark crimson when young. The plant is exceptionally vigorous, capable of reaching 7–8 m. It flowers just before midseason.

'François Poisson' [Barbier, 1902]. *Rosa wichurana* × 'William Allen Richardson'. The lemon yellow buds open into medium-sized (5–6 cm) white flowers with a hint of lemon in the centre that does not fade, distinguishing 'François Poisson' from 'Albéric Barbier'. It is the most double of the white Barbier ramblers and the flowers open fully, showing a mass of quilled inner petals and, sometimes, a button eye. They have a nice sweet-musky scent. The leaves are dark and shiny, and the plant grows vigorously to at least 4 m.

'Henri Barruet' [Barbier, 1918]. The unconventional and inconstant colouring of 'Henri Barruet' has never been popular. When the flowers open, the upper parts of the petals start crimson and peach, overlaid with pink and white in parts, before fading to buff, white, and lilac. It is an astonishing transformation to see on an individual flower, although the colour changes vary according to season and weather. The flowers are scented, medium sized (7–8 cm), and borne singly or in small clusters on a plant which grows to 3–4 m. Yet, the overall effect is of a sparsely blooming climber with scrappy little leaves.

'Jacotte' [Barbier, 1920]. *Rosa wichurana* × 'Arthur R. Goodwin'. 'Jacotte' is very hardy and has always been more widely grown in New England than in its native France. The medium-sized flowers (6–7 cm) are dark copper, even orange, when they first open and fade through peach and buff to pale pink, but the overall impression is of a warm apricot (plate 103). They are semi-double and cupped, so that the whole plant glows with colour when the sun shines through their petals. The flowers are well set off by dark green, glossy, disease-resistant foliage and reddish, very prickly stems. The first flowering is profuse, but the plant is seldom without flowers thereafter. 'Jacotte' grows to 3–4 m.

'Jean Guichard' [Barbier, 1905]. *Rosa wichurana* × 'Souvenir de Catherine Guillot'. Although very like 'Albertine', this cultivar has never enjoyed the same popularity. The flowers are fuller and not as coppery in colour. They are medium sized (7–8 cm), very full, flat, strongly and sweetly scented, and carried in small clusters. The petals are dark salmon pink on the outside, pale rose pink within, and fade eventually to silvery pink. The contrasts give beautiful deep tones to the centre of the flowers. The leaves are larger than many Wichuranas', coppery bronze at first, dark green later. The plant is very vigorous, with long, flexible growths, and it flowers early and very abundantly.

'Joseph Billard' [Barbier, 1907]. *Rosa wichurana* × 'Mme Eugène Résal'. This rose does not impress as a garden plant—the individual flowers are attractive, but few. The flowers are medium to large (7–9 cm), single, and bright, iridescent, crimson red, set off by long stamens and a yellow centre which fades to cream. The crimson fades to magenta and the undersides from pinkish yellow to white. The musk-scented flowers are borne early, singly or in small clusters (up to seven), on a very vigorous plant with dark, glossy leaves.

'Joseph Liger' [Barbier, 1909]. *Rosa wichurana* × 'Irène Watts'. This is an attractive, medium-sized (7 cm) rose, with the full flowers and reflexed petals of its China parent. The buds are dark pink, but the flowers open mother-of-pearl and fade to palest pink or cream. What really distinguishes them, however, is the contrast provided by the dark pink tips to the petals. These have the effect of suffusing the whole of the centre of the flower with pink, which is echoed by the slightly paler pink edges to the pointed, reflexed outer petals. It is a charming and unique combination. The flowers have a sweet, slightly musky scent and come in small clusters of up to seven flowers. The plant is fairly vigorous, with shiny leaves, and grows to about 3 m.

'Jules Levacher' [Barbier, 1907]. *Rosa wichurana* × 'Mme Laurette Messimy'. The small (3–4 cm) scented flowers start from globular buds, whose petals reflex like a cabbage rose, and slowly open into round, full flowers, 4–5 cm across, sometimes with a button eye. The colour is pure deep pink at first, but fades to silvery pink; the pale outer petals contrast with the more intensely pink inner ones. The plant is a vigorous grower with very small, dark leaves and is very free-flowering. It grows to 4 m at Sangerhausen.

'Léontine Gervais' [Barbier, 1903]. *Rosa wichurana* × 'Souvenir de Catherine Guillot'. This famous and popular rambler has often been confused with 'François Juranville'; 'Léontine Gervais' is paler and only semi-double. The buds are coppery red, but the flowers open apricot pink and fade to pale pink and cream or white. The petal-backs are slightly darker. The flowers are about 5 cm across, very strongly scented of sweetness and musk, and borne singly or in short-stemmed clusters of up to about seven. They become rather loose and untidy towards the end of their flowering and do not stand rain well—they do best in cool climates and keep their colour much longer in the shade. The leaves are wonderfully dark and lustrous, and the growing stems are crimson where the sun strikes them and green beneath. The plant has its big flowering fairly early, with a few more flowers later. It is healthy, sinuous, and vigorous and will grow to 5 m.

'Le Poilu' syn. 'Cumberland Belle' [Barbier, 1913]. 'Wichmoss' × 'Moussu du Japon'. The rose of this name at Sangerhausen is the same as 'Cumberland Belle' at Mottisfont. The latter should be a climbing sport of 'Princesse Adélaïde' [Laffay, 1845] which also grows at Sangerhausen but is quite different. I assume therefore that both are correctly 'Le Poilu', although contemporary descriptions of either rose are few. The flowers are 5–6 cm across, rose pink fading to silvery pink, and borne singly or in clusters of up to five on long mossy green stems. They have a rich damask scent and an old-fashioned shape and are early flowering. The plant has bright pale green leaves and grows to about 2.5–3.0 m.

'Maxime Corbon' [Barbier, 1918]. *Rosa wichurana* × 'Léonie Lamesch'. The buds are bright coppery vermilion. As the flowers open, they are a deep coppery yellow washed with red, before passing to apricot, yellow, buff, and cream—flashy colouring inherited from 'Léonie Lamesch'. The centre and the undersides are always paler, and end white. The flowers are medium sized (6–7 cm), double, with neatly imbricated petals like a camellia, very sweet-scented, carried singly or in small clusters (up to seven). They look good against the rich, dark green, glossy, leathery leaves. The vigorous plant grows to 5 m.

'Paul Ploton' [Barbier, 1910]. *Rosa wichurana* × 'Mme Norbert Levavasseur'. The flowers are small (3.0–3.5 cm) and open out into full rosettes which are very double and flat. The colour is a rich, glowing crimson, sometimes with a hint of purple at the centre and, even when fading, always more crimson than pink (plate 105). The backs of the petals are pale pink—quite a contrast. They are borne in large open clusters, some ten to twenty-five in a spray, and start to flower in midseason. The plant is a vigorous, once-flowering, with fine dark foliage, rather puckered but untouched by mildew until late.

'Paul Transon' [Barbier, 1900]. *Rosa wichurana* × 'L'Idéal'. This rose has become confused in the trade with 'Paul Noël', and the true 'Paul Transon' is now rather rare. They are very distinct. 'Paul Transon' never has a mass of little quill-shaped petals radiating out like an apricot-coloured sunburst—that is unique to 'Paul Noël'. 'Paul Transon' has dark pink buds which open to pale salmon pink flowers with an almost coppery or terra-cotta pink centre and fade to creamy pink, keeping the subtle colour grading of its Tea parent. They are strongly tea scented, medium sized (6 cm), double, and open out completely. They are often borne singly, but also in small clusters (three or five) and somewhat sparingly. Enjoy the individual flowers, not the overall effect. The main flowering is midseason, with a few blooms through until late autumn. The plant is a vigorous rambler with dark green, glossy foliage and purplish red young stems. It may get a little mildew late in the year.

'Primevère' syn. 'Primrose' [Barbier, 1929]. *Rosa wichurana* × 'Constance'. The best large-flowered yellow Wichurana Rambler appeared at the end of the Barbier's breeding career. Few roses are so beautiful. The flowers are medium sized (only about 7 cm) but seem much larger (plate 104). They are very full of petals, flat, quilled, and rather muddled, with a really good yellow which lasts, fading only slowly from bright yellow to lemon yellow. The individual roses last longer than most ramblers. I find it produces a few flowers later. The flowers are moderately scented and come singly or in small clusters, typically of three to five. Their long sturdy stems make them excellent for cutting. The leaves are dark and glossy. The plant is a lanky grower, rather bare at the base, with large prickles on the thick, vigorous stems. It grows to 4–5 m.

'René André' [Barbier, 1900]. *Rosa wichurana* × 'L'Idéal'. The influence of the Tea parent is plainly seen in the mixture of colours. When 'René André' first opens, the flowers are bronze, orange, and dark pink, but the yellow hues fade altogether and the flowers end up pale pink, splashed with traces of crimson. The outer petals fade first, so there are at all stages many contrasting shades within each flower. The flowers are medium sized (6 cm), loosely semi-double, and the inner petals are often rather ragged in shape. The flowers come in small clusters and are lightly tea scented. The plant is vigorous, with prickly stems and dark, glossy, bronze green leaves; it grows to 4 m. The first flowering, early in the season, is followed by an occasional bloom later.

'Valentin Beaulieu' [Barbier, 1902]. *Rosa wichurana* × 'Souvenir de Catherine Guillot'. This attractive rose survives at Sangerhausen. The flowers are lightly scented, small to medium sized (5–6 cm), flat, very full of petals, and with a button eye. They open dark pink and fade to medium pink, always darker towards the middle, and are nicely spaced in long loose sprays of five to fifteen. The plant is very vigorous, with lax growth, slender coppery brown branches, and dark, neat leaves. It flowers early in the season.

'Wichmoss' [Barbier, 1911]. *Rosa wichurana* × 'Salet'. 'Wichmoss' was bred for hardiness and the plant certainly has it. The flowers are small (about 4 cm) and semi-double, opening pure rose pink and fading to a beautiful silvery pink. The soft petals spoil in rain. They come in upright clusters of five to twenty-five and have a good scent, a mixture of musk and sweetness. The most arresting feature is the heavy layer of moss which starts with the sepals, runs down the long capsules, the slender pedicels, and stems below until it is transmuted into the dense covering of hard bristles which characterises strongly mossed roses. The moss looks particularly beautiful on the new growth, when it is still crimson and glistens, a striking feature of the plant after flowering. 'Wichmoss' is naturally very prickly and quite bushy, with sturdy upright growth; it can be grown as a 2-m shrub as well as a 4-m climber. Mildew, and sometimes blackspot, may spoil its appearance but never affect its vigour.

OTHER WICHURANA RAMBLERS IN FRANCE

Many nurserymen responded to the huge demand for the new ramblers by breeding a few of their own. This section lists all the other Wichuranas introduced in France which are still in existence, including some very beautiful cultivars introduced by Louis Mermet in the 1930s. One shadowy figure stalks these pages: Laurent Fauque of Orléans, to whom honour is due for such important roses as 'Aviateur Blériot' and 'Miss Helyett'. I have been able to discover nothing about him and his firm, Fauque et fils. I am particularly puzzled because his hybrids were sometimes ascribed to others. The French *Journal des Roses* variously attributed 'Aviateur Blériot', 'Gerbe Rose', and 'La Perle' to Vigneron, 'Francis' to Barbier, and 'Mme Alice Garnier' to Turbat.

'Avenir' syn. 'L'Avenir' [Corboeuf, 1910]. This rose exists now only at L'Haÿ-les-Roses and Sangerhausen. It has small (3.5–4.0 cm), pure white, semi-double flowers in large, erect panicles and a strong musky scent. The plant grows vigorously to 4 m.

'Aviateur Blériot' [Fauque et fils, 1910]. *Rosa wichurana* × 'William Allen Richardson'. This cultivar has been popular since its introduction. The flowers open apricot and fade to pale yellow, cream, and white, becoming increasingly untidy as the petals turn brown (plate 106). The flowers are medium sized (6–7 cm), fairly double, and lightly scented (fruity to me, but some Americans say it reminds them of magnolias) and come in small clusters. The small, neat, glittering leaves are very attractive. The plant grows vigorously to 5 m and flowers early.

'Claude Rabbé' [Buatois, 1941]. This excellent second-generation Wichurana Rambler now exists only in such collections as at L'Haÿ-les-Roses. The strongly scented flowers are medium sized (7 cm), flat, very full, medium pink with a hint of salmon at the centre (and paler at the edges), and copiously carried in medium-sized clusters (five to twelve).

'Diabolo' [Fauque, 1908]. *Rosa wichurana* × 'Xavier Olibo'. 'Diabolo' has a modern look, reminiscent of 'Frensham'. The scentless flowers are fairly large (7–8 cm), single to semi-double, deep crimson with even darker shadings which contrast with the small white centres and the yellow stamens. They come early in the season in medium-sized clusters with long stems on a vigorous, upright, prickly, thick-stemmed plant which grows to 4 m.

'Francis' [Fauque et fils, 1908]. 'Wichurana Rubra' × 'Turner's Crimson Rambler'. The flowers are small (4–5 cm), single or semi-double, bright pink at first, but fading to silvery pink, with a white centre. They are borne in long open sprays of ten to twenty, reminiscent of 'Mrs F. W. Flight', and handsome against the pale green leaves. The plant flowers abundantly, late in the season, and grows to 4–5 m.

'Général Tétard' [Pajotin-Chédane, 1918]. This is not a semi-double sport of 'American Pillar', as is sometimes said, although the description is a good guide to its appearance. 'Général Tétard' is a Wichurana Hybrid with medium-sized (6 cm), musk-scented, single to semi-double flowers which are bright crimson (fading slightly) with white flecks at the centre, a conspicuous exserted style, and petals that recurve (plate 107). They are borne midseason in clusters of ten to twenty-five. The plant has typical Wichurana leaves and sometimes gets mildew on the pedicels. I grow this rose as a 2-m bush, but it will make 4 m as an attractive cheerful climber.

'Gerbe Rose' [Fauque, 1904]. *Rosa wichurana* × 'Baronne Adolphe de Rothschild'. This free-flowering beauty is one of the prettiest and most sweetly scented of all roses. Because it is not overvigorous, it makes a good pillar rose. The flowers are medium sized (8 cm), fairly double, flat, with a ruffled arrangement of petals. They open a pure, rich pink, but fade from the tips to pale pink, so that the centre keeps its darker shadows. The small clusters come early and produce a few flowers until autumn. The stems have few prickles and large, dark leaves. The stiff upright growth reaches about 4 m.

'Jean l'Hoste' [Congy, introduced by Cochet, 1926]. 'Alexandre Girault' × 'Gerbe Rose'. I have seen this undistinguished rose only at Sangerhausen, where it grows slowly to 2.5 m. The musk-scented flowers are medium sized (7 cm), double, and deep pink, with a white centre and paler undersides, and open out to show their stamens. They come in rather congested terminal clusters of three to ten flowers. The leaves are glossy but large.

'La Perle' [Fauque, 1904]. *Rosa wichurana* × 'Mme Hoste'. The medium-sized flowers (7 cm), which are uncannily like 'Symbol Míru', open lemon yellow but fade quickly to cream and white, with a few pink blotches as they die. The outer petals reflex, the middle ones are quilled, and the centre ones fold into a button eye. The flowers are sweetly scented and are borne singly or in small, loose clusters. The dark green leaves and long lithe growths indicate Wichurana descent; the plant climbs quickly to 5–6 m.

'Marco' [Guillot, 1905]. *Rosa wichurana* × 'Souvenir de Catherine Guillot'. The buff-coloured bud opens to a medium-sized (6–7 cm), fully double flower which is creamy white at the edges and a mixture of mother-of-pearl and buff at the centre. It is strongly scented and well complemented by the dark green, shiny leaves. The plant grows vigorously to about 5 m. This attractive rose has recently been reintroduced. Girin introduced a sport in 1911 with red edges to the petals called 'Mme Huguette Despiney'; it is not so attractive.

'Miss Helyett' [Fauque, 1909]. *Rosa wichurana* × 'Ernest Metz'. The unusually large flowers (8–9 cm) are carried singly, occasionally in clusters of up to three. They open deep pulsating pink from a rounded, coral bud, but fade gradually to pearly pink. They are prettiest when the darker pink at the centre is matched by attractively quilled outer petals. The flowers have long stems and a slight scent. The plant has large, glossy, dark leaves; slender growths; and a very vigorous habit. It reaches at least 5 m and is said to be fairly healthy. 'Miss Helyett' flowers early and for quite a long season.

'Mme Alice Garnier' [Fauque, introduced by Turbat, 1906]. *Rosa wichurana* × 'Mme Charles'. The attractive, small (3–4 cm), fully double flowers have neat, quilled, apricot petals which are deep terra-cotta at the centre and paler and pinker at the edges (plate 108). The petal-backs are darker. The blooms have a delicious scent of ripe peaches and come in medium-sized clusters of five to fifteen. The plant has dark pink stems and small, neat, glossy, dark green leaves. A vigorous grower with long, slender, often prostrate stems, 'Mme Alice Garnier' reaches 3–4 m. It flowers reliably throughout the season.

'Mme Charles Lejeune' [Vandevelde, 1924]. 'Dr W. Van Fleet' × 'La Perle'. This rose is pale pink, fading to white, with medium-sized flowers (7–8 cm) on a stiff and upright plant. They come in small clusters of up to seven and have a good, sweet scent but keep their petals too long. At Sangerhausen this plant suffers from blackspot.

'Mme Charles Yojerot' [Thebault-Lebreton, 1921]. Although always described as a Wichurana, the plant at Sangerhausen is closer to the Multifloras. The flowers are small, dark pink, single, and nicely carried on a widely spaced spray. It seems fairly vigorous and healthy, but dull.

'Mme Constans' [Gravereaux, 1902]. This was quite an advanced rose when introduced, although it never has been widely grown. The flowers are medium sized (6 cm), medium pink at first but pale pink later, very full and double, and very freely borne in sturdy clusters of five to ten. The plant is impressive in full flower and in dry weather, when the petals glisten. Rain spoils them. The broad pale green leaves suggest Bourbon heritage, but the flowers are scentless.

'Mme Portier-Durel' [Portier-Durel, introduced by Guillot, 1910]. I have seen this once-popular, now almost-forgotten rose only at Cavriglia, where it is a vision of loveliness in early June. It has elegant, long, loose sprays of pure white flowers and extremely vigorous, long, lax growths (plate 109). The flowers are small (3 cm), but each makes a perfect rosette with a button eye and has a light sweet scent. One curious attribute is the way the sepals reflex completely, long before the bud opens. 'Mme Portier-Durel' is a very hardy plant.

'Renée Danielle' [Guillot, 1913]. This attractive rambler has small (5 cm), fully double, pale buff yellow flowers which fade to ivory and white as they open. The flowers come singly or in small clusters and open rather late in the season, then continue on and off until late autumn. The leaves are handsome, dark, and shiny; the plant, which is almost thornless, grows to about 3 m.

'Souvenir d'Ernest Thébault' [Thébault-Lebreton, 1921]. This rose grows only at Sangerhausen now; it has small, double, dark red, scentless flowers in clusters of five to fifteen. The plant grows to 3–4 m.

'Souvenir de J. Mermet' [Mermet, 1934]. This forgotten beauty has attractive, small to medium-sized (4.5–5.0 cm) flowers which are very well scented, double, rosette shaped, and button eyed (plate 110). The petals are bright, dark pink on their upper sides and palest pink on their undersides, so the button eye provides a particularly effective contrast. The flowers come in clusters of five to fifteen and are best in hot dry weather—the petals spoil in rain. The plant is vigorous, with shiny, bronze green leaves and crimson stems (rather prickly); it flowers again in the autumn.

'Vendôme' [Mouillère, 1923]. This deep crimson red Wichurana grows only at Bagatelle. The flowers are fairly small (5 cm) but fully double and profusely carried in clusters of five to fifteen. The plant is vigorous, with dark, glossy foliage and slender pendulous growths.

'Vîcomtesse de Chabannes' [Buatois, 1921]. Early descriptions of this rose are misleading and exaggerate the flower size and colour. In fact the blooms are medium sized (5–6 cm), rather more than semi-double, and borne in erect clusters of five to ten (plate 111). The colour is bright pale crimson or deep pink and almost white on the undersides, exactly the same shades as 'Alexandre Girault'. Some of the petals have white flecks which run right through from the base to the edge. The flowers have a good fruity scent. The plant is very vigorous, growing to 4–5 m, and covered in deep green, glossy leaves, larger than usual for such ramblers.

Wichurana Ramblers in Germany

WEIGAND OF SODEN

The significance of the new Wichurana Hybrids was not immediately appreciated in Germany. A correspondent of *Rosen-Zeitung* pointed out that the qualities of *Rosa wichurana* and its potential for breeding rambling roses were not recognised for a long time because of its creeping habit (*Rosen-Zeitung* 1898, 61). Ludwig Weigand was the first German to breed Wichurana Ramblers suited to the climate of central Europe.

The Weigand family owned a nursery in the spa town of Soden-am-Taunus, near Frankfurt-am-Main. They produced cut roses, until competition obliged them to diversify into rose breeding. Christoph Weigand (1839–1909) is credited with introducing the first German Wichurana Hybrid, 'Ernst Grandpierre', in 1900, but all the Weigand hybrids were bred by his son Ludwig (b. 1873). In addition to his climbers, Ludwig Weigand also introduced one of the last Hybrid Perpetuals, the splendid 'Ruhm von Steinfurth' (see *Rosenjahrbuch des Vereins Deutscher Rosenfreunde* 1936, III, 93–94). I have grouped all his hybrids together to demonstrate the measure of his achievement.

'Anna Rübsamen' [Weigand, 1904]. The parents of this rose are unknown, but the flowers have the look of 'Turner's Crimson Rambler'. The very full blooms are rich pink at first, fading to pale pink, small (4 cm), and attractive from a distance but prettier still close-up. When they open out, the petals reflex sharply and seem to radiate out from the pale centre. It is an effect which one sees rarely; 'Paul Noël' has the same structure. The airy flower clusters are scented, and the plant grows vigorously to 3–4 m.

'Ernst Grandpierre' [Weigand, 1900]. *Rosa wichurana* × 'Perle des Jardins'. The individual flowers are very attractive, with a hint of a button eye, but fade quickly from cream to pure white. They are medium sized (5–6 cm), very double, strongly scented, and carried in small clusters of three to seven. The typically glossy leaves are a paler, brighter green than normal. The slender plant grows to 3–4 m. It flowers over a very long season, but the overall effect is striking only for a week or so in the middle.

'Frau Albert Hochstrasser' [Weigand, 1906]. The flowers are medium sized (5–7 cm), scented, and very double, with a neat arrangement of petals and a button eye. They open buff yellow but fade quickly to white and hang down in small to medium-sized clusters of five to ten. It has neat glossy leaves and many very large prickles. The plant is vigorous, reaching 4–5 m, and late flowering, with a few flowers until autumn.

'Frau Marie Weinbach' [Weigand, 1906]. This rose has masses of small (4 cm), very double, pure white flowers and a strong musky scent. The petals recurve later to give the flowers a distinctive spiky look. This is attractive because the blooms are regularly imbricated and carried in short clusters, typically of seven to fifteen flowers. The plant has dark glossy leaves and vigorous slender growths which reach at least 4 m.

'Non Plus Ultra' syn. 'Weigand's Crimson Rambler' [Weigand, 1904]. 'Turner's Crimson Rambler' × 'Blanche Rebatel'. This cultivar enjoyed some success as an improved 'Turner's Crimson Rambler'. The flowers are small (4 cm), scentless, double, and bright crimson—a sumptuous colour in cool weather or shade. The flowers are abundantly carried in large, long, stiff, upright clusters of twenty to forty, which droop under the weight of the opened flowers. The bright green leaves have fimbriated stipules and are sometimes susceptible to blackspot. Mildew may affect the pedicels, but the plant grows vigorously to 3–4 m and flowers ten days earlier than its parent. The sport called 'Graf Zeppelin', introduced by Böhm (a Bonn nurseryman, not related to the Czech) in 1910, opens dark pink and fades to pale. Kiese said it flowered late into the autumn and withstood −25°C.

'Schneeball' [Weigand, 1906]. This rose survives only at Sangerhausen. It has clusters of small (4.5 cm), pure white, moderately scented, and lightly double flowers.

'Sodenia' [Weigand, 1911]. This repeat-flowering beauty has small to medium-sized (5 cm), very full flowers which are very bright carmine crimson, a nice contrast to the nearly white undersides. Streaks of white also run through the petals and intensify the colour. The flowers are scentless and come in loose, open clusters of five to fifteen, rather late in the season. The plant is fairly vigorous, with prickly, slender growth; small, glossy leaves; and fimbriated stipules. It is very hardy, even in the Bohemian Erzgebirge.

'Taunusblümchen' [Weigand, 1906]. 'Turner's Crimson Rambler' × 'Blanche Rebatel'. The flowers open deep purplish pink, the colour of 'Zéphirine Drouhin', and fade to medium pink with whiter edges. They are small (4.5 cm), double, with neat circular rows of petals and a sweet musky scent. Each cluster bears ten to twenty flowers, but these are produced in vast quantities and seem to cover the plant with colour. 'Taunusblümchen' grows vigorously to 3–4 m.

'Theodora Milch' [Weigand, 1906]. This is a dainty little rambler—Weigand compared its neatly double flowers to daisies. In fact, its imbricated petals are too broad to justify the analogy, but they are attractive and unusual nevertheless. The flowers are small (3.5 cm), flat, very ordered, and medium pink, fading quickly to pale lilac and white. They are lightly scented, late flowering, and borne in open airy clusters of five to thirty. The leaves are small and glossy, carried on a fairly vigorous plant which grows to 4 m.

'Tricolore' [Weigand, 1906]. The flowers are red, white, and pink—sometimes one colour, sometimes another, but usually an endlessly different combination of all three. They are medium sized (5–6 cm), very double, flat, neatly quilled, lightly scented, and borne in medium-sized clusters, typically of ten. The small, dark leaves are a little susceptible to blackspot, but the plant is vigorous enough, growing to 3–4 m.

OTHER GERMAN WICHURANA RAMBLERS

The discovery and publication of Gregor Mendel's studies of heredity gave a great boost to intelligent plant breeding. His papers were reported in *Rosen-Zeitung* in 1902 and discussed at considerable length. The German who bred some of the world's best ramblers in the 1920s and 1930s was Max Vogel (1867–1934), the director of Sangerhausen.

'Charlotte von Rathlef' [Vogel, 1935]. 'Fragezeichen' × 'American Pillar'. This is a very beautiful, very double, dark pink rose which pales at the edges and comes in small clusters on long stems. It flowers once, in great profusion, and deserves wider cultivation.

'Erna' [Vogel, 1929]. The flowers are small (4 cm), pale salmon pink (darker on the undersides), with a sweet musky scent. The are borne in clusters of five to ten on a fairly vigorous plant with dark, glossy leaves. 'Erna' is a scaled-down 'Albertine'.

'Ernst Dechant' [Vogel, 1928]. This is another very attractive Wichurana, very double, with rows of neat little petals round a large mass of golden stamens. The flowers are musk scented and come in clusters of five to ten.

'Fräulein Oktavia Hesse' [Hesse, 1910]. *Rosa wichurana* × 'Kaiserin Auguste Viktoria'. I consider this the best of all white Wichuranas. The medium-sized flowers (6–7 cm) open with a lemon centre but fade quickly to white (plate 112). They are very freely produced, from early in the season to autumn, in small dense clusters of up to eight. The flowers are full of petals, Tea-shaped at first, but open to show a neat centre and quilled inner petals before reflexing into spiky snowballs. They have a good tea scent. Their only weakness is that they sometimes die badly. The plant is vigorous and very hardy, with long, flexible growths, reaching 5–6 m and covered with dark green, glossy, disease-resistant leaves.

'Frau Liesel Brauer' [Thönges, 1938]. The flowers are among the largest and most elegant of all ramblers (10–11 cm across), but they seem smaller because they stay cupped until they open out their long, irregularly shaped petals. The flowers are semi-double, silvery pink with slightly deeper centres, and moderately scented with a mixture of damask and musk. They come in clusters of three to ten on long elegant stems. The plant is very vigorous, with glossy leaves and lots of large prickles.

'Greta Fey' [Straßheim, 1909]. This cream-coloured, semi-double, small-flowered Wichurana grows only at Sangerhausen.

'Hans Schmid' [Vogel, introduced by Lambert, 1934]. 'Fragezeichen' × 'American Pillar'. This sister-seedling of 'Charlotte von Rathlef' has small (4.5 cm), very double, deep pink, globular flowers in medium-sized clusters of eight to twenty.

'Kleine Rösel' [Vogel, 1929]. Recently reintroduced from Sangerhausen, this rose has small flowers (4 cm) which open mauve crimson, then fade to deep pink with occasional lilac markings. The petal undersides are always paler. The blooms come in flat clusters and are scentless. The plant is vigorous and prickly, with glossy leaves.

'Mühle Hermsdorf' [Dechant, 1928]. A white Wichurana × 'Gruß an Zabern'. The flowers are very strongly musk scented, medium sized (5 cm), well filled, and come in clusters of ten to twenty. The plant is almost thornless, free-flowering, healthy, and vigorous.

'Peter Lambert' [Vogel, 1936]. Vogel named this splendid bright, deep pink Wichurana in honour of Peter Lambert, then the grand old man of German roses. The flowers are medium sized (6 cm), very full, and cabbage-shaped when first open, but scentless. They come in long clusters of five to fifteen. The plant is very vigorous, with glistening leaves and lots of long prickles. It is a mid- to late-season flowerer and very healthy.

'Ratgeber Rose' [Verlag Practischer Ratgeber, 1930]. This rose, named for a popular German magazine, now exists only in such collections as Sangerhausen. The flowers are small to medium sized (4.5–5.0 cm), double, scentless, and light red or dark pink; they come in clusters of five to ten. The plant is late flowering and fairly vigorous.

Wichurana Ramblers in England

Like the Germans, only more so, the English were slow to exploit the possibilities for further breeding inherent in *Rosa wichurana* and 'Turner's Crimson Rambler'. Both Paul firms worked with 'Turner's Crimson Rambler' a little, but few Wichurana Ramblers were bred in England until the 1920s and 1930s, and then mainly by amateurs and small nurseries, never on the scale of Barbier or Van Fleet. One exception was the series of large-flowered hybrids bred and introduced by Chaplin Bros., who took over William Paul's nursery in 1922; 'Chaplin's Pink Climber' is well known, but excellent cultivars like 'Buttermere' and 'July Glory' await reintroduction from such specialist collections as Sangerhausen, where they languish almost forgotten.

Walter Easlea should also be commemorated for 'Easlea's Golden Rambler', 'Thelma', and its incomparable sport 'Melita'. Easlea started his working life as a budder for George Paul when he was sixteen. The next year, his father went to work for William Paul at Waltham Cross, and Walter followed. He remained there for many years, until in 1900 he was able to start his own nursery at Danecroft Rosery, Eastwood, near Leigh-on-Sea. Easlea was a keen rose breeder and built a special glasshouse for his breeding work. Hybrid Teas were his great love; among the popular cultivars he introduced were the white 'Countess of Warwick' [1919] and the cherry red 'Prince of Wales' [1921].

Other English rose nurseries produced a few Wichuranas. Ben R. Cant of Colchester was already an ancient and distinguished firm when it introduced 'Blush Rambler' in 1903. The family business was founded in 1765 and firmly established during the latter part of the nineteenth century by Benjamin Cant (d. 1900). Frank Cant, a nephew of Benjamin, started his own firm at Braiswick in about 1880. He died at Colchester in 1928 but his sons introduced 'Etain' in 1953.

'Blush Rambler' [B. Cant, 1903]. 'Turner's Crimson Rambler' × 'The Garland'. This beautiful rambler is remarkably vigorous and capable of reaching 8 m. The flowers are small (4 cm), scented, single, and borne in large pendulous clusters of twenty to fifty. They open bright medium pink and fade to white, but the flowers have "a wise way of shedding their petals the moment they feel themselves growing old and ugly, so that the large bunches of flowers look fresh and clean from first to last" (Bowles 1914, 76–77). They are well complemented by the pale green leaves and the aura of health and vigour which the whole plant exudes. 'Blush Rambler' has rather stiff, upright growth, few prickles, and blooms only once, rather late in the season, but exuberantly.

'Buttermere' [Chaplin, 1932]. This beautiful late-flowering rambler has very double, medium-sized flowers (6 cm) in pendulous clusters on strong upright stems, five to fifteen in a cluster; the clusters are rather tight, but the flowers open in succession. The flowers have a good scent—a mixture of musk and sweetness. They open buff coloured and hold that colour almost to the end, when they turn to cream and white; the inner petals are always darker and richer and often quilled. The plant has good glossy foliage and lots of prickles and grows vigorously to 4 m.

'Chaplin's Pink Climber' [Chaplin, 1928]. 'Paul's Scarlet Climber' × 'American Pillar'. This popular rose makes a spectacular sight once it is established, and it flowers a week or two earlier than its parents. The semi-double flowers are medium sized (6–7 cm) and a particularly vivid shade of dark pink or carmine, with occasional white flecks. They hold their colour very well, with almost no fading, although they blotch badly in rain. The petal undersides are much paler pink and the flowers have conspicuous pale yellow stamens. They come in large clusters of five to fifteen flowers. The leaves are bright, dark green, and glossy and the plant grows to 4–5 m. A well-grown specimen in full glory is an unforgettable sight—would that it flowered more than once.

'Crimson Conquest' [Chaplin, 1931]. As noted by Courtney Page (1937), 'Crimson Conquest' is "a joyful rose, one that you cannot help stopping to admire." The bright scarlet flowers are medium sized (7 cm) with a delicious, fruity scent. The flowers are attractive on opening, when the pale anthers contrast with the bright red petals, but fade to a duller shade. The petals have a small white patch at the base and a ruffled shape which gives body to the semi-single flower. The flowers come in small (three to five), long-lasting clusters late in the season. The leaves are large, bright green, shiny, and disease-free, although the plant is not completely hardy in cold climates like central Europe.

'Easlea's Golden Rambler' syn. 'Golden Rambler' [Easlea, 1932]. This has the largest flowers and richest colouring of all once-flowering yellow ramblers, but it is not hardy in central Europe or the American Midwest. The flowers are enormous: at 10–11 cm they would do credit to a Hybrid Tea—flat, double, and full of small petals in a muddled arrangement (plate 113). They open dark peachy yellow and turn to bright chrome yellow, fading only very slightly at the edges. The petal edges are sometimes slightly frilled. The individual flowers last well and are very weather-proof. They are strongly and sweetly scented, carried early in the season singly or in clusters of up to about seven. The leaves are distinctive: olive green, glossy, and corrugated. The plant is very vigorous, reaching to 4 m, but inclined to legginess.

'Emily Gray' [Williams, 1917]. 'Jersey Beauty' × 'Comtesse du Cayla'. This is a very English rose—it is not hardy in colder climates and flowers too quickly in hotter ones. The flowers are medium sized (6–7 cm), semi-double, rather cupped, and full of long dark stamens (plate 114). They open apricot and fade to golden yellow; the colour is beautiful at all stages. The flowers are rather loose and have a messy arrangement of irregular and deformed petals when they eventually open out. However, they come early in small, long-stemmed clusters and are strongly tea scented. The leaves are marvellously glossy, large, bronze green, and dark; they would be a good foil for any rose. The plant is vigorous, a stout but leggy grower to 5–6 m. An established plant covers itself with flowers, but it is slow at first and does not repeat.

'Étain' [F. Cant, 1953]. This is a strange name for a shrimp pink rambler, now seldom seen. The flowers are medium sized (5–6 cm), fully double, scented, and borne in large trusses on a vigorous 4-m plant with small, dark green, glossy foliage.

'July Glory' [Chaplin, 1932]. This attractive, very late-flowering Wichurana resembles a dark pink 'Dorothy Perkins'. The flowers are small (3 cm), double, and carried in dense rounded clusters. The leaves are very dark and glossy. The plant is vigorous and grows to 3–4 m.

'Loveliness' [Chaplin, 1933]. I have not seen this vigorous rambler, but its flowers are said to be pale pink-and-white, double, and carried in large clusters. The foliage is small, pale, and glossy, not unlike 'Dorothy Perkins'.

'Lucy' syn. 'Blushing Lucy' [Williams, 1936]. This is said to be a repeat-flowering rose of the 'Dorothy Perkins' type, starting late into flower but continuing through until late autumn. It flowers only once for me. The flowers open a rich medium pink and pale slightly; the centres are always paler (plate 115). They are semi-double, 3.5–5.0 cm across, with a light sweet scent and a hint of musk. They come in long, heavy, pendulous clusters which show up well against the dense, glossy, medium green foliage. The plant is vigorous, with long, flexible growths and a few prickles on the stems. It grows to about 5 m and roots easily from cuttings.

'Monthly Rambler' [Laxton, 1926]. *Rosa wichurana* × 'Semperflorens'. This is a very good rambler with fairly large, pendulous clusters (ten to twenty flowers) of medium-sized (5–6 cm), semi-double flowers: they are a brilliant, rich crimson and hold their colour exceptionally well. It does have a few flowers after the first, exuberant flowering, but not exactly monthly. The foliage reminds me more of *R. multiflora* than *R. wichurana*, but the plant is leafy, fairly vigorous, and very hardy, and grows to about 3 m.

'Nanette' [Hicks, 1926]. Elisha Hicks introduced nine ramblers between 1916 and 1939, but he was a small-scale nurseryman and this is the only one to have survived. Although it did win a Gold Medal from the National Rose Society of Great Britain in 1925, it was never as popular as it merited. The flowers are small to medium sized (5–6 cm), pure white, semi-double, and open out flat, and eventually show a nice boss of stamens (plate 116). They come in long, large, airy clusters, twenty to fifty at a time, starting in midseason and continuing late. They have a strong musky scent. The petals have a distinctive roll which gives the flowers much of their character. The plant is very vigorous and very free-flowering, with shiny green Wichurana foliage.

'Romeo' [Easlea, 1919]. There is more than one rose in cultivation under this name. The one at Sangerhausen is very close to 'Paul Ploton' but fits Easlea's own description well: "its individual crimson blooms are very double, small and attractive, and although it does not show up like Excelsa, it possesses a value all of its own, as every bloom is fit for a small buttonhole" (Easlea 1945). All agree that 'Romeo' resembles a miniature Hybrid Tea in bud.

'Royal Scarlet Hybrid' [Chaplin Bros., 1926]. English breeders in the 1920s introduced many brilliant red ramblers. 'Royal Scarlet Hybrid' has medium-sized flowers (6–7 cm) which are semi-double, lightly scented, and a rich dark scarlet, a remarkable colour in a climber. They come in small clusters of three to eight and are complemented by bright, Wichurana foliage. The plant is hardy and vigorous, growing to 3–4 m; it flowers late in the season.

'Sander's White Rambler' [Sander, 1912]. Sander, Europe's leading orchid nurseryman, was happy to introduce any good plant that came his way, but no one knows who bred this beautiful snow white rambler. It is a late-flowering Wichurana, with long drooping sprays of small (3 cm), fully double flowers that open into flat rosettes. The flowers are strongly and sweetly scented, borne in clusters of ten to twenty, and unusually rain resistant. The plant produces a great number of vigorous long stems shooting up from the base, completely covered with elegant glossy green foliage which is a beautiful foil for the flowers. 'Sander's White Rambler' grows to at least 5 m and has a wonderfully sprawling habit of growth, but it flowers only once.

'Snowflake' [F. Cant, 1922]. Seldom seen now in England, 'Snowflake' remains fairly popular in Germany. The flowers are small (4 cm), semi-double, lightly scented, and pure white; they open out and fold back to resemble snowballs (plate 117). They come in clusters of five to fifteen on long, strong stems. The plant has handsome, dark green, glossy leaves and a vigorous, lax habit, although it reaches 4–5 m in height. It flowers late in the season, but only once.

'Thelma' [Easlea, 1927]. *Rosa wichurana* × 'Paul's Scarlet Climber'. The flowers are a slightly peachy pink at first and fade to carmine and blush pink, but the central petals are always paler and the backs of the petals darken with age (plate 118). The blooms are about 5–6 cm across, fairly scentless, semi-double, with a mass of stamens at the centre. They come in clusters of five to twelve in great quantity and last longer than most roses; the flowers are unaffected by rain or sun. The leaves are beautiful: soft, light, shiny green. The plant is practically thornless and grows vigorously to 3–4 m. Easlea introduced a splendid double-flowered sport called 'Melita' [1934]. It is similar in every way apart from its very full flower, which gives it much greater substance and brightness of colour.

'Weetwood' [Bawden, 1983]. This modern Wichurana Rambler has small (4–5 cm), attractive flowers, which open with a hint of coral at the centre but quickly fade to a pure, pale creamy pink. They have a slight, leafy scent, are full of petals, and are beautifully quartered. 'Weetwood' flowers sparsely and seldom makes a good overall effect, but always has some flowers from midseason until late autumn. The plant is very vigorous even for a Wichurana, and will quickly climb to 5–6 m (more up a tree).

'Windermere' [Chaplin, 1932]. 'Windermere' is one of the handsomest of ramblers. The individual flowers are medium sized (6–7 cm, large for a Wichurana), very full, dark pink or pale crimson, lightly scented, and carried in small sprays of three to eight which have an attractive habit of flopping down. The leaves are dark and glossy; the plant has very prickly, upright stems (the young prickles are conspicuously red) and grows vigorously and strongly to about 3 m.

'Yvonne' [F. Cant, 1921]. This attractive, late-flowering rambler may owe more to 'Turner's Crimson Rambler' than *Rosa wichurana*. The flowers open from neat little buds and are small (4 cm), almost scentless, double, medium pink when first open, but shell pink at the edges and with a darker centre. They come in fairly large, loose clusters of ten to thirty and last very well, although they are not very tolerant of rain. The leaves are dark olive green and glossy, but also have the fimbriated petioles of the Multifloras. The plant grows vigorously to 3–4 m.

Miscellaneous Wichurana Ramblers

No climbing roses were so popular as the Wichurana Ramblers. A survey published in the *American Rose Annual* in 1921 listed the most popular climbing roses in different areas of the United States: "New England prefers 'Dorothy Perkins', with 'American Pillar' and 'Dr W. Van Fleet' second, and 'Silver Moon' and 'Tausendschön' third. The Middle States place 'Dr W. Van Fleet' in the lead, 'Silver Moon' second and 'Dorothy Perkins' and 'Tausendschön' third. 'Dr W. Van Fleet' and 'Silver Moon' are tied for the first place in the South, with 'American Pillar' second and 'Excelsa' third. In the West, 'Tausendschön' comes to the fore, followed by 'Climbing Mme Caroline Testout' and 'Dr W.

Van Fleet'. The Central States give 'Dorothy Perkins', 'Dr W. Van Fleet' and 'Excelsa' first place."

Consider this list of preferences for a moment. None of the roses was introduced before 1900. All were modern. Only one, 'Climbing Mme Caroline Testout', is a climber; the rest are all ramblers. Only one of the ramblers, 'Tausendschön', is a Multiflora. All the others are Wichuranas. No wonder that so many Wichuranas were introduced, even if only a handful survive to this day.

'Blaze' [Calley, introduced by Jackson & Perkins, 1932]. 'Paul's Scarlet Climber' × 'Gruß an Teplitz'. 'Blaze' was the first serious challenger to 'Paul's Scarlet Climber' for the coveted position of everyone's favourite red climbing rose (plate 119). The flowers are medium sized (6–8 cm), semi-double, rather cupped, lightly scented, and carried in great abundance. In 1932 they were considered a brilliant, blazing, scarlet red—we would say glowing crimson red today. They are carried in upright clusters of four to ten on a plant of moderate vigour. The leaves are large for a Wichurana, with rounded leaflets. The plant is reliably remontant.

'Blushing Beauty' [Burbank, 1934]. I have not seen this pale pink Wichurana, which has just been reintroduced to commerce. It is said to be pale silky pink, scented, double, and occasionally remontant. The plant grows to 3 m.

'Coral Fairy' syn. MORcofair [Moore, 1995]. (*Rosa wichurana* × 'Floradora') × 'Hallelujah'. This is a by-product of Moore's miniature rose breeding. The flowers are small (3–4 cm), pink, single (five petals), lightly scented, and borne in large clusters. The plant has dark, glossy leaves and grows to 3–4 m.

'Cracker' [Clark, 1920]. Alister Clark bred several Wichurana Ramblers. The only contemporary description I can trace describes 'Cracker', as: "a vigorous pillar rose, also good as a bush. The flowers are single, about three inches [7.5–8.0 cm] across, of a striking red shade with a distinct white zone, and handsome golden stamens help to make a very attractive variety. The flowers possess a faint sweetbriar fragrance; the foliage is abundant and mildew proof" (National Rose Society of Great Britain *Rose Annual* 1929, 142). The rose still grown at Sangerhausen as 'Cracker' has bright magenta crimson flowers and is 8 cm across, lightly double, strongly scented, borne singly or in small clusters, with prickly wood. There is some doubt as to whether this rose or the cultivar now grown in Australia as 'Cracker' is correctly named.

'Garisenda' [Bonfiglioli, 1911]. *Rosa wichurana* × 'Souvenir de la Malmaison'. This is one of the few Italian-bred climbing roses to become popular in North America. Gaetano Bonfiglioli emigrated to the United States after World War I. 'Garisenda' bears medium-sized (6–7 cm), fully double, pale pink, elegantly quartered flowers in clusters of three to eight rather late in the season. The plant grows to about 4 m.

'Heidekönigin' (Kordapt) syn. 'Pheasant' [Kordes, 1985]. 'Zwergkönig '78' × *Rosa wichurana* seedling. This spectacular modern hybrid has both *R. multiflora* and *R. wichurana* in its ancestry. Initially sold as a ground-cover rose, it is a natural climber, scrambling up with the aid of its long flexible, prickly stems (plate 120). The flowers are medium sized (5.0–5.5 cm), a good medium or dark pink with a hint of coral, and fully double, with a light scent. The flowers have a very round and regular outline and ruffled petals which give them a distinctive charm. It is immensely floriferous, and the splendid, glossy green foliage gives it a look of solidity which contrasts with the frilly petals.

'Pretty Pink' [Barni, 1992]. This modern climber bears medium-sized (5–6 cm), deep pink (fading to pale pink), semi-double flowers in small clusters. The plant has typical Wichurana leaves.

'Refresher' [Clark, 1929]. The American Steve Stevens described this vigorous Wichurana as "a white-flowered 'American Pillar'." Its flowers are small (4 cm) and single and carried in clusters of ten to thirty.

'Ruby Ring' [Clark, 1915]. The name is apt: 'Ruby Ring' has flowers which open out to reveal a big white centre and a narrow edging of deep, unfading crimson or ruby. The lightly scented flowers are small or medium sized (4.5–5.0 cm), single, and borne in long slender clusters of five to fifteen. The leaves are shiny like the Wichuranas, but the thick and upright growth is more reminiscent of the Multifloras. It grows to 2.0–2.5 m.

'Scorcher' [Clark, introduced by Hackett, 1922]. 'Mme Abel Chatenay' seedling. The blazing scarlet, lightly scented flowers are medium sized (8–9 cm), open, lightly semi-double, with loose unkempt petals (plate 121). They come singly or in small clusters rather early in the season and in great profusion, with a few flowers later in the year. The leaves are fairly small, glossy, and quite a dark green. The habit of growth is lanky and stiff and it is probably not hardy in colder areas. It grows to 2.5–3.0 m and looks good as a companion to 'New Dawn'.

'Snowdrift'. There were three Wichurana Hybrids called 'Snowdrift': one introduced by Walsh [c. 1900], another by W. Paul [1913], and the one which is in commerce, introduced by W. R. Smith [1914], which Jäger (1960) describes as "pure white, small, double, in clusters of twenty to thirty, once-flowering, long stems, very large and bright green leaves, fairly vigorous, hardy, to 2½ metres." That description fits the 'Snowdrift' in cultivation in Europe today which has beautiful, cascading panicles of white and a delicious scent, a mixture of sweetness and musk.

'Souvenir d'Adolphe de Charvoik' [1911]. Little is known about the origins of this Wichurana Hybrid. The flowers are small (4.5 cm), pale pink, double, and carried in clusters of five to fifteen on a very vigorous, thornless plant which will grow to 10 m.

'Syringa' [Browning, 1931]. This is a fairly worthless rose, whose flowers are 4–5 cm across, single, pure white, and lightly scented. The blooms come in clusters of five to twenty on an exceptionally vigorous plant which will grow to 5 m, but they are dull.

'Victory' [Undritz, 1918]. 'Dr W. Van Fleet' × 'Mme Jules Grolez'. This rose has attractive, medium-sized flowers (7.0–8.5 cm) which open out nicely to display their quilled and quartered centre (plate 122). The flowers are an attractive pink, with darker tones towards the centre, and fairly well scented. They come in small clusters, early in the season, and drop their petals cleanly when they die. The plant is quite prickly with glossy leaves and a few flowers later; it grows to 3–4 m. 'Victory' anticipates by more than twenty years the race of large-flowered Wichurana Hybrids which were bred from 'New Dawn' in the 1940s and 1950s.

The Brownells

Walter and Josephine Brownell started to take an interest in breeding roses as newlyweds in the early 1900s. They were spurred on by the discovery that all the Hybrid Teas at their summer home in Little Compton, Rhode Island, lost their foliage in August and died during the following winter. There were clearly two problems—hardiness and disease resistance—and the Brownells decided to do something about both.

At first they were not sure how to set about creating better roses, although the publication of Mendel's paper on heredity and cross-breeding gave them a solid theoretical foundation in genetics. It was not until they read, in Ellen Willmott's *The Genus Rosa* (1910–14), that *Rosa wichurana* was both hardy and disease resistant that they decided to use it to develop a range of garden roses which they called "the Brownell sub-zero hybrids." Subzero roses can resist temperatures of less than 0°F (−17.7°C). The Brownells went further, however, intending that their roses should survive unprotected to −15°F (−26.1°C) and, with some earthing up, to −35°F (−37.2°C).

The Brownells' main aim was to produce completely hardy Hybrid Teas which flowered repeatedly and were disease resistant. Although they bred roses for more than forty years, they never succeeded in raising truly hardy roses, largely because *Rosa wichurana* is not as hardy as their study of Miss Willmott had led them to suppose. The Brownells chose three large-flowered Wichuranas as their stud roses: 'Dr. W. Van Fleet', 'Glenn Dale', and 'Mary Wallace', all comparatively healthy and hardy. In 1933 they introduced their first and arguably their greatest climbing rose, 'Mrs Arthur Curtiss James', the first of a race of Wichuranas which may not be completely hardy down to −15°F (−26.1°C) but can nevertheless withstand most severe winters in southern New England. They introduced about ten subzero Hybrid Teas and some forty climbers and shrubs and, by the 1950s, had made an important contribution to the future of garden roses.

The Brownell climbers have their critics. Many flower sparsely. Few repeat. Some are not completely hardy—most do better as creepers than climbers, protected by snow from the worst winter weather. And it could be said that their colours are not bright enough. They are, after all, the roses of an amateur breeder (Josephine Brownell, rather than her husband) who was not a trained horticulturist. But the best are very good indeed.

'Apricot Glow' [Brownell, 1936]. ('Emily Gray' × 'Dr W. Van Fleet') × 'Jacotte'. The flowers are medium sized (7 cm), very full of petals, with a sort-of-quartered centre and a good scent. They open deep apricot, with slightly paler backs, and fade to a pinker tinge as they age. The once-flowering plant is very hardy, with glossy, disease-resistant foliage and extremely prickly stems. It grows to about 3 m.

'Carpet of Gold' [Brownell, 1939]. ('Emily Gray' × 'Aglaia') × 'Golden Glow'. The flowers open from golden yellow buds with a hint of apricot and pale slowly to lemon yellow. They are single or semi-single, with distinctly reflexed petals which create a slightly starry effect and emphasise the size of the central circle of stamens; the flowers themselves are medium sized (7 cm) and sweetly scented. The plant is strong, vigorous, and hardy. It grows to 2.5–3.0 m, but there are too few flowers in both the main flowering and later in the year.

'Copper Glow' [Brownell, 1940]. 'Golden Glow' × 'Break o' Day'. The buds are copper coloured, but the semi-double flowers open out yellow, with red filaments and rather reflexed and spiky outer petals. The flowers are 7–8 cm across and attractive in the bud, but few in number with too few petals. They have a light, fruity scent. The plant is very vigorous, healthy, and hardy, with deep glossy green leaves; it grows to at least 6 m. The Brownells introduced a slightly more orange-coloured sport called 'Orange Everglow' [1942].

'Coral Creeper' [Brownell, 1938]. ('Dr W. Van Fleet' × 'Emily Gray') × 'Jacotte'. This attractive and vigorous climber has medium-sized (8 cm), long-stemmed, lightly double flowers which are a yellowish pink (pinker towards the edges and more yellow towards the centre), with darker backs to the petals and handsome stamens. The overall colour is coral at first, but fades eventually to mother-of-pearl. The blooms have a sweet musky scent and are borne singly or in clusters of up to seven on a very prickly, upright plant (a climber, not a creeper) which has dark glossy leaves and grows strongly to 4 m.

'Elegance' [Brownell, 1937]. 'Glenn Dale' × ('Mary Wallace' × 'Miss Lolita Armour'). The flowers are indeed supremely elegant: long-stemmed, large (12–13 cm), and scented (plate 123). The yellow is on the pale side, and the petals are almost white at the edges, but they stand up well to rain and reflex gracefully. The undersides of the petals are a richer yellow, so the bud is darker than the fully open flower. The foliage is a great asset: large, dark, and glossy. The plant grows to 10 m and has broad red prickles. The exquisite shape of the flowers compensates for their sparse supply. Sometimes the stem-tips are frozen back in cold winters.

'Frederick S. Peck' [Brownell, 1938]. Wichurana Hybrid × 'Mrs Arthur Curtiss James'. The colour is striking, salmon pink in the sunshine, coppery or even coral pink in shade, with dark (almost mahogany) backs to the petals. The flowers are semi-double, with loose petals which add a special grace to the way they open out, and they come on long stems in clusters of two to eight. They also have a good, sweet scent. The plant is slow to get going and is not reliably hardy. However, an established plant acquires considerable strength and vigour. It grows to about 5 m. The dark Wichurana foliage is a bonus.

'Golden Glow' [Brownell, 1937]. 'Glenn Dale' × 'Mary Wallace' seedling. The flowers are medium to large (9–10 cm), have long stems, and open from pointed buds. They are a deep yellow and keep that colour fairly well, even when eventually they open out. They come in small clusters, rather early in the season, and are tea scented. The foliage is large, shiny, dark, and healthy, and the plant grows to at least 6 m.

'Little Compton Creeper' [Brownell, 1938]. This is a very dull rose. The flowers are single, medium sized (6–7 cm), pink at the edges and white in the middle, and borne in small clusters of up to seven. The leaves are small, dark, and glossy. It flowers only once, although the hips are attractive in autumn. It grows to about 6 m.

'Magic Carpet' [Brownell, 1941]. 'Coral Creeper' × 'Stargold'. The medium to large flowers (9 cm) open out from an elegant bud to a fully double centre; the petals reflex abruptly and resemble a starburst. They are a fairly good yellow, rich at first and paler later, with petal-tips tinged with pink or red. They also have a rich, sweet scent. The leaves are small, dark, and glossy and sometimes susceptible to blackspot. The plant is vigorous and reaches 4–5 m. The long flower-stems make it a better climber than ground-cover plant. 'Magic Carpet' is extremely hardy.

'Mrs Arthur Curtiss James' [Brownell, 1933]. 'Mary Wallace' seedling. This remains the best of the Brownell climbers. It is vigorous, early flowering, hardy, and deep yellow and keeps its colour fairly well. The flowers are large (10–12 cm), fully double, and open out flat from elegant buds before they reflex even further. They have a good scent and are carried singly on long stems, which makes it a good cut flower. The leaves are glossy and dark, with a tendency to blackspot; the plant has large prickles and grows to at least 5 m. I have found this cultivar to be firmly once flowering and not overgenerous. The Brownells introduced an orange-coloured sport as 'Golden Orange Climber' [1937]. It perhaps has fewer petals.

'Rhode Island Red' [Brownell, 1957]. I have not seen this dark red, semi-climber which has recently been reintroduced to cultivation. The flowers are large (10 cm), double, cupped, and scented; it has Wichurana leaves and is said to be both free-flowering and remontant.

'Show Garden' syn. 'Everblooming Pillar No. 82', 'Pink Arctic' [Brownell, 1954]. 'Queen o' the Lakes' seedling. This, too, is a semi-climber, with bright deep pink flowers which hold their colour well but acquire a slightly purplish pink tinge with age. They are fairly large (9–10 cm), double, elegantly shaped, lightly scented, and borne throughout the season.

∽ CHAPTER 10 ∾

'New Dawn' and Its Descendants

'New Dawn' was introduced in 1930 as a perpetual-flowering sport of 'Dr W. Van Fleet'. It was a momentous event whose importance cannot be understated: modern climbers begin with 'New Dawn'. The hardy, floriferous, large-flowered climbers we now take for granted were made possible through it. All the leading mid-twentieth-century breeders used 'New Dawn' or its descendants to develop continuously flowering climbers.

Another factor made 'New Dawn' a rose of immense significance to the well-being of the horticultural industry: it was the first plant ever to be patented (U.S. Patent no. 1, 1930). The idea of protecting a plant breeder's intellectual property goes back to the mid-nineteenth century. Alphonse Karr was an early advocate of breeders' rights. In *Journal des Roses* (1887, 51–52) he wrote, "j'ai longtemps combattu pour que la société et les lois reconnaissent la propriété des oeuvres de l'intelligence. Je suis même auteur de la formule 'la propriété intellectuelle est une propriété'. Je voudrais que l'obteneur d'une belle rose pût tirer de son gain honneur et profit comme l'auteur d'un beau livre." (I have long argued that social and legal thinking should recognise rights of intellectual ownership. Indeed, I invented the slogan "intellectual property is property indeed." I want the breeder of a good rose to be honoured and rewarded just as the author of a good book is.) That was extremely advanced thinking in 1887. The United States was the first country to offer these rights to plant breeders, but not until forty-three years later.

According to McFarland (1947), 'New Dawn' is "a Dr Van Fleet that blooms again and again." The mutation could not have happened to a better or more popular rose. 'Dr W. Van Fleet' had for several years been the favourite climbing rose across the United States. Its beautiful, large flowers were quite outstanding, comparable in size to Teas or Hybrid Teas. It was also relatively hardy and exceedingly vigorous. The flowers of 'New Dawn' are identical with 'Dr W. Van Fleet'. It was, however, noticed early on that plants of 'New Dawn' were shorter and more branched than 'Dr W. Van Fleet'; some growers, indeed, thought of it as "a dwarf form, very suitable for growing as a pillar rose" (National Rose Society of Great Britain *Rose Annual* 1933, 179). Nevertheless, it proved a vigorous grower quite capable of reaching 8 m up a tree.

'New Dawn' syn. 'The New Dawn' [Somerset, 1930]. After the first heavy flowering, this rose continues in flower until the winter (plate 124). It is slightly less vigorous than its parent 'Dr W. Van Fleet', but still reaches 5 m in most situations, and more up a tree. 'New Dawn' is a reliable bloomer and a useful cut rose. The colour is darker in the autumn, and paler in high summer, although always more deeply coloured at the centre. 'New Dawn' has spawned a number of sports of its own, as well seedlings. 'Aëlita' [Shtanko, 1952] was introduced as a seedling of 'New Dawn', but the plant now grown at Sangerhausen under this name is identical with 'New Dawn'. 'Probuzení' syn. 'Awakening' [Böhm, 1935] is a fully double sport, but otherwise completely identical to 'New Dawn'. The flower has hundreds of little nib-shaped petaloids in the centre. In favourable conditions it reflexes and becomes a sphere of pink, but the petals are soft and it balls in damp weather and blotches in rain. The bloom appears slightly darker and richer than 'New Dawn' because the petals have more shadows in which to capture and intensify their colouring. 'Weiße New Dawn' [Berger, 1959] is a white sport of 'New Dawn' with crimson-tipped buds. It opens palest pink but quickly fades to pure white. The pale crimson pedicels, red stems and leaf-stalks, together with the small, hard, glossy leaves are a good foil to the flowers.

'New Dawn' is a meagre seed parent—the fruits usually contain only one or two seeds. However, the hips are produced in such quantities and the resultant seedlings are of such quality that the effort of pollinating a large number of flowers is well rewarded. Crossed with Hybrid Teas, 'New Dawn' passed on its characteristic long-flowering, its prolific flower production, and usually its hardiness, too. Breeders saw an opportunity to breed perpetual-flowering climbers for modern gardens, and for thirty years 'New Dawn' was by far the most important parent in the production of new climbers. The most successful breeder was Eugene Boerner, who worked for the megafirm of Jackson & Perkins and was responsible for 'Aloha', 'Coral Dawn', 'Miss Liberty', 'Morning Dawn', 'Parade', and 'Pink Cloud'. 'New Dawn' is itself only one-quarter *Rosa wichurana*; the remaining three-quarters are Tea and Hybrid Tea. Crosses with Hybrid Teas reduced still further the influence of the original species. None of the offspring is as tall and vigorous as 'New Dawn'. They are stiff-growing short climbers, pillar roses, shrubs, and vigorous Hybrid Teas. There are probably many more descendants of 'New Dawn' among the modern climbers (see chapter 11), whose ancestry has never been public knowledge.

'Aloha' [Jackson & Perkins, 1949]. 'Mercedes Gallart' × 'New Dawn'. This popular pillar rose has Hybrid Tea–style buds which open quite flat (about 9–10 cm across) and reflex their petals at their tips, creating a rounded flower (plate 125). The flowers appear deep rose pink, but the inner petals are red and fade to pale crimson, whereas the outer petals start dark and pass to rose pink. All the petals have paler edges. The flowers are strongly scented, drop their petals well, and do not ball. They come in small clusters or occasionally singly. The plant has very glossy leaves, which are dark bronze when young, but always tough and leathery. 'Aloha' is free-flowering, repeats well, is very hardy, and grows to 2.5–3.0 m. Peter Beales introduced an apricot-coloured sport as 'Dixieland Linda' [1996].

'Bantry Bay' [McGredy, 1967]. 'New Dawn' × 'Korona'. This popular shrubby climber has medium to large (9–10 cm), semi-double flowers which open coral pink (with slightly darker backs to the petals), but fade to medium pink. The petals are rather thick and lifeless and look untidy when the stamens brown. The flowers are very lightly scented but are carried prolifically all through summer and autumn, in small clusters on a stiff plant which grows to 2.5–3.0 m. The leaves are healthy, fairly glossy, and large.

'Blossomtime' [O'Neal, 1951]. 'New Dawn' × a Hybrid Tea. The medium to large (10 cm), Hybrid Tea–type flowers are very double, with muddled centres. They open from pointed buds and are a good silvery pink, although the outer petals and the petal-backs are slightly darker. They curl over quite tightly at their tips, giving a rolled effect. The flowers come in clusters of three to seven and are strongly scented. This very hardy plant repeats well all through the season and grows to 2.0–2.5 m.

'Cadenza' [Armstrong, 1967]. 'New Dawn' × 'Embers'. This pillar rose (growing to 2.0–2.5 m) has clusters of medium-sized (6–8 cm), bright, dark scarlet roses which are produced very freely until autumn. They are rather cupped at first but open out eventually and are lightly scented. The individual flowers last a long time, then drop their petals cleanly. The leaves are tough and very glossy, with rather round leaflets.

'Casa Blanca' [Sima, introduced by Kern, 1968]. 'New Dawn' × 'Fashion'. This rose is a good white-flowered climber. The buds have red tinges, but the lightly scented, medium-sized flowers (8 cm) open pure white, semi-double, and eventually flat, with petals that reflex characteristically. They come in small clusters on strong stems and last well, dropping their petals cleanly. The plant has dark green, glossy, medium-sized foliage and grows fairly vigorously to about 4 m. It is very hardy and remontant.

'Coral Dawn' [Jackson & Perkins, 1952]. 'New Dawn' seedling × unnamed seedling. The flowers may start a slightly coral pink, but they open pure rose pink, with pale pink at the edges of the petals. The buds are pointed like a Hybrid Tea's, but often misshapen and split, opening out to muddled centres. The flowers are full, short-petalled, rather cabbagey, medium sized (6–8 cm), and well-scented—a mix of musk and damask. The petals are somewhat soft and subject to rain damage. The flowers come singly or in small clusters. The leaves are broad, glossy, dark, and plentiful. The plant is hardy, remontant, fairly vigorous, prickly, and shrubby; it grows to about 2.5–3.0 m.

'Coral Satin' [Zombory, introduced by Jackson & Perkins, 1960]. 'New Dawn' × 'Fashion'. This cultivar is more coral than 'Coral Dawn'. The flowers open coral pink before fading to deep pink, especially in hot weather, and are always slightly paler on the underside of the petals. The buds resemble Hybrid Teas but open out to medium-sized flowers (9 cm) which are moderately scented and carried in clusters of five to ten. The plant is prickly but has lots of glossy, dark leaves and attractive new growths. 'Coral Satin' flowers freely and repeatedly and grows fairly vigorously to about 2.5 m. It is a very hardy plant.

'Dream Girl' [Jacobus, 1944]. 'Dr W. Van Fleet' × 'Señora Gari'. This richly scented pillar rose with an old-fashioned centre has its admirers. The medium-sized flowers (8 cm) are very full and open out flat to reveal a mass of little petals which are salmon pink at first but fade to pure pink. The flowers tend to hang down under their own weight. They are borne in small clusters which start late in the season and repeat throughout the summer and autumn. The plant has attractive, dark, shiny leaves and is very hardy. It grows to about 3 m.

'Étendard' syn. 'Red New Dawn' [Robichon, 1956]. 'New Dawn' × seedling. The individual flowers are glorious, especially in bud or half open, when they have the classic Hybrid Tea shape. They are bright red, medium sized (8 cm), lightly scented, and most profusely borne in small clusters. The plant has a rigid habit of growth, but handsome, shiny, dark crimson green leaves. It grows stiffly to 4 m and flowers recurrently.

'Étude' [Gregory, 1965]. 'Danse du Feu' × 'New Dawn'. This is very much a Wichurana rose. The buds are coral, and the strongly scented flowers are semi-double, peachy pink but darker outside, and borne in clusters. The blooms are medium sized (8 cm) and very freely borne all through the summer and autumn. The plant is moderately vigorous (3 m), very hardy, and has rich green, glossy leaves.

'Hagoromo' [Suzuki, introduced by Keisei, 1970]. 'Aztec' seedling × 'New Dawn'. The flowers are medium to large (10–11 cm), pale silvery pink (with slightly darker pink undersides), very double, and full. They are lightly scented and usually borne singly on long stems in summer but in small clusters in autumn. The plant has glossy, dark green leaves and is said to grow to 5 m, but I have seen it only as a 2-m shrub.

'Inspiration' [Jacobus, 1946]. 'New Dawn' × 'Crimson Glory'. 'Inspiration' has fairly large (10–11 cm), semi-double flowers which are a good rich pink (fading to pale pink) and scented, but the petals are rather loose, which makes the flowers somewhat formless. The leaves are large, dark, and shiny, and the plant grows fairly vigorously and laxly to about 3 m.

'Miss Liberty' [Jackson & Perkins, 1956]. 'New Dawn' × 'Minna Kordes'. This rose looks more like a Hybrid Tea–type climber than a Wichurana. The flowers are deep pink, not very double, but a fair size (9–10 cm) and borne singly or in clusters of up to ten. They are sweetly scented and produced remontantly. The plant grows to 3–4 m and has dark, leathery leaves, upright growth, and lots of prickles.

'Morning Dawn' [Jackson & Perkins, 1955]. 'New Dawn' seedling × 'Mrs Verschuren'. This attractive and floriferous climber has flowers exactly the same pale pink as 'New Dawn', but larger (11 cm) and more double. The flowers have a good scent but soft petals which spoil in rain. They come singly or in clusters of up to five. The leaves are dark, glossy, and tough, and the plant grows fairly vigorously to 3.0–3.5 m. 'Morning Dawn' is best treated as a pillar rose.

'Morning Jewel' [Cocker, 1968]. 'New Dawn' × 'Red Dandy'. This cheerful, unsophisticated rose has lots of character. The flowers are medium sized (8–9 cm), semi-double, and open out flat—a rich, dark, glowing pink, paler on their undersides, and white towards the base of the petals (plate 126). The petals are rather irregular in shape. There are up to seven flowers in a cluster; they have a fair scent. The leaves are dark and glossy. The plant is very free-flowering and shapely and grows to about 4 m.

'Ohio Belle' [Wyant, 1974]. 'New Dawn' seedling. This cultivar has medium-sized (7 cm), lightly scented, double flowers which are medium pink at their centres and pale pink at the edges. The plant has dark glossy leaves and repeats well; it grows to 3 m.

'Parade' [Jackson & Perkins, 1953]. 'New Dawn' seedling × 'Minna Kordes'. 'Parade' is one of the most impressive of all climbing roses. The flowers are medium to large

(10 cm), slightly cupped, and very full of petals. They are a very vivid pale crimson, with a hint of mauve red on the inner petals; the outer petals are paler, deep rose pink, and all the petals have slightly paler undersides. The flowers droop under their own weight in a charming and characteristic manner. They are richly scented and repeat generously all through the summer and autumn. The plant is vigorous, healthy, and hardy, with lots of dark, glossy leaves with reddish tints.

'Pink Cloud' [Jackson & Perkins, 1952]. 'New Dawn' × 'New Dawn' seedling. The flowers are medium to large (8 cm), fully double, and bright pale crimson or dark pink, with a Tea-rose scent. They come in clusters of between five and fifteen, and those clusters bend under their own weight. A 'Pink Cloud' plant in full flower is a sight of momentous beauty. The leaves are dark and glossy, and the plant grows to about 3 m; the first flowering is profuse, and is repeated throughout the summer and autumn.

'Pink Perpétue' [Gregory, 1965]. 'Danse du Feu' × 'New Dawn'. The flowers are medium sized (7–8 cm), semi-double, and come in medium-sized clusters like a Floribunda, with short, round petals which are pink, with a darker pink (almost carmine) on the undersides (plate 127). The colours fade unattractively in hot weather. Although 'Pink Perpêtue' is free-flowering in summer, it is particularly good in autumn. The flowers have some scent, and tough petals which withstand rain. The plant has small, dark green, semi-glossy foliage and rather rounded leaflets. It grows to about 2 m, or 3 m against a wall.

'Rhonda' syn. 'Ronda' [Lissemore, introduced by Conard-Pyle, 1969]. 'New Dawn' × 'Spartan'. The flowers are medium sized (7–8 cm) and deep medium pink; they hold their colour well (plate 128). They are very full of petals, but of Hybrid Tea form, so that they can be used for exhibition. The flowers are occasionally borne singly but usually in somewhat large clusters, nicely spaced out on strong, upright stems. They are lightly scented and last a long time before dropping their petals cleanly. The leaves are dark green, glossy, and disease resistant. The plant is moderately vigorous and repeats very well. It is hardy to at least −20°C and grows to about 3.5 m.

'Rosy Mantle' [Cocker, 1968]. 'New Dawn' × 'Prima Ballerina'. The unusually large (12–14 cm across) pale coral pink flowers open from elegant buds. The petals, although few, are long, and the outer ones reflex at the tips. The flowers have a sweet scent and are borne in small clusters. The plant has dark, glossy foliage and grows vigorously to about 3 m. It blooms freely, particularly in autumn.

'Temptation' [Jacobus, 1950]. ('New Dawn' × 'Crimson Glory') × 'Dream Girl'. I have not seen this Hybrid Tea–type climber, which has 'New Dawn' on both sides of its ancestry. The flowers are pale pink, with slightly darker petals-backs, medium sized, double, and lightly scented.

'Viking Queen' [Phillips, 1963]. 'White Dawn' × 'L. E. Longley'. This rose was bred for hardiness at the University of Minnesota and has 'New Dawn' on both sides of its ancestry. It has loosely Hybrid Tea–shaped flowers, with petals that tend to reflex in summer but recurve in autumn. They are medium sized (8–10 cm), rich pink, strongly scented, and borne singly or in small clusters. The stems are slender and the pendulous flowers are profusely borne. The plant is very vigorous once established and reliably repeat flowering. It has bright, disease-resistant leaves.

'White Cockade' [Cocker, 1969]. 'New Dawn' × 'Circus'. The buds are dumpy, creamy white, and nicely scented. They open to pure white, medium-sized flowers (8 cm), with strong, thick, rather short petals; the blooms come in small clusters of up to fifteen. The tough, dark, glossy leaves are a fine foil, and the plant is very hardy and very prickly. It can be grown as a shrub with only a little pruning, but will reach at least 4 m against a wall.

'White Dawn' syn. 'White New Dawn' [Longley, introduced by the University of Minnesota, 1949]. 'New Dawn' × 'Lily Pons'. This seedling is often confused with 'Weiße New Dawn', the sport of 'New Dawn'. The flowers are medium sized (7–8 cm), fully double, and sometimes likened to a gardenia in shape. The colour is pure white, without the crimson tints of 'Weiße New Dawn'. The flowers come in small or medium-sized clusters and are attractively set off by glossy foliage. The plant is very prickly and vigorous, reaching 3.0–3.5 m. It repeats well throughout the season.

The Kordesii Hybrids

The Kordesii Hybrids were by far the most significant new race of climbing roses to be developed during the mid-twentieth century. "Never have so many cultivars come from one raiser with such resounding success," commented the English rose breeder Edward Le Grice.

Rosa 'Kordesii' takes its name from the greatest European rose breeder of the twentieth century. Wilhelm Kordes was born in 1891 in Holstein, Germany; he served his apprenticeship in his home country, then worked in Switzerland and France, while learning and networking. In 1912 he crossed the English Channel to work at Bide's Nursery at Farnham and, in the following year, set up on his own account, in partnership with another young Holsteiner, Max Krause. When war broke out in 1914, Kordes and Krause were interned in the Isle of Man as enemy aliens. Kordes's account of his incarceration was typically laconic: "During the war I found time to look at the rose-breeding business from the theoretic side." He acquired a detailed knowledge of rose parentages and ideas for the advancement of rose breeding which were second to none. This knowledge served him well.

After the war, Wilhelm Kordes returned to Germany, where he began to devote some of his enormous energy to building up the German Rose Society as well as his own nursery. During the 1920s and 1930s, he established one of Europe's greatest firms of rose breeders, growers, and retailers. In 1920 they raised no more than 120,000 roses. Their output increased to about 500,000 roses when the Hitler government came to power in 1933 and expanded to 1,100,000 in 1939, when World War II broke out. The 1940s were not an easy time for the Kordes family but, by 1960, W. Kordes' Sohne was once again among the largest European rose nurseries. This was due in part to the development of a new race of roses that came to be known as the Kordesii Hybrids.

Above all, it is as rose breeder that Wilhelm Kordes will be remembered. He and his son Reimer bred some of the world's best-known roses, including 'Crimson Glory' and 'Schneewittchen' ('Iceberg'). Kordes knew that it was through introducing new genes that all the great advances in plant breeding had been achieved. His experiments focused at first upon the native European species and *Rosa rugosa*; his aim was to develop new bush roses for small gardens.

His work on the Kordesii Hybrids began with a seedling which Kordes called a "lucky chance." It was produced on an extremely hardy, trailing rose called 'Max Graf'.

> 'Max Graf' [Bowditch, 1919]. *Rosa rugosa* × *R. wichurana*. This hybrid trails along the ground, occasionally mounding up to about 50 cm but otherwise allowing its long bristly shoots to grow laterally and occasionally to root as it runs (plate 129). For much of the year it is most admired for its disease-resistant foliage, whose rugose surface has inherited a dark shine from *R. wichurana* and which keeps its colour late into autumn. 'Max Graf' has clusters of dark pink flowers in early summer, which fade to medium pink and have a prominent boss of golden yellow stamens. They are 7–8 cm across and have a musky scent. The plant can be trained as a 3-m climber and is very hardy. Its many reddish brown prickles are very attractive against the new growths, which are green before turning red and then brown.

'Max Graf' was thought at the time to be a chance seedling. Some contemporaries claimed it is Jackson Dawson's 'Lady Duncan' reissued under a new name but, because 'Lady Duncan' was considered extinct, this theory could not be tested. Others suggested that it might have *Rosa setigera* in its ancestry. Nevertheless, 'Max Graf' acquired something of a following for its bright green leaves, bristly brown prickles, and habit. It was even recommended as an efficient ground-cover plant, which no rose can truly claim to be. Nurserymen admired its resistance to disease and its hardiness. It was an unusual rose and, as such, attractive to discriminating plantsmen.

Wilhelm Kordes felt that attraction and grew 'Max Graf' for many years, hoping that he could breed from it. But, because it never produced any hips, he concluded that it must be sterile. Then, in 1940 Kordes noticed two hips on his plants from which he raised two seedlings. Only one had any value: its bright crimson, semi-double flowers were set off by dark leaves which clearly owed their glossiness to *Rosa wichurana*. The flowers were fuller and darker than 'Max Graf', and larger too, with reflexed petals; furthermore, the plant had an open habit, not unlike some of the old Lambertiana roses, instead of the densely procumbent shape of 'Max Graf'.

Wilhelm Kordes's seedling proved exceptionally fertile and bred substantially true from seed. This puzzled him. He knew from studying Mendel's laws of heredity that hybrids show a segregation of their determining characteristics so that, in the second generation of crossings, a wide range of differences emerges. However, his seedling was stable. Chromosome counting showed it to be tetraploid, whereas 'Max Graf' is diploid, which led Kordes to suppose it a spontaneous amphidiploid. The seedling was declared a new species and a full description was published as *Rosa* × *kordesii* Wulff, in accordance with the nomenclatural conventions of the time.

A more credible explanation for the origin of *Rosa* 'Kordesii' is that the seedling derived from the pollination of 'Max Graf' by a red Hybrid Tea, following an irregular meiosis in the seed-bearing parent. In due course genetic fingerprinting will no doubt confirm this.

'Kordesii' (= ×*kordesii*) [Kordes, 1952]. The Abraham of modern climbers is itself worth growing for its open, lax habit; dark, glittering foliage; and single, profuse flowering at midsummer (plate 130). The attractive semi-double flowers are cup shaped and deep pink. They are produced abundantly on a shrub which will grow to 2.5 m and are succeeded by vermilion hips. The habit and glossy leaves come from *Rosa wichurana*, the hardiness throughout central Europe from *R. rugosa*. "Not a tip of a shoot has been touched" Wilhelm Kordes wrote enthusiastically in 1949.

Kordes had no doubt that *Rosa* 'Kordesii' would prove itself the founder of a whole new race of roses. He proceeded to raise thousands of seedlings from it and discovered that it produced a certain percentage of repeat-flowering climbers, irrespective of the cross he made. The Kordesii Hybrids have inherited its glossy cheerfulness, bright colours, and dark tough leaves. They may not be refined or elegant, but they are born survivors and had a significant impact on the market for ornamental climbers in such parts of the world as central Europe and the American Midwest. Their strengths are health, hardiness, vigour, and, usually, an ability to flower repeatedly from top to bottom.

Most of his introductions were climbers, although a few were shrubs. Most were red or pink, but Kordes soon produced a good yellow hybrid in 'Leverkusen'; together with 'Hamburger Phönix' it was the first of the new race to be released, in 1954. Thereafter, barely a year went by without one or more new Kordesii introductions. The incomparable 'Dortmund' and 'Wilhelm Hansmann' came out in 1955; 'Aurora', the shrubby 'Bengt M. Schalin', and 'Köln am Rhein' in 1956; 'Ilse Krohn', 'Karlsruhe', and 'Parkdirektor Riggers' in 1957; 'Bad Neuenahr' in 1958; 'Ritter von Barmstede' in 1959; 'Alexander von Humboldt' and 'Raymond Chenault' in 1960; 'Illusion' and the shrub 'Oskar Scheerer' in 1961; 'Morgengruß' in 1962; shrubby 'Gruß an Koblenz' in 1963; and 'Ilse Krohn Superior' and 'Sympathie' in 1964. Their popularity was immediate. Wilhelm Kordes said that, in the early 1950s, his company was selling between 30,000 and 50,000 'Paul's Scarlet Climber' every year; but in 1954 they introduced 'Hamburger Phönix' and three years later were selling 40,000 plants of it against 10,000 'Paul's Scarlet Climber'. Ten years later, his hardy repeat-flowering Kordesii Hybrids were practically the only climbers on the German market.

But the Kordesii Hybrids have their weaknesses too. They have short petals and tend to come in rather tight bunches with little scent. And their bright and brilliant colours, which were so popular in the 1950s and 1960s, do not suit the current preference for softer hues. There was another problem when they made their debut in the 1950s: there were too many Kordesii Hybrids. They were insufficiently distinct. Kordes realised this and stopped introducing them. By then he had bred their healthiness into Hybrid Teas and Floribundas. The dark green glossy Kordesii foliage with its tough, disease-resistant texture became one of the most notable differences between the Hybrid Teas and Floribundas which were raised in the 1940s and 1950s and those introduced in the 1960s and 1970s.

'Alexander von Humboldt' [Kordes, 1960]. 'Kordesii' × 'Cleopatra'. The flowers are a rich scarlet (Kordes called them "a fiery blood red") with occasional white flecks, fully double, and rosette-shaped, with shorter petals towards the centre which give a flat and even shape when fully open. They are only slightly scented, but borne in large clusters against a background of bright glossy leaves. The plant is a shrubby climber (3 m as a shrub but slightly taller against a wall) which makes many basal growths, some of which produce flowers as low as 60 cm from the ground; the effect is then of a pillar of fire.

'Aurora' [Kordes, 1956]. This rose is the only orange-flowered Kordesii Hybrid. At first, the petals are orange on the outside and pinker within, but the overall effect is apricot. When the flowers open out, they also turn to pink. The flowers are not too full and open flat. They come in small clusters and are set off by dark, glossy foliage. The plant is hardy and grows vigorously to 3 m. Although 'Aurora' flowers well and generously, it is not recurrent.

'Bad Neuenahr' [Kordes, 1958]. The flowers of this deep crimson red climber are slightly scented, fairly large (10 cm), and fully double. They are a little too heavy for their stalks and nod their heads, a fine attribute in a climbing rose. The clusters can be enormous, as much as 60 cm across, and are backed by the usual dark glossy leaves of the Kordesii Hybrids. The plant grows to about 5 m, but less as a free-standing shrub.

'Dortmund' [Kordes, 1955]. Seedling × 'Kordesii'. This rose is a most eye-catching short climber when it first flowers and is covered with large (11–12 cm), open, lightly scented, single flowers in large clusters. They are a strong, handsome red, with a large central patch of white and a bright boss of yellow stamens; they radiate their colour in a remarkable way, but are difficult to mix with other colours. The glossy foliage is very dark and healthy. The many orange hips are also attractive, but interfere with reblooming; dead-heading helps to secure an abundant additional flowering. 'Dortmund' makes a bushy climber which scrambles to about 3 m.

'Hamburger Phönix' [Kordes, 1954]. 'Kordesii' × seedling. Its dark, bronze black buds open into medium-sized (7–8 cm), semi-double, dark blood red flowers which are nicely spaced in clusters and not too crowded, like a good modern Floribunda. There is a small patch of white at the base of the petals, which are slightly paler and less brilliant on their backs. The colour does not fade, and the flowers have a slight scent. They repeat well in autumn, especially if dead-headed after the first flowering; otherwise, the flowers develop into large orange hips. The shrub grows to about 3 m and is remarkable for its freedom of flower and its healthy, glossy, dark green foliage.

'Illusion' [Kordes, 1961]. 'Illusion' is a rich scarlet red, with fairly large (8–9 cm) double flowers in large clusters. The leaves are bright green, shiny, and tough; the plant grows vigorously and is very free-flowering. The flowers have a moderate scent which reminded Wilhelm Kordes of the dog rose.

'Ilse Krohn' [Kordes, 1957]. 'Golden Glow' × 'Kordesii'. This was the first white Kordesii Hybrid and the closest to a Hybrid Tea in shape. The flowers are large (12–

13 cm), fully double, high-centred, and pure white; they open from huge elegant buds in small clusters of perhaps three or five. The leaves are large, glossy, healthy, and handsome and droop elegantly when they are young. The plant is very hardy and grows vigorously to 4–5 m high. It has all the qualities for which one could wish, except scent (slight) and remontancy.

'Ilse Krohn Superior' [Kordes, 1964]. There are few examples of a once-flowering rose producing a repeat-flowering sport without a substantive change in habit from a climber to a shrub. 'New Dawn' is one example, and 'Ilse Krohn Superior' is another. It is slightly shorter, flowers earlier, and has larger flowers than 'Ilse Krohn' itself (plate 131). The blooms are also more strongly scented. Their colour is bright white, with a hint of buff in the centre, and the petals are elegantly reflexed. The flowers stand up well to rain. The plant is exceptionally robust and makes fairly vigorous, slender growth to about 3 m. For cold climates, 'Ilse Krohn Superior' is undoubtedly the best large-flowered white climbing rose.

'Karlsruhe' [Kordes, 1958]. 'Kordesii' × seedling. This is not a typical Kordesii Hybrid, nor it is well formed (the bud expands asymmetrically), but 'Karlsruhe' eventually opens out into a many-petalled, flat, open, muddled flower which is exceptionally large (as much as 14 cm across) and an unfading 'Zéphirine Drouhin' pink. It flowers fairly freely throughout the season and has some scent. The plant is very hardy and has many glistening, dark green leaves. It grows to about 3 m.

'Köln am Rhein' [Kordes, 1956]. 'Kordesii' × 'Golden Glow'. This is not the best of the Kordesii climbers and indeed is seldom seen nowadays. The flowers are lightly scented, deep pink, and fairly large (10–12 cm), but only semi-double. They open out flat and rather loosely petalled, but come in large clusters all through the summer and autumn. Profuse flowering is its chief asset. The plant is very hardy and has dark glossy foliage. It grows to about 2.5 m.

'Leverkusen' [Kordes, 1954]. 'Kordesii' × 'Golden Glow'. This rose, the only yellow Kordesii Hybrid, has crinkly, ruffled petals which open out from tight little buds. The fully double flowers are a clear lemon yellow which fades slowly and have an attractive fresh scent. They are carried in graceful clusters of three or four flowers. 'Leverkusen' flowers very freely in its first crop, but is slow to produce a second flush, although it is seldom without a few flowers throughout the summer and autumn. It has small, neat, dark, and glittering leaves, which are somewhat liable to blackspot late in the year. The hips only change to yellow late in autumn. The plant scrambles up to 3–4 m. Two recent colour sports are 'Jolly Dance', which is orange, and 'Laura Louisa' [Riches, 1995], which is more of a coral or salmon pink.

'Morgengruß' [Kordes, 1962]. This popular Kordesii Hybrid was the first to combine pink and yellow in changing tones. It has tight little buds like 'Leverkusen' and is very attractive as it opens its medium to large (8–9 cm) flowers (plate 132). This is because the outer petals are already fully expanded and start to fade to soft creamy pink when the inner ones are still tightly rolled into a dark apricot-coloured cone. Later the whole flower opens out flat, the outer petals reflex, and the colours change to creamy buff. The flowers come in small clusters and are lightly scented. The leaves are healthy, dark green, and glistening, and the plant grows vigorously to 4–5 m.

'Norwich Pink' [Kordes, introduced and named by Morse, 1962]. The semi-double flowers are a bright cerise, measure about 10 cm across, and have a lively knot of pale yellow stamens that increases their brightness (plate 133). The petals are sometimes of uneven length, which gives the flower a charmingly lopsided look, and some of the inner petals have streaks of white in them. The flowers fade to medium pink, but retain the quality of brightness which they have when first open. They are lightly scented. The leaves are dark, glossy, and abundant and the plant grows vigorously, with a dense branching habit, to about 2.5 m. 'Norwich Pink' is seldom out of flower.

'Norwich Salmon' [Kordes, 1962, introduced and named by Morse]. Morse sought permission to introduce 'Norwich Pink' and 'Norwich Salmon' after Kordes had decided not to. 'Norwich Pink' is still available commercially, but 'Norwich Salmon' is now seldom seen. It has medium-sized (6–7 cm), lightly scented flowers which are slightly fuller than semi-double. They open out flat and come in medium-sized clusters. The flowers are a slightly salmon pink, with a yellow base to the petals, fading to pale pink and white, and always paler on the underside. The leaves are thick, glossy, and dark, and the plant makes vigorous, branching growth. It flowers recurrently and reaches about 2.5 m.

'Parkdirektor Riggers' [Kordes, 1957]. 'Kordesii' × 'Our Princess'. The individual flowers are quite small for a Kordesii Hybrid (only about 5–6 cm across) but are borne in fairly large clusters. The colour is a deep, unfading vermilion red, uniformly spread across the petals, with occasional white flecks at the base. This cultivar is very free-flowering and grows as a well-branched plant to at least 3 m, often 5–6 m. It remains one of the most popular of the Kordesii Hybrids, although it is not without faults: the flowers are a hard red and lack luminescence, and the leaves are an equally hard dark green. 'Parkdirektor Riggers' is almost scentless.

'Raymond Chenault' [Kordes, 1960]. 'Kordesii' × 'Montezuma'. The colour is variable: one season the flowers may be a rich, dark cherry red and next year harsh, bright scarlet. The medium-sized flowers (9–10 cm) open flat, semi-double, with no white eye; the loosely held petals are wavy and long. The flowers are nicely held in an elegant open spray and have a prominent circle of stamens. They have only a light scent, but the plant shares the fine, dark foliage of most Kordesii Hybrids and grows vigorously to 3–4 m.

'Ritter von Barmstede' [Kordes, 1959]. 'Kordesii' × unnamed Polyantha. The flowers are medium sized (5–6 cm), semi-double, and borne in clusters which are so large and full of flowers that they may seem overcrowded. The flowers are darkest pink, with slightly paler undersides and a small white eye. The petals have a distinctive waviness (reminiscent of the Polyanthas) and remain on the plant for a long time, although their stamens turn brown fairly quickly. The leaves resemble those of a Wichurana Hybrid: glossy, disease resistant, but rather light green. The plant grows vigorously to about 5 m.

'Rosarium Uetersen' [Kordes, 1977]. 'Karlsruhe' × seedling. In this second-generation Kordesii Hybrid, the potential for glory is fully revealed. The flowers are large (10–12 cm) and the clusters are large, too: a plant in full bloom, rustling its dark pink, ruffled petals, is source of sheer wonderment (plate 134). The undersides of the petals are a more silvery pink, and the flowers fade slightly as they age, which intensifies the beauty of the new flowers and the clusters as a whole. The flowers are very full and double, moderately scented, produced profusely in summer, then intermittently. 'Rosarium Uetersen' responds well to dead-heading and to training; it will grow to 3.5 m if allowed, but may be pruned to 2 m or less. The numerous leaves are large, glossy, and medium green, not the dark green of 'Kordesii'.

'Rote Flamme' [Kordes, 1967]. The rich Turkey red flowers are medium sized (8–9 cm) and fully double, but still have a white centre, not unlike a double form of 'Dortmund' (plate 135). They are borne in small, loose clusters (typically of two to seven flowers) and hang down attractively under their own weight. The flowers, however, are scentless. The leaves are very handsome, large, dark green, glossy, and the plant grows thickly to about 4 m. The first flowering of the year is heavy and spectacular; subsequent flushes are more moderate.

'Rote Max Graf' [Kordes, 1980]. This cultivar was bred as a ground-cover rose and has single, scented, deep glowing red flowers with white flashes at the base of the petals which make a little white circle at the centre. The flowers are about 7 cm across and are borne in fairly large clusters. The bush has neat leaves (rather small) and a lax habit, but grows to about 4 m as a climber.

'Sympathic' [Kordes, 1964]. 'Wilhelm Hansmann' × 'Don Juan'. This second-generation Kordesii Hybrid is rich red, with a dark crimson overlay in places which gives it a sumptuous sheen. This is accentuated by an occasional fleck of white in the petals, especially at their bases. The flowers are of Hybrid Tea shape, fairly well-filled, carried in small clusters like a Floribunda, and freely produced. The lavish main flowering is followed by smaller ones. The flowers seem to stand up well to wind and rain. The bushy, vigorous plant has glossy, rich green leaves and grows to 4 m.

'Wilhelm Hansmann' [Kordes, 1955]. ('Baby Château' × 'Else Poulsen') × 'Kordesii'. The flowers are semi-double, lightly scented, medium sized (about 6–7 cm across), and carried in large broad clusters like a Floribunda. They are bright dark red, with occasional patches of crimson on the upper sides of the petals and, likewise, a few white flecks; they keep their colour well. The leaves are small, dark green, and glittering. The plant will grow to 4–5 m, but can be pruned as a shrub to 1.5–2.0 m.

'Zweibrücken' [Kordes, 1955]. 'Kordesii' × 'Sondermeldung'. This rose can grow to at least 3 m, although Kordes considered it a shrub. The flowers are small to medium sized (5–6 cm), semi-double, crimson red, with small white patches at the base of the petals which help to show off the stamens (plate 136). The petals are slightly wavy with occasional white flecks: the inner petals are smaller than the outer, which has the effect of making the flowers seem rather loosely formed. The blooms are carried in large clusters (up to twenty) and are lightly scented. The leaves are dark green, glossy, and abundant.

Additional Breeding with *Rosa* 'Kordesii' and Its Hybrids

Every Kordesii Hybrid seedling which Wilhelm Kordes introduced is still in cultivation. Most are offered for sale by European nurseries, and many remain widely available. Over the years, the Kordesii Hybrids have been used to breed both climbers and bush roses;

their dark, tough, glittering healthy leaves are considered a great asset. Sam McGredy IV's 'Malaga' [1971], for example, owes its glossy foliage to the presence of 'Hamburger Phönix' among its ancestors. Breeders are reluctant to publish pedigrees in the early years following the introduction of a new cultivar, so many of the climbers of 'Kordesii' descent may be inadvertently listed in chapter 14. The following, however, are known to belong here.

'Bright Fire' syn. PEAxi [Pearce, 1996]. 'Parkdirektor Riggers' × 'Guinée'. Neither parent is clearly present in this English-bred rose, which has vermilion red flowers of Hybrid Tea shape and large, leathery leaves on a vigorous, healthy plant.

'Crimson Descant' [Cants, 1972]. 'Dortmund' × 'Étendard'. This excellent hybrid has elegant buds which open out flat to lightly double, bright red flowers and a good display of yellow stamens. The flowers are large (about 12 cm across) and often carried singly, as well as in small clusters. Its deep green glossy foliage shows off the flowers well, and the plant grows vigorously to about 4 m.

'Louis Jolliet' [Ogilvie, 1991]. This Canadian rose has medium-sized (6–7 cm), double, deep pink flowers in large clusters and a trailing habit, but can be trained up as a climber, about 3 m tall. The flowers have short petals and turn rather quickly to pale pink.

'Schwartzer Samt' [Hänchen, introduced by VEG S-Baumschulen, Dresden, 1969]. 'Alain' × 'Oskar Scheerer'. The flowers are medium to large (7–9 cm), dark, velvety red, and semi-double; they are borne in medium-sized clusters on long, upright stems. The blooms are scentless, but last well when cut. The leaves are dark green, tough, and glossy, and the plant can be treated either as a tall shrub or as a short climber, reaching about 3 m.

'Seppenrade Elfe' [Scholle, 1975]. This hybrid, raised by an amateur, has medium-sized, lightly scented, semi-double crimson flowers in medium-sized clusters. The plant grows to about 2.5 m. Seppenrade is a designated Rosendorf near Lüdinghausen in Niedersachsen. The village rose garden is a considerable achievement—its 1.3 ha contain 10,000 roses and 600 cultivars.

'Shadow Dancer' syn. MORstrort [Moore, 1998]. 'Dortmund' seedling × 'Dortmund'. This rose has lightly scented, medium to large, semi-double flowers in a swirling mixture of dark pink and light pink, with a slight twist to the petals which adds enormously to their character. They are borne in medium-sized clusters on an upright plant which has the dark green, glistening foliage of 'Dortmund' and grows rather stiffly to about 2.5 m.

Felicitas Svedja

Kordes's work was also taken up and developed from 1961 onwards by Felicitas Svedja at the Ottawa Research Station of Agriculture in Canada. Few garden roses survive the Canadian winter in Ontario or Quebec. *Rosa* 'Kordesii' is not winter-hardy at Ottawa, but Svedja used it to breed climbing roses that were both hardier and more floriferous.

She also wanted roses which could easily be raised from cuttings—an important consideration, because such roses would recover when cold weather cut their growth to ground level. And, in the case of those hybrids which flower only once, Svedja sought to extend their single season of bloom so that it exceeded seven weeks. Hardy cultivars usually have only a very short flowering season, whereas repeat-flowering roses flower on new wood, which then freezes back in a Canadian winter.

Svedja's hybrids were named after the pioneers who first explored Canada and branded as the "explorer roses", hence such names as 'John Franklin' and 'Jens Munk'. Unfortunately the parentages of the four Svedja climbers have never been published; all are said to be hybrids between 'Kordesii' and an unnamed seedling of rather complex ancestry. All root very easily from softwood cuttings and produce saleable plants within one year.

'Henry Kelsey' [Svejda, 1984]. This semi-climber grows to about 3 m (more, if its trailing growths are tied in and trained up) and is hardy without any protection in zone 4. The medium-sized flowers (6–7 cm) are slightly fuller than semi-double, bright deep red fading to deep pink, and eventually open up to reveal their stamens. They are borne in clusters of ten to twenty all through the summer and autumn and have a spicy scent. The glossy 'Kordesii' leaves are generally healthy, but occasionally subject to blackspot, and the plant is fairly prickly.

'John Cabot' [Svedja, 1978]. The pale crimson purple flowers are semi-double, medium sized (6–7 cm in diameter), and slightly scented; they open nicely to reveal their stamens and fade slightly as they age. They come in small clusters of three to ten and flower in great profusion for some six or seven weeks, then sporadically. The plant has a densely leafy appearance and mounds up slowly into an arching shrub. In warmer climates the individual growths reach at least 3 m. The long curving spines make 'John Cabot' useful for hedging.

'John Davis' [Svedja, 1986]. 'Kordesii' × ('Red Dawn' × 'Suzanne'). The flowers are an attractive old-fashioned shape, but a very bright pink which fades to a lighter shade with creamy bases to the petals. They are medium sized (8 cm) and fairly double (thirty petals). The blooms open out to show their golden centres, although sometimes the flower is quartered, too. They come in clusters of ten to fifteen, have a slight musky scent, and appear continuously throughout the summer and autumn. The plant has masses of small, glossy, deep green leaves which are occasionally susceptible to mildew and blackspot. The new growths—a beautiful rich red—arch up to about 3 m and are quite prickly. 'John Davis' is extremely hardy, surviving temperatures of −35°C.

'William Baffin' [Svejda, 1983]. This is the strongest of the series, growing vigorously to 3 m or more. The loose, semi-double flowers (about 7 cm across) are a deep, dull pink, with white flashes at the base of the petals and paler undersides. The petals have a tendency to reflex and buckle; the contrast between the upper surface of the petals and the underside gives a distinctive character to the flowers. They come in clusters of ten to twenty-five and appear more-or-less continuously from summer to autumn, but are completely scentless. The foliage is thick, glossy, and fairly resistant to blackspot and mildew.

CHAPTER 12

Climbing Sports

A climbing sport starts as a spontaneous development on a bush rose. It produces larger flowers, which are especially attractive to exhibition growers, but in all other essential characteristics—colour, scent, form, hardiness, and disease resistance—climbing sports remain identical to their bush forms. A sport forms when, suddenly, a stem which is much taller than the rest of the bush grows up, but produces no flowers until the following year, when it blooms on its lateral or secondary growths. The sport is noticed, propagated, and may eventually be introduced as a "Climbing" form of the original bush rose. 'Climbing Pompon de Paris' was first recorded in 1839, although the plant now grown under that name may be a different cultivar; 'Climbing Devoniensis' was introduced in 1858 and has remained in cultivation ever since. These first mutations caused considerable interest and controversy; it was many years before the phenomenon was recognised and understood. Even today, the exact cause of this sporting is unknown, but sports tend to pass on their climbing habit to their seedlings. Thus, sporting may be associated with a genetic mutation.

These mutations arise more frequently than might be expected. They are more likely to be discovered among roses which are extensively grown (such popular cultivars as 'Peace' or 'Queen Elizabeth') or among roses grown for the cut-flower trade (good examples would be 'Liberty', 'Mme Butterfly', and 'Baccará'). Over the years, such eagle-eyed observers as Max Vogel at Sangerhausen, Gianfranco Fineschi in Tuscany, and David Ruston in South Australia have recognised and perpetuated a substantial number of climbing mutants among the roses in their collections.

Some cultivars have achieved more lasting popularity as climbers than in their original form as bush roses. The renown of 'Lady Hillingdon' and 'Mme Edouard Herriot' as climbers far exceeds their reputation as bushes. Conversely, many sports of popular bush roses have failed to acquire a following, and some of the greatest roses have been equally successful in both forms: 'Mme Caroline Testout', 'Lady Sylvia', and 'Étoile de Hollande', for instance.

There is no saying when or whether a particular cultivar will produce a climbing sport. The English nurseryman Walter Easlea (1932, 109) pointed out that a cultivar like 'La France' had been grown for twenty-six years before a climbing form appeared: "on the other hand a rose may be quite a new introduction of only a year or two when a climbing form of it appears. This was so with 'Sunstar' [four years] and 'Irish Fireflame' [three years]." The German rose grower Peter Lambert wrote in the mid-1920s that he could count some 150 climbing sports which had appeared since the mid-nineteenth century; the figure now is closer to 700.

Climbing sports differ enormously, not only between cultivars but also between different clones. Some are better than others, but not always for an obvious reason. Nurserymen will usually tell you which form they are selling, and why; for example, English rose growers preferred the climbing form of 'Ena Harkness' introduced by Gurteen & Ritson [1954] to the one offered by Murrells [1954] because the budwood was cheaper to buy.

Most climbing sports are known by their original names, with the adjunct "Climbing." Thus, the climbing sport of 'Étoile de Hollande' is known as 'Climbing Étoile de Hollande'. There are, however, two exceptions to this rule. First, some introducers choose to give a climbing sport an entirely new name. For example, 'Auguste Kordes' [Kordes, 1928] is a climbing sport of the large-flowered Polyantha rose 'Joseph Guy' [Nonin, 1919]. Second, when roses are known by more than one name in different countries and the sport appears in a country where the bush form of the rose did not originate, "Climbing" is usually attached to the younger name. The climbing forms of 'Schneewittchen' [Kordes, 1958] are 'Climbing Iceberg' because they arose in the United States and the United Kingdom, where the bush form is known as 'Iceberg'.

Today, it is usual to list climbing sports alphabetically under the name of the bush rose from which they sported and then to add "Climbing," often in parentheses. Although this conflicts with the Tokyo Convention (Greuter et al. 1994), I have adopted the practice in this chapter so that they are shown as "*name of bush rose* (Climbing)." This allows those climbing sports which were first raised in France or Germany and are described as "Grimpant" or "Rankende," respectively, to be included in the alphabetical list. (Peter Lambert pointed out that it was incorrect to use the word *rankende* to describe a climbing sport—better words would be *Klimmrosen* or *Kletterrosen*. But there was nothing that even the most influential of German rosarians could do to stop the linguistic development.)

Climbing Teas and Climbing Hybrid Perpetuals

All the roses described in this chapter are the result of chance sports, and they represent a cross-section of the history of bush roses—Teas, Hybrid Teas, Floribundas, and so on. By far the largest comprises Climbing Hybrid Teas. I start with the earliest types of rose to sport—the Chinas, Teas, Bourbons, and Hybrid Perpetuals. Climbing mutants are unknown among the old European roses: there has never been a climbing Gallica, Damask, or Centifolia rose. The propensity to sport arrived with the early introductions from China of such roses as 'Parson's Pink', themselves the product of a mutation centuries ago from tall once-flowering climbers into short repeat-flowering bushes. It follows that any rose which throws up a climbing sport must have the blood of China or Tea roses in its ancestry, a fact which should help us to sort out the taxonomy of many nineteenth-century roses. Climbing Tea roses are especially valuable. The size of their flowers, their exquisite shape, their nodding stems and their ineffable scent make them the queen of flowers.

'Bridesmaid (Climbing)' [Dingee & Conard, 1897]. This sport's large flowers (10–12 cm) are pearly pink, although the deeper buds leave a darker pink mark on the outside of their long elegant petals which seems to infuse the whole flower. The flowers are wonderfully scented and rather too heavy for the slender stalks; they hang down with a suggestion of fragility which gives the plant its overall delicacy.

'Captain Hayward (Climbing)' [W. Paul, 1906]. This Climbing Hybrid Perpetual has large (10–12 cm), loose flowers which open nicely, like a semi-double Gallica (plate 138). They are bright cherry crimson, paler at the edges, and slightly mottled and striped, with a strong, sweet scent.

'Devoniensis (Climbing)' [Pavitt, 1858]. The climbing form of this rose is extremely vigorous, growing in warmer climates to about 5 m. Its elegant buds are pink, but open out into large (9–12 cm), fully double, beautifully shaped, creamy white blooms, with flashes of pink or yellow in them, particularly towards the centre. The blooms have a wonderful tea scent. This sport has a long season of flower, with some recurrence all through the year. The rich red new growths are very handsome.

'Duchesse de Brabant (Climbing)' [c. 1900]. This Climbing Tea opens pale coral pink, then fades to ordinary pink while keeping a slightly darker colour on the outside. It has a delicious, strong tea scent and crimson new growth.

'Gruß an Teplitz (Climbing)' syn. 'Catalunya' [Storrs & Harrison, 1911; Nonin, 1917]. The great virtue of this rose, still unmatched a century later, is its combination of floriferousness and hardiness. Its flowers are medium sized (5–7 cm), cupped, fairly well scented, and a brilliant crimson red. The blooms are continuously produced on a fairly vigorous plant which grows to about 3–4 m. The flowers usually come in threes—hence its English nickname, "Grows in Triplets."

'James Sprunt (Climbing)' syn. 'Cramoisi Supérieur (Grimpant)', 'Agrippina (Climbing)' [Sprunt, introduced by Henderson, 1870; Cochet, 1885]. This climbing sport makes rather leggy growth, scrambling slowly up to as much as 10 m and building up a mass of dense branches. The flowers are medium sized (5–6 cm; larger than the bush form), bright crimson red with occasional white flecks, and a somewhat globular shape. They are lightly scented and appear all the year round in warm climates, with a particularly heavy flush in spring. This sport is often found in old gardens in the Mediterranean region, apparently thriving upon neglect.

'Jules Margottin (Climbing)' [Cranston, 1874]. This Climbing Hybrid Perpetual has deep cerise pink or pale crimson, medium to large (10–11 cm) flowers with a very strong sweet scent—quite delicious. The round buds open out into flat, cabbagey flowers, with one to five in a cluster, often with foliolate sepals. The plant is of moderate vigour and very prickly.

'Lady Hillingdon (Climbing)' [Hicks, 1917]. This Climbing Tea is popular in England because it is fairly hardy against a house wall in towns and sheltered country sites. (It is particularly lovely against a red brick wall.) 'Lady Hillingdon (Climbing)' is one of the most continual flowering of all climbing sports and lasts well when cut. The long pendulous buds open to exquisite apricot yellow flowers which are loosely double and set off by plum purple foliage, prickles, and young stems. The blooms are particularly elegant in autumn and have a rich tea scent. Its grows fairly vigorously to 6–10 m, although the stems are rather thin and need tying in. The namesake of this rose, Lady Hillingdon, is chiefly remembered for her remark, "When my husband lies on top of me, I close my eyes and think of England."

'Maman Cochet (Climbing)' [Lee-Concord, 1909; Howard & Smith, 1915]. This is a classic Climbing Tea, with palest pink flowers which are slightly darker at the centre and with a hint of yellow and cream in the outer petals. The bud is elegantly pointed, the flowers about 10 cm across and moderately scented, but the plant is not especially vigorous, growing to no more than 2.5 m high.

'Mrs Herbert Stevens (Climbing)' [Pernet-Ducher, 1922]. This is a wonderful rose for a warm, dry climate. The pendulous buds are large and pure white, with no hint of colour on their outside (plate 137). The flowers open large (10–12 cm) and pure white but sometimes have a suggestion of green or buff towards the centre. They are fully double, strongly scented, and have noticeably long, thin petals. The leaves are large and sometimes rather sensitive to mildew, but the plant remains a very free-flowering climber, easily reaching 6 m.

'Niphetos (Climbing)' [Keynes, Williams & Co., 1889]. This elegant white Climbing Tea opens from palest pink buds into large (9–10 cm), long-petalled, globular, strongly scented flowers which are produced on laterals all along the length of the longer shoots, which easily reach to 6–8 m. It is a fine glasshouse climber in cool climates and repeats well. The bush form was an important parent of hardy Hybrid Teas.

'Old Blush (Climbing)'. Origin unknown. The semi-double or double flowers are pink at first, but deepen towards pale crimson so that there is an attractive contrast between the darker outer petals and the paler inner ones. The distinctive twist of the reflexed petals and the rather weak pedicels add to their charm. The flowers are larger than the bush form (6–7 cm) and have a tea scent. The spring flowering is spectacular, and the plant grows to about 4 m.

'Papa Gontier (Climbing)'. Climbing sports have arisen many times from this bush; they include Hosp [1898], Gouchault [1902], Turbat [1902], Vigneron [1903], Chevrier [1904], and Chase [1905]. This famous old Tea rose is deep pink, with darker undersides but paler edges to the petals and a hint of orange yellow towards the base, a very Tea-rose combination. The flowers are little more than semi-double, but open very attractively and are strongly tea scented. It grows fairly vigorously to 3 m.

'Perle des Jardins (Climbing)' [Henderson, 1889]. The flowers are large, globular, and pale yellow, with those hints of darker yellow and apricot which are one of the great attractions of the Teas. The blooms are also strongly scented. The leaves are dark and the growth slender, but it will easily reach 3 m.

'Pompon de Paris (Climbing)' syn. 'Rouletti (Climbing)'. The flowers are fairly small (3.0–4.5 cm), double, and bright pink with perky petals and almost no scent (plate 139). However, they are carried in extraordinary profusion on a plant which grows to 4–5 m (more against a house) and hang down on long wands which are covered in flowers for their entire length. The leaves are neat, small, almost miniature, and borne at short intervals on rather zigzag stems. It is one of the earliest roses to flower and the first show is spectacular. There are only a few flowers later.

'Pride of Reigate (Climbing)' [Vogel, 1941]. This is a Sangerhausen speciality which has never been offered for sale. It makes a very striking climber, laden with pure crimson flowers with pale pink stripes (plate 140). They are firmly held, 10–12 cm across, and strongly scented. There is only an occasional rebloom, but this is a good rose which ought to be more widely known and grown.

'Setina' syn. 'Hermosa (Climbing)' [Henderson, 1879]. This Climbing China rose is very floriferous, a splendid sight during its first early flowering. The flowers are small to medium sized (5–6 cm), double, with masses of short, broad petals, which are light, bright pink, with a hint of mauve. The flowers have a fair scent, and the plant grows vigorously in warm climates to about 4 m.

'Souvenir de la Malmaison (Climbing)' [Bennett, 1893]. This sport is usually described as a Climbing Bourbon. The flowers are large (10–12 cm; even larger than the bush form), flat, quartered, creamy pink (slightly pinker at the centre), and supremely beautiful when well grown (plate 141). The scent is intriguing: the English rosarian Reverend Joseph Pemberton (1920) referred to its "peculiar perfume, a kind of beery smell." The plant grows lankily to about 5 m and repeats fairly well.

'Souvenir de Pierre Notting (Climbing)' [F. Cant, 1913]. This Climbing Tea carries large (about 10 cm across), shapely, very full flowers which hang heavily down on slender stems and have a delicious tea scent. They open apricot yellow with hints of gold and copper, then fade to creamy pink, although the petals are edged carmine pink throughout. This is a very floriferous climber, carrying its flowers in small clusters with the typical reddish leaves and young wood.

'White Maman Cochet (Climbing)' [Knight, 1907]. This Climbing Tea is identical to 'Maman Cochet', of which it is a pure white sport. It is a great stand-by in warm climates.

Climbing Hybrid Teas

The Hybrid Teas are roses of supreme elegance and floriferousness, and they have proved by far the most successful and enduring of all climbing roses. It has become fashionable to deny their beauty and to denigrate the good sense of those who choose to grow them. In such countries as the United States and Australia, many lovers of heritage roses practice a form of cultural apartheid between themselves and the great majority of gardeners who recognise the virtues of the Hybrid Tea. This is both ridiculous and offensive: the Hybrid Teas have given us most of the world's most beautiful and popular roses.

Sports among the Hybrid Teas were relatively uncommon until the twentieth century. Their introduction was a factor of the enormous expansion of Hybrid Tea numbers during the early 1900s. By the 1920s the climbing sports were being introduced in large numbers. In 1927 the English rosarian Walter Easlea wrote, "Had I a garden long enough I would have a long walk arranged with pillars of these lovely roses on either side. Such a walk would be a joy from June to October, yielding far more pleasure than the pergola, with its very short season of blossoming." Many of the best Climbing Hybrid Teas were introduced in the 1930s: 'Dame Edith Helen' and 'Independence' in 1930; 'Étoile de Hollande' in 1931; 'Mrs Pierre S. du Pont' and 'Talisman' in 1933; 'Dainty Bess' and 'Lady Sylvia' in 1935; 'Betty Uprichard' and 'Margaret McGredy' in 1936; 'Mevrouw G. A. van Rossem' and 'Mrs Sam McGredy' in 1937; 'Mrs Tresham Gilbey' in 1938. They offered all the virtues of the Hybrid Teas while bringing to the climbing roses a wider range of colours and a greater elegance of flower than ever before. Their blooms were generally larger than the bush types and, because Hybrid Teas already produced the largest roses, this meant that the blooms on Climbing Hybrid Teas were even larger than anything that had gone before. Had they but flowered repeatedly, the Climbing Hybrid Teas would immediately have established themselves as by far the most important group of climbing roses.

More than any other group of climbing roses, success with Climbing Hybrid Teas depends in large measure upon proper cultivation. Flowers are produced upon the laterals which develop from the characteristic, long, extended growths. It is essential to tie in those growths so that laterals are encouraged to develop and then to prune them back after flowering to encourage them to flower again. Rose growers were slow to realise this. Throughout the 1920s and 1930s, apologists explained that Climbing Hybrid Teas were wonderful roses but only flowered once. The American Rose Society encouraged experiments to increase their floriferousness (*American Rose Annual* 1940) and discovered that plants need a mixture of good feeding and regular deadheading throughout the growing season. Even the most recalcitrant once-flowering rose was coaxed into flowering for at least three months, while the once-flowering ramblers like 'Excelsa' and 'Gardenia' still flowered only once. Climbing Hybrid Teas also perform better in warm climates and when there is plenty of water to encourage new growth; they are more satisfactory in irrigated gardens in Western Australia or southern California than in northern Europe.

There are about 250 Climbing Hybrid Tea cultivars in existence, most of which I have seen, studied, and photographed. Unfortunately, space does not allow me to describe them all in the detail they deserve. Some 150 will have to be left with only the most basic mention. I have divided the remaining cultivars into two groups: fifty which are fairly widely available commercially in some part of the world, and about another fifty which are now less commonly grown but perhaps deserving of greater currency. I start with those most widely available.

'Alec's Red (Climbing)' [Harkness, 1975]. This has large (12–14 cm), strongly scented, bright red, double blooms, borne either singly or in small clusters.

'Baronne Edmond de Rothschild (Climbing)' [Meilland, 1974]. This vigorous climber has very large (14–16 cm), strongly scented, bright cherry red flowers with pale pink undersides and vigorous glossy foliage. This rose is a very handsome and impressive sight in full flower.

'Bettina (Climbing)' [Meilland, 1958]. This popular climber has fairly large, scented, double flowers of a charming mixture of colours—salmon pink at the centre and buff yellow at the edges.

'Blessings (Climbing)' [Gregory, 1972]. This climber has elegant, double flowers, which are fairly well scented; they open coral pink and change to rose pink, although the outer petals are often darker.

'Blue Girl (Climbing)' syn. 'Kölner Karnival (Climbing)' [Kyle, 1977]. The bush form of this rose was one of several attempts by Kordes to breed a large-flowered, strongly scented, lilac mauve Hybrid Tea. The climber is excellent, its flowers as much as 15 cm across, and beautifully shaped.

'Blue Moon (Climbing)' syn. 'Blue Monday (Climbing)', 'Sissi (Climbing)' [Jackson, 1978]. This is another good and popular blue rose (actually lilac mauve) which is double, strongly scented, and about 12 cm across. It is a sport of 'Mainzer Fastnacht' [Tantau, 1965].

'Captain Christy (Climbing)' [Ducher sœurs, 1881]. Why is this wonderful rose not more widely grown? It is one of the earliest and the largest of all climbing rose sports. The flowers are pale creamy pink at their ruffled edges, darker towards the centre, and strongly tea scented. Of only moderate vigour, it repeats well and makes an unforgettable free-growing shrub.

'Carina (Climbing)' [Meilland, 1968]. This opulent, rich pink, and generously proportioned rose has large flowers (14–15 cm) with long petals, borne singly on a vigorous plant. It has two weaknesses—only a moderate scent and a tendency to spoil in rain—but it makes a fine choice for a warm, dry climate.

'Château de Clos Vougeot (Climbing)' [Morse 1920]. This is still a popular climber due to its silky dark scarlet crimson flowers which fade to blackish purple. The blooms are large (10–12 cm), full, open, paeony-shaped, and very highly scented. It is one of shorter-growing climbing sports, about 2.5 m high, and is best considered a pillar rose.

'Chrysler Imperial (Climbing)' [Begonia, 1956]. The crimson red, velvety, large (13–15 cm), double flowers open from a pointed bud and have a sweet, spicy scent. Excellent in hot climates, the plant grows to about 4 m.

'Columbia (Climbing)' [Vestal, 1923; Lens, 1929]. This remains one of the best and most floriferous of the climbing sports. The flowers are very large (15 cm), full, well-shaped, strongly scented, and a rich pure pink.

'Comtesse Vandal (Climbing)' [Jackson & Perkins, 1936]. This rose is beautiful in bud, and as it first expands, 'Comtesse Vandal' reveals a medley of colours—buff on the upper side of the petals and deep apricot pink on the undersides. It is still popular worldwide, although in cool climates it gets mildew and in hot ones its flowers fade quickly to dirty white.

Climbing Sports

'Crimson Glory (Climbing)' [Millar, 1942; Richardson, 1944; Jackson & Perkins, 1946]. 'Crimson Glory' is a sumptuously rich crimson Hybrid Tea, with a scent as opulent as its colour. The weak stalks are a defect which becomes a virtue in the climbing form. The flowers, always larger than the bush form, are about 10–12 cm across and produced all through summer and autumn. It is not a very vigorous sport, only about 2.0–2.5 m high.

'Dainty Bess (Climbing)' [Van Barneveld, 1935]. This is one of the most continual-flowering of all climbing sports. The single flowers are short-lived but freely borne. They are pale lilac pink, with just a hint of coral when they open and darker undersides. They owe their distinctive beauty to maroon filaments and yellow stamens.

'Double Delight (Climbing)' syn. AROclidd, 'Grimpant Double Delight' [Christiensens, 1982]. The flowers are carried singly or in small clusters on long stems. They open creamy white but the outer petals have a broad band of cherry crimson on their tips, so that the effect of the open flower is of a blanched centre ringed by layers of cerise. The flowers are large (up to 15–16 cm across) and extremely sweetly scented. The 'double delight' is to the eye and the nose.

'Eden Rose (Climbing)' [Meilland, 1962]. The flower opens very deep pink, almost pale crimson (some people describe the colour as "Tyrian rose" or "clear cherry red"), but it fades to a medium pink and always has a slightly paler underside to the petals. It is very strongly scented, elegantly shaped in the Hybrid Tea style, and opens out to about 12–14 cm across. This rose is a classic beauty.

'Ena Harkness (Climbing)' [Gurteen & Ritson, 1954]. Like 'Crimson Glory' the climbing form has the great advantage of weak flower-stalks, which means that the pendulous flowers can be better appreciated. They are large (12–13 cm across), bright unfading crimson, strongly scented, and elegantly shaped (plate 142). The first flowering occurs rather early in the season and is spectacular; thereafter you are seldom without at least a few flowers on an established plant.

'Étoile de Hollande (Climbing)' [Leenders, 1931]. This crimson Hybrid Tea is elegantly shaped, is very sweetly scented of damask, and blooms steadily from spring to autumn. It is also one of the most vigorous of climbing sports, easily reaching 7 m. The buds often have split centres, but they open out very attractively. I would never want to be without its vigour, colour, and sumptuous scent in my garden.

'First Prize (Climbing)' [Jackson & Perkins, 1976]. This exhibition rose is still one of the top cultivars for warm climates. The flowers are enormous (as much as 20 cm across), elegant in bud and spectacular as they open out, magnolia pink, slightly paler towards the centre, and lightly scented. The plant is very vigorous, with rather a lanky habit of growth. It produces a generous first flowering and intermittent blooms thereafter.

'Fragrant Cloud (Climbing)' [Collin, 1973]. The flowers are well shaped, bright orange vermilion, and very strongly scented. The climber is not too vigorous (3 m); it gives an excellent show in later spring, but repeats sparingly. The colour turns blotchy red in hot weather.

'Frau Karl Druschki (Climbing)' [Lawrenson, 1906]. This old rose still has some of the largest flowers (15–17 cm) you will ever see: pure white, lightly double, with elegant long petals, beautiful at all stages, although only lightly scented (plate 143). In its day,

'Frau Karl Druschki (Climbing)' was a top exhibition rose but it also makes a very dependable garden rose. It is said to grow up to 4 m, but I have never seen it taller than 2.5 m. It is extremely hardy and grows well on its own roots.

'General MacArthur (Climbing)' [Dickson, 1923]. The climbing form of this early Hybrid Tea has semi-double, cup-shaped, medium red flowers with a strong, sweet scent. It flowers rather sparsely after the first flush. Nevertheless, it is still fairly widely available and commonly seen in old rose gardens.

'Golden Dawn (Climbing)' [Armstrong, 1935; Le Grice, 1947]. 'Golden Dawn' has deep yellow buds which open to pale yellow flowers. It is never really golden, but the flowers are very full and rain resistant. The climber is healthy and not very vigorous (2.5 m high) but a good autumn-flowerer.

'Grand'mère Jenny (Climbing)' [Meilland, 1968]. The flowers are like a deeper, richer 'Peace', apricot yellow with light crimson shadings, but strongly scented and fairly large (12–13 cm). When half open, the bloom is one of the most handsome of Climbing Hybrid Teas. The plant is vigorous and healthy.

'Josephine Bruce (Climbing)' [Ross, 1968]. The climbing form is very prickly, but fairly vigorous (3 m) and has a most abundant first flowering (plate 144). The dark crimson flowers are larger and even more sumptuous than in the bush form.

'Lady Sylvia (Climbing)' [Stevens, 1933]. The strongly scented flowers are large (11–12 cm) and elegantly shaped; they are pale pink at the edges and slightly deeper pink towards the centre and at the base of the inner petals. 'Lady Sylvia (Climbing)' grows to at least 6 m high, and flowers best when the new wood is tied in horizontally.

'La France (Climbing)' [Henderson, 1893]. The flowers are large (12–13 cm), beautifully pointed when they first open, silvery pink (slightly darker on the outsides of the petals), and elegantly reflected with the sweet damask scent that rose lovers appreciate (plate 145). It is a stiff upright grower (with rather short internodes) to about 5 m, thrives in almost any soil and position, and repeats quite well. The petals are fairly soft, so the plant does best in warm, dry weather.

'Landora (Climbing)' syn. 'Sunblest (Climbing)', 'Clinora' [Orard, 1978; Tantau, 1978]. This is the best modern yellow Climbing Hybrid Tea (plate 146). The yellow is pure and dark; the strongly scented flowers are elegantly shaped and relatively large (11–13 cm). The plant grows fairly vigorously to about 4 m.

'Michèle Meilland (Climbing)' [Meilland, 1951]. Nothing can match the promise of its half-open flower—pearly pink at the edges, but with a hint of apricot at the heart. It opens out to a pure pale pink. The flowers are large (10–12 cm), not too double, and strongly scented. The plant grows to 3–4 m tall and is a reliable performer, whatever the weather or the climate.

'Mme Abel Chatenay (Climbing)' [Page, introduced by Easlea, 1917]. This large rose (10–12 cm) is full of reflexed petals which are pale silvery pink on the upper side and dark salmon pink on the underside. The flowers are tea scented and carried singly on long stems—perfect for cutting. The plant is sometimes susceptible to blackspot and mildew, neither of which affects its ability to flower well and repeatedly throughout the summer and autumn. It grows to 3–4 m high.

'Mme Butterfly (Climbing)' [Smith, 1926]. This sport is deep pearly pink with a hint of buff yellow at the centre. That said, the climbing forms of 'Ophelia' and 'Mme Butterfly' now in commerce are so alike that I find it difficult to distinguish them. Both are healthy, vigorous, strongly scented, and exceptionally floriferous.

'Mme Caroline Testout (Climbing)' [Chauvry, 1901]. Often found against the walls of old houses (mine included), the flowers are large (12–14 cm) and fat (globular and blowsy). They are bright silvery pink and slightly darker on the underside of the petals, which are nicely reflexed at the tips. They stand up well to rain and are fairly well scented. The plant is rather a scraggy and prickly grower, but vigorous (as much as 6 m high), and is apparently immune to most diseases.

'Mme Edouard Herriot (Climbing)' [Ketten Bros., 1921]. The colour has been described as coral, salmon pink, terra-cotta, strawberry rose, prawn red, and flame pink (plate 147). The colour is shaded and blended with many other vivid shades and hues and is more intense towards the centre of the flower. The lightly double, well-scented flowers are elegant in bud but rather loose and untidy when open. They are borne in great profusion early in the season. The new leaves are bronze red, and the older leaves somewhat liable to blackspot. It grows vigorously to 5–6 m on a somewhat scraggy, prickly plant and produces a few later flowers.

'Mme Jules Bouché (Climbing)' [Bigot, 1938]. There is a splendid specimen of this sport draped over the gateway to Professor Fineschi's Roseto at Cavriglia. The flowers are large (12–13 cm), white at the edges, cream or palest buff towards the centre, and strongly scented. At its best, this rose is a vision of loveliness.

'Mrs Aaron Ward (Climbing)' [Pernet-Ducher, 1907]. The large flowers (11–12 cm) are peachy buff and noticeably paler (almost white) at the edges, but vary in colour from year to year and are darker in autumn. The flowers are double and very attractive, with a light sweet scent.

'Mrs Pierre S. du Pont (Climbing)' [Hillock, 1933]. Its shapely red buds open to a slightly peachy yellow and the flowers fade to lemon, but the overall impression is of pure, deep yellow. The flowers are fairly large (10–12 cm), lightly double, and fruit scented. It grows to 5 m wound around metal columns at Bagatelle.

'Mrs Sam McGredy (Climbing)' [Buisman, 1937]. The orange apricot flowers have redder undersides to the petals. They are large (10–12 cm), lightly double, and open out to reveal handsome red filaments. Like many Irish roses, they are short-lived, but are borne in considerable profusion over a long time. The foliage is crimson at first and may get blackspot later. The plant is rather prickly and grows vigorously to about 5 m.

'Ophelia (Climbing)' [Dickson, 1920]. 'Ophelia' set the standard by which all Hybrid Teas should be judged for excellence. The flowers of this sport are perfectly shaped and double, with long petals which are white at the edges and palest pearly buff at the centre. The plant is also exceptionally vigorous (up to 6 m) and one of the most continual-flowering of all climbing sports.

'Papa Meilland (Climbing)' syn. MEIsarsar, 'Grimpant Papa Meilland' [Stratford, 1970; Meilland, 1976]. One of the best of the dark red velvety climbers, this sport has large flowers (10–12 cm) which are strongly scented and individually borne. The blooms hold their colour well and drop their petals cleanly. The plant grows vigorously to about 4 m and flowers intermittently after the first fine flowering.

'Pascali (Climbing)' [Anderson, 1978]. This sport of a plain, sturdy, tough-petalled white seedling of 'Queen Elizabeth' is perhaps a little short on charm, but it has a good scent and grows strongly to at least 6 m.

'Paul Lédé (Climbing)' [Low, 1913]. This Climbing Hybrid Tea has medium large (9–10 cm), buff pink flowers, individually and abundantly borne on short drooping stems early in the season and occasionally thereafter. The edges of the flowers fade to pale yellow, while the centre remains almost raspberry pink. They have a strong tea scent. The true old cultivar is seldom seen in cultivation today, its place being taken by an inferior, sugar pink impostor.

'Peace (Climbing)' syn. 'Mme A. Meilland (Climbing)' [Brandy, 1950; Kordes, 1951]. The climbing form of the world's best known rose is a stupendously vigorous climber, growing quickly to 6–8 m (plate 148). It flowers spectacularly early in the season, but only occasionally thereafter. The pink-and-yellow flowers are very large (16 cm) and carry their beauty from the opening bud right through to the blowsy full flower. Although I find it strongly scented, others disagree.

'Queen Elizabeth (Climbing)' [Whisler, introduced by Germain, 1957]. The climbing sport of this famously vigorous bush rose is a vigorous climber, growing 5–6 m tall. The flowers are borne at the end of long stiff stems and resemble the parent plant in every way: medium pink, tough petalled, strongly scented, and about 12 cm across. After the main flush come a few later flowers.

'Sheer Elegance (Climbing)' [De Vor, 1995]. This sport is a vigorous climber whose large flowers (15–16 cm) have the classic Hybrid Tea shape. They open orange pink and fade to pale pink, but always have a dark edging to the petals which emphasises their elegance. The scent is an unusual mixture of musk and fruitiness.

'Shot Silk (Climbing)' [Knight, 1931; Low, 1935]. The blend of cherry pink and yellow made this rose instantly popular, but the colours lose some of their vitality with age. Although not the most vigorous of climbing roses at 2.5 m tall, this sport flowers early and late and repeats fairly well. The flowers are also honey scented and the plant nearly thornless: "one of the most satisfactory of all the climbing roses," according to the English rosarian Albert Norman (1953).

'Sonia Meilland (Climbing)' syn. 'Sonia (Climbing)' [Meilland, 1975]. The coral pink buds on this vigorous climber have all the appearance of a classically elegant Hybrid Tea, but open out into flat dusky pink flowers with old-fashioned, quartered centres. They are also strongly scented, with a rather an unusual, fruity scent.

'Spek's Yellow (Climbing)' syn. 'Golden Scepter (Climbing)' [Walters, 1956]. This was introduced as an *unfading* dark yellow rose, which is true only in cool climates. Here its none-too-double form is an asset, but it opens out too quickly in hot climates, where the petals reflex into a spiky mess. It is strongly scented and vigorous (up to 5 m) in a lanky sort of way, with few flowers later.

'Super Star (Climbing)' syn. 'Tropicana (Climbing)' [Blaby, 1965; Jackson & Perkins, 1971]. This Hybrid Tea climber has a peculiar orange red sheen, from the presence of pelargonidin in its chemistry. It seems almost luminous in the late evening light. The buds are elegantly pointed, and the flowers are large (14 cm) and very sweetly scented. The climbing form is vigorous (4–5 m), but it can be a niggardly bloomer.

'Sutter's Gold (Climbing)' [Weeks, 1954]. The buds are vivid vermilion, but the flowers open bright yellow. The blooms are about 13 cm in diameter and are borne singly on exceptionally long rigid stems. When they open out, they recurve their petals rather abruptly and take on a pink tinge, but they do have a wonderful, distinct scent. This sport is not very free-flowering, although it is one of the earliest climbers to flower.

'Tiffany (Climbing)' [Howard, 1958]. This dark pink Hybrid Tea makes a good climber because its flowers hang down on weak stalks. The buds are finely shaped and held on long stems. They open into large (about 13 cm across), fully double, and very strongly scented flowers, although the blooms tend to look rather bedraggled after heavy rain. This sport produces only a few flowers after the main flush.

The following are fifty or so Climbing Hybrid Teas that are particularly deserving of wider cultivation.

'Astrée (Climbing)' [Croix, 1960]. This peachy pink climber (pink towards the tips of the petals, and apricot towards the centre) has large and well-scented flowers which open out flat with ruffled centres; the blooms are attractive at every stage of growth. This sport is seldom seen outside France.

'Break o' Day (Climbing)' [Brownell, 1944]. This rose is a climbing sport of one of the subzero Hybrid Teas. The flowers are pale pink with an apricot centre, full, and fairly large. It makes a good, healthy plant and flowers profusely, but repeats little. 'Break o' Day (Climbing)' is still seen in East Coast gardens of the United States.

'Cathrine Kordes (Climbing)' [Krohn, 1938]. The flowers are large (12 cm), very double, globular (but with long petals), sweetly scented, very bright pale crimson, with slightly lighter undersides. This sport is completely hardy in central Europe, but it grows well in hot climates, too. This rose is still seen in German gardens and is worth reintroducing.

'Charlotte Armstrong (Climbing)' [Morris, 1942]. The bush form of this sport was one of the parents of 'Queen Elizabeth'. The climber has pointed buds, tough petals, and a good scent. The colour is very dark pink, with yellow towards the base of the petals. I have seen it in such gardens as San Jose Heritage Rose Garden in California, at David Ruston in South Australia, and at Bagatelle and L'Haÿ-les-Roses in Paris, France.

'Cherry-Vanilla (Climbing)' [Fineschi, c. 1990]. This is a spectacular, early-flowering, and very floriferous climber. Its very large flowers (15–17 cm across) open lemon yellow, but change to white while developing deep pink edges to the petals. The flowers are elegant and double and have a curious, sweet, musky scent. The buds are quite small and give no suggestion that the flowers are so large.

'Christine (Climbing)' [Willink, 1936]. The small flowers are intensely bright yellow, many petalled, shapely, and freely produced. They also have an unusual, rather fruity, scent. The plant grows to only 2.0–2.5 m—good as a pillar rose.

'Christopher Stone (Climbing)' [Marsh's Nurseries, 1942]. This is a rose for hot climates. The very large flowers (12–13 cm) are scented, semi-double, and bright crimson to cherry red. The petals are wavy and very attractive when the sun shines through them. The plant grows extremely tall (at least 7 m). Margaret Snyder (1949), Dr McFarland's head gardener at Breeze Hill in Philadelphia, wrote, "To me size does not denote perfection but there is something about these huge blossoms that makes you pause and admire." This sport is still available in California and Australia.

'Condesa de Sástago (Climbing)' [Vestal, 1936]. This rose is deep raspberry red on the upper side of the petals and deep yellow underneath. The strongly scented flowers are also very full of petals—very beautiful as they open but rather untidy in wet climates. This sport is still available in Germany.

'Dame Edith Helen (Climbing)' [Howard & Smith, 1930]. The glowing pink flowers are very large (13–15 cm), with lots of petals and a very strong scent. It grows magnificently in warm climates, where it can open out. In parts of Queensland 'Dame Edith Helen (Climbing)' fared so well that a special exhibition class was made for it (National Rose Society of Great Britain, *Rose Annual*, 1951). In 1960, the English rose breeder Jack Harkness wrote that "it was the most lovely pink rose of all to me."

'Dr F. Débat (Climbing)' [Barni, 1955]. The flowers are very large (15–17 cm), deep pink at the centre, and paler towards the edges. They are beautiful at every stage but simply unbelievable when they open out flat. Long popular in France, and rightly so, this sport deserves to be known and grown much more widely.

'Elizabeth Harkness (Climbing)' [Harkness, 1972]. This rose has large (13–14 cm), elegant, pale yellow flowers, which fade to white with a hint of buff or pink at the centre; it produces a piercingly sweet scent. In shape, colour, and delicacy it harks back to the earliest Hybrid Teas and indeed to the Climbing Teas. Never widely grown, it is still offered by one or two European nurseries but should be much better known.

'Feu Joseph Looymans (Climbing)' [Western, 1935]. This extremely handsome Pernetiana is quite commonly seen in California gardens and should be grown more in other warm climates. The flowers are large (11–12 cm), cupped, semi-double, with long petals and a good sweet scent. Their charm is in the colour—apricot in the centre and buff yellow towards the edge.

'Forty-Niner (Climbing)' [Moffet, 1952]. This rose has a striking colour combination: cherry crimson on the upper side of the petal and yellow on the underside. The flowers are fairly large, scented, and open out attractively to reveal a mass of regular petals. 'Forty-Niner (Climbing)' is still available in France and Australia, but nowhere else.

'Gail Borden (Climbing)' [Jackson & Perkins, 1960]. This sport grows at Sangerhausen in Germany and has very fine, very full, and large flowers (13–14 cm) with long petals. The colour is coral at first, fading to pink, with white undersides, a handsome combination. The blooms have a good scent, too.

'Gloria di Roma (Climbing)' [Fineschi, c. 1990]. This sport has huge, strongly scented, many-petalled, scarlet and pale crimson flowers and, so far as I know, grows only at Cavriglia in Italy. It would be a wonderful climber in any Mediterranean type of climate. The bush form was an important floristry flower in Hungary, still accounting for more than half the cut-rose production in the 1960s.

'Golden Rapture (Climbing)' syn. 'Geheimrat Duisberg (Climbing)' [Armstrong, 1941; Knackfuß, 1954]. The flowers are deep yellow at first, fading to lemon yellow. They are strongly scented, about 13 cm in diameter, with the elegant form of the 'Ophelia' tribe to which 'Golden Rapture' belongs. The plant is a very vigorous climber with large glossy leaves, and is still seen in older gardens in Europe and North America.

Climbing Sports

'Granada (Climbing)' [Swim & Weeks, 1964]. This is a remarkable bicolored rose—red at the edges and yellow at the centre—but with hints of pink and white as well. The large, scented flowers are semi-double, so they show this extraordinary colouring when they open out; they are also freely produced on a vigorous plant which grows to about 3 m. This sport is grown only in Australia, so far as I can discover.

'Harry Wheatcroft (Climbing)' [Mungia, 1980]. Harry Wheatcroft's ebullient personality is well commemorated by this very striking striped rose, bright orange vermilion, with bold yellow flecks and stripes. It is available from specialist nurseries in the United States.

'Ivory Fashion (Climbing)' [Williams, 1964; Earing, 1968]. Elegant, slender buds open up into large (12–13 cm), semi-double flowers, whose long white petals (cream at the base) enclose the crimson filaments like a magnolia. They expand fully, reflexing their petals like a nun's starched wimple, holding on a long time and dropping cleanly. Hardy, weather resistant, good in all climates, scented, healthy, vigorous, and a good repeater—'Ivory Fashion (Climbing)' is all these things. I have seen this image of fluttering beauty only at the Roseto di Cavriglia in Italy.

'Josephine Baker (Climbing)' [Orard, 1983]. This intensely sweet-scented, rich crimson Hybrid Tea has never had the popularity it deserves, either as a climber or as a bush rose. The flowers are large (10–11 cm)and borne singly on long stems. I have seen it only in France and Australia.

'Karl Herbst (Climbing)' [c. 1980]. This sport has large (10–12 cm), strongly scented, many-petalled flowers of an intense crimson scarlet. It produces a good first flowering, with some intermittent flowers thereafter. It is available in France.

'Kordes' Perfecta (Climbing)' [Japan Rose Society, 1962]. The buds are exquisitely shaped, high pointed with neatly reflexed petals. The flowers are creamy pink, fading to palest pink, but neatly tipped with crimson; they are also large (9–10 cm), strongly scented, and usually borne in clusters. The climbing form is occasionally seen in Europe, but otherwise widely available only in Australia.

'Lady Forteviot (Climbing)' [Howard, 1935]. This is one of the most vigorous (and prickly) of climbing sports, easily reaching 7–8 m (plate 149). The flowers are a beautiful apricot at first, but they fade to yellow and are always slightly darker on the backs of the petals. They open out attractively, being only really semi-double, and are very sweetly scented. A few later flowers follow the rapturous first flowering. This rose is available from several nurseries in Europe and the United States.

'Lady X (Climbing)' [Ruston, 1970]. The climbing form of a popular bedding rose is a wonderful sight when covered with enormous mauve pink-flushed flowers bulging with petals. It also has a good, slightly fruity scent. This sport is extremely vigorous and probably grows best in warm, dry climates.

'Los Angeles (Climbing)' [Howard & Smith, 1925]. The climbing form of this striking rose was a great improvement on the rather feeble original. The colour is a great mix of pink, orange, salmon, yellow, apricot, gold, and flame, fading eventually in hot weather and opening out to cream and pink. The flowers are large (10–11 cm), well-shaped (very regular), strongly scented, and borne on long stems. It is a moderate grower (about 2.5 m high) and much more free-flowering than most Climbing Hybrid Teas.

'Maria Callas (Climbing)' syn. 'Miss All-American Beauty' [Meilland, 1969]. This is a deep pink, classic Climbing Hybrid Tea with large (11–12 cm), full flowers, borne singly, and with a rich tea scent. It grows particularly well in warm climates, but is a vigorous grower anywhere, and fairly good at producing additional blooms after the first main flowering. It is still quite widely available, especially in France, but not in the United States.

'Max Krause (Climbing)' [Moreira da Silva, 1940]. This is an enormous and ravishingly beautiful Climbing Hybrid Tea. The blooms are strongly scented and buff yellow with apricot backs to the petals, which give the flower a wonderful depth of colour. The flowers are packed with petals but in warm weather open out slowly and continue in beauty for several days. They are freely produced on a fairly vigorous plant. I have seen this sport only at Sangerhausen.

'Mme Henri Guillot (Climbing)' [Meilland, 1941]. This sport is one of the finest Pernetianas. The flowers are enormous (14–15 cm), semi-double, and crimson coral but slightly more yellow on the backs of the petals. They are produced very freely at first, but only intermittently thereafter, on a vigorous plant which quickly reaches 5 m. It is still available from a few nurseries in France and England.

'Mme Pizay (Climbing)'. This rose is a vigorous, lanky grower with few prickles. It bears lots of large (11 cm) apricot-coloured flowers which fade charmingly to buff (but remain always deeper on the backs of the petals). They open out flat with many short, broad petals and have a strong tea scent. This rose grows at Sangerhausen, but is not available in commerce.

'Mount Shasta (Climbing)' [Knight, 1968]. This is a mighty white-flowered climber, with large (13–15 cm), scented, many-petalled flowers which nevertheless open out into great white cups, often with a hint of buff or primrose at the centre. It grows vigorously to at least 5 m, and a bush in full flower is a sight to marvel at. This rose is available commercially, but only in Australia; it ought to be grown in similar climates around the world.

'Mrs Henry Bowles (Climbing)' [Dobbie, 1929]. The flowers of this strongly scented Hybrid Tea are exceptionally large, even by today's standards, as much as 15–16 cm across when they open out from the elegant buds. The flowers are absolutely packed with rich pink petals, with a hint of peach at the base. It makes a fairly vigorous climber at Sangerhausen, but is no longer available in the trade.

'Mrs Tresham Gilbey (Climbing)' [Vogel, 1938]. This rose, too, survives only at Sangerhausen, where it was found as a sport. It is particularly free-flowering when it first opens, covering the bush with bright pink flowers flushed with salmon, a slightly harsh colour, but one that catches the eye. The flowers are large (10–11 cm), sweet scented, and shapely.

'Picture (Climbing)' [Swim, 1942]. This Climbing Hybrid Tea is still available from several nurseries around the world. Its flowers are classically elegant Hybrid Teas, pale pink (darker towards the centre), with a creamy underside and a fairly good scent. It is a moderate grower, perhaps 2.5 m high, and repeats well.

'Pilar Landecho (Climbing)' syn. 'Marquesa de Urquijo (Climbing)' [Folgado, 1954]. This yellow climber is still available commercially but does best in warmer climates. The flowers have reddish markings on the bud and the outer petals, which tend to reflex as they open. There is a distinct fruit scent.

'President Herbert Hoover (Climbing)' [Dixie, 1931; B. R. Cant, 1937]. The large, lightly double, strongly scented flowers are suffused with pink, cream, apricot, and occasional streaks of carmine. The plant grows very vigorously to at least 5 m and is particularly good in warm climates such as those of South Africa and the southern states. This sport is still available from a few nurseries but, because it proved difficult to bud, many nurseries dropped it from their lists. It roots fairly easily from hardwood cuttings.

'Président Leopold Senghor (Climbing)' [Meilland, 1982]. This is one of the better modern crimson Climbing Hybrid Teas, with very large (14–15 cm), deep velvety flowers, individually borne on long stems. It is sold only by a handful of French nurseries.

'Président Vignet (Climbing)' [Vogel, 1942]. This rose is a Sangerhausen speciality, never offered for sale, but an attractive sight when covered with its strongly scented, double, crimson flowers which turn to cherry red as they open and fade. It makes a sturdy, upright plant, growing to about 2.5 m.

'Princesse Margaret d'Angleterre (Climbing)' syn. 'Princess Margaret of England (Climbing)' [Meilland, 1969]. This is a handsome climber, pure medium pink with a hint of apricot at the centre, later fading to silvery pink when the flowers begin to look blowsy. The buds are long and elegant, and the long petals reflex gracefully. The flowers come singly on long stems and keep well when cut. It repeats well throughout the season. It grows in the Paris rose gardens but is sold only in Australia. According to the *Australian Rose Annual* (National Rose Society of Australia 1992, 40), this sport is a "delicious pink Hybrid Tea climber that just keeps coming."

'Radiance (Climbing)' [Griffing, 1926]. The climbing form is now rather rare, although it is still grown in North America, Europe, and Australasia. The flowers are fairly large (10–11 cm), fat with petals, sweetly scented, and medium pink with a hint of salmon; the colour is slightly darker pink on the outside of the petals, which gives extra depth to the flowers. The plant is vigorous and particularly good in hot climates; it was for many years one of the most reliable roses in the southern states.

'Richmond (Climbing)' [Dickson, 1912]. This sport is a very vigorous, tall-growing climber with rich crimson flowers which are held on long stems. The medium-sized (8–9 cm) flowers are slender, not overfull, and very attractive in bud or when half open, but this is a rose which does best in cooler climates like England and British Columbia. It is intensely sweet-scented. 'Richmond (Climbing)' is available from several European nurseries.

'Rina Herholdt (Climbing)' [Bal Raj Arora, c. 1975]. I have not seen the climbing form, but the original bush is a very beautiful rose, not only for its long buds and large full flowers, but because they are ivory white with a conspicuous bright pink edge to the petals, thicker on the upper side than on the undersides. Many people find bicolors difficult to like; this one is so neatly drawn that no one could fail to be beguiled.

'Rouge Meilland (Climbing)' [Meilland, 1954]. The bush form of this rose is a good cultivar for hot climates. The climbing form has enormous flowers (15 cm) of brilliant red, fading (rather unevenly) to crimson—very spectacular in full flower. This sport is still available in France.

'Signora (Climbing)'. I have seen this climbing form only at Saverne in Alsace. It makes a vigorous, upright plant, with enormous flowers (15–16 cm) borne singly on very long stems. Their overall colour is deep salmon, but they are paler and pinker in the centre and darker and redder at the edges, with yellow at the base of the petals. They are also strongly scented and good in wet weather, even though Domenico Aicardi bred the bush form for the Mediterranean climate.

'Silver Jubilee (Climbing)' [Cocker, 1985]. 'Silver Jubilee' proved to be an important rose, because it was much used by breeders as a parent. Its flowers are large (11–12 cm), broad with nicely reflexed petals, and fairly well scented (plate 150). The colours change as the flower opens, but the inner petals tend to be pale pink at their tips and peach-coloured at their bases, whereas the outer petals are crimson lake at their tips and pink or salmon pink at the bases. The climbing form disappeared from commerce almost as soon as it arrived.

'Snowbird (Climbing)' [Weeks, 1949]. This American speciality is not grown outside the United States and Canada. This rose is a lovely, vigorous Hybrid Tea with ivory white flowers fading to pure white (plate 151). The flowers have a pale yellow centre at first and are fully double. They are only 10–11 cm in diameter, but look bigger because they have so many petals. They are said to be strongly scented, but I have not found this to be the case. Nevertheless the flowers look like great white snowballs when well grown, as at the Huntington Botanical Gardens in San Marino, California.

'Soraya (Climbing)' [Barni, 1960]. This climber was quite widely available until the mid-1990s. The flowers are large (14–15 cm), double, and very bright orange vermilion fading to crimson lake, but always slightly darker on the backs of the petals. There is little scent. The individual flowers are carried on long stems, and the plant as a whole grows fairly vigorously to about 4 m.

'Souvenir de Claudius Pernet (Climbing)' [Western, 1925; Schmidt, 1932; Gaujard, 1933; Square, 1937]. The climbing form is stunning, with huge (15 cm), richly scented, many-petalled globes which hang down beautifully. Their colour is pure bright yellow at first, then the tips of the petals pale to lemon, while the centre of the flowers, as they open, reveal tints of buff and gold. This sport is particularly successful in warm, dry weather, where its flowers can open out fully, although it is also very hardy.

'Souvenir de Georges Pernet (Climbing)' [Pernet-Ducher/Gaujard, 1927]. This is a sumptuous beauty, with large (14 cm), globular, heavy, very full flowers which hang down under the weight of their petals. The flowers are a dark rich pink, almost red towards the centres, which have a distinctive spiralling arrangement of their petals. The blooms are very fragrant. The bush form is a weak grower, but the climbing sport is notably vigorous. It is still available from a few European nurseries.

'Souvenir of Wootton (Climbing)' syn. 'Climbing Wootton' [Dingee, 1899]. This rose was a very early Hybrid Tea and is one of the few climbing sports which is now more than a century old. The flowers are large (11–12 cm across) and deep pink or pale crimson with just a hint of purple when they open. They are cupped, strongly and sweetly scented, and carried singly or in small clusters up to five. The plant is fairly vigorous (growing to 2.5–3.0 m high) and very hardy, although it was also widely used at first as a forcing rose. It has an abundant first flowering rather early in the season, with one or two light flushes later in the year.

'Sterling Silver (Climbing)' [Miyawaki, 1963]. The flowers are large (12–13 cm across) and have the classic pointed shape and reflexed petals. They are pure mauve on the inside of the petals and a slightly darker, lilac mauve, on the outer edges. The blooms are extremely strongly scented.

'Tchin-Tchin (Grimpant)' [Meilland, 1995]. The climbing form of this stunning orange red Hybrid Tea is widely grown in France.

'The Doctor (Climbing)' [Dyess, 1950]. The flowers on the climbing form are huge and sumptuous; at 15–17 cm, they are among the largest exhibition roses ever raised. The flowers are a pure silky pink, very strongly scented, and not too full of petals, which is why this sport does well in England. The plant produces only a few flowers after the first flush, I find.

Climbing Hybrid Teas in Danger of Extinction

So far, I have described only two-fifths of the Climbing Hybrid Tea roses in existence, and by and large these represent the best-known and more widely grown sports. The remaining 150 cultivars are, for the most part, grown only locally in one or two countries or regions of the world. They get only the barest descriptions, but I can vouch for the beauty and vigour of many, including 'Climbing Olé' at David Ruston's nursery in South Australia, 'Climbing Ville de Paris' at Cavriglia in Italy, and 'Climbing Oklahoma' at the Huntington Botanical Gardens in California. In addition to those which follow, some additional 200 Climbing Hybrid Teas are now extinct.

'American Heritage (Climbing)', creamy apricot.
'Angelus (Climbing)', white with a creamy heart, grown at Sangerhausen.
'Anne Marie Treschlin (Climbing)', apricot pink, strongly scented.
'Anvil Sparks (Climbing)', orange red with yellow streaks, well named, scented, grown in Germany and South Africa.
'Apotheker Georg Höfer (Climbing)', a Sangerhausen speciality, coppery red, large, scented.
'Asso di Cuori (Climbing)', dark red, scented, grown in Italy.
'Augustus Hartmann (Climbing)', medium crimson, sweetly scented, at Cavriglia only.
'Avon (Climbing)', dark red, fairly double, sweetly scented, grown in Australia.
'Baccará (Climbing)', orange red, medium sized, nice red new leaves, grown in Germany (Westfalenpark, Dortmund) and South Australia (David Ruston).
'Ballet (Climbing)', deep pink, large, full flowers, very vigorous, seen in German gardens.
'Bel Ange (Climbing)', large, scented, pink.
'Best Wishes (Climbing)', red-and-yellow bicolor, variegated leaves.
'Bewitched (Climbing)', rich pink and sweetly scented, available in California.

'Caledonia (Climbing)', large, attractive white flowers, borne singly, available in California.

'Capitaine Soupa (Climbing)', medium to large, fairly bright pink, grown only at Sangerhausen.

'Caprice (Climbing)' syn. 'Lady Eve Price (Climbing)', apricot yellow, grown by David Ruston.

'Carla (Climbing)', pink, with a hint of salmon, grown and sold in France.

'Champs Elysées (Climbing)', dark red, large, not very vigorous, grown in Adelaide Botanic Garden.

'Charles Mallerin (Climbing)', dark red, large, available in South Africa.

'Chicago Peace (Climbing)', dark, rich pink and yellow, available in Australia.

'Christian Dior (Climbing)', elegant, scarlet cut-flower rose.

'Cochineal Glory (Climbing)', large, red, and lightly double, grown at Sangerhausen.

'Confidence (Climbing)', peachy pink, scented, grown at Bagatelle.

'Coral Fiesta (Climbing)', orange crimson, available in Italy.

'Critérion (Climbing)', bright, pale crimson, very vigorous, available in France.

'Daily Mail Scented Rose (Climbing)', dark red and velvety, sweetly scented, grown in Australia and at Sangerhausen.

'Dame de Coeur (Climbing)', pale crimson red, available in Belgium and France.

'Dearest (Climbing)', attractive peachy pink, strongly scented, available in Australia.

'Destin (Climbing)', bright red, strongly scented, available in France.

'Editor McFarland (Climbing)', semi-double, bright deep pink, rather formless, grown in Australia.

'Elli Knab (Climbing)', silvery pink with dark pink undersides, large, sweetly scented, grown at Sangerhausen.

'Ellinor Le Grice (Climbing)', large, elegant, scented, yellow, grown in Australia.

'Elvira Aramayo (Climbing)', brilliant orange, with scarlet and yellow flashes, grown at Sangerhausen.

'Eminence (Climbing)', mauve, scented, available in France.

'Ernest H. Morse (Climbing)', bright crimson, scented, grown at Sangerhausen, now available in England.

'Festival (Climbing)', large, red, scented, grown at Cavriglia (but may not be correctly named).

'Flaming Sunset (Climbing)', orange, with yellow petal-backs, rather reflexed petals, grown by David Ruston.

'Fontanelle (Climbing)', large, pale yellow, scented, grown by David Ruston.

'Freiburg II (Climbing)', pale pink, with darker undersides, very vigorous, grown at Sangerhausen.

'Fritz Thiedemann (Climbing)', orange red, scented, grown in several German gardens.

'General-Superior Arnold Janssen (Climbing)', glowing cherry crimson, paler on inner petals, grown at Sangerhausen.

'George Dickson (Climbing)', bright crimson red, scented, sold in Europe.

'Germiston Gold (Climbing)', dark yellow, strongly scented, available in South Africa.

'Golden Emblem (Climbing)', good yellow, particularly in hot climates, listed by David Ruston.

'Golden Masterpiece (Climbing)', deep yellow, fading to lemon, elegant buds and strongly reflexed petals, available in California.

'Golden Ophelia (Climbing)', cream with a golden yellow centre, sold in New Zealand.

'Golden Talisman (Climbing)', sport of 'Talisman', medium yellow, listed by David Ruston.

'Grandpa Dickson (Climbing)', bright yellow, large, not very vigorous, grown at Cavriglia.

'Gwynne Carr (Climbing)', pearly pink, large, scented.

'Hadley (Climbing)', light crimson, scented, sold in California and Australia, and grown in several European gardens.

'Helen Traubel (Climbing)', elegant apricot, fading slightly to pink, sold in Australia.

'Hermann Robinow (Climbing)', good pink, silvery at edges, deeper in middle, strong scent, grown at Sangerhausen.

'Home Sweet Home (Climbing)', large, full, pink, sold in England.

'H. V. Machin (Climbing)', light crimson, large (bush form was an exhibition rose), grown at Sangerhausen.

'Independence Day (Climbing)', apricot, with a hint of brown, scented, sold in France and grown in Belgium and Italy.

'Irish Fireflame (Climbing)', fiery apricot, with scarlet backs, single, scented, continually flowering, sold in England.

'J. B. Clark (Climbing)', cerise pink, large, grown at Sangerhausen and L'Haÿ-les-Roses.

'John Russell (Climbing)', crimson, with darker markings, scentless, grown at Sangerhausen.

'Jonkheer J. L. Mock (Climbing)', pink (outside deeper), long-stemmed, scented, sold in the United States, and grown at Sangerhausen.

'Julien Potin (Climbing)', deep yellow, then lemon yellow fading to cream, scented, grown by David Ruston.

'Kaiserin Auguste Viktoria (Climbing)', famous, creamy white, beautiful, good repeat-flowering but not very vigorous.

'Kardinal Schulte (Climbing)', bright red, large, scented, grown at Sangerhausen.

'Kronenbourg (Climbing)', maroon red and yellow, sold in India.

'Lady Rose (Climbing)', orange pink and orange red, scented, available in France.

'Lal (Climbing)', pink, medium-sized, pendant flowers with a damask scent, grown at Sangerhausen.

'Laurent Carle (Climbing)', crimson and strongly scented, grown at Sangerhausen and L'Haÿ-les-Roses.

'Liberty (Climbing)', brilliant crimson, strongly scented, long stems, the bush form was an important glasshouse variety, grown in several European gardens. The name made it popular in the United States.

'Louise Catherine Breslau (Climbing)', coral pink, yellow on undersides, large and attractive, grown at L'Haÿ-les-Roses.

'Louisiana (Climbing)', white, with a slight scent, available in India.

'Louis Pajotin (Climbing)', large, pearly pink, more apricot on the outside of the petal, grown at L'Haÿ-les-Roses.

'Lucy Cramphorn (Climbing)' syn. 'Maryse Kriloff (Climbing)', red, good scent, grown at several gardens in Germany.

'Lyon Rose (Climbing)', pink, yellow, coral, and apricot; large; striking; grown at Sangerhausen and L'Haÿ-les-Roses.

'Manou Meilland (Grimpant)' syn. MEItulimonsar, pink with a hint of lilac, scented, available in France.

'Mardi Gras (Climbing)', dark red, some scent, grown by David Ruston.

'Marie-Claire (Climbing)', red bud, orange crimson flowers with yellow undersides, rather gaudy, part of the breeding programme which produced 'Peace', grown in several European countries.

'Mary Hart (Climbing)', orange red, strongly scented, grown by David Ruston.

'McGredy's Triumph (Climbing)', scented, bright red, grown at Sangerhausen.

'McGredy's Yellow (Climbing)', pale yellow, moderate height, free-flowering, available in Australia.

'Message (Climbing)' syn. 'White Knight (Climbing)', white, shapely, grown by David Ruston.

'Mevrouw G. A. van Rossem (Climbing)', large, orange and yellow, strong scent, moderate vigour, free-flowering, available in England.

'Miss Universe (Climbing)', red, orange, and yellow, available in France.

'Mister Lincoln (Climbing)', dark velvety red, very strongly scented, quite widely available in Australia.

'Mme Louis Lens (Climbing)', large, white, scented, grown at Sangerhausen.

'Mme Ségond Weber (Climbing)', pink with a slightly darker outside, scented, grown at Sangerhausen.

'Mojave (Climbing)', orange or apricot with red flashes, grown by David Ruston.

'Montezuma (Climbing)', deep pink, paler at edges, good in hot dry climates, grown by David Ruston.

'Mrs C. V. Haworth (Climbing)', orange apricot fading to cream, semi-double, scented, grown at Sangerhausen.

'Mrs Henry Winnett (Climbing)', red to crimson, some scent, grown at Sangerhausen.

'Mrs W. J. Grant (Climbing)' syn. 'Belle Siebrecht (Climbing)', pale pink, nodding, scented, and available again from European nurseries. The bush form was a famous old beauty, incorrectly called 'Belle Siebrecht' in the United States.

'My Love (Climbing)', deep red, strongly scented, sold in England.

'New Year (Climbing)' syn. BURyear, orange, medium-sized.

'New Yorker (Climbing)', crimson, lightly double, lightly scented, sold by several European nurseries.

'Odette Foussier (Climbing)', pale pink or mother-of-pearl, large, scented, grown at L'Haÿ-les-Roses.

'Oklahoma (Climbing)', large, dark crimson red, strong, sweet scent.

'Olé (Climbing)', scarlet, full, with ruffled petals, very floriferous, but not too vigorous, grown by David Ruston.

'Orchid Masterpiece (Climbing)', pinkish mauve, large, scented, recently introduced in the United States.

'Paradise (Climbing)', mauve with bright pink petal-tips and a very light scent.

'Percy Thrower (Climbing)', pale pink, vigorous, sold in Australia.

'Peter Frankenfeld (Climbing)', deep pink, available from several Australian nurseries.

'Petula Clark (Climbing)', bright red, grown in several German gardens.

'Pink Peace (Climbing)', rich pink and very sweetly scented, sold in the United States and Australia.

'Pink Pearl (Climbing)', rich pink, good scent, sold in California.

'Princesse de Monaco (Climbing)', white and pink, very vigorous, sold in Australia.

'Radar (Climbing)', vermilion-lake, scented, grown at L'Haÿ-les-Roses.

'Rapture (Climbing)', pale apricot or coral pink, elegant, scented, grown by David Ruston and at Sangerhausen.

'Raymond Chevalier Appert (Climbing)', semi-double, pale crimson, grown at L'Haÿ-les-Roses.

'Red Favourite (Climbing)', bright dark red, semi-double, little scent, grown by David Ruston.

'Red Queen (Climbing)', large, red, grown at Cavriglia.

'Red Radiance (Climbing)', light crimson or cherry red, strong scent, sold in California, grown by David Ruston.

'Red Talisman (Climbing)', long buds, cherry red, fruity scent, extremely vigorous, sold in the United States.

'Rio Rita (Climbing)', large, scented, crimson, grown (as 'Climbing E. G. Hill') at Sangerhausen.

'Romance (Climbing)', pale pink, little more than semi-double, medium sized, sweet scent, vigorous, grown at Sangerhausen.

'Rose Gaujard (Climbing)', bright cherry crimson with silvery pink undersides, large, sold in France.

'Rose Marie (Climbing)', large, silvery pink, sold in Australia and grown at Sangerhausen.

'Rouge Meilland (Climbing)', bright red, good in hot climates, sold in Europe, grown in Australia.

'Roundelay (Climbing)', dark red, shapely, available in England and California.

'Royal Queen (Climbing)', white, scented, vigorous, available in The Netherlands.

'Royal William (Climbing)', dark red, scented, fairly new; the bush is a popular bedding rose.

'Samouraï (Climbing)' syn. 'Scarlet Knight (Climbing)', bright red, large, scentless, sold in Australia and South Africa.

'Santa Anita (Climbing)', rich pink, medium to large, rather concave leaves, grown at Sangerhausen.

'Schlössers Brillant (Climbing)' syn. 'Detroiter (Climbing)', bright red, scented, grown at Sangerhausen.

'Seika (Climbing)' syn. 'Olympic Torch (Climbing)', red, with white patches when first open, available in Japan.

'Shocking Blue (Climbing)', pale mauve, grown in Germany and South Africa.

'Show Girl (Climbing)', pale crimson, fading to medium pink, attractive, grown by David Ruston.

'Silver Lining (Climbing)', silvery pink, scented, available in commerce shortly.

'Sleigh Bells (Climbing)', creamy white, large, scented, sold in California.

'Solitaire (Climbing)', pale yellow, pink edges, moderately vigorous, available in commerce shortly.

'Souvenir de Mme Boullet (Climbing)', bright yellow, available commercially, but sometimes another (apricot-coloured) rose is sold in its place.

'Stefanovitch (Climbing)', dark red, strongly scented, very vigorous and prickly, grown at Sangerhausen.

'Sultane (Climbing)', red, with yellow backs, scented, available in France.

'Summer Sunshine (Climbing)', bright, unfading yellow, sold in England.

'Suspense (Climbing)', red, with yellow undersides, grown at Cavriglia.

'Suzon Lotthé (Climbing)', palest pink, with a hint of buff, strongly scented, grown by David Ruston.

'Talisman (Climbing)', scarlet flowers with yellow backs, fading to pale crimson and orange, early flowering, fairly vigorous with flowers intermittently after the first profuse flush, fairly widely available, especially in Europe.

'Tassin (Climbing)', Turkey red, large, scented, sold in Australia, grown in Europe.

'Texas Centennial (Climbing)', orange and red, becoming pinker with age, strongly scented, very tall and lanky, sold in California, grown in Europe.

'Tzigane (Climbing)', red, with yellow undersides, sold in Australia.

'Victoria Harrington (Climbing)', dark red, turning to vivid crimson and opening flat, many petals, grown in California.

'Ville de Paris (Climbing)', bright yellow, fading to lemon, extremely tall and lanky, sold in California, grown in Australia and Italy.

'Virgo (Climbing)', large, elegant, white, fairly widely available.

'Wendy Cussons (Climbing)', cherry purple, strongly scented, sold in England.

'Wenzel Geschwind (Climbing)', crimson, medium sized, looks like a Hybrid Perpetual, grown at Sangerhausen.

'Whisky Mac (Climbing)', bronze apricot, attractive, sold in Australia.

'White Christmas (Climbing)', white, medium sized, scented, sold in South Africa.

'White Knight (Climbing)' syn. 'Message (Climbing)', large, elegant, white, grown by David Ruston.

'White Masterpiece (Climbing)', very large, scented, white, sold in Japan.

'Young Venturer (Climbing)', peach coloured, sweetly scented, grown at Cavriglia.

Climbing Floribundas

The Floribundas arose from continually backcrossing the Polyanthas to the Hybrid Teas, after about 1910. The Polyanthas were thereby transformed from dwarf, twiggy bushes with small flowers into strapping shrubs with clusters of much larger flowers. So distinct were these Hybrid Polyantha roses that in 1934 the American meganursery Jackson &

Perkins coined a new term for them, "Floribunda." Twenty years later, the Floribundas were accepted worldwide as a distinct new category of rose.

The early Floribundas tended to be scentless. They compensated by an extraordinary range of bright colours, which suited the mood of the 1950s and 1960s, when they were developed by such masters as François Meilland, Matthias Tantau, Wilhelm and Reimer Kordes, Sam McGredy IV, Eugene Boerner, and Gordon Von Abrams. Floribundas also had a reputation for flowering more freely and in greater quantity than the Hybrid Teas. The practice of backcrossing them to the full-petalled, pointed Hybrid Teas continued to the end of the century, so that many recent Floribundas are in effect cluster-flowered Hybrid Teas.

There are fewer climbing sports of Floribundas in commerce than of Hybrid Teas. This may in part be explained by competition from modern climbers bred specifically to flower repeatedly all through the season. But the Climbing Floribundas include some of the most beautiful, floriferous, and colourful of all climbers. Personally, I should never wish to be without 'Climbing Iceberg', 'Climbing Gruß an Aachen', 'Grimpant Edith de Martinelli', and 'Climbing Rimosa'.

'Alain (Grimpant)' [Delforge, 1957]. This is a splendid red climber, the best of its type. The flowers are semi-double, bright Turkey red, very slightly scented, and profusely carried in neat clusters on a very and healthy vigorous plant that will grow to 4 m in the open, but much higher against a building (plate 152).

'Allgold (Climbing)' [Gandy, 1961]. This sport is medium sized (7–8 cm), of medium vigour, and medium yellow—an average good climber (plate 153). The flowers open yellow but fade quickly to lemon, cream, and white. It is, however, fairly floriferous, and the dark, disease-resistant foliage is a splendid foil to the flowers. It will grow to 5 m in a warm climate.

'Angel Face (Climbing)' [Haight, 1981]. The climbing form is popular in the United States and Australia. It is not available in Europe, although grown at Cavriglia. The medium to large flowers (10–11 cm across) are a deep, rich mauve, running to purplish crimson at the edges, and look very attractive when their wavy petals open out. They are also strongly scented. The plant is fairly vigorous, grows to about 3.5 m, and repeats well.

'Arthur Bell (Climbing)' [Limes, 1979]. This bright yellow, semi-double climber, often the earliest to flower, is particularly popular in England. The flowers fade to lemon yellow at the edges but retain a richness of hue. They are also strongly scented and nicely set off by the shiny foliage. The blooms are carried on a very leafy, vigorous plant, but its habit of growth is upright and unbending and it tends to look bare towards the base.

'Auguste Kordes (Climbing)' [Kordes, 1928]. The floriferousness of the bush form, 'Joseph Guy', has been transmitted to the climber, which is a mass of colour when it first flowers and seldom without flower thereafter (plate 154). The colour is dark carmine or pale crimson, but its flowers then fade, to end up pink or even pale pink. The semi-double flowers come in large clusters and have a musky scent. The stems are almost thornless and the plant grows very vigorously to about 5 m. The plant has two additional virtues—it is very hardy and one of the earliest to flower.

'Betty Prior (Climbing)' syn. COOprior [Cooper, 1995]. The scentless flowers are medium pink (darker on the undersides), wavy, and distinctly notched at the apex, but little more than single.

'Charleston (Climbing)' [Rumsey, 1966]. A good Floribunda, with large flowers (9–10 cm) borne singly in small clusters on rather stiff upright stems. The flowers open yellow, but soon take on a bright vermilion flush and quickly turn pure red. Like so many descendants of 'Masquerade', however, they have little scent. The plant grows vigorously to 5–6 m.

'Chorus (Climbing)' [Meilland, 1986]. The flowers of this striking climber are bright vermilion, fading slightly to dark orange and always slightly paler in the centre. They are carried in small clusters and are fairly large (about 11 cm), but are poorly scented.

'Circus (Climbing)' [Armstrong, 1961]. Not very vigorous, little more than a pillar rose normally, this climber has beautiful flowers which open dark salmon, with yellow centres, but fade to pink and white in a way that holds all the colours harmoniously together. They are medium sized (8–9 cm), with a strong fruity scent, and carried in fairly large clusters.

'Dauphine (Grimpant)' [Gaujard, 1959]. This attractive climber is seldom seen outside France. The flowers are dark pink or pale crimson, borne in small clusters, and lightly scented. The plant grows vigorously to 5 m and has only a few prickles.

'Diablotin (Grimpant)' syn. 'Little Devil (Climbing)', DELposar [Delbard, 1970]. The flowers are bright vermilion orange (slightly paler towards the base of the petals), medium sized (about 7–8 cm), scentless, and only really semi-double. This sport is vigorous (growing to 5 m at Bagatelle) and still sold in France.

'Edith de Martinelli (Grimpant)' [Orard, 1983]. This truly magnificent Climbing Floribunda is almost unknown outside France. It has large flowers (12 cm) in small clusters (plate 155). They are very full, rounded, held horizontally, vermilion-lake (slightly pinker on the underside), and borne in amazing profusion on a vigorous plant which quickly reaches 5 m.

'Fashion (Climbing)' [Jackson & Perkins, 1951; Mattock, 1955]. The flowers of 'Fashion' are quite distinctive, a really bright, pure shade of orange when they first open, although they fade first to coral and then to pale pink, with yellow backs which pass almost to white. They are fairly well scented, open out double, and are borne in comparatively large clusters. The plant has a reputation for susceptibility to blackspot and rust. The Mattock sport is said to be the better of the two, but it is apparently sold only in Australia. Each is only of moderate vigour and repeats well.

'Fashionette (Climbing)' [Noack, 1962]. This excellent Climbing Floribunda is grown only in Germany. The flowers are full of petals, about 8 cm across, and pink with a hint of coral; they open out to an old-fashioned centre. They have a good scent and are carried in small clusters on a vigorous, prickly plant. The deep green, glossy leaves are also very handsome.

'Firecrest (Climbing)' [Le Grice, 1969]. This is a cheerful, reddish vermilion Floribunda climber with fully double flowers in medium-sized clusters. Hardy and vigorous, 'Firecrest (Climbing)' is still seen in some European collections.

'Goldilocks (Climbing)' [Jackson & Perkins, 1951]. This was a popular climber when it first came out. Its buds are like little Hybrid Teas. The flowers open out double, scented, and deep yellow, although they fade to lemon, cream, and white and the petals recurve to create a spiky look. The plant is of moderate vigour, growing to 3 m high, and repeats fairly well.

'Gruß an Aachen (Climbing)' [Kordes, 1937]. 'Gruß an Aachen' is often proclaimed as the first of the Floribundas, although its putative parents are both Hybrid Teas. The climbing sport makes a very vigorous climber, of the Multiflora type, with pale pink buds which open to large (10–12 cm across), full, white flowers. The flowers also have a hint of buff and mother-of-pearl in them; these colours, when combined with the mass of petals (sometimes almost imbricated, sometimes almost quartered), make for great beauty. The blooms also have a strong, sweet damask scent. The bush is vigorous (5 m), very hardy, and amazingly floriferous in its first flowering, with additional flowers produced intermittently thereafter.

'Iceberg (Climbing)' [Cant, 1968]. There are several sports of 'Iceberg', the best white Floribunda ever bred. Cant's form is the best, with large (9–10 cm), pure white flowers, but with a hint of pink in the half-open flower (plate 156). Cant's sport has distinctive incurved petals and more of them than in the bush form. The flowers are also strongly scented. The plant grows fairly vigorously to about 5 m and, after the first spectacular flowering, is never without one or two flowers for the rest of the year. Its bright green leaves suffer, like the bush form, from blackspot, but that never seems to affect its vigour or floriferousness.

'Independence (Climbing)' syn. 'Kordes' Sondermeldung (Climbing)' [Baldacci, 1960]. The climber is fairly vigorous (about 4 m high), with flowers that are orange scarlet, fairly large (12 cm), and lightly scented. Although the colour does not blend easily with others, this rose has its admirers.

'Kalinka (Climbing)' syn. 'Pink Wonder (Climbing)', MEIhartforsar [Meilland, 1976]. This Climbing Floribunda has beautiful medium pink flowers which open with a hint of coral at the centre and pale to pure rose pink. The flowers have an old-fashioned shape with a muddled centre. They are only about 11–12 cm across, but their shape and the size of the clusters make them seem larger. The blooms are also very strongly scented. The plant is almost thornless and grows to about 4 m.

'Lilli Marleen (Grimpant)' syn. PEKlimasar [Pekmez, 1982]. This sport produces large quantities of dark, bright, Turkey red flowers in small clusters, which give an overall impression of great profusion when they first flower (plate 157). The flowers are medium sized (10 cm), slightly scented, and carried on a dense but fairly vigorous plant which grows to about 3 m. 'Grimpant Lilli Marleen' and 'Grimpant Alain' are the best red Climbing Floribundas.

'Masquerade (Climbing)' [Dillian, 1958]. Like the bush, the flowers of the climbing form open bright yellow before turning pink and deep crimson, but they are larger, about 8–9 cm in diameter (plate 159). The scentless flowers are borne in large, spacious clusters on a vigorous plant, about 4 m high. I find that the sport repeats well, and regard it as a better plant all-round than its bush form.

'Pasadena Tournament (Climbing)' syn. 'Red Cécile Brunner' [Marsh, 1945]. This

Chapter 12

California speciality shows no resemblance to its reputed parent, but it makes a very vigorous and excellent climber. The plant is almost thornless. The flowers are cherry crimson, medium sized (8 cm), fully double, and strongly scented. It looks to me like a China hybrid.

'Pernille Poulsen (Climbing)' [Poulsen, 1976]. This attractive pink climber has buds like a Hybrid Tea, but they are borne in large clusters like the Floribundas. The buds open out so that the flowers appear little more than semi-double. The blooms are about 10 cm across, fairly well scented, and set off by dark green, glossy leaves.

'Playgirl (Climbing)' syn. MORclip [Moore, 1993]. This climber is fairly vigorous (3 m) and carries a remarkable profusion of deep pink or crimson, single flowers, with a few thereafter all through the year in warm climates. The scentless flowers are about 8 cm across, with notched and wavy petals, and carry a superb, large boss of yellow stamens at the centre. The foliage is brilliantly dark and glossy.

'Porthos (Climbing)' syn. LAPadsar [Bois, 1976]. The flowers measure about 9 cm across. They are a bright, hard red, long-lasting, and profusely carried on strong upright growths. They have little scent, but are substantial and tough flowers which stand up well to heat, cold, and rain. The dense, vigorous plant grows to about 3.5 m.

'Prince Igor (Climbing)' [Meilland, 1985]. The flowers of this Floribunda are a bright vermilion red. They have a good scent.

'Redgold (Climbing)' syn. 'Rouge et Or (Grimpant)' [Pekmez, 1984]. The flowers are a good rich yellow, thickly edged with bright vermilion red. The combination is fairly arresting as the flowers start to open, but the colours later fade. The flowers are scentless, about 9 cm across, and borne either singly or in small clusters.

'Rimosa (Climbing)' syn. 'Gold Badge (Climbing)', 'Gold Bunny (Climbing)' [Meilland, 1991]. This rose is spectacular and very healthy in continental Europe and Australia, less so in cool damp climates. The flowers are medium to large (11 cm), fully double, and deep rich yellow; they hold their colour well (plate 158). They are nicely scented and profusely borne in small clusters. The plant reaches up to about 4 m and repeats fairly well.

'Rosenmärchen (Climbing)' syn. 'Pinocchio (Climbing)' [Parmentier, 1951]. The flowers are small to medium (about 6 cm), semi-double to double, and distinctly musk scented. Their colour is intriguing; the flowers open pink, with a hint of yellow at the base, then take on a crimson hue, especially at the edges, a tendency which this sport passed on to its descendant 'Masquerade'. It is a good repeater.

'Rusticana (Climbing)' syn. 'Poppy Flash (Climbing)', MEllénasar [Paolino, 1975]. This climber sported from an orange vermilion Floribunda, a colour popular in the 1960s and 1970s. Its flowers are medium sized (8–9 cm), scentless, and carried in small clusters. The plant grows to 3–4 m.

'Sarabande (Climbing)' syn. MEIhandsar [Meilland, 1968]. This cheerful vermilion climber makes an attractive splash when it first flowers. The flowers are carried on upright stems in small clusters, but they have little scent. They are bright orange red, slightly paler towards the base of the petals, and single, with occasionally an extra petal or two. Growth is fairly vigorous, to about 4 m.

'Spartan (Climbing)' [Martinez, 1958; Kordes, 1960]. The strongly scented flowers are large (11–12 cm), deep, full, many petalled, often with muddled centres which give them a special charm. The colour is deep, radiant coral, not perhaps the subtlest of colours, but less insistent than many 1960s Floribundas. The plant makes thick, vigorous, hardy growth, and lots of it, to about 5 m tall. 'Climbing Spartan' is one of the most productive of climbing sports.

'Sun Flare (Climbing)' syn. 'Yellow Blaze' [Burks, 1987; Jackson & Perkins, 1987]. This is an attractive climber, whose medium-sized (7–8 cm), scentless flowers are pure yellow at the centre and lemon yellow at the edge. It has rather small leaves and conspicuously long prickles and grows to about 3 m.

'Tip Top (Climbing)'. I first saw this rose at Bagatelle in 1986, but do not know the introducer. It has semi-double, scented, coral pink flowers which are paler on the outside of the petals; the flowers open out very attractively. The growth is fairly vigorous, and it has a very abundant first flowering.

'Trumpeter (Climbing)' [c. 1997]. The climbing form of this popular bedding rose has medium to large, bright vermilion flowers and glossy reddish foliage.

'Winifred Coulter (Climbing)' [Jarvis, c. 1968]. This exceptionally vigorous climbing sport is much admired by visitors to the Huntington Botanical Gardens in California, where it is spectacular on the great trellised pergola. The strongly scented flowers are pale crimson, white at the base of the petals, and paler on the backs (plate 160). They open out flat and are borne in great profusion during the main flowering.

'Woburn Abbey (Climbing)' [Brundrett, 1972]. This sport is an Australian speciality. The flowers are vermilion red with orange edges and orange backs to the petals, so that the overall effect is of orange splashed with red (plate 161). The flowers are medium sized (10 cm) and borne in clusters—very attractive during the first flush of flowers. The bush form had a reputation for susceptibility to blackspot and mildew, but neither is a problem in hot, dry climates, where the climbing form flourishes.

'Yellowhammer (Grimpant)' [Dorieux, 1976]. This French speciality has medium-sized (8 cm), shapely, golden yellow flowers in small clusters. The flowers are scented and last well as a cut flower. The plant seems to be of only moderate vigour, growing to perhaps 3 m high at most.

Lesser-Known Climbing Floribundas

The remaining Climbing Floribundas are only occasionally seen. Some have been popular in the past, but are now superseded by better cultivars. Those that are still in commerce are usually only locally available, in one or two countries at the most. France, in particular, has a large number of Climbing Floribunda sports which have not been taken up in other parts of the world. Some of the better ones, for instance, 'Grimpant Edith Martinelli', I have tried to describe fully in the previous section, but this section still contains a number of highly desirable Climbing Floribundas which ought to be more widely known and grown, including 'Climbing Bernina', 'Climbing Moulin Rouge', and 'Climbing Princess Michiko'.

'Bernina (Climbing)', large, pale yellow, fully petalled flowers, fading almost to white, medium scent, grown by David Ruston.

'Bibiche (Climbing)', bright vermilion flowers with short petals, borne in large clusters, grown at Bagatelle.

'Cocorico (Climbing)', semi-double, medium sized, red, dark at the edges, more orange in the centre, grown by David Ruston.

'Cognac (Climbing)', peach fading to pink, burnt orange undersides, semi-double, and attractive, grown at Sangerhausen.

'Concerto (Climbing)', semi-double, bright Turkey red, grown by David Ruston.

'Curiosa (Climbing)', salmon pink, with paler undersides, attractive, grown at L'Haÿ-les-Roses.

'Europeana (Climbing)', large clusters of very full, small to medium-sized flowers, intense dark red with no trace of orange or crimson, very beautiful, sold in France.

'Feuerschein (Climbing)', bright red, 6–7 cm in diameter, scentless, borne in a cluster of three to six, dark leaves, very prickly stems, vigorous, grown at Sangerhausen.

'Feurio (Climbing)', scarlet vermilion, double, vigorous, long flower stems, grown at Sangerhausen.

'Floradora (Climbing)', bright orange scarlet, fading to pink, the precursor of the screaming vermilion Floribundas of the 1950s and 1960s, grown in several European gardens.

'Florence Mary Morse (Climbing)', bright scarlet, handsome, grown at L'Haÿ-les-Roses.

'Floriane (Climbing)' syn. 'Tender Night (Climbing)', MEIlaursar, medium sized, Turkey red, with dark glossy leaves, grown in France.

'Forever Amber (Climbing)', orange scarlet, fading to pink, scented, excessively vigorous, grown at the Huntington Botanical Gardens in California.

'Frau Astrid Späth (Climbing)', pale glowing crimson, semi-double, beautiful, grown at Sangerhausen (plate 162).

'Guitare (Climbing)', orange and yellow, strong scent, sold in India.

'Hein Evers (Climbing)', pure bright red, no scent, 6 cm across, borne in a cluster of five to eight, lightly double, glossy leaves, grown at Sangerhausen.

'Kathleen Ferrier (Climbing)', salmon pink, fading to pure pink, large clusters, good scent, grown at Bagatelle.

'Kimono (Climbing)', medium pink, borne in large clusters, sold in France.

'Korona (Climbing)', bright orange scarlet, single or semi-double, scentless, grown at Sangerhausen.

'Mercedes (Climbing)', orange scarlet and yellow, shapely, a David Ruston speciality.

'Minuette (Climbing)', extremely attractive, white flowers, exquisitely formed, with crimson edges.

'Moulin Rouge (Climbing)', spectacular Turkey red flowers in great abundance, should be better known (plate 163).

'Nina Weibull (Climbing)', dark, unfading red, scented, sold in Belgium.

'Orangeade (Climbing)', bright orange red, semi-double, sold in England.

'Orange Sensation (Climbing)', bright orange, red tips to petals, semi-double, sold in France.

'Princess Michiko (Climbing)', orange pink, semi-double, sold in Japan.
'Pußta (Climbing)' syn. 'New Daily Mail (Climbing)', dark red, semi-double, sold in France.
'Ruth Leuwerik (Climbing)', bright scarlet, strongly scented, sold in France.
'Samantha (Climbing)', bright red, grown at Cavriglia.
'Sunsprite (Climbing)', bright yellow, large clusters, scented, sold in California.
'Sweet Repose (Climbing)', pink and yellow, fading to cream, grown by David Ruston.
'Tantau's Triumph (Climbing)', semi-double, a shade of scarlet that was once much admired, light scent, prickly, grown at Sangerhausen.
'Tiki (Climbing)', light pink, with slightly darker edges, shapely, grown by David Ruston.
'Wettra (Climbing)', red, scentless, fairly large clusters, available in Benelux.
'Zambra (Climbing)' syn. MElalfisar, nasturtium orange, semi-double, sold in South Africa.
'Zorina (Climbing)', salmon orange, medium sized, scented, sold in South Africa.

Climbing Polyanthas

The first Polyanthas were neat, compact, dwarf shrubs with small, pale flowers. Crosses with other roses led to looser, taller growth and greatly increased the colour range. Most important was the influence of 'Turner's Crimson Rambler', which introduced a range of crimson and purple tones unknown among the Hybrid Teas and a tendency to lack scent. Crosses with Tea roses gave rise to the exceptional 'Mlle Cécile Brunner' and 'Clothilde Soupert', whereas 'Orléans Rose' initiated a huge range of colour mutations which were in due course also represented by climbing sports.

Climbing sports of Polyanthas look just like Multiflora Ramblers. To that extent, therefore, the roses listed below should be considered as an adjunct to those listed in chapter 7. They share all their essential characteristics, including a tendency to mildew among some of the older cultivars. Certainly, when it comes to choosing Multiflora Ramblers for the garden, no selection would be complete unless it included some of the Climbing Polyanthas.

'China Doll (Climbing)' [Weeks, 1977]. This is a vigorous climber, with rather tight clusters of small (5 cm), double, bright pink flowers. The blooms are paler at the edges and on the backs of the ruffled petals, which give them great beauty and substance. This sport has little scent and few flowers after the main flowering, but the glossy leaves are attractive and the plant is thornless.

'Clothilde Soupert (Climbing)' [Dingee & Conard, 1901]. No early Polyantha has such large flowers; they are about 10 cm in diameter, with long reflexed petals, a beautiful deep mother-of-pearl in the centre which fades to white at the edges. They are deliciously scented of tea and are carried in small clusters, typically of five flowers. The plant grows vigorously to about 3 m and is rather prickly, with soft leaves somewhat prone to mildew. It is very remontant.

'Gloria Mundi (Climbing)' syn. 'Prinses van Oranje (Climbing)' [de Ruiter, 1933; Lens, 1934]. The blazing orange scarlet flowers are quite unmistakable in the garden. They are double and well set off by light green leaves, but completely scentless. They come in large clusters, often more than fifty flowers, and appear more-or-less continuously. The plant grows to about 2.5 m and often carries mildew, but this seems not to affect its vigour. According to *Rosenjahrbuch des Vereins Deutscher Rosenfreunde* (1955), it is not entirely hardy.

'Margo Koster (Climbing)' [Crombie, 1962]. This rose is salmon orange (paler on the undersides), scentless, and semi-double to double. When it opens out, the recurved petals give it a slightly globular shape. The flowers come in clusters of up to thirty and are borne continuously, especially on the new wood. They have a very slight scent and some susceptibility to mildew. The plant is vigorous, growing to about 3 m, with attractive leaves which start a soft, pale green and turn darker with age.

'Mlle Cécile Brunner (Climbing)' [F. P. Hosp, 1894]. This beautiful Climbing Polyantha has very elegant slender buds which open out into small flowers (5 cm), usually with reflexed petals and sometimes with a button eye. The flowers are coral pink in the centre and pinkish white at the edges, fading especially quickly in the sun. They are borne in large clusters of up to one hundred flowers (typically twenty to thirty) and are strongly scented. The plant is very vigorous, reaching 8 m. This Climbing Polyantha repeats so well that it is seldom out of flower.

'Orange Triumph (Climbing)' [Leenders, 1945]. 'Orange Triumph' is definitely on the crimson or pink side of red—a dull, scentless, semi-double rose with somewhat glandular stalks. The flowers are small (about 5 cm) and held upright in clusters of twenty to thirty. The plant grows to about 2 m and produces only a few flowers after the main flush.

'Pinkie (Climbing)' [Dering, 1952]. The flowers are medium pink (fading to pale pink, with streaks of white towards the centre), semi-double, up to 7 cm across, with long petals that reflex. They come in medium-sized clusters with no scent that I can detect, although others disagree. The plant is thornless, has glossy foliage, and grows thickly to about 2.5 m in the open, twice that against a wall. It flowers tirelessly throughout summer and autumn and is especially popular in Australia.

'Red Explorer' [Penny, 1928]. This rose is very much a Multiflora Rambler. It has rich deep pink, double flowers which fade slightly. They measure about 4 cm and have a slightly musky scent. The blooms are carried in medium-sized clusters, typically of five to twenty flowers, on a vigorous plant with beautiful pale green leaves. It reaches about 3.5 m and is gently remontant.

'Teschendorffs Jubiläumsrose (Rankende)' [Teschendorff, 1930]. The pale crimson or deep pink flowers fade to medium pink. They are about 4 cm across, fully double, lightly scented, and carried in clusters of five to twenty. The Multiflora foliage is a beautiful foil.

'Triomphe Orléanais (Climbing)' [Turbat, 1922]. 'Triomphe Orléanais' reminds me of 'Dorothy Perkins'. The flowers are semi-double, about 4–5 cm across, and almost scentless. They open pale crimson and fade to deep pink, but their incurved petals do not drop off when they have faded—that is, it does not die well. The clusters have twenty to forty flowers and make an acceptable display, but there is no repeat flowering.

Climbing Sports

The following Climbing Polyanthas are still in cultivation, but are seldom seen for sale:

'Chatter (Climbing)', light red, semi-double, grown at Sangerhausen.

'Happy (Climbing)', crimson flowers in dense clusters, grown in Germany.

'Holstein (Climbing)', semi-single, crimson with a white eye, rather large flowers (10 cm) in large clusters, grown at Sangerhausen.

'Jackie (Climbing)', pale yellow, fading to cream and white, double, strictly speaking a climbing miniature, still sold in Europe and Australasia.

'Johanna Tantau (Climbing)', medium-sized, semi-double, pale pink flowers fading rather unpleasantly to white.

'Marie-Rose (Climbing)', reddish pink, double, light scent, almost thornless, grown at Sangerhausen.

'Miniature (Climbing)', very small, very full, pale pink flowers fading to white, in clusters of about ten, and a fairly strong musky scent. This sport has little value apart from its historical interest.

'Miss G. Messmann (Climbing)' syn. 'Baby Rambler (Climbing)', clusters of cupped crimson flowers, like a paler version of 'Turner's Crimson Rambler', grown at Sangerhausen.

'Mrs W. H. Cutbush (Climbing)', semi-double, pink with a white centre, late-flowering, liable to mildew, grown at L'Haÿ-les-Roses.

'Torch (Climbing)', small, semi-double, bright orange scarlet with a white centre, occasionally seen in gardens.

Large-Flowered Climbers

Bourbons and Hybrid Perpetuals

The large-flowered climbing roses come in many forms. The earliest were Bourbons and Hybrid Perpetuals with enough extra vigour to enable them to be grown at least as pillar roses.

'Adèle Frey' [Walter, 1911]. Walter introduced this dark red climber as a Climbing Hybrid Tea; in fact, it more closely resembles a Hybrid Perpetual. The flowers are 9 cm across and have a light, sweet scent. The plant is very prickly and not very vigorous.

'Ards Pillar' [Dickson, 1902]. This pillar rose has scented, medium-sized (10 cm), pale crimson flowers. It is late flowering and not especially vigorous.

'Ards Rambler' [Dickson, 1908]. Originally described as rosy carmine or orange carmine, the plant now grown at Sangerhausen as 'Ards Rambler' has very bright red, semi-double, lightly scented flowers.

'Ards Rover' [Dickson, 1898]. The straggly habit, prickly stems, and tendency to mildew which characterise this popular and vigorous Hybrid Perpetual–type climber are all redeemed by the opulent, dark crimson flowers profusely borne in midseason and thereafter sporadically. They are large (12 cm), substantial, double, and sweetly scented. When well grown, the foliage too is large and handsome.

'Mikado' [Kiese, 1913]. Lanky, prickly 'Mikado' looks more like a Bourbon or Hybrid Perpetual than a climber. Its handsome, semi-double flowers have a sumptuous, sweet damask scent; they are pale crimson at first, fading to dark pink. The plant is very vigorous and early flowering. It grows still at Sangerhausen.

'Miss Marion Manifold' [Adamson, introduced by Brundrett, 1911]. The flowers of this handsome Hybrid Perpetual–type rose have a very rich scent and are large (10 cm), full, and rather globular, borne in clusters of one to four. They open a good deep crimson, then fade to dark pink; the undersides are much paler, almost silvery pink. The plant is nearly thornless and very hardy but grows especially well, to about 4 m, in warm climates.

'Paxton' syn. 'Sir Joseph Paxton' [Laffay, 1851]. This vigorous Bourbon rose is usually grown as a climber. The flowers are dark pink, medium to large (8–9 cm), fully double and open flat to a quilled and sometimes quartered shape. They are strongly scented and come in clusters of one to six. The very prickly plant repeats well in autumn and grows vigorously to about 3 m.

'Prince Stirbey' [Schwartz, 1871]. A very vigorous Hybrid Perpetual (with a trace of Tea rose in it), 'Prince Stirbey' is best grown as a climber, as at Sangerhausen. The flowers open out large (9–10 cm), flat, fully double, and dark pink or pale crimson (medium pink on the petal-backs) with a strong scent. The plant grows to 4–5 m and repeats well.

'Robusta' [Soupert & Notting, 1887]. A Climbing Bourbon (with a trace of Noisette), this rose bears clusters of five to ten musk-scented flowers. The blooms are double and small (5 cm) and open mother-of-pearl then fade to white. It is a vigorous grower (3–4 m) which should not be confused with the scarlet 'Kordes' Robusta' [1979].

'Souvenir de Nemours' [Hervé, 1859]. This Bourbon hybrid has very attractive, scented, medium pink flowers which are slightly paler on the undersides of the petals and have a tendency to reflex. The medium-sized (6.0–6.5 cm), usually single blooms are rather pendulous. The plant grows vigorously to about 3 m.

'Souvenir de Pierre Dupuy' [Levet, 1876]. This is a very vigorous Hybrid Perpetual, possibly crossed with a Tea. The flowers are medium sized (8 cm), crimson (with an occasional white stripe on their petals and paler undersides), very full, globular, and very sweetly scented. They are borne singly or up to four in a cluster on a very prickly, bushy plant which grows to about 3 m.

'Surpassing Beauty' syn. 'Woolverstone Church Rose'. The English rosarian Humphrey Brooke reintroduced this Hybrid Perpetual–type climber in 1980 from the Suffolk church where it had grown for a hundred years. It is a classic crimson beauty with a very strong, sweet scent. The heavy flowers open red and darken with age, ending up purple (but redder on the outside); they have masses of short petals and muddled centres. The leaves have a red tinge when young.

'Zéphirine Drouhin' [Bizot, 1868]. Although traditionally described as a Bourbon, I consider 'Zéphirine Drouhin' a cross between a Boursault and a Hybrid Perpetual. It is hardy, thornless, strongly scented, early flowering, and has beautiful crimson new growths. The flowers are fairly double, flat, medium sized (8 cm), and bright cherry pink, fading only slightly, with streaks of white towards the centre. It will make 2 m as a bush, and twice that on a wall. Its sport 'Kathleen Harrop' [Dickson, 1919] has rose pink flowers with dark backs, but fewer petals and less vigour. Much better is another sport, 'Martha' [Zeiner, 1912]; its petals are exactly the same colours as 'Kathleen Harrop', but the flower is fuller, so the petal-backs reflect deeper tones into the heart of the flower. All three cultivars flower profusely and regularly into autumn.

Once-Flowering Climbers with Large Flowers

Many of the early twentieth-century climbers were once-flowering Hybrid Teas, for instance, 'Cupid' [Cant, 1915]. Others were the result of experiments with unusual species, notably *Rosa foetida*. The best remain popular even today.

'Allen's Fragrant Pillar' [Allen, 1930]. 'Paul's Lemon Pillar' × 'Souvenir de Claudius Denoyel'. The elegant buds and large (10–11 cm), loosely double flowers of this Hybrid Tea–type climber are bright cherry red, flushed with golden yellow, and open out to show their stamens. They are borne recurrently on long stems, usually singly, and have a rich, sweet scent. The plant has typical Hybrid Tea–type leaves and grows fairly vigorously to about 3 m.

'Allen's Golden Pillar' [Allen, 1932]. This is another Hybrid Tea–type climber with large (8–10 cm), full, dark yellow flowers (orange on the back of the petals), and glossy leaves. It flowers heavily, but only once, and grows to about 3 m.

'Birthday Present' [Toogood, 1950]. 'Guinée' × 'Rouge Mallerin'. This Hybrid Tea–type climber is seldom seen today, even in its native Australia, perhaps because it flowers only once. The flowers are lightly double, Hybrid Tea shaped, strongly scented, and dark red. The plant is very vigorous, and the one flowering is most prolific.

'Chaplin's Pink Companion' [Chaplin, 1961]. 'Chaplin's Pink Climber' × 'Opéra'. This rose is very attractive during its one long flowering (plate 164). The flowers are small (5 cm), semi-double, scented, pale salmon pink, and carried most abundantly in clusters of up to fifteen flowers. The plant grows vigorously to about 4 m and is mildly susceptible to mildew. It grows best in an open position.

'Chastity' [F. Cant, 1924]. The large (10 cm), elegant, strongly scented, semi-double, pure white flowers of this Hybrid Tea–type climber come in nicely spaced clusters of four to six. The petals are broad and rather reflexed, with a wide boss of yellow stamens. The plant has pale green leaves (sometimes susceptible to mildew) and very prickly stems. It flowers early but only once and grows vigorously to about 5 m.

'Čsl. Legie' [Böhm, 1933]. 'Paul's Scarlet Climber' × 'Jan Böhm'. This Hybrid Tea–type climber, named for the Czechoslovak Legion, is best described as a darker, more double 'Paul's Scarlet Climber'. It still grows at Sangerhausen.

'Cupid' [B. R. Cant, 1915]. The flowers of this overrated Hybrid Tea–type climber are large (12 cm), single, and scented. They open peachy pink, with crinkly petals, but fade quickly to shell pink and white (plate 165). The blooms come in small clusters and are attractively set off by the pale stamens. Autumn brings enormous hips, like small, bright orange pears with long, persistent calyces; they last well into winter. The plant is vigorous and prickly, flowers once, and is rather susceptible to late spring frosts. It grows gawkily to 5 m.

'F. Ferrer' [Pahissa, 1935]. This scented, scarlet, Hybrid Tea–type climber survives only at Sangerhausen, where its rich red, medium-sized flowers (8–9 cm) appear singly and continue through to autumn. It is not a heavy bloomer—Pahissa always preferred quality to quantity.

'Parkfeuer' [Lambert, 1906]. This remarkable and very distinctive climber is a seedling of *Rosa foetida* 'Bicolor'. The flowers are medium sized (6–7 cm), single or semi-single, and bright crimson red, set off by golden stamens. They are borne on short stems in small clusters very early in the season and do not repeat. The lanky, hardy plant has handsome young purple leaves and no prickles; it grows very vigorously to at least 8 m.

'Rustica' [Barbier, 1929]. This very early-flowering hybrid of *Rosa foetida* has bright yellow, semi-double flowers which hold their colour well and fade only slowly to buff yellow. The lightly scented flowers are well held, singly or in upright clusters of two or three, and are medium sized (7–8 cm). The plant is a shrubby climber that will grow to 3 m. The leaves are dull and liable to blackspot, and the stems are very prickly.

The Druschkis

The incomparable early Hybrid Tea 'Frau Karl Druschki' [Lambert, 1901] was widely used to impart hardiness and vigour to new roses. Some proved so vigorous ('Mme Grégoire Staechelin' is the best known) that they are unquestionably climbing roses.

'Apeles Mestres' [Dot, 1925]. 'Frau Karl Druschki' × 'Souvenir de Claudius Pernet'. This beautiful Hybrid Tea–type climber has enormous, pale yellow flowers, rather sparsely produced early in the season, but sweetly scented, elegantly shaped, and fully double. It grows strongly and lankily to 4–5 m, and occasionally flowers again later in the year.

'Marguerite Carels' [Nabonnand, 1922]. 'Frau Karl Druschki' × 'General MacArthur'. The size and sheer class of both its parents are visible in this Hybrid Tea–type climber. The flowers are very large (12–14 cm) and open from large, pointed buds on long, strong stems. They are bright pink, fading to pale pink, but always darker towards the centre of the flower, and have a distinctly fruity scent. The plant is vigorous, not too prickly, and is said to flower recurrently; it certainly flowers very profusely in summer.

'Mme Grégoire Staechelin' syn. 'Spanish Beauty' [Dot, 1927]. 'Frau Karl Druschki' × 'Château de Clos Vougeot'. 'Mme Grégoire Staechelin' is the most popular of the once-flowering Hybrid Tea–type climbers, and rightly so. The large (13–14 cm), lightly double, pendulous flowers have a unique charm which comes from the distinctive frilly, ruffled wave of their petals. They are clear creamy pink, with darker pink undersides to the petals and redder markings on the outer petals, as well as being slightly paler in the centre. They are sweetly scented and borne in such profusion that the English botanist Patrick Synge once called them "sumptuous, even voluptuous, billowing in masses along the branches" (Gault and Synge 1971). It grows quickly and vigorously to 5–7 m. The plant flowers notably early, with fairly dark glossy leaves. Large pinkish orange hips usually follow in autumn.

'Mock's Rosa Druschki' [Mock, pre-1935]. This sweet-scented pillar rose has elegant Hybrid Tea–type buds, although the glossy leaves suggest some *Rosa wichurana* in its ancestry. The flowers are medium to large (8–9 cm), a good rose pink, fading slightly, and borne two to ten in a cluster.

'Schloß Seußlitz' [Dechant, 1933]. 'Frau Karl Druschki' × 'Harison's Yellow'. The flowers of this unusual hybrid are creamy yellow, fading to white, medium sized (6–7 cm), semi-double, and flat. They come in small clusters on an extremely hardy but once-flowering plant which grows to 7–8 m and is remarkable for its bristliness, great vigour, and early flowering.

'Soleil d'Orient' [Croibier, 1935]. 'Frau Karl Druschki' × 'Mme Edouard Herriot'. This Hybrid Tea–type climber has lightly double, bright pink flowers with a hint of coral and long, silky petals which reflex at the tips (plate 166). The flowers have a good scent and are large (9–10 cm), substantial, and borne on long stems. The plant is not very floriferous and does not always repeat, but grows vigorously to about 3.5 m.

'Studienrat Schlenz' [Lambert, 1926]. 'Mrs Aaron Ward' × 'Frau Karl Druschki'. This vigorous and tall Hybrid Tea–type climber grows at Sangerhausen. The flowers are an attractive rose pink, but are slightly darker on the backs of the petals. The blooms are fully double and scented, but the plant flowers only once.

Alister Clark

Alister Clark wanted to breed garden roses that would flourish in the hot, dry climate of Australia; look good on the bush; and keep well when cut. We examined his experiments with *Rosa gigantea* in chapter 3. Now it is time to consider his other crosses. Clark was an amateur, with no long-term strategy for his breeding; provided the plants grew well, their size and floral form were acceptable. His hybrids are an idiosyncratic selection. All are Hybrid Tea–type climbers, unless otherwise indicated, and much hardier than Clark's Giganteas.

'Amy Johnson' [Clark, introduced by National Rose Society of Victoria, 1931]. 'Souvenir de Gustave Prat' seedling. This vigorous climber has lightly double, long-stemmed flowers. They are pale pink at the edge of the petals and at the base of the petals as they age, but darker pink towards the centre of the flower. The petals are distinctly wavy, and the inner ones are quite short. The flowers open out well to reveal red anthers. They have a good, sweet scent. The plant has rather corrugated leaves, and grows to 4–5 m; it flowers recurrently.

'Billy Boiler' [Clark; introduced by National Rose Society of Victoria, 1927]. The deep, glowing red flowers of this pillar rose are loosely semi-double and strongly scented. This rose is not as good as 'Black Boy', from which it was bred.

'Black Boy' [Clark, introduced by National Rose Society of South Australia, 1919]. 'Étoile de France' × 'Bardou Job'. This excellent crimson climber is justly very popular in its native Australia. It should be more widely grown in hot climates, where it also tolerates light soils. The flowers are a pure, unfading, bright crimson with dark maroon markings on the upper sides of the petals and occasional white flecks at the base. The flowers are elegantly pointed, medium sized (7–8 cm), lightly double, and moderately scented. The foliage is small, sparse, and no stranger to blackspot, but the plant still grows quickly and vigorously.

'Countess of Stradbroke' [Clark, introduced by Hazelwood, 1928]. 'Walter C. Clark' seedling. This is a handsome, velvety, dark crimson rose of unusual depth and richness, with large (10–11 cm), classically elegant, sweet-scented flowers borne singly or in small clusters. The plant is moderately vigorous and repeats well.

'Daydream' [Clark, introduced by Hazelwood Bros., 1925]. 'Souvenir de Gustave Prat' × 'Rosy Morn' or 'Gwen Nash'. This is an extremely attractive and sweetly scented climbing rose, with fairly large (9 cm), single to semi-double flowers which open pearly pink and fade almost to white (plate 167). The ruffled petals and the reddish gold stamens add to its elegance; Clark likened it to a water lily. The hardy plant grows bushily to about 3 m; it blooms very profusely in midseason and then intermittently.

'Emily Rhodes' [Clark, introduced by National Rose Society of Victoria, 1937]. 'Golden Ophelia' × 'Zéphirine Drouhin'. Not one of Clark's best introductions, this pillar rose (growing to 3 m high) has lightly scented, semi-double, vermilion pink flowers with rather reflexed petals. It does, however, repeat well.

'Gwen Nash' [Clark, introduced by National Rose Society of New South Wales, 1920]. 'Rosy Morn' × 'Scorcher'. Alister Clark called this repeat-flowering pillar rose the most beautiful thing in decorative pinks he could hope to produce. The medium to large (8–9 cm), lightly scented flower is elegantly semi-double with very reflexed petals. It opens mother-of-pearl, but fades to pale pink, with white streaks and a white centre. The flower has a good boss of yellow stamens, but this is sometimes hidden behind a petaloid stamen—a defect.

'Janet Morrison' [Clark, 1936]. 'Black Boy' seedling. 'Janet Morrison' has medium to large (8–9 cm), semi-double flowers in small clusters. They are a bright cherry carmine and have an unusual scent, of cloves. The plant is vigorous, repeats well, and grows to about 3 m, but it is not one of Clark's best roses.

'Margaret Turnbull' [Clark, 1931]. This vigorous pillar rose has attractive, large (11 cm), double flowers which open out to reveal a peachy pink centre and pure pink outer petals. The flowers are lightly scented and borne both freely and recurrently.

'Mrs Harold Alston' [Clark, 1940]. 'Sunny South' seedling. The fairly double, dark pink flowers of this pillar rose fade slightly as they age, when the petals also begin to show a darker flecking. It grows to about 2 m and repeats well.

'Mrs Hugh Dettman' [Clark, introduced National Rose Society of Victoria, 1930]. The pillar rose now grown under this name has exquisite fully double flowers which are very sweetly scented and a beautiful buff colour. The outer petals fade almost to white but the base of the petal is always much darker, especially towards the middle of the flower. The overall effect is reminiscent of 'Buff Beauty'. It flowers only once, but very prolifically.

'Mrs Norman Watson' [Clark, introduced by Geelong Horticultural Society, 1930]. 'Radiance' × 'Gwen Nash'. This is a very vigorous climber with large flowers (12–13 cm) borne on long upright stems. The petals are pale pink at the edges of the flower, but cherry pink at the centre. The plant grows to 3–4 m.

'Nora Cuningham' [Clark, introduced by Hackett, 1920]. 'Gustav Grünerwald' seedling. This handsome climber has large (10 cm), lightly scented, deep pink flowers with white centres and attractive red stamens. They are slightly more than single and borne singly or in small clusters on long stems. The plant comes into flower early, and repeats well; it grows with moderate vigour to about 4 m.

'Princeps' [Clark, 1942]. One of Clark's last introductions, this classic red climber is matched by a rich, traditional red-rose scent. The lightly double flowers are a good deep crimson, fading slightly, and paler on the underside of the petals. They are profusely carried on long stems early in the season, but do not repeat. The plant grows strongly to 5 m.

'Queen of Hearts' [Clark, introduced National Rose Society of Victoria, 1919]. 'Gustav Grünerwald' × 'Rosy Morn'. 'Queen of Hearts' has large (11 cm), semi-double, richly scented flowers which open deep pink and fade to pale pink. The petals open out and lie flat around the yellow stamens. The leaves are dark and glossy. The very prickly plant is said to be remontant and healthy, and it grows vigorously to about 3 m.

'Ringlet' [Clark, introduced by Brundrett, 1922]. 'Ernest Morel' × 'Betty Berkeley'. This putative hybrid between a Tea rose and a Hybrid Perpetual has produced a cluster-flowered climber which grows fairly vigorously to 4 m (plate 168). The scented flowers are single, medium sized (6 cm), and white with pink edges, rather like 'Frühlings-morgen' and other Scotch hybrids. The pink edging is marbled or flecked, not a con-tinuous strip of colouring. The plant has bright green leaves and few prickles, and it repeats well.

'Sunday Best' [Clark, introduced by National Rose Society of Victoria, 1924]. 'Frau Karl Druschki' seedling. This very hardy climber has light red flowers—a good colour—which fade to deep pink and are offset by white centres. They are slightly more than single and often have a petaloid stamen or two in the centre, which may spoil the overall effect. The flowers are borne in small clusters on a dense, rather angular plant with large prickles. It grows to 4 m and occasionally has a few later flowers. "The queen of the early bloomers," wrote Margaret Snyder from Pennsylvania in 1949.

'Sunny South' [Clark, 1918]. 'Gustav Grünerwald' × 'Betty Berkeley'. The habit of this vigorous bush or small climber is very upright, with growths that are slender and quite floriferous. Its long stems rise up in elegant masses. The buds are slim and shapely and open out very attractively to well-spaced, semi-double flowers, which are deep pink (fading to pale pink) at the tips and peachy pink at the base of the petals. It has a long flowering period and was once much used in Australia for hedging.

Hybrid Tea–Type Climbers

Many of the early repeat-flowering climbers were vigorous Hybrid Teas, and they include some of the best of all climbers. I particularly commend 'Allen Chandler', 'Colcestria', and 'Lorenzo Pahissa'.

'Allen Chandler' [Chandler, introduced by Alfred Prince, 1923]. 'Hugh Dickson' seedling. This Hybrid Tea–type climber is still the best red-flowered semi-double climber. The lightly scented flowers are brilliant crimson scarlet and large (12–14 cm), with wavy petals and sometimes a white base behind the handsome, broad boss of sta-mens. They are borne in small clusters (typically three flowers) on long stems, abundantly produced early in the season. The plant is seldom without flowers until winter; it has large, orange red hips and typical Hybrid Tea–type leaves. It grows vigorously to 5 m.

'Australian Beauty' [Kerslake, 1911]. Unfortunately this is just another scented, crim-son Hybrid Tea–type climber, somewhat undistinguished and prone to disease. A good name—pity about the rose.

'Böhms Climber' [Böhm, pre-1935]. This crimson Hybrid Tea–type has little to distinguish itself. The flowers are medium sized (6–7 cm), pale to medium crimson, and sweetly scented.

'Captain Thomas' [Thomas, introduced by Armstrong, 1938]. 'Bloomfield Completeness' × 'Attraction'. This pillar rose grows to 2.5–3.0 m high. The flowers open cream and fade to white with a yellow base to the petals. They are attractive at all stages, but keep their colour better in shade. The flowers are single, have handsome red filaments, and are borne in small clusters on long, strong stems. The leaves are many and glossy. The plant blooms continuously until late autumn.

'Červanky' [Böhm, c. 1935]. This Hybrid Tea–type climber grows at Sangerhausen, where it is said to have large, double, yellow flowers.

'Colcestria' [B. R. Cant, 1916]. One of the best of the once-flowering Hybrid Tea–type climbers, 'Colcestria' has large flowers (11–12 cm), very full of silvery pink petals which are a richer pink on their backs. The flowers are borne singly or in threes and hang down under their own weight. They have a strong damask scent and slightly reflexed petals. The plant grows to about 3 m.

'Comte de Torres' [Schwartz, 1906]. 'Kaiserin Auguste Viktoria' × 'Mme Bérard'. The old accounts of this Hybrid Tea–type climber describe a pale salmon pink flower which is large and double. The plant still grown at Sangerhausen is a short climber or pillar rose whose pale cream flowers open from red buds and come three to ten in a cluster. It is late flowering, with purple new growths and large prickles.

'Dr Renata Tyršová' [J. Böhm, 1937]. Like a very vigorous Hybrid Tea, this rose has large (10–11 cm), heavy, rather globular flowers borne singly or in clusters of up to three. They are silvery pink with lots of rather soft petals (best in hot, dry climates) and a damask scent. The plant grows to 3–4 m.

'Edda' [Lodi, 1929]. 'Reine Marie Henriette' × 'Boncenne' (a crimson Hybrid Perpetual). This Hybrid Tea–type climber produces large (9–10 cm), very double, pale pink flowers with a slightly darker centre. It still grows at Sangerhausen.

'Effective' [Hobbies, 1913]. 'General MacArthur' seedling × 'Paul's Carmine Pillar'. Another early Hybrid Tea–type climber in light, bright crimson, 'Effective' has long buds which open to large (10 cm), cupped, lightly double, and strongly scented flowers. The blooms are carried singly or in clusters intermittently throughout the season.

'Flash' [Hatton, introduced by Conrad-Pyle, 1938]. 'Rosella' × 'Margaret McGredy'. Quite a novelty when first introduced, the flowers of this striking pillar rose are bright crimson on one side and bright yellow on the underside. They are globular, lightly scented, medium to large (9–10 cm), and borne somewhat sparingly. The plant has deep glossy foliage and grows bushily to 2.5 m.

'Gartendirektor Julius Schütze' [Kiese, 1920]. 'Mme Jules Gravereaux' × 'Pharisäer'. This Hybrid Tea–type climber with large (9 cm), rich pink, strongly scented flowers now grows only at Sangerhausen.

'Gavá' [Munné, 1934]. 'Souvenir de Claudius Denoyel' × 'Souvenir de Claudius Pernet'. This dark pink climber still survives in England and Germany. The flowers are medium to large (7–8 cm), Hybrid Tea–shaped, sweetly scented, and fully double.

'Geschwind's Gorgeous' [Geschwind, 1916]. Introduced posthumously and still grown at Sangerhausen, this prickly climber bears medium-sized flowers (7 cm) in small clusters (one to three). They are bright pale crimson, paler underneath, and lightly double. The flowers open to show their stamens. This rose is neither gorgeous nor worthy to bear Geschwind's name.

'Glarona' [Krüger, introduced by Kiese, 1922]. This opulent beauty has large (9–10 cm) cabbagey flowers, borne one to three in a cluster, with muddled centres and a very strong sweet scent (plate 169). They are rose pink with paler outer petals (almost white) and so heavy that they nod their heads. The plant grows vigorously to 3 m and has noticeably broad leaves and rounded leaflets.

'Golden Crest' [Archer, 1948]. This Hybrid Tea–type pillar rose was popular in England in the 1950s. The flowers are medium sized (8–9 cm), double, lightly scented, and bright yellow with paler edges. The plant has handsome dark leaves and repeats well; it grows to about 2 m.

'Gold Rush' [Duehrsen, 1941]. This rambler has elegant, scented, medium-sized (6–8 cm) flowers in small clusters which open golden yellow but fade to lemon. The dark green, shiny leaves suggest *Rosa wichurana* ancestry. The plant grows vigorously to 3–4 m and occasionally repeats.

'High Noon' [Lammerts, 1946]. 'Sœur Thérèse' × 'Captain Thomas'. This very vigorous, slightly tender plant grows to 6 m and produces elegant, lightly double, Hybrid Tea–type buds. Buttercup yellow at first, then fading to lemon and cream, they open into rather shapeless, medium to large flowers (9–11 cm) with long petals and a good fruity scent. They are borne singly or in small clusters on a stiff, scraggy shrub which has few leaves and suffers from blackspot. Although seldom without flowers, 'High Noon' is not very floriferous.

'Irène Bonnet' [Nabonnand, 1920]. This attractive Hybrid Tea–type climber has elegant, sweet-scented, long-stemmed flowers which hang down on weak pedicels. They are pink with paler edges and open into a diaphanous mass of petals. The plant is vigorous, but best in hot, dry climates.

'La France de '89' [Moreau-Robert, 1889]. 'Reine Marie Henriette' × 'La France'. This bushy climber bears small clusters (one to six flowers) of large (8–9 cm), full, heavy flowers which hang down under their own weight like Hybrid Perpetuals. They are rich pale crimson or cherry red (silvery pink on the undersides) and have a very rich sweet scent. The plant grows to about 3 m and repeats well. Moreau-Robert said it was named to honour the centenary of "la grande et mémorable date de 1789."

'Les Rosati' [Gravereaux, 1906]. This vigorous Hybrid Tea–type climber has elegant dark pink buds and bright carmine flowers. I have seen it only at L'Haÿ-les-Roses, where it was bred.

'Ley's Perpetual' [Ley, 1936]. This vigorous rambler has large (10–12 cm), full, pale apricot yellow buds. Cupped at first, they then open out very attractively and fade to buff and cream. The plant grows fairly vigorously to 5 m.

'Lorenzo Pahissa' [Pahissa, 1941]. Seedling × 'Marí Dot'. At its best, no rose can match the ethereal loveliness of 'Lorenzo Pahissa'. The scented, creamy pink flowers are very large (13–15 cm) and elegant at every stage of growth, hanging down on long stems and lasting a long time (plate 170). The plant makes strong, upright, vigorous growth (2 m as a shrub and twice that as a climber) and repeats well.

'Louis Bruyère' [Buatois, 1941]. Still grown at L'Haÿ-les-Roses, this Hybrid Tea–type climber has medium to large (7–9 cm), double, deep cerise pink flowers which open flat. They are paler on the undersides of the petals and at the centre, but neither the flower nor the plant, which grows to about 4 m, is in any way exceptional.

'Mady' [Gemen & Bourg, 1925]. This beautiful Hybrid Tea–type climber should be reintroduced from Sangerhausen. The large (10 cm), creamy white, tea-scented flowers are a mass of ruffled petals like some of the modern English roses, but are borne singly and held upright on strong stems and pedicels (plate 171). The plant's habit is also upright; it grows moderately vigorously to about 2.5 m and is one of the last of its type to flower.

'Mercedes Gallart' [Munné, 1932]. 'Souvenir de Claudius Denoyel' × 'Souvenir de Claudius Pernet'. The very large, double, strongly scented flowers of this excellent Hybrid Tea–type climber are borne on long stiff stems. They come recurrently on a strong, vigorous, healthy plant with good shiny foliage. "No other climber gives the same result at its best," declared the American rosarian J. Horace McFarland (1947). The colour combination of bright purplish pink and pale cerise has always attracted comment, and critics say it is better in autumn.

'Nubian' [Bobbink & Atkins, 1937]. This Hybrid Tea–type climber has large (9–10 cm), dark crimson flowers borne singly or in small clusters and a good, rich scent. The plant is moderately vigorous, growing to 3 m, and is said to repeat. It is not as good as 'Guinée', which has more, better-shaped flowers.

'Professor Dr Hans Molisch' [Mühle, 1923]. This Hybrid Tea–type climber has medium to large, very full, silvery pink flowers in small clusters. The plant is very prickly and, I believe, grows only at Sangerhausen.

'Professor Erich Maurer' [Tepelmann, 1939]. The slender growths of this Hybrid Tea–type climber hang down under the weight of the flowers. The blooms are very large, as much as 15 cm across, semi-double, a bright dark pink (paler towards the centre), and lightly scented. The petals reflex fairly abruptly, so that a fully opened flower has rather a starry look, but the overall effect is attractive.

'Réveil Dijonnais' [Buatois, 1931]. This remarkable hybrid of *Rosa foetida* is said to be bred from 'Eugen Fürst' × 'Constance'. 'Réveil Dijonnais' makes a fine pillar rose and does especially well in hot, dry climates. The flowers are scented, semi-double (occasionally single), large (10–12 cm), and usually come in short-stemmed clusters of up to five (plate 172). They are a curious, bright orange crimson overlaid with bright yellow and with a golden yellow centre that fades slightly as the flower ages. There are often yellow streaks in the outer parts of the petals, which also have yellow backs. All in all, this rose has a very distinct coloration. The leaves are thick, glossy, bronze green, and subject to blackspot. The plant flowers early and fairly profusely, then more occasionally. It produces thick brown stems and bears short prickles.

'Souvenir de Claudius Denoyel' [Chambard, 1920]. 'Château de Clos Vougeot' × 'Commandeur Jules Gravereaux'. The large (12 cm), richly scented flowers of this Hybrid Tea–type climber are bright crimson with darker velvety marking on the petals; they keep their colour well and look more substantial than they really are. 'Souvenir de Claudius Denoyel' is said to be a sparse bloomer and not very vigorous, but I have seen it 4 m high on a wall and covered in its large, slightly pendulous flowers.

'Vîcomtesse Pierre du Fou' [Sauvageot, 1923]. 'L'Idéal' × 'Joseph Hill'. This cross between a Tea-Noisette and a Hybrid Tea produced an excellent climber of most unusual colour. The flowers are medium to large (8–9 cm), double, and strongly scented; they open a wonderful bright coral red, with yellow towards the base of the petals, and then fade to pink and cream. The bush is vigorous, stout, and rather bushy; it grows to 3–4 m and carries beautiful bronze red new leaves. The flowers come singly or in small clusters early in the season and recurrently thereafter. The plant is slightly susceptible to mildew, but this does not affect its vigour or floriferousness.

'Winsome' [Dobbie & Co., 1931]. The origins of this slender, vigorous climber are unknown. Its loosely double flowers are a bright pale crimson, medium sized (8 cm) and tea scented. They come in small clusters on long stems, abundantly at first and then more occasionally. The plant is hardy and grows to 3 m.

Modern Climbers

Several strains have emerged over the last fifty years, above all the Floribunda-type climber and a fashion for unusual colours—bright scarlets and oranges, red-and-yellow multi-colours, and striped roses in shades of red, pink, and white. Before we look at the work of individual breeders, families, and companies, I devote a section to other good modern roses. What follows is of necessity a miscellany.

'Anne Dakin' [Holmes, 1974]. A touch of *Rosa wichurana* shows in the glossy leaves and flexible stems of this Hybrid Tea–type climber. The medium-sized flowers (6–7 cm) are bright coral, fading slightly to medium pink, ruffled, and occasionally quartered. They come in small clusters (typically five to nine flowers) on a vigorous, healthy plant which grows to 3–4 m. 'Anne Dakin' is an underestimated rose.

'Apollo XI' [Leenders, 1970]. The reddish buds on this good Hybrid Tea–type climber open to large (11 cm), medium yellow flowers. They are profusely borne on a handsome, vigorous plant which grows to 3 m. As with many Leenders roses, it is not as well known as it deserves to be.

'Aunt Ruth' [Jerabek, 1995]. I have not seen this climber, which is said to have medium-sized, semi-double, pink-and-white flowers in clusters of varying sizes. It is the best known of several climbers raised by an elderly American amateur. Others include the velvety red 'Jules' [1997] and 'Paulspride' [1996], which opens yellow and fades to pink.

'Autumn Sunlight' [Gregory, 1965]. 'Danse du Feu' × 'Goldilocks (Climbing)'. This Floribunda-type of climber with well-scented, medium-sized (6–7 cm), double flowers is noted for its unusual and rather variable colour. The flowers are normally bright golden orange (fading to a dull lake pink), but sometimes vermilion or dark pink and always paler towards their centre. They come in small clusters on a vigorous plant that grows to 3 m and repeats reliably.

'Black Magic' [Hamilton, 1953]. 'Guinée' seedling. I have not seen this rose, but it still grows in Australia. It is said to produce strongly scented, deep crimson Hybrid Tea–type flowers in late spring and, very occasionally, later in the year.

'Brindis' [Dot, 1962]. 'Climbing Orange Triumph' × ('Phyllis Bide' × 'Baccará'). A dull Floribunda-type climber, 'Brindis' has small clusters of scentless, single flowers. They measure 5–6 cm across and are crimson with a white centre. The plant grows lankily and flowers sparsely.

'Conquistador' [Pineau, 1983]. This cultivar is a Floribunda-type of climber, with small clusters of distinctively scented, semi-double, medium-sized (7 cm), vermilion flowers. The prickly plant grows upright to 3–4 m, and the shiny leaves suggest 'Kordesii' ancestry.

'Copacabana' [Dorieux, 1966]. 'Coup de Foudre' seedling (perhaps with 'Kordesii' origins). This scentless Floribunda-type climber has handsome, medium-sized (8 cm), vermilion brown flowers in small clusters, although it may produce up to twenty flowers in a cluster when well grown. The plant has dark leaves, grows vigorously to 3–4 m, and repeats well.

'Corolle' [Dot, 1962]. 'Danse du Feu' × 'Cocktail'. 'Corolle' is a vigorous Floribunda-type climber with lightly scented, red, semi-double, medium-sized (6–7 cm) flowers and glossy Wichurana foliage. Fairly similar to 'Fugue', its 1960s cheerfulness is enhanced by bright sunlight.

'Crimson Cascade' syn. FRYclimbdown [Fryer, 1991]. This modern climber has lightly scented, rich, dark red, Hybrid Tea–style flowers, measuring about 10 cm across. It grows fairly vigorously to 3 m and repeats well. I find 'Crimson Cascade' an excellent cut flower, as the blooms last a long time in water.

'Denyse Ducas' [Buatois, 1953]. This yellow Hybrid Tea–type climber survives at L'Haÿ-les-Roses. It has elegant buds and large flowers (11 cm) which open out nicely. The plant grows gawkily to about 4 m.

'Don Juan' [Malandrone, 1957]. 'New Dawn' seedling × 'New Yorker'. For several years 'Don Juan' was the leading dark crimson–flowered climber, and it is still widely available. The Hybrid Tea–type flowers are medium to large (10–11 cm), double, and very sweetly scented. They are carried singly or in small clusters on a vigorous, prickly, upright bush which grows to 5 m. The tough, dark green foliage is a good foil. 'Pink Don Juan' [Nelson, 1996] was introduced as a pink sport of 'Don Juan', but its flowers are smaller and only semi-double.

'Dreaming Spires' [Mattock, 1973]. 'Arthur Bell' seedling × 'Allgold'. The flowers of this reliable and very attractive early-flowering yellow climber are strongly scented, medium sized (8 cm), lightly double, bright yellow at first, but fading quickly as they open out to reveal red filaments (plate 173). They are borne in small clusters and open from elegant buds. This rose repeats quite well and grows to about 3 m.

'Elizabeth Heather Grierson' syn. MATtnot [Mattock, 1986]. 'Bonfire Night' × 'Dreaming Spires'. This deliciously scented climber has pale pink flowers, with darker coral-pink buds and slightly darker petal-backs. They are lightly double and open out attractively. The flowers are borne in small clusters on a neat upright climber with rather brittle wood.

'Expreß' [VEG S-Baumschulen, 1984]. 'Queen Elizabeth' × 'Gruß an Heidelberg'. This modern climber has large (11 cm), lightly scented, double flowers which are light coral pink, fading slightly. They are usually borne singly, but there may be up to four in a cluster, and they have very long flower stems. The plant is very vigorous and grows to 3–4 m, but is somewhat lacking in personality.

'Flashfire' [Little, 1992]. 'Altissimo' × 'Playboy'. I have not seen this amateur-raised climber. It is said to have bright orange-red, single flowers in small clusters.

'Fourth of July' syn. WEKroalt, 'Crazy for You' [Carruth, 1999]. 'Roller Coaster' × 'Altissimo'. I consider this cheerful, floriferous rose the best of the recent striped climbers (plate 174). The flowers are medium sized (7 cm), semi-double, scented, and last well. Their colour is variable, but is basically crimson splashed with white or pink. They come is small clusters on a healthy, vigorous plant which grows to 3–4 m and repeats well.

'Freedom's Ring' [Dykstra, 1994]. 'Stars 'n Stripes' × 'Paradise'. Not the best of the modern striped climbers, the flowers of 'Freedom's Ring' are semi-double, small (3–4 cm), lightly scented, and basically red with pale pink stripes. The flowers have a passing resemblance to 'Ferdinand Pichard'. They are carried in small clusters on a prickly bush of unexceptional vigour which reaches 3 m.

'Gladiator' [Malandrone, 1955]. 'Charlotte Armstrong' × ('Pink Delight' × 'New Dawn'). Exhibition-quality, bright pink flowers are the attraction of 'Gladiator'. They are Hybrid Tea–shaped, lightly scented, and borne on long stems, usually singly. The bush grows vigorously to 4 m and produces some repeat flowering.

'Golden Future' syn. HORanymoll [Horner, 1997]. ('Anytime' × ['Liverpool Echo' × ('Flamenco' × *Rosa bella*)]) × ('Korresia' × 'Kiskadee'). This amateur-raised rose of complex pedigree has pleasantly scented flowers which are medium yellow (fading to lemon yellow), paler on the petal-backs, double, and medium to large (10–11 cm). It grows stiffly to about 3 m.

'Golden Showers' [Lammerts, 1956]. 'Charlotte Armstrong' × 'Captain Thomas'. Bred nearly fifty years ago, this rose is still one of the best yellow climbers. The lightly double flowers quite often open from a split bud. Flat, scented, and medium yellow (fading to lemon yellow), the blooms are carried singly or in clusters. The filaments are red. The flowers appear early in the season and repeat well. They have long slender stems, are good for cutting, and associate well with purples and crimsons, especially clematis. The bushy plant grows vigorously, reaching 3–4 m, with handsome, spoon-shaped, glossy leaflets (sometimes susceptible to blackspot). 'Golden Showers' does best in cool, wet climates (the flowers stand up well to rain) and is not completely hardy in central Europe.

'Goldfassade' [Baum, 1967]. This excellent rose bears small clusters (up to ten) of rich yellow flowers which are full, large (11 cm), and richly scented (plate 175). The flowers open out well and take on a red tinge as they fade. This rose has good, dark, glossy leaves and repeats well.

'Hassi Messaoud' [Hémeray-Aubert, 1961]. This rose is one of the better Floribunda-type climbers. It has full, dark scarlet, medium-sized (6–7 cm) flowers which open out well, although they tend to scorch in hot weather. They come in clusters (typically seven) on a vigorous plant which grows to 4–5 m and repeats well.

'Heinrich Blanc' syn. HELklewei [Hetzel, 1994]. At its best, 'Heinrich Blanc' is a very attractive pillar rose or short climber (plate 176). The scented flowers are palest pink, fading to white, medium sized (5–6 cm), cabbage shaped, and carried in small clusters. It grows to 2.5–3.0 m and repeats well.

'Honour Bright' [Eacott, 1950]. ('New Dawn' × 'Allen Chandler') × ('Climbing Mrs W. J. Grant' × 'Climbing Richmond'). The flowers of this Hybrid Tea–type climber are bright pale crimson, semi-double, 9–10 cm across, and pleasantly scented. They open out attractively and are borne singly or in small clusters (up to five) on a prickly, upright plant which grows to 3 m and repeats well.

'John Grooms' [Beales, 1993]. The flowers of this undistinguished pillar rose open salmon pink and fade to pink. They are medium sized and lightly double. The plant reaches 3 m.

'Joseph's Coat' [Armstrong, 1963]. 'Buccaneer' × 'Circus'. The best of the multi-coloured climbers, this cultivar has semi-double flowers which change slowly from yellow (with red edges) through orange to red and crimson. They are medium sized (7 cm), lightly scented, and borne in small clusters (typically seven flowers). The plant has good, dark, glossy foliage and grows to 2–3 m. The flowering is spectacular at first, thereafter intermittent.

'Leaping Salmon' syn. PEAmight [Pearce, 1983]. [('Vesper' × 'Aloha') × ('Paddy McGredy' × 'Maigold')] × 'Prima Ballerina'. This Hybrid Tea–type climber is popular in England. The shapely flowers are very large (12–13 cm), coral pink, and sweetly scented. They are well complemented by dark glossy green foliage but tend to ball in rain. The plant is moderately vigorous and grows to 3 m

'Liane' [Cocker, 1989]. Sold mainly in Germany, this salmon pink climbing rose has large (10–12 cm), Hybrid Tea–type buds and full, sweet-scented flowers. They open vermilion orange and fade to pinkish yellow. The flowers are borne singly and are well complemented by shiny, dark leaves. The plant grows to 3 m.

'Ludvik Večeřa' [Večeřa, 1981]. This very hardy rose looks like a seedling of 'Paul's Scarlet Climber' (plate 177). It has large clusters of almost scentless, medium-sized (8 cm), double, bright vermilion red flowers, which are rather short on charm.

'Meg' [Gosset, 1954]. 'Paul's Lemon Pillar' × 'Mme Butterfly'. This stiff, gawky, brittle climber enjoys an inexplicable popularity. Its flowers are large (12–13 cm), semi-single, and barely scented, with prominent dark stamens (plate 178). Their colour is peach at first (salmon or copper on the petal-backs), fading to pale pink and white. They open wide and come in small clusters. The plant grows with moderate vigour to 2.5–3.0 m and occasionally produces a small second flowering.

'Messire' [Laperrière, 1963]. 'Danse du Feu' seedling. This Floribunda-type climber looks fairly like its parent. The flowers are scarlet red, medium sized (8 cm), and borne singly or in small clusters. The fairly vigorous but unexceptional plant grows to 3 m and flowers recurrently.

'Mona Lisa' [Malandrone, 1956]. 'Mrs Sam McGredy' × ('Mrs Sam McGredy' × [seedling × 'Captain Thomas']). Behind this intriguing name lie large flowers (10–11 cm) of the Hybrid Tea type. They are full of petals but open out flat, salmon pink fading to rose pink, and strongly scented. The plant grows vigorously to 4 m and repeats well.

'Mountain Snow' [Austin, 1985]. Not one of David Austin's best creations, this sweet-scented, white rambler holds its petals, dies badly, and blotches to crimson in the rain. That said, its sprays of small (3–4 cm), semi-double flowers and dark green leaves have their admirers. The plant grows to about 4 m.

'Nachsommer' [Wänninger, 1990]. This amateur-raised, moderately vigorous pillar rose has clusters of strongly scented, fully double, coral pink flowers (fading rather unattractively) like an early Floribunda. The glossy leaves suggest *Rosa wichurana* ancestry.

'Nouvelle Europe' [Gaujard, 1964]. 'Miss France' × 'Vendôme'. The small clusters of this Floribunda-type climber carry lightly scented, medium-sized flowers (7–8 cm) which are orange vermilion at first, but fade to lake pink and creamy pink at the edges. They are fully double and have a Hybrid Tea shape. The plant grows fairly vigorously to 3–4 m.

'Opaline' [Clause, 1982]. 'Opaline' is a very attractive Hybrid Tea–type climber, with sweetly scented, elegant, apricot pink flowers. The blooms are slightly paler (almost transparent) at the edges and do not have too many petals. The large, dark, healthy leaves are bonus. The plant grows to 4 m.

'Orange Velvet' [Williams, 1986]. 'Climbing Super Star' × 'Swarthmore'. This cultivar has fine Hybrid Tea–type flowers which are vermilion red with crimson patches, fading to lake pink (paler on the petal-backs). They are large (12 cm), upright, and lightly but sweetly scented. The plant grows stiffly to 4 m.

'Orfeo' [Leenders, 1963]. 'Curly Pink' × 'Guinée'. Now seldom seen, 'Orfeo' has bright crimson Hybrid Tea–type flowers which fade slightly to deep cerise. They are large (11–12 cm) and full, with reflexing petals and a very sweet scent. The flowers have weak stems, so that they tend to hang down—always an asset in a climber. The plant grows to about 4 m.

'Pelé' [Benardella, 1979]. This handsome Hybrid Tea–type climber has huge flowers (15 cm) which are pale pink, fading to mother-of-pearl at the edges. They have very long stems, long petals, and a medium scent. The plant has upright growth and lush crimson foliage. It repeats reliably, but is a fair-weather rose susceptible to rain damage.

'Pimbonson' [Muraour, 1953]. This unexciting cerise pink, semi-double climber grows only at L'Haÿ-les-Roses.

'Pink Ocean' [Verschuren, 1980]. 'Pink Showers' × 'Alexander'. This pillar rose has sweetly scented, Hybrid Tea–type flowers which are salmon pink at first, fading to pale pink. The plant grows stiffly to about 2.5 m.

'Pink Showers' [Verschuren, 1974]. 'Carla' × 'Golden Showers'. This Hybrid Tea–type climber has small clusters of medium-sized (7–9 cm), coral pink flowers. The bush is very prickly and has very vigorous, lanky, upright growth.

'Red Flare' [Mansuino, 1954]. 'Reine Marie Henriette' × 'Paul's Scarlet Climber'. Despite its old ancestry, this rose has a modern look to it (plate 179). The flowers are a bright rich crimson, fading only slightly, lightly and sweetly scented, medium sized (6–9 cm), and double. They come singly or in small clusters on a vigorous plant which grows to 3–4 m. This is a good rose, with some repeat flowering, spoilt only by its susceptibility to rain damage.

'Red Fountain' [Williams, 1975]. 'Don Juan' × 'Blaze'. This interesting hybrid has clusters of dark red, almost crimson, flowers which are medium sized (6–7 cm), fully double, repeat flowering, and fairly well scented. The plant has large, dark green leaves and grows vigorously to 3–4 m.

'Renae' [Moore, 1954]. 'Étoile Luisante' × 'Sierra Snowstorm'. 'Renae' is a pleasing Floribunda-type climber with small, rather tight clusters of pink flowers which fade to white. They are medium sized (6 cm), semi-double, open, and strongly scented. The lax, thornless plant grows vigorously to about 4 m and repeats so well that it seems to be constantly in bloom.

'Roberta Bondar' [Fleming, 1993]. 'King's Ransom' × 'Buff Beauty'. Bred by an amateur from the Niagara Peninsula in Canada, this hardy modern climber bears small clusters of medium yellow, scented, medium-sized (6–7 cm), double flowers on a shrubby, vigorous bush.

'Rosendorf Schmitzhausen' [Cocker, 1977]. This handsome, dark red climber seems to be grown only in Germany. The flowers are Hybrid Tea shaped, fully double, and lightly scented. The plant grows strongly to 3–4 m; repeats well; and has dark, healthy leaves.

'Rosenfest' [GPG Roter Oktober, 1981]. 'Dortmund' seedling × seedling. One of the better roses to be bred in East Germany, 'Rosenfest' bears pale crimson or cherry red flowers (rather more vermilion in some seasons) in small clusters (plate 180). They are fairly scented, medium sized (8–9 cm), semi-double, and open out to display quite a broad circle of stamens. The plant has large, glossy leaves with rounded leaflets. It grows to 3 m, but also makes a good bush.

'Schloß Dryberg' [GPG Roter Oktober, 1981]. 'Lydia' × 'Le Rêve'. This Floribunda-type climber is rather ordinary. It produces small, tight clusters of medium to large flowers (10 cm) which are bright yellow at first and fade a little (plate 181). They have a slightly foetid scent of parsley. The plant has many large prickles and the small, disease-prone leaves of *Rosa foetida*. It grows to about 3 m, and every so often it produces a few, many-petalled flowers of sumptuous colour and size.

'Sif' [Lundstad, 1969]. 'Trämland' × 'Royal Gold'. This Floribunda-type climber has orange salmon flowers which fade to pink. They are medium sized (9 cm), full, rounded, and scentless. The plant grows fairly vigorously to 4 m and repeats well.

'Snow Goose' syn. AUSpom [Austin, 1996]. This shrubby climber has exceptionally long sprays of small (3–4 cm), white flowers with many narrow petals, opening from pink-tipped buds. The flowers have a strong musky scent. The plant makes a very attractive overall effect; it grows to about 2.5 m and has neat, dark leaves.

'Soldier Boy' [Le Grice, 1953]. Seedling × 'Guinée'. 'Guinée' was widely used to breed red climbers, but few matched its sumptuous dark crimson. 'Soldier Boy' has medium to large (10 cm), single, scarlet flowers with little scent. At first, the blooms are freely produced in small clusters, and then intermittently. The plant is fairly healthy and grows to 2.5–3.0 m.

'Soleil Levant' [Mondial Roses, 1956]. 'Danse du Feu' seedling. This scentless, scarlet- or orange-flowered, single, Floribunda-type climber has little to recommend it, apart from for the simple cheerfulness of its flowers.

'Teide' [Dot, 1948]. 'Texas Centennial' × 'Guinée'. Now surviving only in such gardens as Sangerhausen, this Hybrid Tea–type climber has full, medium-sized (8–9 cm), bright crimson flowers.

'Water Music' [Bell, 1982]. 'Handel' seedling. Like is parent, the distinctive feature of this Australian Floribunda-type climber is the dark pink edge to the pale pink flowers. The flowers are medium sized (7–8 cm), double, and lightly scented.

'White Pillar' [Hay, 1958]. Another Australian rose, this has clusters of large, double, bright, silvery white flowers and handsome light green leaves. The hardy, healthy plant grows strongly to 4 m.

CHARLES MALLERIN

Mallerin was a French engineer who bred roses as a hobby and enjoyed considerable success, especially after he took early retirement. Hybrid Teas were his main interest. Mallerin is best remembered for 'Beauté', 'Charles Mallerin', and 'Mrs Pierre S. du Pont'. His climbers also include two of the great classics: 'Danse du Feu' and 'Guinée'. But his later crimson climbers, 'L'Africaine' and 'Sénégal', both of which he considered an improvement on 'Guinée', deserve to be more widely grown.

'Cascade' [Mallerin, 1951]. 'Holstein' × 'American Pillar'. This rose resembles an early Floribunda-type of climber, rather reminiscent of 'Evelyn Fison'. The flowers are medium sized (5–6 cm), nearly single, and bright crimson with white patches in their centres. The clusters are large, rather full, and freely borne on an upright, vigorous plant which reaches 4 m.

'Danse des Sylphes' [Mallerin, 1957]. 'Danse du Feu' × 'Toujours'. This scentless, Floribunda-type climber has small to medium-sized flowers (5–6 cm) in small clusters—typically three to five in a bunch, later often single. They are fully double and have a rounded outline. The outer petals are reddish crimson but the inner petals open vermilion and their tips fade unattractively in hot weather. The first flowering is spectacular and is followed by lesser flushes all through summer and autumn. The plant grows vigorously to 3–4 m.

'Danse du Feu' syn. 'Spectacular' [Mallerin, 1953]. 'Paul's Scarlet Climber' seedling. The colour of this Floribunda-type climber was a novel one among climbers—bright vermilion. The flowers also have occasional streaks of white and crimson, most noticeably on the inmost petals, which are the most exposed when the flower opens out flat. The flowers are medium sized (6–7 cm), little more than semi-double, faintly scented, and borne singly or in small clusters, in great profusion at first, and then intermittently throughout the summer. The leaves are large, shiny, and dark green (rather more bronzed when young). The plant grows to 3–4 m and does well in light shade. 'Danse du Feu' has produced several colour sports over the years, including the bright red 'Amazone' [Delforge, 1961] and the cherry pink 'Anne Jackson' [Jackson, 1973].

'Feu d'Artifice' [Mallerin, 1935]. *Rosa foetida* hybrid × 'Colette Clément'. This cultivar is a Hybrid Tea–style climber. The nearly single, bright vermilion red flowers are large (9–10 cm) and lightly scented. The plant grows fairly vigorously to 3 m and has deep green, glossy foliage, but is neither floriferous nor remontant. Too often confused with 'Feuerwerk' [Tantau, 1962], the real 'Feu d'Artifice' is still grown at Sangerhausen. 'Réveil Dijonnais' [Buatois, 1931] is similar to 'Feu d'Artifice' but better.

'Guinée' [Mallerin, 1938]. 'Souvenir de Claudius Denoyel' × 'Ami Quinard'. This is the best known of Mallerin's dark red climbers and very popular worldwide, although it is not hardy in New England or central Europe. The flowers are very deep, rich crimson with dusky highlights like the finest velvet. They have an intensely sweet scent, are medium sized (8–9 cm) and fairly double, but open out flat, at which point the yellow stamens show off the wavy petals perfectly. The plant is vigorous and fairly prickly, with nondescript foliage which is somewhat sensitive to mildew. The flowers come in clusters of one to three, early in the season and abundantly, but only occasionally later. Their colour is lost against brick or stone, but is stunning against a white wall.

'Impératrice Rouge' syn. 'Red Empress' [Mallerin, 1956]. ('Holstein' × 'Décor') selfed. Very much in the Hybrid Tea mould, this rose has long, stiff, upright stems, each carrying a single, perfectly shaped, pale crimson flower. They are large (10–11 cm), double, and scented. The bush is vigorous, upright, and gently repeat flowering; it grows to 4–5 m.

'L'Africaine' [Mallerin, 1952]. 'Guinée' × 'Crimson Glory'. 'L'Africaine' was the last of Mallerin's crimson Hybrid Tea–type climbers. The flowers are large (10–11 cm), elegant, very dark red, and usually borne singly. This cultivar flowers early in the season and abundantly, but does not repeat. The flowers come on long stems, hang their heads, and have rather a light scent for such a deep crimson rose.

'Love' [Berthe Mallerin, 1935]. 'Hadley' × 'Ami Quinard'. This Hybrid Tea–type semi-climber was bred by Mallerin's wife. It has medium to large (10–11 cm), semi-double, crimson flowers with a good sweet scent, but is otherwise not very distinguished. The plant is of moderate vigour and grows slenderly to about 2.0–2.5 m; it flowers early but is not reliably remontant.

'Rubis' [Mallerin, 1948]. 'Mme G. Forest-Colcombet' seedling. Not the darkest of Mallerin's line in red climbers, 'Rubis' is nevertheless one of the most strongly scented. The flowers are large (9–10 cm), double, and bright red with some crimson markings. The plant is a vigorous grower but flowers only once.

'Sénégal' [Mallerin, 1944]. 'Guinée' seedling. 'Sénégal' is very deep crimson—the darkest red climber I have ever seen and a definite improvement on 'Guinée'. The Hybrid Tea–style flowers are only small to medium sized (6–7 cm) and not produced in great abundance. Moreover, they tend to brown in the sun. Nevertheless, they have good rich scent, and the plant grows vigorously to about 5 m.

MARCEL ROBICHON

In the 1950s and 1960s Marcel Robichon of Pithiviers, France, raised some fine climbers. All are still widely grown and sold in France but seldom abroad. The best are very good indeed. Robichon was particularly interested in breeding the perfect large-flowered red climber.

'Aurore Sand' [Robichon, 1963]. 'Mme Moisans' × 'Odette Joyeux'. The peachy pink colouring of this Hybrid Tea–type climber is unusually charming. The flowers are large (11 cm), double, sweetly scented, and open out attractively. The plant grows vigorously to about 4 m.

'Belle d'Orléans' [Robichon, 1958]. Seedling × 'Kordes' Sondermeldung'. This reddish crimson Floribunda-type of climber resembles Robichon's 'Étendard' (see chapter

10). The large (10–11 cm), scentless flowers have a Hybrid Tea shape and are borne in very large clusters (up to twenty). The glossy foliage is fairly disease-free. The plant flowers recurrently and grows vigorously to 4–5 m.

'Guirlande Fleurie' syn. 'Flower Garland' [Robichon, 1968]. 'Valenciennes' × 'Paul's Scarlet Climber'. This cultivar's parentage explains everything—a brilliant red rose borne in large clusters of lightly double flowers which open out well. The blooms are Hybrid Tea shaped, medium sized (7 cm), and barely scented, but last well as cut flowers. The leafy plant grows vigorously to 5 m and is reliably remontant.

'Intervilles' [Robichon, 1962]. 'Étendard' seedling. The influence of *Rosa wichurana* is quite apparent in the dark, glossy leaves of this brilliant red climber (plate 183). The flowers have a Hybrid Tea shape before opening out fully and are profusely carried in small clusters. They are medium sized (7–8 cm), lightly double, gently scented, and tough-petalled. The healthy plant grows vigorously to about 4 m.

'Odette Joyeux' [Robichon, 1958]. 'Lady Sylvia' seedling. Size is everything with 'Odette Joyeux'. The flowers are great pink cabbages, as much as 16 cm across, and usually borne singly (plate 182). They have a good damask scent and are slightly darker pink on the petal-backs. The plant is remontant, but otherwise unexceptional, and grows vigorously to 4 m.

'Orientale' [Robichon, 1946]. 'George Dickson' × 'Mrs Pierre S. du Pont'. This is a Hybrid Tea–type climber. The flowers are bright pink, large (12 cm), richly scented, and late flowering. They are carried singly on long, strong stems and sometimes have a quartered pattern of petals. The plant may suffer from mildew and has rather gawky growth, but the flowers (which repeat) are glorious.

'Trophée' [Robichon, 1969]. 'Valenciennes' × 'Étendard'. I have seen this rose only at Saverne, which means it must be very hardy. 'Trophée' is a vigorous, remontant climber with clusters of bright red, medium to large (10 cm), lightly double, scentless flowers. The plant is vigorous and grows to about 4 m.

'Valenciennes' [Robichon, 1957]. 'Paul's Scarlet Climber' seedling. 'Valenciennes' is more crimson, less red, than many of Robichon's climbers, and fades to cherry red. The flowers are medium sized (8 cm), scentless, semi-double, and borne in small clusters held upright on long stems. The plant is vigorous, repeats well, and grows to 5 m, but it can get a little leggy.

'Voie Lactée' [Robichon, 1949]. 'Frau Karl Druschki' × 'Julien Potin'. The influence of 'Frau Karl Druschki' is clearly detectable in this handsome, short climber. The flowers are creamy white, large (10–11 cm), double, and, surprisingly, very sweetly scented. However, they do tend to ball in wet weather. The plant grows vigorously to about 3 m and repeats intermittently.

THE HOUSE OF MEILLAND

The Meillands have been by far the most successful rose breeders in France since 1945, the year in which Francis Meilland introduced 'Peace' ('Mme A. Meilland'). Since then, they have introduced hundreds of superb roses, bred and selected in response to demand.

The family has never specialised in climbing roses, but issues them from time to time when competition makes it essential to bolster their market share. By the 1990s, the fashion for tall shrub roses with old-fashioned shapes and scents saw a series of beautiful Meilland introductions under the broad categories of Grimpants or Romanticas. Many are too bushy to be considered true climbers, and so I have had to exclude such wonderful shrubs as 'Gîtes de France' [1994], 'Domaine de Courson' [1995], 'Colette' [1996], 'César' [1996], 'Michka' [1998], and 'Mon Jardin et Ma Maison' [1998]. But others, for instance, 'Sorbet' and 'Kir Royal', keep alive the Meillands' reputation for producing climbers of exceptional beauty.

'Arielle Dombasle' syn. MEIhourag [Meilland, 1992]. Not one of Meilland's better climbers, 'Arielle Dombasle' has small clusters of salmon yellow, medium-sized (7 cm), semi-double flowers. The petal-backs are pure yellow. The plant grows to about 3 m and, in my experience, is susceptible to blackspot.

'Benvenuto' [Meilland, 1967]. ('Alain' × 'Guinée') × 'Cocktail'. 'Benvenuto' bears lightly scented, semi-double, medium-sized (7–8 cm) flowers in small clusters. They are very dark red, with just a hint of yellow at the base of the petals, but the edges of the petals turn very dark as they age, almost black. The petal-backs are yellow. Sometimes the flowers burn in the sun. The first prolific flowering is followed by intermittent flowerings. The plant grows thickly and lushly, like an overgrown Floribunda, to 3 m. The wood is covered with many short prickles.

'Cassandre' syn. MEIdeuji [Meilland, 1989]. It is difficult to explain the charm of this pale crimson Floribunda-type climber which grows with moderate vigour to about 3 m (plate 184). The flowers come in small clusters and are medium sized (6–7 cm). They have little scent. Yet, they also have a beautiful circular outline and attractively ruffled petals. And they are not too stiff-stemmed, holding themselves sideways and outwards for appreciation.

'Clair Matin' syn. MEImont [Meilland, c. 1964]. 'Fashion' × (['Kordes' Sondermeldung' × 'Orange Triumph'] × 'Phyllis Bide'). Despite its complicated ancestry, the attraction of 'Clair Matin' lies in its simplicity. The flowers are semi-double, round, medium sized (6–7 cm), and salmon pink, fading to pale pink. They open from coral buds, and the petal-backs remain darker than the open flower. The flowers come in small clusters (typically of three to seven) and are sweetly scented. The plant grows to 2 m as a shrub (4 m as a climber) and seems to be constantly in flower. It responds well to good cultivation.

'Cocktail' [Meilland, 1957]. ('Kordes' Sondermeldung' × 'Orange Triumph') × 'Phyllis Bide'. 'Cocktail' is a variable rose: stunning at first, but plain dull later. The flowers are single, scented, small (5 cm), and carried in large clusters (up to twenty of them). They are at their best when they open, with a bright yellow base and orange red petals. However, the flowers soon fade to crimson and white, and the petals hold on unattractively for some time after the stamens have died. 'Cocktail' is a rose for hot climates—in fair weather the flowers are extremely handsome as they open, whereas they tend to blotch in rain. The flowers last well when cut. The plant is bushy, but flowers profusely and recurrently, and it reaches 4 m.

'Exploit' syn. MEllider, 'All In One' [Meilland, 1984]. 'Fugue' × 'Iskra'. This scentless, scarlet Floribunda-type rose bears medium-sized (7 cm), lightly double flowers in small, upright clusters and grows vigorously to 3–4 m. The leaves are glossy, with rather round leaflets.

'Fandango' syn. MEljade [Meilland, 1989]. This attractive rose might be called a 'Clair Matin' with more petals. The buds open first into full flowers (9 cm across) and then manage to open out flat, while retaining their charm at all stages. The colour is pink with a hint of shrimp, "rose azalée," say the French authorities. The plant grows fairly quickly to 3 m.

'Fugue' [Meilland, 1958]. 'Alain' × 'Guinée'. This was one of Mme Meilland's earlier climbers, and it is still worth growing today. The lightly scented flowers are medium sized (8–9 cm) and pure crimson red (plate 185). They are fully double, but open out to reveal their stamens and become rather cup shaped. Later the blooms tend to turn black at their petal-tips. They come in small clusters on a healthy plant which grows vigorously to about 3 m and is very floriferous.

'Iskra' syn. MEIhati, 'Sparkling Scarlet' [Meilland, 1968]. 'Danse des Sylphes' × 'Zambra'. Rather a 1960s rose, 'Iskra' has clusters of medium-sized (6–7 cm), semi-single, scentless flowers of bright vermilion, like a Climbing Floribunda. The colour is slightly paler on the petal-backs. The plant grows luxuriantly to about 3 m and flowers intermittently after the first abundant flush.

'Kir Royal' syn. MEInibur [Meilland, 1995]. This shrubby climber has exceptionally attractive flowers which open dark pink with a mass of ruffled petals, then turn to pale pink at the edges and acquire a charming sprinkling of crimson spots and markings. The flowers are medium sized (6–7 cm) and only lightly scented, but freely borne. The plant grows fairly vigorously to 3 m and is very healthy.

'Looping' syn. MEIrovonex [Meilland, 1977]. (['Zambra' × 'Danse des Sylphes'] × 'Cocktail') × 'Royal Gold'. 'Looping' is a fine rose which deserves to be more widely grown. The flowers are medium to large (8–9 cm) and quite strongly scented (plate 186). Although double, they open out well to show their red filaments. The colour is unusual: orange or peachy at first, turning more pink at the edges as it opens out. The plant grows well to 3–4 m and flowers remontantly, but has a tendency to blackspot.

'Paprika' syn. 'Gavroche', MEIriental [Meilland, 1992]. 'Centenaire de Lourdes' × 'Picasso'. This Floribunda-style climber is something of a throwback to the 1960s. It has medium-sized (7–8 cm), single, scentless flowers in small clusters. Their colour is vermilion with paler undersides to the petals. The plant has dark glossy leaves and grows to 3 m.

'Pierre de Ronsard' syn. MEIviolin, 'Eden Rose 88' [Meilland, 1988]. ('Danse des Sylphes' × 'Handel') × 'Climbing Pink Wonder'. This has become a very popular, shrubby climber for hot, dry climates, where its heavy, overpetalled flowers can open slowly. The flowers are large (10–12 cm) and hang down under their own weight. Their shape is variable: sometimes flat and muddled and sometimes cupped and imbricated. The colour also varies: typically, creamy white with distinct crimson edges to the petals, but sometimes just pink all over. The flowers are sweetly scented. The foliage is bright green and the bush has thick, sturdy, short-jointed stems. It grows to about 2.5 m; the tallest example I have seen reached 4 m in the centre of Melbourne.

'Polka 91' syn. MEItosier, 'Scented Dawn', 'Lord Byron' [Meilland, 1991]. 'Golden Showers' × 'Lichtkönigin Lucia'. Another shrubby climber, 'Polka 91' struggles to reach 2.5–3.0 m in height. The scented flowers are exquisite: deep apricot, fading to palest buff at the edges. This shows off their most distinctive feature—the wavy edges of the petals which build up like layers of paper. The plant flowers heavily and repeatedly.

'Royal Show' [Meilland, 1983]. 'Kordesii' must be in the ancestry of this handsome rose; it produces a mass of completely scentless, red, Floribunda-type flowers. They are a deep bright vermilion, with just a hint of crimson in the bud, medium sized (7–8 cm), and fully double (with somewhat short petals) and come in large clusters of eight to twenty. The leaves are dark green, with rich beetroot new growths. The plant exudes vigorous growth to 5 m. The combination of dark flowers and dark leaves means that it looks best against a white wall.

'Sorbet' syn. MEIpeluj [Meilland, 1992]. 'Sorbet' has a most curious colour: basically lemon, it fades to pink as it ages, thus giving it a unique two-tone effect. Aside from that, the flowers are fairly ordinary: medium to large (9–10 cm), like a dumpy Hybrid Tea in shape, and lightly scented. They come singly or in clusters of up to six on a vigorous, healthy plant which grows to 3 m.

MAURICE COMBE

Although a prolific rose breeder, Maurice Combe from Grenoble, France, was not a professional, and most of his roses were introduced by Minier or Vilmorin. Their form and colours reflect the fashions of the 1950s and 1960s, when they were bred. This was the era of cheerful, bright Floribundas and Hybrid Teas, when fifty or more plants of the same rose were planted in a single bed. Flowering in red, scarlet, vermilion, crimson, and orange, Combe's "grimpants" were their climbing equivalents. They survive in such gardens as L'Haÿ-les-Roses, Bagatelle, and Cavriglia, but their commercial popularity is waning fast. All flower repeatedly and grow to 3–4 m.

'Alpin' [Combe, 1960]. 'Danse du Feu' × 'Toujours'. This orange red climber has Hybrid Tea–type flowers borne singly or in small clusters early in the season. They are medium sized (6–7 cm), lightly scented, and double. The outer petals often have a brown cast which is most unusual and very attractive; the petals later recurve and give the flower a broad, rolled appearance.

'Balcon' [Combe, 1960]. 'Danse du Feu' seedling. 'Balcon' is a Floribunda-style rose, with medium-sized (6–7 cm), semi-double, scentless, scarlet flowers.

'Barricade' [Combe, 1968]. 'Barricade' has medium to large (8–9 cm), scentless, lightly double flowers in small clusters, like a Floribunda. They are vermilion or orange. The petals tend to blacken at the edges and recurve.

'Brandon' [Combe, 1959]. This dark red climber has large (8–9 cm), double, classic Hybrid Tea–type flowers borne singly on long, upright stems. The plant, too, has the neat, sturdy, erect growth of the Hybrid Teas.

'Cordon Rouge' [Combe, 1970]. Not one of Combe's better roses, this has clusters of medium-sized (6–7 cm), fully double flowers which are brilliant vermilion but seldom open out completely, despite having rather short petals.

'Cortège' [Combe, 1976]. 'Cortège' bears very attractive, medium-sized (6–7 cm) flowers, singly or in small clusters, on slender stems. Their colour is quite variable—basically a pale orange, but often red in the bud (and on the outer petals), and occasionally fading to soft apricot cream.

'Danse du Printemps' [Combe, 1954]. This very vigorous climber has medium to large (7–8 cm) and long-stemmed clusters of double or semi-double flowers in pale crimson. Although this rose is impressive in full flower, it repeats only sparingly.

'Frénésie' [Combe, 1965]. 'Frénésie' is another of Combe's Floribunda-type climbers with lightly scented flowers that open deep vermilion brown (paler on the petal-backs) and fade to orange.

'Iséran' [Combe, 1965]. 'Iséran' has the short petals of the Floribundas in a Hybrid Tea–type shape and looks best when the flowers open out. They are medium to large (8–9 cm), full, and lightly scented, usually orange or pale scarlet but sometimes more crimson in cooler weather.

'Le Chamois' [Combe, 1954]. This early Floribunda-type climber has medium-sized, semi-double, crimson flowers in small upright clusters. It has slightly larger flowers (but fewer of them) than 'Danse du Printemps', of which it appears to be a sister-seedling.

'Portail Rouge' [Combe, 1973]. I have seen this crimson Hybrid Tea–type climber only at Cavriglia, where it has large (9 cm), scented flowers and distinctive beet purple new leaves and stems.

PAUL CROIX

Paul Croix has produced a steady trickle of introductions from Bourg Argental in the Department of Loire. His hybrids are often rather unusual, and all are very different from each other. The best—'Croix Blanche', 'Declic', and 'Sourire d'Orchidée'—are very good indeed.

'Astral' [Croix, 1983]. I have seen this sumptuous, large-flowered, Hybrid Tea type of climber only at Cavriglia. The flowers are very deep crimson.

'Croix Blanche' [Croix, 1984]. This beautiful short climber has very large (12–13 cm), pure white, Hybrid Tea–type flowers of great elegance. Opening from creamy white buds, the flowers usually come singly, occasionally in small clusters. The blooms tend to crumple and lose their petals quickly in wet weather, so this is a rose for warm, dry climates. The plant has vigorous, lush growth; large, dark green leaves; and rather prickly stems. It makes very upright growth to about 3 m.

'Croix d'Or' [Croix, 1985]. I have seen this rose only at Bagatelle, where it bears large (11–12 cm), cabbage-shaped globes of rich golden yellow—a beautiful colour.

'Declic' [Croix, 1988]. This beautiful and highly floriferous climber should be much better known. It carries large clusters of very strongly scented, medium-sized (6–7 cm), lilac pink flowers very early in the season (plate 187). It has glossy green leaves and grows to 5–6 m. A plant in full flower is a wonderful sight.

'Minouchette' [Croix, 1970]. Not one of Croix's better hybrids, 'Minouchette' has clusters of medium-sized (5–6 cm), pale pink flowers like a Floribunda. It is a vigorous grower and repeats well.

'Murmure' [Croix, 1970]. 'Luna Park' × 'Moulin Rouge'. 'Murmure' bears medium-sized (6–7 cm), bright red or scarlet flowers in small clusters. It grows as a stiff and upright plant.

'Sourire d'Orchidée' [Croix, 1985]. This shrubby climber has very spacious clusters of medium-sized (6–7 cm), semi-double flowers. The unopened buds are pink. The flowers open pale pink and fade to white, although the overall effect is of mother-of-pearl and the petals are slightly darker underneath. The flowers have handsome stamens of uneven length and a sweet musky scent. The clusters have typically five to ten flowers, but can carry up to thirty. The large-leaved plant is bushy, vigorous, and fairly healthy. 'Sourire d'Orchidée' is a rose of sweet simplicity.

GEORGES DELBARD

The personality and achievements of Georges Delbard dominated French horticulture in the latter half of the twentieth century. From the remote village of Malicorne in Allier, he built up one of the largest horticultural industries in Europe, with three hundred employees and garden centres throughout France. Delbard, who died in 1999, is perhaps best known as a breeder of fruit—pears, cherries, soft fruit, and, above all, apples. His 'Tentation' and 'Estivale' apples achieved international success within a few years of being released. As a rose breeder, Delbard kept ahead of his French competitors by studying trends in other countries and introducing his own lines to match or forestall them. His early climbers, produced by his hybridisers Joseph and André Chabert, show the influence of 'Kordesii' in their hard colours and dark, glossy foliage. In the 1970s he switched to softer tones and, by the late 1990s, when the hybridising was in the hands of his son Guy, Delbard introduced roses with more complex shapes and masses of petals in the old-fashioned style.

'Altissimo' syn. DELmur, 'Altus' [Delbard-Chabert, 1966]. 'Ténor' seedling. Variously described as "blood red" and "lacquer red," 'Altissimo' is one of the most popular of modern climbers. The flowers are single, large (10–12 cm), uniformly and unfadingly red, with no white centre and no difference between the upper and undersides of the petals (plate 188). This increases the impression of size and sumptuousness they give. The flowers come in small clusters (occasionally singly) and are very slightly scented. They are borne intermittently on a vigorous, healthy plant which has large, dark leaves and grows to 3 m. The largest flowers are borne in cool weather. Heirloom Roses of St. Paul, Oregon, introduced a "smoky Mandarin orange" sport of 'Altissimo' called 'Dorothy' in 1997.

'Blanche Colombe' syn. DELgribla [Delbard, 1995]. 'Blanche Colombe' carries white, medium-sized (8–9 cm) flowers of supreme shapeliness all through the summer and autumn. There is a hint of lemon in the bud, which is high-centred like a classic Hybrid

Tea, but it eventually opens out fully with strongly reflexed petals. The flowers are almost invariably borne singly on stems up to 75 cm long—very elegant and useful for cutting. 'Blanche Colombe' is one of the best white modern climbers of moderate height (3 m) and is less prickly than 'White Cockade'.

'Campanile' syn. DELtrut, 'Campanela' [Delbard-Chabert, 1967]. ('Queen Elizabeth' × 'Provence') × ('Sultane' seedling × 'Mme Joseph Perraud'). This beautiful climber has large (10–11 cm), scented, dark pink, globular flowers of the old Hybrid Tea type, but very full of petals and sometimes borne in small clusters, as well as singly. The lush plant has large leaves and grows vigorously to 3 m. It is very hardy but flourishes in hot climates, too. 'Campanile' is always very free-flowering and repeats well.

'Dune' syn. DELgrim [Delbard, 1993]. This good yellow climber has never been a great commercial success. The flowers are attractive, medium to large (8–9 cm), lightly double, and strongly scented. They pale slightly as they age. The plant grows vigorously to 4 m and repeats well.

'Grimpant Delbard' syn. DELpar, 'Delbard's Orange Climber' [Delbard-Chabert, 1963]. 'Danse du Feu' × ('Gloria di Roma' × 'La Vaudoise'). 'Grimpant Delbard' bears pleasant, medium-sized (7–8 cm), cupped, lightly double, orange red flowers in small clusters. They last well, but tend to fade a little, and have a light scent. The leaves are dark green and healthy. The plant repeats well and grows vigorously to 3–4 m, but this is not the most distinctive or stylish of Delbard's roses.

'Messire Delbard' syn. DELsire, 'Grandessa' [Delbard, 1975]. ('Danse du Feu' × 'Guinée') × (['Ténor' × 'Fugue'] × ['Delbard's Orange Climber' × 'Gloire de Dijon']). Despite its complex ancestry, 'Messire Delbard' is a fairly ordinary rose, with medium-sized (7–8 cm), lightly scented, dark red flowers in small clusters on long, stiff, upright stems. The leaves are large and healthy, and the plant grows vigorously to 3–4 m.

'Nahéma' syn. DELéri [Delbard, 1999]. This climber has scented, pink flowers in the old-fashioned style—cupped and full of petals. The plant is said to be healthy, free-flowering and bushy, eventually reaching 3 m.

'Neige Rose' [Delbard-Chabert, 1955]. 'Neige Rose' has large flowers (11 cm). The blooms are very attractive with their ruffled petals, pure dark pink at the centre and on the petal-backs, and paler towards the edges. They are lightly scented and borne in small clusters on a vigorous plant which grows to 3–4 m.

'Obélisque' syn. DELmot [Delbard-Chabert, 1967]. 'Danse du Feu' × ('Orange Triumph' × 'Floradora'). 'Obélisque' is a shrubby climber with long, upright clusters of pale geranium-lake flowers which are paler towards the centre. They are semi-double, lightly scented, and abundantly borne through to autumn. The plant is hardy, with handsome, dark, glossy leaves. It grows to about 3 m.

'Paname' [Delbard-Chabert, 1959]. 'Danse du Feu' seedling. The flowers of 'Paname' are medium to large (10 cm), double, sweetly scented, and a deep rich pink (although the undersides of the petals are buff apricot). They have a Hybrid Tea shape at first, then open out flat and broad like a Floribunda. The flowers are borne singly on long, strong stems right through to autumn. 'Paname' is a shrubby plant which grows to about 3 m.

'Papi Delbard' syn. DELaby [Delbard, 1995]. 'Papi Delbard', the breeder's masterpiece, was named for Georges Delbard himself. It has very large (12–13 cm), old-fashioned flowers which are so full of petals that they hang down slightly (a good thing—it means you can look into them). They are borne singly or in small clusters on long stems. The flowers are apricot coloured with a darker base to the petals and a creamy underside. This glorious combination of colours is matched by a rich fruity scent. The plant is healthy and grows vigorously to 3–4 m.

'Parure d'Or' syn. DELmir [Delbard, 1968]. ('Queen Elizabeth' × 'Provence') × ('Sultane' × 'Mme Joseph Perraud'). This short, upright climber produces small clusters of lightly double, medium-sized (7–9 cm), scented flowers on long, stiff stems. They are a rich golden yellow with broad crimson piping and rather ragged edges to the petals which serve to emphasise the colour contrast. The colouring, vigour, health, and attractiveness of the flowers at all stages are reminiscent of 'Peace'. The plant grows to 2.5–3.0 m and repeats well.

'Phare' syn. DELgo [Delbard-Chabert, 1961]. 'Danse du Feu' × 'Flora' seedling. This bright vermilion red Floribunda-type has medium-sized (8 cm), double flowers in small clusters at the end of long, straight stems. They fade to light crimson and repeat through to autumn. The plant grows to 3 m.

'Phenomène' [Delbard, 1989]. I have seen this rose only at Cavriglia, where it produces clusters of attractive, medium-sized (6–7 cm), apple-scented, semi-double flowers which open cream and fade quickly to white.

'Puerta del Sol' syn. DELglap [Delbard, 1970]. ('Queen Elizabeth' × 'Provence') × ('Michèle Meilland' × 'Bayardère'). This rose bears small, loose clusters of lightly scented, medium-sized (7–8 cm), double flowers which are peachy yellow and nod down attractively. The plant grows to 3–4 m.

'Rose Céleste' syn. DELroceles [Delbard, 1979]. ('Queen Elizabeth' × 'Provence') × ('Sultane' × 'Mme Joseph Perraud'). 'Rose Céleste' has small clusters of lightly scented, long-lasting, semi-double, light pink flowers (slightly darker in the centre) which open out to reveal their yellow stamens. The healthy and remontant plant grows to about 3 m.

'Salammbô' syn. DELperl [Delbard, 1994]. 'Grimpant Delbard' × 'Perle Noire'. Named after Flaubert's Carthaginian princess, 'Salammbô' has medium-sized (7–8 cm), lightly scented flowers borne in small, long-stemmed clusters. The blooms are bright crimson red and keep their colour well. The plant is fairly healthy and grows to about 3 m.

'Sensass Delbard' syn. 'Sensass', DELmoun [Delbard-Chabert, 1973]. ('Danse du Feu' × ['Orange Triumph' × 'Floradora']) × 'Ténor' seedling. This rose has scentless, bright scarlet red, medium-sized (6–7 cm) flowers in small clusters. It makes a scrawny climber, growing to 3 m high.

'Tarzan' [Delbard-Chabert, 1955]. 'Tarzan' is surprisingly delicate; the flowers are pearly pink (slightly darker on the undersides), semi-double, medium-sized (6–7 cm), scented, and freely borne (plate 189). They open out attractively and are complemented by dark, glossy leaves. The plant grows to 4 m and repeats well.

'Ténor' syn. 'Tenor', DELcap [Delbard, 1963]. This is yet another of Delbard's medium-sized (7–8 cm), semi-double Floribunda-type climbers in red—a bright and velvety red, but scentless and humdrum nevertheless.

'Tropique' syn. DELjis [Delbard-Chabert, 1956]. 'Tropique' has medium-sized (6–7 cm), fairly double flowers borne singly or in small clusters on long stems. They are velvety crimson red and repeat well. The small, glossy leaves suggest some relationship to 'Kordesii'.

'Zénith' syn. DELzen [Delbard, 1980]. ('Danse du Feu' × 'Ténor' seedling) × ('Flora-dora' × 'Incendie'). This rose is a good, short Floribunda-type climber, with clusters of lightly scented, semi-double vermilion flowers which fade only slowly (plate 190). It grows stoutly to 2.5 m.

ANDRÉ EVE

André Eve's best and most inventive crosses have been with *Rosa filipes* (see chapter 2), but he has issued a few other climbing roses from his nursery at Pithiviers, France. 'Albert Poyet' is the best.

'Albert Poyet' [Eve, 1978]. This excellent Hybrid Tea–type modern climber has fairly large (10 cm), fully double flowers of a most unusual colour. They open cherry pink, but creamy in the middle; the outer petals then turn to crimson and the inner ones to pale pink. The flowers have only a light scent but are borne repeatedly in small clusters. The plant is vigorous, bushy, and leafy, growing to 5 m tall.

'Mme Solvay' [Eve, 1992]. 'Mme Solvay' has large clusters (up to twenty flowers) of medium-sized (7 cm), loosely held, semi-double flowers. The crimson petals have flashes of white towards the base and are very recurved, which gives the sweetly scented flowers a spiky look. The plant grows slenderly to about 5 m.

'Red Parfum' [Eve, 1969]. This Floribunda-type climber has medium-sized (7 cm), hard-red flowers and glossy leaves which suggest 'Kordesii' antecedents. They are rather too sparse, but the plant grows vigorously to 4 m.

'Shirpa' [Eve, 1975]. 'Shirpa' is a lightly double Hybrid Tea–type climber. The medium to large flowers (11–12 cm) are dark coral pink, shading to yellow at the base of the petals, and open out to show their stamens (plate 191). The plant has large leaves and broad leaflets and grows stiffly to about 4 m.

JACKSON & PERKINS

Jackson & Perkins, now part of the Bear Creek group, has been one of the world's leading rose breeders for more than a hundred years. 'Dorothy Perkins' was named after the first president's daughter. Jean Henri Nicolas, Dennison Morey, and Bill Warriner were each in charge of breeding and were responsible for some of the finest twentieth-century bush roses, as well as the following climbers.

'America' syn. JACclam [Warriner, 1976]. 'Duftwolke' × 'Tradition'. This popular modern climber has strongly scented, medium to large (10 cm), double, Hybrid Tea–shaped flowers borne in small clusters. They are salmon pink, with paler undersides, and fade with age. Although 'America' flowers repeatedly, there are long periods between flowerings. It makes a neat, sturdy, upright plant of only moderate vigour, no more than 3 m. 'Pearly Gates' syn. WEKmeyer [Meyer, 1999] is a soft pink sport, and 'Royal America' [Cooper, 1994] a white one, both identical in every other way to 'America'.

'Butterscotch' syn. JACtan [Warriner, 1986]. ('Buccaneer' × 'Zorina') × 'Royal Sunset'. Now seldom seen, 'Butterscotch' has small clusters of all-but-scentless, bronze orange, medium-sized flowers (9 cm) which are rather loosely petalled.

'Dream Weaver' syn. JACpicl [Zary, 1996]. This Floribunda-type climber has attractive pink flowers with darker coral shades at the base of the ruffled petals. They are medium sized (8–9 cm), well scented, and borne in clusters. The plant grows to 2.5–3.0 m and repeats well. This rose is a good modern addition to the ranks of short climbers.

'Dr J. H. Nicolas' [Nicolas, 1940]. 'Charles P. Kilham' × 'Georg Arends'. This pillar rose has fat, nodding buds which open out into large (10 cm), very double, pink, cabbagey flowers with somewhat short, incurved petals. The flowers have a strong, rich damask scent and come in clusters of three or four. The plant is hardy and healthy, with very prickly stems and large round leaves. It grows slowly to 2.5 m and repeats throughout the summer and autumn but is not very vigorous; in some ways it resembles a Hybrid Perpetual more than a climber. This cultivar's name commemorates a charming Franco-American rosarian and hybridiser who was one of the great characters of rose growing in the 1930s.

'Dynamite' syn. JACsat, 'High Flyer' [Warriner, 1992]. Seedling × 'Sympathie'. 'Dynamite' is a 'Kordesii' derivative, with small clusters of fully double, Turkey red flowers which measure 12 cm across and have little scent. The foliage is dark and glossy in the 'Kordesii' manner, and the plant grows stiffly to 2.5–3.0 m.

'Golden Cascade' [Morey, 1962]. ('Captain Thomas' seedling × 'Joanna Hill') × 'Lydia'. Seldom seen now, this was a good medium yellow, Hybrid Tea–type climber in its day, with large (11–12 cm), lightly scented, double flowers in small clusters. The plant has typical Hybrid Tea foliage, repeats well, and grows vigorously to 4 m.

'June Morn' [Nicolas, 1938]. 'Mme Grégoire Staechelin' × 'Souvenir de Claudius Pernet'. The medium to large (8–9 cm), strongly scented flowers of this Hybrid Tea–type climber open pale crimson with yellow undersides. The flowers are very striking at first, but less so later when the colours fade to medium pink and white; the inner petals never open fully, which means that there is always a contrast between them and the reflexed outer petals. The flowers are borne in tight clusters of up to five and drop their petals neatly. The plant has large glossy leaves (with a tendency to blackspot) and makes a good pillar rose, growing to 3 m high. The first heavy and long-lasting flowering is followed by occasional later blooms.

'King Midas' [Nicolas, 1941]. Launched as a Wichurana Rambler, this rose is more of a Hybrid Tea climber. The lemon yellow, medium-sized (9–10 cm), and strongly tea-scented flowers are loosely double and have golden stamens. Very popular when first launched, 'King Midas' is an easy and vigorous grower that flowers early, repeats intermittently, and reaches 4–5 m.

'Lace Cascade' syn. JACarch [Warriner, 1992]. 'Iceberg' × 'Prairie Fire'. 'Lace Cascade' is an interesting rose, with the very hardy *Rosa arkansana* as one grandparent. The flowers are white, double, medium sized (7–8 cm), and lightly scented. The buds are elegant, but the petals eventually reflex into a starry ball. The flowers are borne singly or in small clusters on a bushy plant which grows to 2 m and has glossy, dark green leaves.

'Royal Gold' [Morey, 1957]. 'Climbing Goldilocks' × 'Lydia'. This popular modern climber has fully double, deep yellow flowers of the Hybrid Tea type with conspicuous yellow stamens. They are large (10–11 cm), scented, and borne singly or in small clusters. The plant repeats, but only after a long interval, and grows moderately vigorously to about 3 m. 'Royal Gold' gives its best in a warm climate.

'Royal Lavender' [Morey, 1961]. 'Lavender Queen' × 'Amy Vanderbilt'. This vigorous climber has never had the popularity it deserves. Its medium-sized flower (8 cm) is cupped at first, then open out to a nice rosette, almost like a waterlily, to show its stamens. The flowers are lavender pink, deeper on the underside of the petals, paler inside, and sweetly scented. They come in small, tight clusters on a fast-growing plant which grows to 4 m and repeats intermittently.

'Royal Sunset' [Morey, 1960]. This cultivar is a California speciality—at the Berkeley Rose Gardens a vast semi-circular pergola is planted entirely with 'Royal Sunset'. Its buds are burnt orange. The flowers are semi-double and deep apricot, slightly darker on the outside of the large petals, and with a strong, sweet scent (plate 192). This rose is an immensely vigorous climber, capable of 10 m, with very thick stems and large, deep green foliage. Hearty, outsized, exuberant, but attractive, too, 'Royal Sunset' should be better known in Europe and Australia.

'Tempo' [Warriner, 1975]. 'Ena Harkness (Climbing)' × unnamed Kordesii Hybrid. As with his much later 'Dynamite', the influence of 'Kordesii' is clearly seen in the bright Turkey red flowers and the hard, dark, glossy leaves. 'Tempo' has small clusters of medium-sized (9–10 cm) Hybrid Tea–type flowers which are fully double, short-petalled, and very lightly scented. The flowers last a long time and keep their colour well. The plant grows slowly to about 2.5–3.0 m, repeats well, and is very hardy.

W. KORDES & SOHNE

The story of the Kordes family, Germany's leading rose breeders for nearly a century and raisers of the 'Kordesii' rose, is told in chapter 11. From the 1920s onwards, however, both Wilhelm Kordes and his son Reimer bred many other roses—shrubs, Hybrid Teas, Floribundas, and climbers. Such early climbers as 'Louis Rödiger' and 'Werner Dirks' were by-products of Wilhelm's experiments with *Rosa rubiginosa*, but many of their recent introductions are large-flowered, repeat-flowering modern climbers, often with a trace of 'Kordesii' in them. They are among the world's best today.

'Antike '89' syn. 'Antique', KORdalen [Kordes, 1988]. ('Grand Hotel' × 'Sympathie') × (unnamed seedling × 'Arthur Bell'). 'Antike '89' is a Climbing Floribunda type resembling an improved 'Handel'. The flowers are pale pink or white, with a bright red edging—very striking when the flower is half open. The flowers are large (13 cm), fully double, and elegant in the bud. The plant grows slowly to 2.5–3.0 m and repeats well.

'Burg Baden' [Kordes, 1955]. Still occasionally seen, 'Burg Baden' has medium-sized (5–6 cm), single flowers which are pale crimson or dark pink and slightly paler at the base of the petals. They come in large clusters on a shrubby climber that reaches about 2.5 m.

'Copper Arch' syn. KORhurtlen [Kordes, 1991]. I have not seen this modern climber, but it is said to have large, pink flowers and to be very hardy.

'Evergold' [Kordes, 1956]. This climber bears deep yellow, medium-sized flowers and has glossy, dark leaves. It is in still grown in Japan.

'Goldener Olymp' syn. 'Olympic Gold', KORschnuppe [Kordes, 1984]. Seedling × 'Goldstern'. This popular, short (2.5 m), and very hardy climber has sumptuous, richly scented, large (11–13 cm) flowers full of wavy petals. They open a rich peach and fade to butterscotch and pale yellow, especially at the petal edges, which adds to their allure. Sometimes they come in small clusters, sometimes singly. The leaves are attractive and dark green. The plant is fairly vigorous, upright, and bushy, and it repeats a little. 'Goldener Olymp' is good in rain.

'Gruß an Heidelberg' syn. 'Heidelberg' [Kordes, 1959]. 'Minna Kordes' × 'Floradora'. Once popular, this large-flowered (8–9 cm) climber with fiery carmine petals (paler underneath) now shows a susceptibility to blackspot and rust. The lightly scented flowers have muddled centres but open from elegant, pointed buds. They keep their colour well and are freely produced, singly and in clusters, right through until late autumn (plate 193). The leaves are dark and glossy, and the plant grows vigorously to 3 m. Wilhelm Kordes (1960) thought it "better grown as a free bush."

'Harlekin' syn. KORlupo, 'Kiss of Desire' [Kordes, 1986]. The scented, pure white flowers are brightly tinged with crimson edges to the petals. They are large (9–10 cm), double, elegant, borne in small clusters, and set off by handsome dark green foliage (plate 194). The shrubby plant grows to 3–4 m and repeats quickly. 'Harlekin' is the best of the bicolors, with darker edges, larger flowers, and more petals than 'Handel', as well as being more floriferous.

'Louis Rödiger' [Kordes, 1935]. 'Daisy Hill' × ('Charles P. Kilham' × 'Mevrouw G. A. van Rossem'). This beautiful and unusual rose has apricot orange, semi-double flowers, with very attractive, short incurved petals and a strong, distinctive fruity scent. The plant grows vigorously to about 5 m and has lots of large prickles and dark leaves. Like many roses with *Rosa foetida* in the background, this cultivar is very hardy and flowers notably early. Louis Rödiger (1855–1927) was a rose nurseryman at Langensalza-Ufhoven. His firm was founded in 1881, and three members of the family were Bürgermeister of Ufhoven. They did much to earn the town's status as a "Rosendorf."

'Lucinde' syn. KORtaly [Kordes, 1988]. 'Lucinde' is a fine, vigorous, shrubby climber. The blooms open very bright yellow and pale slightly. The flowers are 8–11 cm across, double, and Hybrid Tea shape. They come singly or in small clusters and have a good fruity scent. The plant grows to 2 m as a bush, twice that as a climber.

'Maigold' [Kordes, 1953]. 'Poulsen's Pink' × 'Frühlingstag'. 'Maigold' was a by-product of William Kordes's experiments with the native German *Rosa spinosissima* to produce hardy shrubs. The flowers are medium to large (9 cm), loosely double, with crimson filaments and a strong fruity scent. They open deep apricot, with coppery hints and dark golden yellow undersides to the petals, but fade eventually to pale yellow. The flowers are borne singly or in clusters of up to seven, on an extremely prickly plant with thick brown stems and bright pale leaves. 'Maigold' reaches 3–4 m as a climber up a wall and flowers very early in cool climates—hence its name. There are always a few later flowers.

'Manita' syn. KORberuhig [Kordes, 1996]. This Floribunda-type climber has small clusters of moderately scented, medium to large flowers (9 cm) which are lightly double, wavy petalled, and medium pink fading to silvery pink. The plant reaches 2.5 m as a bush, but 4 m as a climber. It is very winter hardy and repeats well, but is perhaps not the most exciting of modern pink roses. The dark green leaves are handsome.

'Morgensonne '88' syn. KORhoro [Kordes, 1988]. 'Morgensonne '88' is one of those climbers which opens rich yellow but fades quickly to cream. The flowers are medium to large (8–10 cm), double, and nicely scented; they open from red-tinted buds (plate 195). The plant is quite floriferous and remontant, very vigorous, and grows strongly to about 3 m. Its leaves are dark and shiny but it is not the best of modern yellow cultivars.

'Ramira' syn. 'Agatha Christie', KORmeita [Kordes, 1988]. 'Ramira' is a short-growing climber (3 m) or vigorous bush, with Hybrid Tea–type flowers which are large (9–10 cm), pink, elegantly shaped, and lightly scented. They are borne singly or in small clusters and repeat well. The plants has shiny, dark, 'Kordesii' leaves. Kordes described it as a pink 'Sympathie', which is apt.

'Rosanna' syn. KORinter [Kordes, 1982]. This cultivar is a pink pillar rose. 'Rosanna' has large (10–11 cm), full, Hybrid Tea–type flowers with a hint of coral at first and a strong scent. The very hardy plant grows fairly vigorously to about 2.5–3.0 m and repeats well.

'Salita' syn. KORmorlet [Kordes, 1987]. 'Salita' has a most striking colour—flaming orange scarlet, not unlike 'Super Star'. The flowers are medium to large (8–9 cm), elegant, double, Hybrid Tea shaped, and borne singly or in small, loose clusters. They are beautifully set off by dark shiny green leaves which are richly crimson when young—as are the new growths. The plant is a moderate grower to about 3 m, and it flowers continuously.

'Summer Wine' syn. KORizont [Kordes, 1985]. This is an unusual rose. The flowers are single but, once seen, charm everyone with their elegant petals and prominent red stamens. They open from neat, conical, pointed, bright coral buds into nicely scented flowers of pale coral pink which fade to rose pink; the petal undersides are darker at first but also fade to pale pink. The plant grows slenderly to about 3.5 m, with rather coarse foliage and large prickles. It can also be grown as a bush. 'Summer Wine' repeats fairly well throughout the summer and autumn.

'Tradition '95' syn. KORkeltin [Kordes, 1995]. From its very glossy dark leaves and bushy habit with lots of regrowth, this bright red climber looks like a 'Kordesii' descendant. The flowers are medium sized (7–8 cm), semi-double, and lightly scented and retain their colour quite well, paling only slightly. The come in small clusters like a Floribunda, with leaf bracts at the base of the pedicels. The plant is rather prickly, but grows vigorously to 2.0–2.5 m and is very hardy.

'Werner Dirks' [Kordes, 1937]. 'Mrs Pierre S. du Pont' × 'Daisy Hill'. This Macrantha hybrid has clusters of medium to large (10 cm), double, creamy white, sweetly scented flowers in midseason. The very vigorous and prickly plant grows to 5 m. This rose grows still at Sangerhausen.

Almost all these Kordes climbers may be grown as shrubs. Others which are too short and shrubby to be treated here, even as pillar roses, are 'Angela' [1984], 'Flammenspiel' [1974], 'Lichtkönigin Lucia' [1966], and the scarlet crimson Rugosa Hybrid 'Kordes' Robusta' [1979].

MATTHIAS TANTAU, FATHER AND SON

The Tantaus are second among German rose breeders only to their friends and neighbours the Kordes. Matthias Tantau Senior was an innovative breeder between the wars, and his 'Direktor Benschop' is still deservedly popular. His son, also Matthias, bred some of the greatest and most strongly scented bush roses of the 1950s and 1960s, including 'Prima Ballerina', 'Super Star', and 'Duftwolke'. Climbers were not his particular interest, so his introductions were irregular and very different from one another. All are good, but 'Lawinia' is perhaps the best.

'Direktor Benschop' syn. 'City of York' [Tantau, 1945]. 'Dorothy Perkins' × 'Professor Gnau', a Hybrid Tea. This once-flowering, Floribunda-type of rambler has buff yellow buds which open into small (5 cm), scented, semi-double, creamy white flowers with prominent stamens at the centre (plate 196). The plant grows vigorously to 5 m and has beautiful, dark, glossy foliage. The flowers are too small and cupped to be attractive, however; this prolific flowerer is best seen as a mass, from a distance, not close-up.

'Dukat' [Tantau, 1955]. 'Mrs Pierre S. du Pont' × 'Golden Glow'. One of Tantau's best climbers, 'Dukat' has large (11 cm), full, sweetly scented, Hybrid Tea–type flowers which open out from red-tipped buds into a mass of reflexed petals. The overall effect is yellow, but the flowers are pale lemon at the tips and golden yellow at the centre. The plant is vigorous but otherwise unremarkable, growing rather stiffly to 4–5 m.

'Goldstern' [Tantau, 1966]. This cultivar is a Hybrid Tea–type climber with large (12 cm), double, strongly scented, rain-resistant flowers which keep their deep yellow colouring very well as they open and only fade very slightly just before their petals curl back and fall. The red stamens intensify the rich colour. The plant grows bushily to 3 m and repeats well.

'Herman Löns' [Tantau, 1931]. 'Ulrich Brunner fils' × 'Red Letter Day'. This rose was one of the earliest Floribunda-type climbers. The flowers are medium sized (8 cm), single, crimson, scentless, and not very exciting. 'Herman Löns' grows to about 4 m and is still available in Germany.

'Lawinia' syn. TANklewi [Tantau, 1980]. 'Lawinia' has large, pendulous clusters of medium to large (9–10 cm) pink flowers of an intense, bright hue, slightly translucent at the edges and darker at the centre of each flower (plate 197). They are profusely borne and richly scented, opening from shapely buds into long-petalled hemispheres. The plant has dark green leaves, repeats well, and grows bushily to 2.5–3.0 m.

'Santana' [Tantau, 1984]. Tantau seldom publishes pedigrees, but 'Kordesii' must be among the forebears of 'Santana'. The flowers are dark vermilion red, double, medium to large (10 cm), with little or no scent, and borne in small clusters. The plant is fairly vigorous and very healthy, with dark, glossy leaves. It grows to 2–3 m and has a reputation for hardiness and rain tolerance.

'Schneewalzer 87' [Tantau, 1987]. Most commentators describe 'Schneewalzer 87' as "pure white"; in fact, it is palest lemon, with a mother-of-pearl centre. The flowers are very large (13–15 cm), shaped like Hybrid Teas, lightly scented, and borne singly or in small clusters. They are well complemented by dark, healthy 'Kordesii' foliage. The plant is a sparse flowerer after the fine first display, and the blooms spoil in wet weather.

'Solo' [Tantau, 1956]. A Floribunda-type climber, 'Solo' has small, loose clusters of medium-sized (8 cm), fiery crimson flowers. They are set off by healthy, dark green leaves (red at first). The plant is free-flowering and hardy, repeats well, and grows rampantly to 5 m.

Noack

Noack is a young firm in Gütersloh, Germany, which has issued a stream of prize-winning roses since the 1980s. They cover every type of rose, with a speciality in landscaping roses. Many, however, have not attained the popularity and currency which they deserve. Indeed, some have far too limited a distribution. Two Noack climbers (both shrubby) which I have not seen are 'Ravensberg' [1986], with bright, dark red flowers, and 'Deutsches Rosarium Dortmund' [1995], with pink ones. Noack's climbers are a mixed lot, and 'Goldregen' and 'Momo' are among the best of all modern introductions.

'Goldregen' [Noack, 1985]. 'Goldregen' is a tall (5 m) and lanky grower with large flowers (10–13 cm) of Hybrid Tea shape. They are held very upright, but open out nicely, being only lightly double. Their deep yellow fades to pale lemon and they have a fairly strong scent—rather fruity. This rose is reliably remontant.

'Lybelle' [Noack, 1984]. This short-growing Floribunda-type climber bears medium to large flowers (9 cm) in clusters of five to ten. They are heavy, which make them hang down and increases their opulence. The lightly scented flowers open a good, clear pink, but tend to fade with age and develop red blotches in wet weather.

'Momo' [Noack, 1995]. This superb crimson rambler seems at first like a throwback from the 1900s, but close examination immediately reveals its superiority. 'Momo' carries huge clusters (thirty to sixty flowers) in great profusion and is constantly pumping up new flowering branches, so that it is never out of flower. The flowers are small (3.5 cm), very bright cherry crimson, very double, and often quartered. They also have reddish pedicels and new stems. All are set off by very dark, handsome, glossy, narrow, small, Wichurana leaves.

Jack Harkness

R. Harkness & Company of Hitchin, England, were famous for their roses—above all for 'Ena Harkness', which they introduced but did not breed—for many years before Jack Harkness started raising new cultivars in the 1960s. Jack Harkness was an inspired creator who included the development of new climbers among his declared objectives. In the event, he introduced only a handful, and only one, 'Compassion', has been a runaway success. Even that is surprising, however, because 'Compassion' suffers from serious weaknesses.

'Breath of Life' syn. HARquanne [Harkness, 1980]. 'Red Dandy' × 'Alexander'. The large (10–11 cm), full, circular flowers of 'Breath of Life' open out apricot and are strongly and sweetly scented. The half-open bud can look exquisite, when the colour is pale coral and the central petals are neatly spiralled. The flowers are borne one to three in a cluster on a short, prickly, vigorous plant which repeats well and grows to 3 m. 'Breath of Life' spots badly in rain but is nevertheless popular in England.

'City Girl' syn. HARzorba [Harkness, 1993]. 'Armada' × 'Compassion'. This rose was commissioned by St Paul's Girls' School in London to commemorate the school's centenary. It has rather wide silky petals, which are pale salmon (fading to pink), but the flower is nearly single, and it has proved a commercial disappointment.

'Compassion' syn. 'Belle de Londres' [Harkness, 1972]. 'White Cockade' × 'Prima Ballerina'. 'Compassion' has a wonderful, strong, sweet scent and beautiful, large (12 cm), rounded, salmon pink flowers when they first open. However, they fade to an unattractive buff white and hold onto their petals for too long. The blooms also spoil in rain. They are borne singly or in small clusters on a vigorous plant which is very free-flowering and recurrent. It reaches 3.0–3.5 m but the stiff habit and thick, fat growths are unattractive and difficult to train. 'Highfield' [Harkness, 1980] is a pale yellow sport of 'Compassion'. The flowers are smaller and only semi-double, but it has the same sweet scent as its parent. The petals of 'Highfield' reflex unattractively—an inferior rose.

'Della Balfour' syn. HARblend, 'Desert Glo', 'Renown's Desert Glo', 'Royal Pageant' [Harkness, 1994]. 'Rosemary Harkness' × 'Elena'. The colouring of this somewhat coarse climber is surprisingly old-fashioned: its deep yellow flowers with pink edges are reminiscent of 'Peace'. They are sweet scented and large (10–11 cm) and have an attractive wave to their petals. The plant is stout, stiff, and fairly vigorous, with large thick leaves. It reaches no more than 3 m.

'High Hopes' syn. HARyup [Harkness, 1994]. 'Compassion' × 'Congratulations'. 'High Hopes' has elegant, medium-sized (6–7 cm), semi-double, well-scented flowers borne singly or in small clusters at the end of long stems. Pink at first, they open out flat, fade to palest peach, and blotch in the rain. The plant is stiff, very upright, and not excessively floriferous; it grows to 3 m.

'Penny Lane' syn. HARdwell [Harkness, 1998]. This is the first of a new generation of Harkness climbers with smaller flowers and an old-fashioned shape. The flowers are apricot buff and strongly scented but not very free-flowering.

'Perpetually Yours' syn. HARfable [Harkness, 1999]. This rose is an improvement on 'Penny Lane', with cream-coloured flowers which turn to white, but it is still not conspicuously floriferous.

Mention should be made of 'Mary Mine' [Harkness, 1973], bred from 'Queen Elizabeth' × 'Buccaneer'. This cultivar is classified in the United States as a Grandiflora but grown as a climber in parts of England. It has pleasant, strongly scented flowers which open apricot and pale to pink at the edges, with darker undersides to the petals. Another Harkness rose is HARpippin, with large, peachy yellow flowers. The rose has never been introduced (it suffers from blackspot), but Betty Hussey has two plants against the walls of Scotney Castle in Sussex. Peter Harkness tells me that they would call it 'Betty Hussey' if Harkness ever introduced it.

Sam McGredy IV

Sam McGredy was the last of his family to breed roses and the most successful. His skill was to see opportunities that others missed. The stream of beautiful, short-growing, ever-blooming climbers that he introduced from Northern Ireland in the 1960s and 1970s were intended to counter the hard colours of the all-powerful Kordesii Climbers. 'Dublin Bay' and 'Handel' are still among the most popular and widely grown of all roses, whereas, for sheer quality, 'Casino' and 'Santa Catalina' run them close. Indeed, McGredy's climbing roses are all uniformly excellent.

'Casino' syn. 'Gerbe d'Or' [McGredy, 1963]. 'Coral Dawn' × 'Buccaneer'. 'Casino' produces large flowers (10–11 cm), best seen when they open fully and the mass of small, loose, dark yellow inner petals contrasts with the larger, paler outside ones. The flowers tend to come singly, like specimen Hybrid Tea roses, at their first flowering, and then in clusters like Floribundas later in the year. They have a fairly strong, rather fruity scent. The upright, hardy plant has large, glossy leaves and grows vigorously to 3–4 m.

'Danny Boy' [McGredy, 1969]. 'Uncle Walter' × 'Milord'. This superb rose opens an unusual shade of bright orange vermilion and fades eventually to salmon pink. The sweetly scented flowers are medium sized (8–9 cm) and have the shape of a Hybrid Tea before they open out. The flowers are sometimes borne singly but usually in small clusters. 'Danny Boy' is a vigorous, upright plant which grows rather stiffly to 5 m and repeats well.

'Dublin Bay' syn. MACdud [McGredy, 1975]. 'Bantry Bay' × 'Altissimo'. Why is this short, scentless Floribunda-type climber one of the most widely grown roses throughout the world? The answer lies not in its shortcomings, but in its virtues. The flowers are medium to large (10–11 cm), attractive both as buds and when opened out. They are a very pure dark red, enhanced by slightly darker patches on the petal-tips which give them a sumptuous outline. The plant is very healthy, constantly throwing up new stems and flowers, so that it seems never out of flower. The flowers of 'Dublin Bay' will open in cool weather, but can also tolerate great heat, and they are complemented by dark green, glossy foliage.

'Galway Bay' syn. MACba [McGredy, 1966]. 'Gruß an Heidelberg' × 'Queen Elizabeth'. 'Galway Bay' is an unusual colour. The flowers are apricot at first, then fade to pink, but the colour is always darker on the outside of the petals and towards their edges. They open, often from split buds, into a cabbagey shape and have a good fruity scent. The blooms are medium to large (10 cm) and borne in small clusters on a healthy, vigorous plant. It grows to 3 m and repeats well, constantly throwing up new flowering stems from the base. Red young leaves enliven the dark green, glossy foliage.

'Grand Hotel' syn. MACtel [McGredy, 1972]. The flowers of 'Grand Hotel' are Turkey red, with dark crimson petal-tips. They are lightly double, medium to large (9–11 cm), and scentless, but the thick petals seem to glow with velvety sheens and shadows. The flowers are borne upright on stout stems, singly or in small clusters (up to five), and keep coming all through summer and autumn. The plant has tough, dark, glossy leaves and grows to 5 m. It is very hardy.

'Handel' [McGredy, 1965]. 'Columbine' × 'Gruß an Heidelberg'. 'Handel' was the first hardy modern climber to have two-toned flowers: cream, fading to white, edged with deep pink or crimson. It was a startling combination—a half-open 'Handel' flower, at its best, provides one of loveliest shapes and colour contrasts of any rose. The colour is especially dark at the very edge of the petals, which shows up their form and colour. The petals are very wavy and curvy, which gives the flower a distinctive shape and contributes enormously to its beauty. The flowers are medium to large (8–10 cm), lightly double, shapely in bud, well scented, and freely recurrent. The plant sends up endless new stems from the base, clothed with clean, dark, shiny leaves; it grows vigorously to 5 m. A fair-weather rose, 'Handel' is best in cool, dry weather, and is now outclassed by two Kordes roses, 'Harlekin' and 'Antike '89'.

'Malaga' [McGredy, 1971]. ('Danse du Feu' × 'Hamburger Phönix') × 'Copenhagen'. This dark pink beauty is the least known of McGredy's climbers. The flowers are large (11–12 cm), double, very sweetly scented, and Hybrid Tea shaped, but usually carried in small clusters. 'Malaga' is prettiest when the flowers open out to display their muddled centres. The plant has large glossy leaves, makes lots of new growths, repeats well, and reaches 2.5–3.0 m.

'Santa Catalina' [McGredy, 1970]. 'Paddy McGredy' × 'Gruß an Heidelberg'. 'Santa Catalina' is one of the sensations of late May at Bagatelle in Paris. Wound round metal cones to 5 m, it creates a confection of fluttering, semi-double, open flowers. The blooms are pale pink when they open out flat but dark pink on the buds and petals-backs, and the petals reflex along their sides to give the flowers their distinctive shape (plate 198). They are lightly scented and borne in small clusters. The plant is has dark green, glossy leaves and repeats well after the first profuse flowering.

'Schoolgirl' [McGredy, 1964]. 'Coral Dawn' × 'Belle Blonde'. This prickly brute (the prickles are large and plentiful) bears flowers of great beauty. They are large (12 cm), lightly double, richly scented, and usually carried singly like Hybrid Teas. Their colour is an unusual combination of shades—the outer petals are pink with peachy undersides, whereas the inner petals are pale coral with dark apricot undersides. The flowers open out to reveal a crown of red filaments. The plant has dark green, glossy foliage, grows vigorously to 3–4 m, but is apt to become bare and leggy at the base. 'Schoolgirl' is not the most productive of climbers, but is strongly recurrent.

'Swan Lake' [McGredy, 1968]. 'Memoriam' × 'Gruß an Heidelberg'. Best described as an elegant, white-flowered 'Gruß an Heidelberg', 'Swan Lake' has small clusters of medium-sized (8–9 cm), elegantly shaped, very full flowers which are white with a blush of pink at the centre. They are lightly scented and popular in northern Europe, where their rain-resistant petals excel. This vigorous bush has dark green leaves, grows to 3 m, and repeats well.

CHRISTOPHER WARNER

Chris Warner is a retired teacher from Devon who has developed a range of small climbing roses known as Patio Climbers. Reaching no more than 2–3 m, Warner's climbers are clothed to the ground with bright flowers and luxuriant foliage.

'Devon Maid' [Warner, 1976]. 'Casino' × 'Elizabeth of Glamis'. This climber antedates the Patio Climbers. It has small clusters of sweetly scented, pink roses and grows to about 4 m.

'Gloriana' syn. CHEwpope [Warner, 1998]. 'Laura Ford' × 'Big Purple'. 'Gloriana' has small (5–6 cm), Hybrid Tea–type flowers in rich purple, a most attractive and unusual shade. The plant grows to 2.5 m.

'Good As Gold' syn. CHEwsunbeam [Warner, 1994]. 'Anne Harkness' × 'Laura Ford'. One of Warner's best introductions, this cultivar bears large clusters of small (3 cm), attractive, double, Hybrid Tea–shaped flowers. The flower is dark yellow at first. When it opens out, the anthers turn first brown, then black, and the flower becomes less attractive, especially as the petals begin to bleach. This rose does not die well. The flowers have a fruity Pernetiana scent. The plant has red stems; small, dark, glossy leaves; some prickles; and vigorous, upright growth to 2.5 m.

'Lady Barbara' [Warner, 1987]. 'Red Planet' × ('Elizabeth of Glamis' × ['Galway Bay' × 'Sutter's Gold']). A conventional modern pillar rose, 'Lady Barbara' has beautiful orange flowers (yellow on the petal-backs) which are shaped like Hybrid Teas, lightly double, and scented. Beautiful cut in bud, they fade unattractively later. The plant grows stiffly to 2.5–3.0 m and has a reputation for being a tardy and miserly flowerer.

'Laura Ford' syn. CHEwarvel, 'King Tut', 'Normandie' [Warner, 1989]. 'Anna Ford' × ('Elizabeth of Glamis' × ['Galway Bay' × 'Sutter's Gold']). 'Laura Ford' has masses of small (3–4 cm), lightly scented, deep yellow flowers opening out from scrolled buds; later they acquire a pink edge. They are very abundantly borne in small clusters on a vigorous, upright plant with lots of small, dark, glossy leaves. It reaches 2.5–3.0 m.

'Little Rambler' syn. CHEwramb [Warner, 1994]. ('Mlle Cécile Brunner' × 'Baby Faraux') × ('Marjorie Fair' × 'Nozomi'). Quite different from Warner's other small ramblers, this cultivar has elegant, open sprays of small (2–3 cm), double, pink flowers (lilac pink in cool weather). They are strongly scented and freely borne on a bushy, tiny-leaved plant which eventually reaches 2.5 m.

'Nice Day' syn. CHEwsea [Warner, 1992]. 'Seaspray' × 'Warm Welcome'. The flowers of this attractive Patio Climber are salmon pink in bud; they open to peach-coloured flowers (slightly darker on the petal-backs) before eventually fading to pink. The blooms are small (3–4 cm), full, shapely, and lightly scented, and they last well as cut flowers. The plant has masses of small, dark, glossy leaves and grows bushily to 2.5 m.

'Open Arms' syn. CHEwpixcel [Warner, 1995]. 'Mary Sumner' × 'Laura Ashley'. The scented, semi-double flowers of 'Open Arms' are peachy pink in the bud; they open pale pink and fade to dirty white as the stamens go brown. They are borne in large clusters on a vigorous, bushy plant which reaches 2.5–3.0 m and is well clothed with small, dark, glossy leaves.

'Rosalie Coral' syn. CHEwallop [Warner, 1992]. ('Elizabeth of Glamis' × ['Galway Bay' × 'Sutter's Gold']) × 'Anna Ford'. Very much a Warner rose, this cultivar has large, neat clusters of small (4 cm), lightly scented, semi-single flowers. The blooms are orange with yellow petal-backs and fade eventually to pink. They show up well against the small, dark green and crimson leaves, which have a sort of bluish glaze to them. The bushy plant grows to 2.0–2.5 m.

'Warm Welcome' syn. CHEwizz [Warner, 1991]. ('Elizabeth of Glamis' × ['Galway Bay' × 'Sutter's Gold']) × 'Anna Ford'. I shall never forget the impression this cultivar made when it first appeared in the Royal National Rose Society's trials. The plant was covered from top to bottom with clusters of small (3 cm), semi-single, lightly scented, bright orange flowers. The blooms were set off by dense, dark, small, glossy leaves, and the plant grew to 2 m within three years. It won the society's highest award, the President's International Trophy, and has gone on to be grown worldwide.

POULSEN AND OLESEN

The Danish rose-breeding Poulsens more-or-less invented Floribunda roses. Since then, they have tended to follow fashion rather than create it. Nils Poulsen was a reliable breeder, and his 'Copenhagen' is still a good rose. Since the 1980s his son-in-law Mogens Olesen has also produced some excellent shrub roses. Their climbers, however, are rather a mixed bag.

'Calypso' syn. POULclimb, 'Berries 'n' Cream' [Olesen/Poulsen, 1997]. One of several new striped climbers introduced in recent years, 'Calypso' has large clusters of small to medium (5–6 cm), semi-double, lightly scented flowers which are basically crimson, splashed with pink stripes (much paler on the petal-backs). The plant has large leaves and reaches 3–4 m. It is fairly vigorous, almost thornless, very floriferous, and a good repeater. I find that the flowers blotch in rain.

'Copenhagen' [Poulsen, 1964]. 'Hakuun' × 'Ena Harkness'. 'Copenhagen' was Nils Poulsen's first rose. It is a Hybrid Tea–type climber with large (12–14 cm), shapely, double, scented, scarlet flowers borne in small clusters. The plant has lots of very large foliage (dark green, but coppery at first), grows to 2.5–3.0 m, and repeats well, but tends to become a bit leggy.

Chapter 13

'Jazz' syn. POULnorm [Olesen/Poulsen, 1997]. 'Jazz' is a pleasant enough rose, but not a great improvement on what has gone before. Its sweet-scented flowers are rich crimson, shapely, and borne singly or in clusters of up to fifteen. They are medium sized (8 cm), fairly double, opening out nicely and flat, and keeping their colour well. The petals towards the centre are smaller, which sometimes gives the flowers a camellia effect. The plant has rather large glossy leaves, with broad leaflets, and grows well to about 3 m.

'Night Light' syn. POULlight [Poulsen, 1982]. 'Westerland' × 'Pastorale'. The colour of this scraggy, prickly climber is a remarkable mixture of deep yellow and crimson. The flowers open bright yellow and turn slowly to red, starting with the outer edges of the outer petals until the whole flower is crimson. As they are borne in medium-sized, spacious clusters, the contrasts between the older and newer flowers is remarkable. The blooms are medium sized (8 cm), double, scented, and rain-resistant.

Olesen has recently introduced two additional climbers: 'Flamenco' syn. POULtika, 'Northern Lights' [1997], whose pink flowers have an old-fashioned shape, and 'Ragtime' syn. POULtime [1997], whose semi-double, dark pink flowers have pale undersides.

JAPANESE ROSES

Roses do not have the popularity in Japan which they enjoy in most Western countries. The roses of Seizo Suzuki, the leading modern Japanese breeder, have been introduced by Keisei. The only one available outside Japan (but not in Europe) is 'Fure-Daiko'.

'Fure-Daiko' syn. 'Piñata' [Suzuki, 1974]. ('Goldilocks' seedling × 'Sarabande') × 'Golden Giant' seedling. 'Fure-Daiko' is best described as 'Joseph's Coat' with larger Hybrid Tea–shaped flowers. The flowers open deep yellow from vermilion buds, but acquire more redness as they age, especially on the petal-tips. The are medium sized (6–7 cm), semi-double, and long lasting. The plant is moderately vigorous, very floriferous, and grows to 3 m.

Suzuki has introduced several other climbing roses. 'Honoho-No-Nami' [1968], bred from 'Danse du Feu' × 'Aztec', has lightly double, vermilion, Hybrid Tea–type flowers. 'Shin-Setsu' [1969], bred from ('Blanche Mallerin' × 'Neige Parfum') × 'New Dawn' seedling, has large, fully double, pure white Hybrid Tea–type flowers; I have seen this rose at Westfalenpark, Dortmund. 'Bonbori' [1973], bred from 'Golden Slippers' × ('Joseph's Coat' × 'Circus'), is orange, with an apricot yellow underside.

Cultivating Climbing Roses

Too many books about roses ignore the pleasures of gardening and emphasise the labour and commitment it requires. Here are some of the chapter headings of one book published in the 1920s—as a turn-off for rose growing, it cannot be bettered: Manures for Rose Beds, Preparing Beds for Roses, Planting the Roses, Pegging Down Roses, The Summer Management of Roses, Rose Suckers and How to Deal with Them, Feeding Roses, The Winter Management of Roses, Rose Diseases and How to Recognise and Treat Them, Rose Pests and the Remedies against Them, Pruning Roses, Budding and Grafting Roses, until one comes nearly to the end with The Year's Work in the Rose Garden. This list is not exceptional among rose books. Jobs had to be found to keep the gardener busy in winter—the Protestant work ethic has a lot to answer for.

A combination of feeding, pruning, training, and spraying can translate a dull performer into a star, but none of these is essential. We all know of deserted or ill-maintained gardens where climbing roses have survived or thrived on neglect for many years. There are, however, some simple actions which will increase the pleasure you get from your roses. The first thing to remember is that climbing roses need at least a couple of years to get up to a fair height and as many as seven years before they approach their maximum size.

All roses like a deep, rich, fertile soil, but so do most plants. The fact is that roses will grow well enough and give satisfaction in a wide variety of soils and situations. Feeding roses is not essential but helps them to grow quicker; nutrients are best applied just before and during the main growing season. It matters not whether the nutrient is organic manure or inorganic fertiliser.

Roses do not need protection from sun and heat, but they do respond to watering by putting on new growth. Watering is therefore advisable in hot climates; it prevents summer dormancy, so that plants continue to flower. In cold climates, some climbers may need protection in winter. There are two principal ways of minimising winter-kill, and both are laborious. One is some form of protective cladding—traditionally straw, but today more commonly horticultural insulating fleece. The other involves dismantling the climber, taking the stems down, and earthing them over until spring—more work for the gardeners.

Roses are susceptible to fungal infections, notably blackspot, mildews, and rust. The incidence of these diseases differs around the world, and well-grown roses are less susceptible. Disease may weaken a plant, but I have never seen one killed by any of these fungi; thus, a relaxed attitude towards disease control is always an option. If you wish to use approved fungicides, there are two golden rules: first, choose a systemic one which will prevent infection; second, spray as early in the season as you can. Prevention is always better than cure. Recent trials by the Royal National Rose Society in England have shown that a preventative spray in late winter, when the dormant leaf buds are just starting to expand, followed by another spray one month later, will protect most roses all through the year.

The ease with which so many rambling roses can be raised from cuttings undoubtedly accounts for their universality in cultivation. 'American Pillar', 'Albertine', and 'Goldfinch' flourish in modest and neglected gardens throughout the world. The success rate with Wichuranas and Multifloras is almost 100 per cent. *Rosa multiflora* itself is widely grown from cuttings as a rootstock, and the Wichurana Rambler 'Dr Huey' is popular for the same purpose in much of North America and Australia. Young woody cuttings (10–30 cm long) should be stuck into the ground in damp weather in autumn. Rooting powder is seldom necessary. Softwood cuttings may also be tried in spring, either under mist or at home on a windowsill by putting a plastic bag over the pot.

Much nonsense has been written about pruning. There are only two rules: the first is "If in doubt, don't." You cannot underprune a climbing rose, but you can most certainly overprune one. More roses are killed by overenthusiastic pruning than by anything else. Goethe said that the "*der schrecklichste der Schrecken*" (the horror of horrors) was the gardener with his knife. The second rule is "Do it only if you want to." The main reason for pruning is aesthetic. Tailor and shape your roses to fit your intentions and the available space. The only proviso is that you ought to cut out dead or dying wood, stems that are beginning to look woody and threadbare. I once asked a leading English rose nurseryman *when* I should prune my roses. He replied "Well, I start at the end of October, and hope I can finish by Easter."

The ancient wisdom was to cut old ramblers to the ground after they had flowered—not the whole plant, but the long branches which had borne this year's flowers. I consider this an unnecessary chore at a time of the year when most gardens are too hot to work in. These long wands will in any case flower again next year, although not as freely as the newer growths. The best advice is to wait until winter and then cut out any wood which is dying back or growing where it is not welcome. If the ramblers are trained to a support, then this is also the best time to tie them in.

Climbers build up a more permanent framework, although they take much longer to develop than ramblers. Pruning consists of no more than the periodical removal of anything which is dying back or exceeding its bounds. The received wisdom is that one should encourage new growths to sprout low down on the plant, but there is no sure way of doing this, short of pruning the whole plant very severely, which is much more likely to cause its demise. Indeed, many climbers flower very well for years on end with no pruning at all.

Most climbing roses need some form of support. Although this may differ according to the stiffness or suppleness of their growth, it is the nature of that support which determines the pruning. Most climbers are fine against a wall but, because they encourage mildew, it is best to avoid growing such susceptible cultivars as 'Dorothy Perkins' against a wall. All types of climbers will quickly grow up a small tree, for instance, an old apple tree, in which case pruning is probably unnecessary. Most of the ramblers may be grown as large, free-standing bushes: I grow 'Albertine', 'Madeleine Selzer', and 'Général Tétard' in mixed borders and just cut any bits which seem to be dying back. I do this in winter when the plants are leafless and I can see their structure more clearly. The simplest support is to tie a rose into a pole; this may be seen at Sangerhausen in Germany and David Ruston's garden in South Australia. The effect is intensified if the rose is wound around the pole, as at L'Haÿ-les-Roses and La Bonne Maison in France. A structure made from several poles tied together at the top or an iron pyramid is better still if covered with several plants of the same rose. Catenaries are popular in England (Regent's Park, The Gardens of the Rose, and Wisley); trelliswork is widely seen in the United States (Brooklyn Botanic Garden and the Huntington Botanical Garden) and France (L'Haÿ-les-Roses); and the best fan-trained climbers I have seen are at Cavriglia in Italy. Remember, too, that the flexible stems of ramblers make very attractive weeping standards.

Glossary

amphidiploid interspecific hybrid having a complete diploid chromosome set from each parent; also called allotetraploid

blackspot any of several closely related fungal diseases characterised by black spots or blotches, especially on the leaves

chlorosis diseased condition in green plants marked by yellowing or blanching, especially of the leaves

corymb indeterminate flat-topped or convex inflorescence, where the outer flowers open first (cf. umbel)

corymbose resembling or forming a corymb

cuneate inversely triangular, wedge shaped

cyme more-or-less flat-topped and determinate inflorescence, with the central or terminal flower opening first

eglandular without glands

excorticate having the skin worn off

fimbriate bordered with a fringe of slender processes

foliolate bearing leaflets

glabrous smooth, hairless

glaucous having a powdery or waxy coating, usually blue or bluish grey, which gives a frosted appearance and tends to rub off

imbricate closely overlapping in a regular pattern, encircling the centre

inflorescence arrangement of flowers and their accessory parts

laciniate irregularly and finely cut, as if slashed

lanceolate lance shaped; narrowly ovate with the broadest point below the middle, tapering to a spearlike apex

obovate ovate, but broadest above rather than below the middle, thus narrowest towards the base rather than the apex

obovoid oval, but broadest below the middle; obovate in cross-section

pedicel stalk supporting an individual flower

Glossary

peduncle stalk supporting an inflorescence

petaloid small straplike petal, usually formed at the centre of a flower

petiole stalk supporting a leaf

procumbent trailing loosely or lying flat along the surface of the ground, without rooting

pubescence short, fine, soft hairs

rachis axis of a compound leaf or a compound inflorescence, as an extension of the petiole or peduncle, respectively

remontant flowering twice or more in a season, in distinct phases

rugose wrinkled by irregular lines and veins

scandent climbing

stipule leafy or bractlike appendage at the base of a petiole, usually growing in pairs and soon shed

stolon prostrate or trailing stem which takes root and gives rise to plantlets at the apex and sometimes at nodes

stoloniferous producing stolons

tomentose with densely woolly, short, rigid hairs

tomentum tomentose pubescence

umbel a flat-topped inflorescence like a corymb, but with all the flowered pedicels arising at the same point at the apex of the main axis

villous with shaggy pubescence

Bibliography

Aicardi, Domenico. 1951. *Le Rose Moderne*. Rome, Italy.

Allison, Sally. 1993. *Climbing and Rambling Roses*. Auckland: Moa Beckett.

American Rose Society. 1916– . *American Rose Annual*. Shreveport, La.: American Rose Society.

Betten, Robert. 1919. *Die Rose, ihre Anzucht und Pflege*. 4th ed. Frankfurt-an-der-Oder, Germany: Druck und Verlag von Trowitzsch & Sohn.

Bhatcharji, B. S., Courtney Page, and Amal Chandra Pal. 1933. *Practical Rose Growing in India*. Calcutta: Thacker, Spink & Co.

Boulenger, G. 1931. François Crépin et les roses. *Bulletin du Jardin botanique de l'Etat. Bruxelles* 9 (2): 78–83.

Bowles, E. A. 1914. *My Garden in Summer*. New York: Dodge Publishing.

Buist, Robert. 1847. *The Rose Manual*. Philadelphia: Carey & Hart.

Bunyard, George. 1904. *England's National Flower*. Maidstone, U.K.: Simpkin, Marshall, Hamilton, Kent & Co.

Cayeux, Henri. 1929. *Rosa gigantea* et ses hybrides. *Journal of Heredity* 20: 305–307.

Cochet-Cochet, P. C. M., and S. J. Mottet. 1925. *Les Rosiers*. 5th ed. Paris: Octave.

Crépin, François. 1888. Description d'une nouvelle rose asiatique. *Bulletin de la Société royale de Botanique de Belgique* 27 (2): 20–23.

Crépin, François. 1889. Nouvelles observations sur le *Rosa gigantea* Collett. *Bulletin de la Société royale de Botanique de Belgique* 28 (2): 11–14.

Curtis, Henry. 1850–1853. *The Beauties of the Rose*. 2 vols. London: Groombridge.

Dickerson, Brent C. 1992. *The Old Rose Advisor*. Portland, Ore.: Timber Press.

Dickerson, Brent C. 1999. *The Old Rose Adventurer: The Once-Blooming Old European Roses and More*. Portland, Ore.: Timber Press.

d'Ombrain, Rev. H. H. 1928. *Roses for Amateurs*. 5th ed. Edited by Walter Easlea. London: L. Upcott Gill.

Easlea, Walter. 1896. *The Hybridisation of Roses*. Edinburgh, U.K.: R. & R. Clark Ltd.

Easlea, Walter. 1932. *National Rose Society of Great Britain Rose Annual* 1932: 109.

Easlea, Walter. 1945. *National Rose Society of Great Britain Rose Annual* 1945: 38.

Ellacombe, H. N. 1982. *In a Gloucestershire Garden.* 2d ed. London: Century.

Elliott, R. G. 1920. *The Australasian Rose Book.* Melbourne: Whitcombe & Tombs.

Ellwanger, H. B. 1893. *The Rose.* Rev. ed. New York: Dodd, Mead & Co.

Farrer, Reginald. 1916. *Journal of the Royal Horticultural Society* 41: 106.

Forestier, J. C. N. 1922. *Bagatelle et ses jardins.* 2d ed. Paris: Maison Rustique.

Foster-Melliar, A. 1905. *The Book of the Rose.* 3rd ed. London: Macmillan.

Garnett, T. R. 1990. *Man of Roses: Alister Clark of Glenara and His Family.* Sydney: Kangaroo Press.

Gault, Millar S., and Patrick M. Synge. 1971. *The Dictionary of Roses in Colour.* London: Ebury Press.

Geier, M. 1936. *Rosenjahrbuch des Vereins Deutscher Rosenfreunde* 1936 (III): 79–80.

Geschwind, R. 1863. *Die Hybridation und Sämlingszucht der Rosen.* Vienna: Druck.

Geschwind, R. 1884. *Die Theerose und ihre Bastarde.* Leipzig: Voigt.

Gravereaux, J. 1902. *Les Roses cultivées à l'Haÿ en 1902.* Paris: Rousset.

Greuter, W., F. R. Barrie, H. M. Burdet, W. G. Chaloner, V. Demoulin, D. L. Hawksworth, P. M. Jørgensen, D. H. Nicolson, P. C. Silva, and P. Trehane, eds. 1994. *International Code of Botanical Nomenclature (Tokyo Code).* Königstein, Germany: Koeltz Scientific Books.

Hariot, P. A. 1903. *Le Livre d'or des Roses.* Paris: Laveur.

Harkness, Jack. 1960. *National Rose Society of Great Britain Rose Annual* 1960.

Harkness, Jack. 1978. *Roses.* London: Dent.

Harvey, N. P. 1951. *The Rose in Britain.* London: Plant Protection Ltd.

Henry, Augustine. 1902. Wild Chinese roses. *Gardener's Chronicle* ser. 3 (32): 438–439.

Henslow, T. G. W. 1934. *The Rose Encyclopaedia.* 2d ed. London: Vickery, Kyrle.

Hoffmann, J. 1905. *Rosenbuch für Gartenliebhaber.* Berlin: Paul Parey.

Hole, S. R. 1901. *A Book about Roses.* 18th ed. London: Arnold.

Irvine, Susan. 1997. *Rose Gardens of Australia.* Ringwood, Australia: Viking.

Jäger, A. 1960. *Rosenlexikon.* Leipzig: Zentral-Antiquariat der Deutschen Demokratischen Republik.

Jamain, H., and E. Forney. 1873. *Les Roses: Histoire, Culture, Description.* Paris: Rothschild.

Jekyll, Gertrude. 1902. *Roses for English Gardens.* London: Country Life.

Johnson, Hugh. 1979. *The Principles of Gardening: The Science, Practice and History of the Gardener's Art.* London: Mitchell Beazley.

Journal des Roses. 1877–1914. Melun, France: Cochet.

Keays, Mrs Frederick Love. 1935. *Old Roses.* New York: Macmillan.

Kingdon-Ward, Frank. 1952. *Plant Hunter in Manipur.* London: Jonathan Cape.

Kingsley, Rose. 1908. *Roses and Rose Growing.* London: Whittaker.

Kordes, Wilhelm. 1928. 'Emile Nérini'. *Rosen-Zeitung* 126.

Kordes, Wilhelm. 1956. *Das Rosenbuch.* 7th ed. Hannover: Schaper.

Bibliography

Kordes, Wilhelm. 1960. *National Rose Society of Great Britain Rose Annual* 1960: 48.

Krüssmann, Gerd. 1974. *Rosen, Rosen, Rosen.* Hamburg: Parey.

Ledlie, R. 1923. *A Handbook of Rose Culture in India.* Calcutta: Thacker, Spink & Co.

Lee, Charles. 1881. *Gardener's Chronicle* 16: 183.

Leroy, André. 1954. *Histoire des Roses.* Paris: Baillière.

Lester. F. E. 1942. *My Friend the Rose.* Harrisburg, Penn.: McFarland.

Loudon, John. 1844. *Arboretum et Fruticetum Britannicum; or the Trees and Shrubs of Britain, Native and Foreign, Hardy and Half Hardy.* . . . London: Longman, Brown, Green, and Longman.

Mansfield, T. C. 1946. *Roses in Colour and Cultivation.* 2d ed. London: Collins.

McFarland, J. H. 1923. *The Rose in America.* New York: Macmillan.

McFarland, J. H. 1930. *Modern Roses.* New York: McFarland.

McFarland, J. H. 1947. *Roses of the World in Color.* 3rd ed. Boston: Houghton, Mifflin.

National Rose Society of Australia. 1928– . *The Australian Rose Annual.* Melbourne: National Rose Society of Australia.

National (Royal National) Rose Society of Great Britain. 1907– . *Rose Annual.* London: National Rose Society of Great Britain.

Nicolas, J. H. 1930. *The Rose Manual: An Encyclopaedia for the American Amateur.* New York: Doubleday.

Nietner, Theodor. 1880. *Die Rose: ihre Geschichte, Arten, Kultur und Verwendung.* Berlin: Parey.

Norman, Albert. 1953. *Successful Rose Growing.* London: Collingridge.

Ohwi, Jisaburo. 1965. *Flora of Japan.* Ed. Frederick G. Meyer and Egbert H. Walker. Washington, D.C.: Smithsonian Institution.

Osborn, Arthur. 1927. The wild roses: the newer species. *National Rose Society of Great Britain Rose Annual* 1927: 44–56.

Page, Courtney. 1937. *National Rose Society of Great Britain Rose Annual* 1937: 42.

Pal, B. P. 1966. *The Rose in India.* New Delhi: Indian Council of Agricultural Research.

Parkman, Francis. 1866. *The Book of Roses.* Boston: Tilton.

Paul, A. W. 1888. *The Rose Garden.* 9th ed. London: Kent.

Paul, A. W. 1902. Roses for autumn blooms. *Journal of the Royal Horticultural Society* 26: 478–487.

Paul, A. W. 1907. *On the Derivation of Some Recent Varieties of Roses: Report of the Third International Conference on Genetics.* London: Spottiswoode.

Pemberton, J. H. 1920. *Roses.* 2d ed. London: Longman, Green.

Phillips, R., and M. Rix. 1993. *The Quest for the Rose.* London: BBC Books.

Phillips, R., and M. Rix. 1997. *Conservatory and Indoor Plants.* London: Macmillan.

Poulsen, Svend. 1955. *Poulsen on the Rose.* London: MacGibbon & Kee.

Pyle, R., J. H. McFarland, and G. A. Stevens. 1930. *How to Grow Roses.* New York: Macmillan.

Rivoire, A., and M. Ebel. 1933. *Roses et Rosiers.* Paris: Baillière.

Rosenjahrbuch des Vereins Deutscher Rosenfreunde. 1934– .

Rosenzeitung des Vereins Deutscher Rosenfreunde. 1886–1933.

Sanders, T. W. 1899. *Cultivated Roses.* London: Collingridge.

Sanders. T. W. 1931. *Roses and Their Cultivation.* 14th ed. London: Collingridge.

Shepherd, R. E. 1954. *History of the Rose.* New York: Macmillan.

Singer, Max. 1885. *Dictionnaire des Roses.* Brussels: Lebèque.

Smith, Walter S. 1932. *Practical Hints on Rose Culture in India.* Allahabad, India: Indian Press.

Snyder, Margaret. 1949. *American Rose Annual.* Shreveport, La.: American Rose Society.

Snyder, Margaret. 1953. *American Rose Annual.* Shreveport, La.: American Rose Society.

Société Française des Rosiéristes. 1896– . *Les Amis des Roses: Bulletin de la Société Française des Rosiéristes.* Lyon: Société Française des Rosiéristes.

Stern, F. C. 1960. *A Chalk Garden.* London: Faber.

Stevens, G. A. 1933. *Climbing Roses.* New York: Macmillan.

Sulzberger, R. 1891. *La Rose.* Namur, Belgium: Charlier.

Thomas, A. S. 1950. *Better Roses.* Sydney: Angus & Robertson.

Thomas, G. C. 1924. *Roses for All American Climates.* New York: Macmillan.

Thomas, Graham Stuart. 1965. *Climbing Roses Old and New.* London: Phoenix.

Thomas, Graham Stuart. 1994. *The Graham Stuart Thomas Rose Book.* Portland, Ore.: Timber Press.

Ungarische Rosenzeitung, edited by Ernst Kaufmann. 1889–1896.

Vergara, M. 1892. *Bibliografia de la Rosa.* Madrid: Tello.

Westcott, Cynthia. 1952. *Anyone Can Grow Roses.* Toronto: Van Nostrand.

Williams, A. H. 1913. Wichuriana ramblers. *National Rose Society of Great Britain Rose Annual* 1913: 91–103.

Willmott, Ellen. 1910–1914. *The Genus Rosa.* 2 vols. London: John Murray.

Young, James. 1923. *Rose Growing in New Zealand.* Auckland: Whitcombe & Tombs.

Young, Norman. 1971. *The Complete Rosarian.* London: Hodder & Stoughton.

Index

Bold page numbers indicate main descriptions of cultivars. *Italic* plate numbers indicate illustrations. *Passim* indicates numerous mentions of the plant over the range of pages given.

Index